FODOR'S®
GREECE
1985

Fodor's Greece:

Area Editor: Peter Sheldon

Editorial Contributors: Frances Howell, Robert Liddell, Ira Mayer, Paul Strathern, David Tennant

Editor: Richard Moore

Assistant Editor: Thomas Cussans

Cartography: C. W. Bacon, Alex Murphy

Drawings: Lorraine Calaora

Fodor's Travel Guides
New York

All the following Guides are current (most of them also in
the Hodder and Stoughton British edition).

**FODOR'S COUNTRY
AND AREA TITLES:**

AUSTRALIA, NEW
ZEALAND AND
SOUTH PACIFIC
AUSTRIA
BELGIUM AND
LUXEMBOURG
BERMUDA
BRAZIL
CANADA
CANADA'S MARITIME
PROVINCES
CARIBBEAN AND
BAHAMAS
CENTRAL AMERICA
EASTERN EUROPE
EGYPT
EUROPE
FRANCE
GERMANY
GREAT BRITAIN
GREECE
HOLLAND
INDIA, NEPAL, AND
SRI LANKA
IRELAND
ISRAEL
ITALY
JAPAN
JORDAN AND HOLY
LAND
KOREA
MEXICO
NORTH AFRICA
PEOPLE'S REPUBLIC
OF CHINA
PORTUGAL
SCANDINAVIA
SCOTLAND

SOUTH AMERICA
SOUTHEAST ASIA
SOVIET UNION
SPAIN
SWITZERLAND
TURKEY
YUGOSLAVIA

CITY GUIDES:

AMSTERDAM
BEIJING,
GUANGZHOU,
SHANGHAI
BOSTON
CHICAGO
DALLAS AND FORT
WORTH
GREATER MIAMI
HONG KONG
HOUSTON
LISBON
LONDON
LOS ANGELES
MADRID
MEXICO CITY AND
ACAPULCO
MUNICH
NEW ORLEANS
NEW YORK CITY
PARIS
ROME
SAN DIEGO
SAN FRANCISCO
STOCKHOLM,
COPENHAGEN,
OSLO, HELSINKI,
AND REYKJAVIK
TOKYO
TORONTO
VIENNA
WASHINGTON, D.C.

FODOR'S BUDGET SERIES:

BUDGET BRITAIN
BUDGET CANADA
BUDGET CARIBBEAN
BUDGET EUROPE
BUDGET FRANCE
BUDGET GERMANY
BUDGET HAWAII
BUDGET ITALY
BUDGET JAPAN
BUDGET LONDON
BUDGET MEXICO
BUDGET
SCANDINAVIA
BUDGET SPAIN
BUDGET TRAVEL IN
AMERICA

USA GUIDES:

ALASKA
CALIFORNIA
CAPE COD
COLORADO
FAR WEST
FLORIDA
HAWAII
NEW ENGLAND
PACIFIC NORTH COAST
PENNSYLVANIA
SOUTH
TEXAS
USA (in one volume)

GOOD TIME TRAVEL GUIDES:

ACAPULCO
MONTREAL
OAHU
SAN FRANCISCO

CONTENTS

CONTENTS

SUPPLEMENTS

EUROPE AND
DON'T MISS

Now you can sail the legendary QE2 to or from Europe—and fly the other way, free! That means you can begin or end your European vacation with five unforgettable days and nights on the last of the great superliners. And get a free British Airways economy-class ticket between London and most major U.S. cities.

For only $499 extra per person, you can fly a specially reserved British Airways Concorde between London and New York, Miami or Washington, D.C.

Only the QE2 offers four top restaurants and five lively nightspots. A glittering disco, a glamorous casino and a 20,000-bottle wine cellar. The famed "Golden Door Spa at Sea,"® with yoga and aerobic dance, a gym and jogging deck, saunas, swimming pools and Jacuzzi® Whirlpool Baths.

• Wide choice of crossings between England and New York, some calling on Boston, Philadelphia or Port Everglades, as well.
• Cunard's choice European tours—varying in length, attractively priced, either escorted or independent—all include a QE2 crossing.
• 20 percent discount at Cunard hotels—including London's fabulous Ritz—and at Inter-Continental Hotels throughout Europe.
• Enchanting QE2 and Vistafjord European cruises, which may be combined with a crossing.

For all the facts, including any requirements or restrictions, contact your travel agent or Cunard, Dept. F84, P.O. Box 999, Farmingdale, NY 11737; (212) 661-7777.

CUNARD

Certain restrictions apply to free airfare and Concorde programs.
All programs are subject to change. See your travel agent.

THE QE2:
THE MAGIC.

FOREWORD

Greece has everything to offer to the visitor—whether he is in search of sun and sand, art and history or just a good time. And prices are still reasonable within a vast range of holiday possibilities, from inexpensive to luxury; there is, however, a general lack of solid comfort and outstanding food.

It is a land of contrasts where the influences of all the waves of invaders which flowed and ebbed across Greek soil can still be seen. There are Byzantine towns, Venetian fortresses and Frankish monuments, as well as the glorious remains of ancient Greece itself, or the ruins of the Minoan era on Crete. It is not necessary to be a scholar of history or archeology to feel the closeness of ancient Greece.

The islands have gained in importance as tourist centers, especially Corfu and Rhodes, which rank high in the modern tourist trade, but which have suffered from the hotel-elephantiasis which first afflicted the western Mediterranean and then spread throughout most of the region. The huge increase in hotel development has been needed to cope with the fact that the track beaten by tourism gets longer and broader each year. Package tours now blanket the whole of Greece. Happily the lesser islands and mainland beaches are sufficiently numerous for some to remain the sweet-scented peaceful havens they always were. But even they are in danger of being engulfed in the tide of concrete. Moreover, Greece has become one of Europe's leading centers for sailing and yachting besides providing all traditional and recent nautical sports.

In this guide, we have naturally devoted considerable space to the history and mythology of ancient Greece and its world-renowned sites. But we also have included practical information for the yachtsman who wants to cruise the Aegean, the sportsman who wants to swim, fish, play golf or ski, or just the easy-going wanderer who wants nothing more than a pleasant spot with sunshine by day and congenial cafés by night.

Last, but far from least, we must mention the Greeks themselves who brought western civilization to its first flowering in antiquity.

They are good linguists and the English-speaking tourist will find no difficulty in making himself understood, even in outlying villages.

*

All prices quoted in the Guide are based on those available to us at time of writing, mid-1984. Given the volatility of European costs, it is inevitable that changes will have taken place by the time this book becomes available. We trust, therefore, that you will take prices quoted as indicators only, and will double-check to be sure of the latest figures.

*

We wish especially to acknowledge the help of Peter Sheldon, our Area Editor for Greece, who has once more put his deep knowledge of, and love for, this fascinating country at our disposal.

We also extend our sincere thanks to the many individuals and organizations who helped in collecting material contained in this book. Our gratitude goes especially to the Greek National Tourist Organization in Athens, together with the Director of the London office and his staff.

*

Be sure to double check all opening times of museums and galleries on the spot. We have found that such times are liable to be changed with no notice at all, due to staff illness, strikes, fire and Acts of God, and you could easily make a trip only to find a locked door.

The hotels and restaurants that appear in our lists are only a selection of the many available. Restrictions of space prevent us from including more, although there are often other establishments with facilities similar to those we have actually included. Do bear in mind also that, in highly individualistic Greece, frequent changes in management and ownership often result in drastic reversals of standards. Consequently, we genuinely welcome letters from our readers. Errors are bound to creep into any Guide, but your letters will help us to pinpoint trouble spots. Our two addresses for letters are–

In the USA: Fodor's Travel Guides, 2 Park Avenue, New York, NY 10016
In Europe: Fodor's Travel Guides, 9/10 Market Place, London W1, England.

TWA to Europe. *(Why not get the*

Over the next several hundred pages, you're going
to be faced with any number of tough decisions.
Like what to see in Europe. When to see it. Where
to stay. Where to eat. And so on.

Fortunately, deciding how to fly there won't be
one of them. Who else but TWA?

TWA has convenient nonstops to more
European countries than anyone else. With our
great TWA low fares.

easy decisions out of the way first.)

At TWA's JFK Airport Flight Center, only a short hallway stands between you and your connecting TWA overseas flight.

Finally, there's TWA Getaway® Vacations — by far the most popular vacation choice in America. With over 100 value-packed tours. And a vacation style to fit yours.

So call your travel agent or TWA.

Now that wasn't so hard, was it?

You're going to like us

FACTS AT YOUR FINGERTIPS

Planning Your Trip

$P£ **MONEY.** As all considerations of costing your trip depend on understanding the Greek currency, here are a few vital statistics to help you along. The monetary unit is the *drachme*. It is divided into 100 *lepta*. There are 1, 2, 5, 10, 20 and 50 drachmes and 50 lepta coins and banknotes of 50, 100, 500, 1,000 and 5,000 drachmes.

At time of going to press there were 110 dr. to the U.S. $ and 155 to the £ sterling. Daily exchange rates are prominently displayed at all banks. You'll get a better exchange rate at banks than from hotels or stores.

WHAT IT WILL COST. Continuing inflation everywhere, periodic devaluations in various places, and fluctuations in nearly all currencies make accurate budgeting long in advance an impossibility. Prices mentioned throughout this book are indicative only of costs at the time of going to press. Keep a weather eye open for fluctuations in exchange rates, both when planning your trip and while on it.

Inflation continues for the third year at about 25%, partly offset by a rise in the dollar exchange rate. Judicious choosing and advance booking can still ensure good value even for limited budgets, but meals are not always up to western standards in the same category.

We give details of hotels and restaurant costs later in this section. There are no regional price differences, variations within the five hotel categories depend on location—part of town; near or far from a beach—as well as on the extras—airconditioning, swimming pool, sauna, etc. Groups invariably receive substantial discounts. The better-class resort hotels insist on half board.

Off-season rates are 15–20% lower from April 15 to May 31, and from September 15 to October 31; they are up to 40% lower in the few seaside hotels which stay open from November 1 to April 15—excluding, of course, Christmas and Easter holidays.

A word of warning: seaside taverns, despite their deceptively simple appearance, are often classified A or B, charging accordingly. Make sure of the category, which must be prominently indicated, and in the lowlier places follow the Greek custom—go into the kitchen to select the fish, have it weighed and priced. By far the most economic meals are the set menus in

3

A to C hotels—there are none in outside restaurants—but they are of the dreary international variety which wrongly calls itself French.

For those who are budget minded, the package tour, bought through a travel agency or airline company normally takes care of your transportation, accommodation, meals, tips. It may, or may not, include excursions and entertainment, so check carefully on this. Outside of your quoted tour fare then, your only expenses are likely to be for postage, drinks, gifts and personal shopping.

The pay-as-you-go, go-where-you-please tourist, who wants to follow his own fancy, is of course more difficult to budget. His tastes may call for deluxe, expensive, moderate or inexpensive traveling. "Deluxe" as here used, means staying in the best hotels; renting a comfortable car; taking the best seats everywhere and visits to nightclubs. Expensive travel involves staying at good hotels, eating at good restaurants but not always at the most expensive ones, indulging in nightlife and orchestra-seat entertainment, traveling by small self-drive car, golf, tennis and nautical sports. Moderate means rooms and meals in comfortable establishments, sightseeing tours, but economical entertainment. Inexpensive does not necessitate any hardship, but it does mean meals in popular taverns, second class travel on boats or trains, local buses, swimming on free beaches, and depending for interest on museums and *kafenia* (coffee-houses) and your own eyes.

Following these guidelines, a day for two people could cost in each category, and in drachmes

Deluxe—42,000
Expensive—24,000
Moderate—10,350
Inexpensive—5,700

As a sample of the way such a day is made up, here is the Moderate breakdown in drachmes for two people:

Double room, half board, tax and service charges	3,400
Lunch or dinner at tourist restaurant, wine	2,200
Transportation, sightseeing, excursions	1,300
Sports and refreshments	1,200
Evening entertainment (Festival tickets or disco)	1,300
10% for contingencies	950
	10,350

Some Miscellaneous Costs. An *ouzo* costs from 35 to 90 dr.; a bottle of beer from 45 to 100 dr.; a bottle of local wine 120 to 500 dr.; half a liter of *retsina* 50 to 80 dr.; a Coke from 35 to 90 dr.; American coffee 70 to 120 dr., and Greek coffee 45 to 75 dr.

A haircut costs from 250 dr. at the most basic barber to 1,000 dr. at a posh hotel. Hairdressers charge from 500 to 1,500 dr.

WHEN TO GO. The main tourist season in Greece runs from about the beginning of April to the end of October, with the peak coming in July and August. For most British and American holiday-seekers the country is at its best from April to June and from September through October. Some of the islands, like Rhodes, Corfu and Crete cater for tourists all year round, but on the many rainy days offer little entertainment; it is pleasant but hardly sufficient that the daily average temperature through the year is about 71°F. Athens, in July and August, can make sightseeing hard work, but winter is pleasant.

July and August are not only the hottest months, but also the most tourist-ridden and expensive. On the other hand, for sun-worshippers the coast of Attica and the Aegean islands are quite bearable—a northerly wind, the *meltémi*, attenuates the midsummer heat. This is also the liveliest season, when Athenians flee their badly polluted city and crowd such fashionable spots as Corfu, Crete, Mykonos, Rhodes, etc. Therefore, if you intend to take your Greek vacation at the height of summer, plan well in advance to avoid disappointment. Count also on paying much higher prices during July and August.

Average maximum daily temperatures in degrees Fahrenheit and Celsius:

Athens	Jan.	Feb.	Mar.	Apr.	May	June	July	Aug.	Sept.	Oct.	Nov.	Dec.
°F	55	57	61	68	77	86	92	92	84	75	66	59
°C	13	14	16	20	25	30	33	33	29	24	19	15

Thessaloniki												
°F	48	54	57	68	77	86	90	90	82	72	61	52
°C	9	12	14	20	25	30	32	32	28	22	16	11

Off-Season Travel. This has become more popular in recent years as visitors have come to appreciate the advantages of avoiding the crowded periods. Transatlantic sea and air fares are cheaper and so are hotel rates. Even more important, you have a wider choice of accommodation in the tourist centers and more attentive service. Moreover, the Greeks are friendlier when not swamped by tourists. Spring is particularly delightful for nature lovers, fall is best for bathing, the sea being warm and the beaches empty; both seasons are the least exhausting for sightseeing. Winters are cold inland but fairly mild by the sea; except in Athens, there is little entertainment on the many rainy days.

SEASONAL EVENTS that attract foreign visitors to Greece include a full program of music and drama festivals, folklore events, and some international sports contests. The events summarized here are more fully described in the chapters covering the regions of Greece.

Religious ceremonies play a major role in Greek life and, fittingly, the new year commences with the feast of St. Basil when, according to an old Byzantine custom, the *Vassilopita,* a cake containing a coin, is sliced; the coin bestows good luck on the finder. A more solemn note is struck on **January** 6, when the Blessing of the Water at the celebration of Epiphany is especially impressive at Piraeus, the port of Athens. Carnival starts ten Sundays before the date fixed for Easter, gathering momentum through **February.** The Patra carnival processions are held on the two Sundays before Lent, usually early in **March.** On Shrove Monday, a holiday, there is a general exodus into the country; Thebes stages an amusing parody of a highland (Vlach) wedding. Military parades commemorate the outbreak of the War of Independence, on the Feast of the Annunciation, March 25, 1821. On Palm Sunday, Messolongi commemorates the heroic sortie of its defenders in 1826, during the War of Liberation.

To the Orthodox faith Easter is more important than Christmas and Greek Easter does not coincide with Protestant or Catholic Easter week. It is usually in **April.** Good Friday is kept as a day of mourning throughout the nation and in Athens the highest church dignitaries and members of the Government participate in the funeral procession. During Saturday midnight service, held in all churches, the light of resurrection is passed by candle from one to the other. General jubilation commences and continues on Easter Sunday. The traditional lamb-roasting takes place outdoors, followed by dancing, quite often in regional costumes. Visitors are welcomed at these festivities and made guests in Greek homes. Do as the Greeks do and try to get into the country where the most typical festivities are held at Arahova and Livadia not far from Delphi. Monday being a nationwide holiday, you are sure to get your fill of brotherhood and rejoicing. It is also at Arahova, the mountain town known for its handicrafts and wine, that on St. George's Day takes place the *mikro panegyri,* a "small celebration" which lasts all day and where you can witness the costumed dancing contest of old men. On the same day, dancing at Aharnés, just outside Athens.

The Sound and Light spectacle at the Acropolis of Athens, in Corfu and at the Palace of the Grand Masters in Rhodes is presented nightly in Greek, French or German from April through October.

The traditional *trata* is performed by the fisherfolk on Tuesday after Easter, at Megara. The same custom survives on the nearby island of Salamis. During the second half of **May** Macedonia enters the picture: Edessa holds a two weeks Flower Festival—a delayed action carnival. Langadas, near Thessaloniki, and Agia Eleni, near Seres, perform on May 21, feast of St. Constantine and St. Helen, the heretical Byzantine ceremony of the *anastenarides.* Its outstanding feature is the barefooted dancing on burning embers, holding icons.

In late **June** some special artistic events usually provided by renowned foreign orchestras and performers, are the curtain raiser to the cheapest of the world's acclaimed artistic manifestations, the International Athens Festival, which lasts well into September. It provides adequate value with performances of orchestral and chamber music, operas, ballets, as well as classical tragedies and comedies in the ancient Herodes Atticus open-air theater, on the slopes of the Acropolis.

The Epidaurus Festival presents ancient drama every weekend from mid-**July** through August. During the summer performances take place in the ancient theaters of Dodóni in Epirus, Philippi and Thassos in Macedonia, though to call them festivals (as the Olympus Festival, divided between the castle of Platamonas and the ancient theater of Dio), seems an overstatement. Navy Week in early July is celebrated in various ports, most originally at Agria near Volos and Plomari on Lesbos.

From early July to mid-September a Wine Festival is held in the park of the famous Byzantine monastery of Daphni, just outside Athens. You can taste dozens of wine from all parts of Greece. Deafening orchestras enliven several outdoor tavernas. A similarly bibulous festival at Alexandróupoli, Thrace, lasts from early July to mid-August.

A miscellany of expositions, musical and theatrical performances, lectures and folkloric events characterize the Epirotika at Ioanina, the Prose and Art Festival at Lefkáda, and the Hippokratia at Kos, in **August.** This is also a month of religious festivity. On the 6th, the Feast of the Savior, the people of Corfu island make their annual pilgrimage to the islet of Pontikonissi, where a fair is held afterwards. The hundreds of small boats converging upon it offer a sight to remember. Five days later on the same Corfu island, St. Spyridon is honored by a sumptuous procession, followed by festivities. The spotlight moves to the Aegean: there is a nationwide pilgrimage to Tinos (Cyclades) on August 15, to the miraculous icon of the Holy Virgin. You can witness picturesque processions on Ionian Zákynthos in commemoration of its patron saint, St. Dionysios, on August 24.

An international Sailsurfing competition is held in the Halkidiki and the International Fair at Thessaloniki opens in **September** for two weeks, accompanied by a Song Festival and followed first by a Greek Film Festival, then by the Dimitria Festival of Byzantine Music and Drama to October 26, St. Dimitrios' Day, while the second National Day on the 28th brings President and government to Thessaloniki for a big military parade.

 WHERE TO GO. With the annual number of tourists at two for every three inhabitants, Greece has risen to the top of the tourist league. Travelers today encounter all the comforts and facilities to which they are accustomed in this land of bold contrasts. Historically, the ancient Greek civilization, almost everywhere in evidence, is in sharp opposition to that of Byzantium, of the Norman and Frankish overlords and the maritime republics of Genoa and Venice. Strangely enough, nearly 500 years of Turkish rule left relatively few traces.

Scenically, the wild peaks of the Pindos range, or the mythological Olympos and Parnassos mountains are a world apart from the lush islands of Corfu, Zákynthos and Rhodes. Holiday-wise, the sleepy sun-soaked siesta of a coastal beach contrasts with a trip over the rugged mountain roads of Central Greece to the monasteries of Meteora or a leisurely island-hopping cruise on a chartered yacht. And contrasts of physical comfort range from the luxury category of the country's leading hotels to the rough-and-ready joys of some village's local taverna.

Greece is a sizeable country: its 51,173 square miles of land *plus* the sea lanes of the Aegean make it larger than Great Britain or Alabama; it has a population of over nine million. Distances are made to appear longer by the country's many mountain ranges and the vast area of the island groups. You will find that each region has its own character and traditions, its own attractions and charm.

Ionian Islands. Scattered along the western coast of Greece lie the islands which derive their name from mythological Io, one of Zeus' numerous loves. They were never subjected to Turkish rule and the graciousness and civilized formality of Venetian life still lingers on there. For British visitors the most interesting sights are the traces of the Protectorate which lasted half a century (1814–64), an interlude that has left the strongest mark on Corfu where graceful Regency palaces and monuments blend harmoniously into the fairytale setting; Zákynthos has long been known as the Flower of the Levant; Ithaki is the fabled home of Odysseus; and Lefkada is enlivened by an annual summer art festival. Kefalonia features good beaches, a wooded mountain, prehistoric and Venetian ruins.

Athens, Attica and Delphi. In 1834, Athens was chosen as the capital of the re-born Greek nation and since then it has grown from a derelict Turkish smalltown into one of Europe's largest and liveliest cities. This 20th-century badly-polluted boom town is dominated by the 5th-century B.C. Acropolis, a perpetual shrine of classic beauty, symbol of western civilization. The Plaka, the old quarter, just below the Acropolis, is crowded with *tavernas* and all sorts of evening entertainment. The National Museum is a tantalizing collection of masterpieces of the Greek archaic and classical periods and the Byzantine and Benaki museums will dazzle the visitor with their icons and exuberant peasant costumes.

From Mt. Ymitos (Hymettus) you overlook almost the whole of Attica; the Saronic Gulf, Salamis and Aegina, the plain of Marathon and Cape Sounio. The Monastery of Daphni, a few miles west, is the finest Byzantine monument in southern Greece.

Beyond Thebes and Livadia, in the midst of splendid mountain scenery, lies Delphi, seat of the most important oracle of ancient Greece and of the then-known world. The sacred precincts, in a singularly dramatic and numinous setting, remain impressive even in ruins.

The Peloponnese. Joined to the Greek mainland by the isthmus of Corinth, this mulberry-leaf shaped peninsula (hence its other name: Morea) is a tourist "must" second only to Athens and Delphi. It includes the ancient sites of the panhellenic Isthmian and Olympic games; the historic cities of austere Sparta and licentious Corinth; the antique theater of Epidaurus where Greek drama is presented each summer in a genuine setting, and the pre-historic site of Mycenae. Byzantine and medieval remains abound in splendid natural surroundings such as the Argive plain and the bay of Nafplio. Suntan can be easily acquired at numerous excellent beaches, especially on the west and south coast.

Epirus. Facing the Ionian Islands is Epirus, meaning "the solid land", whose port Igoumenitsa is the first mainland stop of the ferry boats from Italy. The provincial capital Ioanina, superbly situated on a lake promontory, retains a strongly oriental character. Parga is an outstandingly picturesque coastal village, while a Sunday excursion to the mountain village of Métsovo will acquaint you with undiluted Greek Folklore. To the south are the remains of the most ancient oracle, Dodona, and near medieval Arta the extensive ruins of Nikopolis, the Roman city Octavian built to commemorate his victory over Mark Anthony and Cleopatra at nearby Actium. If you have a rod with you, on the way you'll catch some trout without much effort in the scenic Louros river.

Thessaly. Volos is an industrial town and a terminal of a car and train ferry to Syria. It is sited below wooded Mt. Pilio which is easily accessible and shelters a score of picturesque villages many of which have now become summer resorts. There you can enjoy lusty village dancing on most Sundays. Ancient customs are still very strong around Larissa, the main city, and the excursion on to Tempe, a formidable defile six miles long, should not be missed. A unique experience for seasoned mountaineers is the ascent of Mitikas, highest peak of the Olympos chain. Lesser fry will restrict themselves to driving up to one of nature's wonders, the monasteries of Meteora, perched on gigantic rocks.

Macedonia and Thrace. Macedonia evokes Alexander the Great and Thessaloniki the Byzantine Empire of which there are many splendid vestiges in this modern city of nearly three quarter of a million inhabitants. The Museum contains—among other priceless exhibits—the recent finds from the "Tombs of Gold" at Vergina. The attractive seafront, studded with restaurants and cafes, is lively till late at night. Nearby Langadas is the scene of the firewalking ceremony of the *anastenarides*.

In the west, prosperous Kastoria, the "fur-city", has over 70 tiny Byzantine churches dating from the 11th to the 19th century. In the east, Kavala is an important tobacco center. The Turkish minority in Thrace introduces a colorful element. The Athos peninsula, home of a few hundred monks, has an autonomous status and can be visited for a day by men only and by permission obtainable from the Ministry of Foreign Affairs. These regulations must be strictly observed. Its 20 monasteries are treasure houses of Byzantine art.

The Aegean Archipelago. Comprised of 1,425 islands which are divided into several distinctive groups: the Argo-Saronic islands, easily accessible from Athens; the Sporades, as their name implies, scattered north of the central islands; the Cyclades, where Mykonos has developed into an international playground. In nearby Delos, the famous, weatherworn lions seem to stand guard over the sacred island, mythological birthplace of Apollo and Artemis. The eastern islands, off the Turkish coast, consist of sizeable Samos, Hios and Lesbos; and the Dodecanese, of which Rhodes is the most famous.

Halfway between three Continents, Crete boasts the earliest European civilization—that of the Minoan kings who introduced American plumbing and French super-bikinis 3,000 B.C., as you will be able to ascertain by visiting their palace and the museum at Iraklio.

In these islands you find a great variety of landscapes from volcanic, spectacular Thira to peaceful Paros and wooded Samothrace. Island life is just as varied: the sophistication of Rhodes contrasts sharply with the hard life on rocky Kalymnos and Symi whose surplus sponge-divers have settled in Florida. Since the Roman conquest of Greece the archipelago has seen Byzantine, Genoese and Venetian conquerors, followed by the Turks and some of the islands (such as Rhodes which was under Italian rule) achieved union with Greece only after World War II.

Caves. About 7,000 caves honeycomb the mountainous regions and several of these eerie, iridescent forests of stone have been opened to the public. Some have provided primitive man with the earliest form of shelter in which prehistoric artifacts have been found; others are remarkable for the variety of their colorful stalactites and convoluted stalagmites. Outstanding are: the Glýfada sea-cave at Pýrgos Dirou in the southern Peloponnese; the Perama cave near Ioanina in Epirus; the Drongorati caves and the Melissani sea-cave on Kefalonía; the Koutouki cave near Peania in Attica; Kokines Petres at Petralona, Halkidikí, where man found shelter 260,000 years ago.

SPAS, HOT SPRINGS. The thermal stations are gradually regaining the remarkable position they held 2,000 years ago in the Roman empire. An increasing number of foreign patients has in recent years benefited from the curative properties of the watering places, which have the added advantage of being mostly situated close to famous antiquities. Details of the facilities which these spas provide and of the disorders which they each cater for—from rheumatism to skin diseases—can be obtained from the *Greek National Tourist Organization*. The thermal establishments open from May through October.

 HOW TO GO. You have now decided *when* you want to visit Greece, and probably have a fair idea of *where* you wish to travel in that country. Now is the time to seek the advice of a travel agent. Even experienced travelers will find it advantageous to do so. He can help you avoid standing at station ticket windows and information offices, when you would rather be using your vacation time to see the sights. For package tour bookings and transportation reservations his charge to you will be the same as you would pay direct, as he receives a commission from carriers and tour operators. If he works out for you an individual itinerary, he will make a service charge on the total cost of your trip—usually 10 to 15%. If you don't know a reputable one, write to the *American Society of Travel Agents,* 4400 MacArthur Blvd., NW, Washington DC 20007; or the *Association of British Travel Agents,* 55 Newman St., London W1.

For further detailed information, contact the *Greek National Tourist Organization* (*GNTO*): in the **United States**—Olympic Tower, 645 Fifth Ave., New York, NY 10022; 611 W. Sixth St., Los Angeles, Calif. 90017; 168 N. Michigan Ave., Chicago, Ill. 60601.

In Canada—2 Place Ville Marie, Suite 67, Esso Plaza, Montreal, Quebec H3B 2C9.

In Great Britain—195–197 Regent St., London W1R 8DL.

Tour Operators. There are dozens of firms organizing holidays to Greece, ranging from luxurious art cruises to package camp-outs. The National Tourist Organization of Greece annually publishes *Travel Agent's Manual,* giving an itinerary, list of representatives in the U.S. and Greece, and all the major tour operators sending tours to Greece, and, for each, their tours for that particular year. The itineraries and prices listed here are representative of those offered by established operators; while specifics may vary from year to year, similar tours can always be found.

American Express combines Athens and classical Greece with a 5-day islands cruise for a total of 12 days, beginning at $795, plus airfare. *TWA's Aegean Adventure* runs for two weeks, covering Athens, the Greek Isles and Turkey, with land and sea arrangements $629–698. *International Weekends,* 1170 Commonwealth Ave., Boston, Mass. 02134, offers a one-week charter to Athens for $599, including airfare, hotel and some sightseeing.

From Britain, *Timsway Holidays,* Penn Place, Rickmansworth, Hertfordshire WD3 1RE, specializes in wide-ranging Greek holiday packages, with accommodations from 1st class hotels to bed and breakfasts and self-catering villas. *Cox & Kings* Ltd., 46 Marshall St., London W1, offers guided botanical tours of Cyprus and Crete from £585 for 15 days.

Among the classically-oriented tour operators are *Swan* (*Hellenic*), 237 Tottenham Court Rd., London W1P 0A1, who run cruises in connection with the *Hellenic Travellers Club*, accompanied by distinguished classical scholars who give lectures on board ship and at the various sites visited. These are exceptionally popular and it's wise to book a long way ahead. Approximate cost for two weeks, depending on cabin, ranges from £775 to £1,755. They also have excellent guided tours of Thrace and Macedonia in their *Art Treasures* program.

Olympic Holidays, 17 Old Court Place, Kensington High St., London W8 4PL, offer a huge variety of holidays in all parts of Greece, as well as cruises around the islands.

Roughing It. The National Tourist Organization of Greece, the Hellenic Touring Club and some private individuals have set up over 100 camping sites in some of the most attractive parts of the country. Those of the GNTO are usually the best sited and equipped. Fees per night are: adults 80–100 dr.; children 40–50 dr.; tent or caravan 80–120 dr. Camping is forbidden outside the organized camping sites.

Camping and Caravaning in Europe is published in the U.K. by A.A. Publications and is available in the U.S. through Rand McNally. It contains much useful information.

The Greek Youth Hostels Association, Dragatsaniou 4, Athens, is affiliated to the International Youth Hostel Federation and members are admitted to its 30 hostels throughout the country. The fee for joining in Greece is 300 dr. Members may stay at a hostel for five consecutive days; bed 120–180 dr.; bed-sheets an additional 35 dr.; breakfast 70–90 dr. To join in North America write to: *American Youth Hostels Inc.,* 1332 I St. NW, 8th Floor, Washington, D.C. 20005; or *Canadian Youth Hostels Assoc.,* 333 River Rd., Vanier City, Ottawa, Ontario. In Britain, contact the *Youth Hostels Assoc.,* 14 Southampton St., London WC2.

More comfortable are the YMCA, Omirou 28, Athens and Platia Han, Thessaloniki; the YWCA, Amerikis 11, Athens; Agias Sofias 11, Thessaloniki; summer only—Synikia Timiou Stavrou, Rethymno, Crete. Prices from 120 dr. in dormitories to 750 dr. in a single room with shower. Breakfast and one meal, 400 dr.

The Federation of Greek Excursionist Clubs, Dragatsaniou 4, Athens, runs summer colonies for legitimate artists and art students on the islands of Mykonos, Idra and Rhodes, and at Delphi.

In many parts of the country simple accommodation is available in private houses. The charges range from 500 dr. for a double room without bath up to 1,400 dr. for a double room with bath. Inquire of the Tourist Police in the area concerned.

 WHAT TO TAKE. Airline baggage allowances to most countries are figured by size rather than by weight. In First Class, two pieces, each up to an overall measure of 62 inches (length, width and height added together); in Economy Class, two pieces, neither one over 62 inches and both together not over 106 inches. Carry-on, underseat baggage up to 45 inches for either class. Extra charges for oversize can be very high. Some airlines make special provision for bicycles and skis, so inquire separately. Within Europe, many bus lines and international trains restrict the free baggage allowance to 55 pounds and porters are increasingly scarce these days.

Travel simply: Greece is an informal country, where one rarely dresses for dinner outside Athens and bikinis may be worn at any beach. In summer men wear lightweight slacks, open-neck shirts and sandals. Women prefer simple cotton dresses or slacks. Sunglasses, a flashlight for grottos, camping and monasteries; a pocket knife, thermos bottle and a towel or two will come in handy, as well as a hat with a visor or broad brim against the sun in summer. All hotels down to C category offer laundry facilities, but results vary greatly. Dry cleaning in all towns and resorts. Pharmacies stock a wide range of American and European drugs, cosmetics and suntan lotions. For roughing you'll need your own soap and a roll of toilet paper (small country or island hotels don't supply them).

Baggage by Air. The very first thing is to make sure your baggage is distinctive. If you have bought one of the mass-produced varieties, put some colored tape or other very easily spotted marking on it. You'll be amazed how many suitcases exactly like yours roll along that conveyor belt.

Don't pack valuables—jewelry, important papers, money and travelers checks—in your checked baggage. They should be close to you at all times.

Lock each item and put name and address labels both inside and outside.

Ensure that the check-in clerk puts the correct destination on the baggage tag and fixes it on properly.

Check that he puts the correct destination on the baggage claim tag attached to your passenger ticket.

If, by unlikely chance, your baggage doesn't appear on arrival, tell the airline representative immediately, so they have the details necessary to start their tracing system straightaway.

PASSPORTS. Americans. Major post offices and many county courthouses process passport applications, as do U.S. Passport Agency offices in various cities. Cost for adults is $35 for the passport itself plus a $7 processing fee when applying in person, $20 plus processing fee for those under 18. There is no extra fee when renewing or applying by mail. Adult passports are valid for 10 years, others for five years. Also needed: either a previous passport not more than eight years old or birth certificate/proof of citizenship; two identical photographs 2-inches square, full face and black and white or color; and proof of identity. Allow four to six weeks for processing, though in an emergency Passport Offices can have a passport readied within 24 to 48 hours.

British Subjects. You must apply for passports on special forms obtainable from main post offices or a travel agent. The application should be sent or taken to the Passport Office according to residential area (as indicated on the guidance form) or lodged with them through a travel agent. Apply at least 5 weeks before the passport is required. The regional Passport Offices are located in London, Liverpool, Peterborough, Glasgow and Newport. The application must be countersigned by your bank manager or by a solicitor, barrister, doctor, clergyman or justice of the peace who knows you personally. You will need two full-face photos. The fee is £15: passport valid for 10 years.

British Visitor's Passport. This simplified form of passport has advantages for the once-in-a-while tourist to most European countries (Yugoslavia and Eastern European countries presently excepted). Valid for one year and not renewable, it costs £7.50. Application may be made at main post offices in England, Scotland and Wales and at the Ministry of Health and Social Security offices in Northern Ireland. Birth certificate or medical card for identification and two passport photographs are required—no other formalities.

Visas. Not required. Nationals of the US and most American countries have to apply for a residence permit after a stay of two months; British subjects and Europeans, after three months.

Health Certificate. Not required for entry into Greece.

Getting to Greece

FROM NORTH AMERICA

 BY AIR. The Greek national flag carrier, *Olympic Airways,* and *TWA* operate daily flights from New York as well as Boston and Los Angeles to Athens with Boeing 747 jets. The majority of the flights are non-stop, taking about 9 hours eastbound and 10½ hours westbound.

The most economic fare from the U.S. is either a direct charter (for example, those offered by *International Weekends,* mentioned in the package tour section) or getting a regularly scheduled APEX flight to London and booking further passage from there. There are many package tours to choose from out of London—often at prices much lower than those available in the U.S.

Tour operators who have booked entire blocks of seats on scheduled flights offer economy-fare passage even for those not buying an entire package, and these can be as cheap as charter travel. Unless you want stopovers, which can only be got by taking one of the much more expensive regular flights, you will save greatly by picking one of the various types of excursion or package fares.

BY SHIP. Of the almost extinct liner services *Cunard's QE 2,* sailing to northern Europe has first- and tourist-class accommodation. You can also arrange for a fly/sail combination (flying one direction and going by ship the other). Increasingly limited freighter travel can also be found through *Freighter Travel Service,* 201 East 77 St., New York, NY 10021 or *Pearl's Freighter Tips,* 175 Great Neck, NY 11021.

The most popular alternative for travelers to Greece seeking to spend time on the water is to take a short Mediterranean cruise around various Greek ports and/or one that takes in, say, Greece, Turkey, Israel and Egypt. Among those offering such cruises are *Paquet,* 1370 Avenue of the Americas, New York, NY 10019 and *Royal Viking,* 630 Fifth Avenue, New York, NY 10111. In the latter instance, cruises can begin in San Francisco, Fort Lauderdale or New York before continuing across the Atlantic.

FROM GREAT BRITAIN

BY AIR. Olympic Airways and British Airways operate pool services to Greece, the former using the Airbus, the latter Tristars or Boeing 737s. Most services go to Athens, but there are also non-stop flights to Thessaloniki and Corfu as well as through flights to Crete and Rhodes by Olympic only. Flying time to Athens from London is about 3½ hours, about 30 minutes less to Corfu and Thessaloniki.

The APEX fare to Athens from London for 1985 is likely to be around £195 with variations according to season. Charter flights are also available but you must have at least basic accommodation booked (and can prove it) before you can use these to Greece. Charter flights are, of course, much cheaper and it is often well worthwhile taking the basic accommodation offered with these, although you do not have to occupy it. Charter fares to Athens for 1984 are likely to be around £165 to £190, slightly less to Corfu.

APEX and charter fares do not allow any stop-overs en route. If you want to do that then you must take the full fare which is around the £350 to £400 mark.

BY TRAIN. To travel all the way from the U.K. to Athens is for the rail enthusiast, as it requires some stamina. There are no through services from the continental Channel ports or indeed from Paris either.

The most convenient routes by train are from Dortmund (in northwest Germany) or Munich or Venice, the last being the quickest at around 38 hours. The others take between 48 and 52 hours from the start. These trains certainly connect with services from London, but in each case you must also allow an additional 15 to 20 hours travel. Through carriages, including 2nd class couchettes, operate on the three above routes from the starting points, and there are buffet services part of the way.

BY BUS. From London there are several direct services to Athens, some operating throughout the year, others in summer (May to September) only. *Supabus* has a year-long service departing Friday evenings, changing coaches in Munich, and arriving in Athens three days after initial departure. Buses also leave on Sat. during Nov. and Dec., and Sun. during Jan. through Mar. Approximate cost is £107 return (1984 figure).

There are other services such as by *Euroways* (part of the long-established Wallace Arnold group in England) taking the same time, basically, but traveling via Italy (Milan). And there are some Greek-owned operations which involve only one night stopping, the others traveling. These are cheaper but are very tiring. The U.K. government has tightened up the rules governing coach operations between London and Athens requiring more drivers and a change of coach at Milan. *Always check* on the operator for these cheaper services and find out about how many drivers are carried (two minimum, three unless there are changes en route) and also how long the stops are along the way.

BY CAR. The shortest route from Britain, if you want to drive all the way, is from Ostend via Nurnberg, Munich, Salzburg and Klagenfurt to Ljubljana in Yugoslavia, then along that country's only through highway to Beograd and Skopje, connecting with the Greek motorway at the border station of Evzoni. The scenically lovelier Adriatic highway turns inland before Albania and connects with the Greek roads at Niki. Both about 1,900 miles.

Car-Sleeper Expresses. Some 825 miles and two or three days of driving can be saved by crossing from Dover to Ostend and boarding the summer express from Brussels to Ljubljana (Yugoslavia). Driving may be greatly reduced by using the Paris-Milan and Milan-Brindisi car-sleeper and then a car-ferry to Corfu, Igoumenitsa or Patra. While the car-sleeper is apparently expensive, it whittles down somewhat when set off against the expenses of gasoline and hotels. It is obviously more advantageous for a party of four than two. The RAC and AA provide bookings and information.

See also below, *By Car from the Continent*.

FROM THE CONTINENT

 BY AIR. Athens is connected to all major European and Middle Eastern cities by daily flights. There are also direct flights from several of these cities to Corfu and Thessaloniki. Charter flights in connection with inclusive holidays operate to Athens, Corfu, Thessaloniki, Crete, Rhodes and several of the smaller islands.

 BY TRAIN. As mentioned in the section on travel from the U.K. the main train connections to Greece are from Germany and Italy. The following trains operate these—

Hellas Express—Dortmund—Dusseldorf—Cologne—Stuttgart—Munich—Salzburg—Ljubljana—Zagreb—Belgrade—Nij—Thessaloniki—Athens.

Akropolis Express—as above, but starting at Munich.

Venezia Express—Venice—Trieste—Ljubljana and then as above.

In addition you can take the train to Brindisi (good connections from Turin, Milan and Rome) then the overnight ferry to Patra and either train or coach to Athens.

 BY SHIP. There are numerous services from Adriatic ports—Trieste, Venice, Ancona, Brindisi, Bari, Rijeka, to Corfu, Igoumenitsa, Patra and Iráklio (Crete); very few call at Piraeus (Athens). Not all of the lines service all of these ports. All ships from Italy and Yugoslavia are ferries.

 BY CAR. If you're driving overland through Europe you may cross the frontier into Greece from Yugoslavia, via Bitola (border stations Medzitlija-Niki) or at Gevgelija-Evzoni. A detour through Bulgaria can be made from Nis via Sofia-Thessaloniki, crossing the border at Promahonas. You could drive the length of Yugoslavia as far as Albania on the scenic Dalmatian corniche, about the same distance when coming from Italy. It is not possible to enter Albania except as a member of an accredited travel group. No one can take in a private car and American citizens are totally barred. So go, if you will, as far as Dubrovnik, then turn inland to join the motorway at Skopje.

Car-Sleeper Expresses. Useful services for motorists from interior continental countries en route for Greece are: Paris-Milan, about 12½ hours; Milan-Brindisi, 15 hours; Düsseldorf-Milan, 14 hours. Mostly summer services running two or more times weekly.

Car Ferries. Many shipping lines, both Greek and Italian, sail daily between various Italian east coast ports—Venice, Ancona, Bari, Brindisi and Otranto—and Greece. Mainland destinations include Igoumenitsa and Patra, but rarely Piraeus while the principal island destination is Corfu. The shipping lines are the *Achaic, Adriatica, Fragline, Hellenic Mediterranean, Ionian, Karageorgis, Marline* and *Minoan.* Some ferries also continue on to Crete and Cyprus and from there to Alexandria in Egypt and Haifa in Israel.

There are also twice-weekly sailings from Dubrovnik in Yugoslavia to Corfu and Igoumenitsa.

Four car ferries ply every week between the ports of Volos in Thessaly on the east coast of Greece and Tartoush in Syria.

Most boats are airconditioned and have three cabin classes as well as a large number of aircraft-type seats in the observation saloon, besides restaurant, bar and swimming pool.

Arriving in Greece

CUSTOMS. The dual flow Green and Red System operates at most customs posts; Green if nothing to declare, Red even if in doubt. Duty free for passengers arriving from an EEC country are 300 cigarettes or 75 cigars, 1.25 liter of alcoholic beverages or 4 liters of wine, 75 gr. perfume; gifts up to a total value of 11,000 dr. Passengers from any other countries can bring in 200 cigarettes or 50 cigars, 1 liter of alcoholic beverages or 2 liters of wine, 50 gr. perfume and gifts up to a total value of 2,500 dr.

Cats and dogs require a health and rabies inoculation certificate issued by a veterinary authority in the country of origin stating that inoculations took place not more than 12 months (for cats 6 months) and not less than 6 days prior to arrival. Health clearance at port of entry.

Foreign banknotes in excess of $500 (about £250) must be declared for re-export. There is no restriction on travelers' checks. Only 3,000 drachmes may be imported or exported.

At the end of your stay you may take out, duty free, almost any amount of souvenirs and gifts. For purchases of archeological items etc., you will have to obtain an export license.

Staying in Greece

 THE LANGUAGE. English presents no problem in the better hotels and restaurants; even in modest establishments, someone is usually able to cope. Yet it is useful to possess a smattering of everyday phrases and words—some of which will be found in the Vocabulary at the end of this book. But the written alphabet is not the same as the one you are used to back home, so let us get that out of the way first. Without a fair mastery of the letters, you will find that many of the signs around you are simply incomprehensible.

The ancient Greek alphabet of 24 letters has remained unchanged and you won't find it difficult to recognize A, E, I, K, M, N, O, T, Y and Z. The letter B is pronounced V; H reads like EE; P like R, and X is a guttural CH; Π stands for P and Ξ for X.

Let's see the remaining letters: Δ = D, Γ = G, Λ = L, Ω = O, Σ = S, Θ = TH, Φ = PH, Ψ = PS. The letter C does not exist in Greek and is substituted by K, except in the name Pórto Carrás—and surely nobody expects a Greek shipowner to abide by the rules and regulations in his own home!

Though now able to read ΑΘΗΝΑ, ΘΕΣΣΑΛΟΝΙΚΗ, ΟΛΥΜΠΙΑ, and even some mysterious advertisements like ΜΠΑΤΕΡΙΑ (battery), don't think you've mastered the language! Although demotic (*dimotikí,* vernacular Greek) was officially imposed in 1977, most educated people, several authors and newspapers still speak and write in *kathomilouméni,* which is more akin to ancient Greek; but both follow the same rules of pronunciation, which differ considerably from the Erasmic—the Greek taught in classics' classes in American and British schools and universities. Biblical (*koiné*) Greek, yet another variation, is still read in church.

But this should not worry the normal traveler. What may well prove a problem is the confusion over the naming of places, and we must now try to explain the morass of variations which you will find in print, on maps or on signposts.

Place Names. To make the signposts, maps and travel handouts comprehensible to tourists from all nations, indications are given in Greek as well as Latin characters, but phonetically according to the modern Greek pronunciation, which differs not only from the ancient Greek, but even more from the latinized forms mainly used in English, French and German.

As if it were not enough that many villages, mountains and rivers are called differently by the locals from the classical names favored by officialdom, *dimotikí* has changed most endings of names. Hence the confusing (how often we find ourselves using that word!) variety of indications, about evenly divided between the old and the new, even for the capital itself; thus Athina (new) as well as Athine (old). Names that reverberated through history for millenia have been deprived of their final "n" or "s". Pólis (town) has not been spared and has been reduced to póli, yet an "s" has often been added to the endings of the names of mountains and rivers. We give the new demotic form first in the text under the main entry, with the generally-used anglicized name in brackets, and then employ the generally-used name throughout the text for such familiar places as Athens and Corinth. AE and AI have been replaced by E (Aegina = Egina); EI, H, OI, and Y by I (but not consistently, Y is creeping back again, for some inexplicable reason more in the islands, while Olympia and Olympos have always remained sacrosanct); the guttural Greek X, often rendered in Latin CH or KH is now spelled H (Achaia = Ahaia, Chios = Hios); the Greek aspirate ('), which equalled the Latin H, was abolished as an afterthought in 1983 (Heraklion = Iráklio); GH and RH become simple G and R (Aghios = Agios, Rhodes = Rodos); PH becomes F (Phaestos = Festos).

Though neither the Greek capital letters nor the Latin characters are accented, we have stressed the relevant syllable when the name first occurs, as well as in the tourist vocabulary, as otherwise you might not be understood.

Street Names in most towns and resorts are likewise indicated in both alphabets, but following the Greek habit, only in the possessive case of the name, omitting *odós* (street), but not necessarily *leofóros* (avenue) or *platía* (square); 3 Stadium Street thus becomes "Stadiou 3." Renaming streets is a favorite pastime of Greek municipalities.

 HOTELS. There are six official categories of hotel in Greece, graded according to the level of comfort and service offered. These grades are L, A, B, C, D and E. They relate to our own grading system—(L) Luxury, (E) Expensive, (M) Moderate, (I) Inexpensive—thus: (L) = L; (E) = A; (M) = B; (I) = C and D. The official E, the rockbottom grading, exists mostly in remote areas and though clean is probably better avoided and does not figure in our own listings. The Luxury grading, is generally below the equivalent grading in other western countries, though above its Balkan counterparts, and usually not what most of our readers would expect from Luxury establishments; the international chains are notable and creditable exceptions to this generalization. The lower gradings are mostly of strictly utilitarian sameness, lacking any individual features or atmosphere.

The price range of these categories is as follows: (L) 4,500 to 11,000 dr. single, 6,000 to 13,000 double; (E) 2,000 to 3,500 dr. single, 2,500 to 4,000 double; (M) 1,300 to 1,800 dr. single, 1,700 to 2,500 double; (I) 900 to 1,300 dr. single, 1,200 to 1,700 double.

Hotels are open all year round in the towns, though most close from November to April 15 in the beach resorts. (L) and (E) are nearly always airconditioned, (M) sometimes are and even (I) occasionally.

The few pensions are not distinguishable with the naked eye; by some quirk of officialdom they are graded one category above the price they are authorized to charge. Some will be listed together with the (I) hotels, while the rather expensive service flats will join the (E)s. At the lower end are almost 50,000 rooms in authorized private houses. These village guest houses are divided into three categories, with prices ranging from 500 to 1,400 dr. for a double room. The roughly one half in A and B categories are often grandiloquently advertized as flats or apartments. They differ from hotels mainly in providing cooking facilities, but little or no service. In the high season they are popular with Greek families. Because of the smallness of the units, no lists are available. Careful inspection is indicated; even more so for C category and the 150,000 unauthorized rooms, which are sometimes even cheaper, but rarely cleaner. In view of the unpredictable side effects, being a paying guest in a Mediterranean household should be by choice and not as a last resort. There are also over 100 holiday camps and organized camping sites.

All hotels listed have been opened or at least modernized subsequent to 1960 and thus have showers, even in the (I) category. Most (E) and (M) resort hotels insist on half board, full board available on demand. Not all (I) hotels have restaurants, which will be stated in each case. (I)s are rarely referred to by travel agencies, yet those listed are adequate for basic needs.

Reservations for the summer season should be made well in advance. A confirmation is necessary, especially if any deposit has been paid. As few hotels bother to answer individual letters, it is advisable to make arrangements through a travel agency. Overbooking is a major problem in the summer—be sure you have a written confirmation of your reservation.

Picturesque villages have been dolled up by the GNTO as traditional settlements far from the hubbub of the crowded popular resorts. On the islands of Hios, Kefalonia and Thira, in the Peloponnese and on Mt. Pilio, otherwise largely abandoned villages have been restored and modern conveniences installed. Rooms are rented at (M) category prices, whilst a whole house comes to between 10,000 and 25,000 dr. a week. Local craftsmen are encouraged and a local village atmosphere is maintained.

Villas. Renting a villa or apartment may be pleasant and economical for a long vacation, but it is chancy to rely on the uniformly glamorous advertisement photos. Only reputable agencies should be used. Among those in the U.S., try *Interchange/Villas International*, 213 E. 38 St., New York, N.Y. 10016. In addition, the GNTO, 645 Fifth Ave., New York, N.Y. 10022, publishes a list of Greek agents with whom you may deal directly.

In the UK: *Corfu Villas Ltd.*, 43 Cheval Place, London SW7; *Timsway Holidays*, Penn Place, Rickmansworth, Herts. (tel. 0923-771266). And, again, the GNTO can advise.

 HOLIDAY VILLAGES. These are on commercial lines, catering mostly to foreign visitors. Some of them offer package holidays, including charter flights from various points of Western Europe or boat from

Italy. Accommodation is in bungalows, bamboo huts or tents. They have their private beach, dance band and other entertainment and they offer organized excursions, sailing, underwater fishing, etc. Rates range from 500 dr. bed and breakfast in the Eros bamboo village to 6,000 dr. full board, including wine, per day in the luxury hotels of the Club Méditerranée.

Angistri, island off Egina. Apply: STS Ltd., Filellinon 1, Athens 118.

Club Méditerranée, at Corfu (three sites), Euboea (Gregolimano), and Egio-Lambiri, 18 miles east of Patra. Apply: Club Méditerranée, 8 Rue de la Bourse, Paris; 40 Conduit St., London, W1; Syngrou Ave. 302, Athens.

Club Poseidon, Loutraki, 50 miles from Athens. Apply direct.

Engazi—Z. Plage (Bungo huts), Diakofto, Peloponnese, 110 miles from Athens. Apply direct.

Eros Beach, Petalidi Messinias, south coast of the Peloponnese, between Kalamata and Koroni. Apply Ippokratous 71, Athens 144.

Hercules Beach, Poros, Kefalinia, 27 miles from Argostoli. Apply: Kalamaki Beach, Filellinon 4, Athens 118.

Kalogria Beach, 25 miles beyond Patra. Apply Arvanitis, Kalogria, Metohi.

Lassi Holiday Center (only for youths under 25) on Kefalonia; eight-bed bungalows. Apply at Argostoli.

Libero Camping, five miles before the Corinth Canal. Apply: Libero Tours, Ag. Konstantinou 2, Athens.

Pirgi Village, ten miles north of Corfu town. Apply: Mastoras Travel, Sophocleous 23, Athens.

Sikyon Beach, Xylokastro, 75 miles from Athens. Apply direct.

 RESTAURANTS. Although we include (L) meals prices below—they are for meals in Luxury hotels— the scarcity of worthwhile restaurants restricts our usual listing of (E) Expensive, (M) Moderate, and (I) Inexpensive. The price ranges within these gradings, for lunch or dinner, are as follows: (L) 1,500 to 3,000 dr.; (E) 1,200 to 2,000 dr.; (M) 600 to 1,200 dr.; (I) 300 to 600 dr. Breakfast will range (L) 160 to 300 dr.; (E) 140 to 220 dr.; (M) 120 to 180 dr.; (I) 100 to 120 dr. These prices are for one person, inclusive of taxes and tips, but exclusive of beverages.

Only hotels offer set menus; they are unimaginative but at the lower end of the (M) price range. At the seaside try the open-air tavernas, where you walk into the kitchen and choose your own dishes. Breakfast is served continental style.

Service is sometimes slow and uncertain in the lesser places; don't be shy, call loudly for the waiter by saying *"garçon, parakaló."*

 TIPPING. Hotel bills include a service charge of 15%. For a longer stay, an extra 10% might be divided among chambermaid, porter and room service. Except for the hotel menus, restaurants list somewhat confusingly two prices for each dish, without and with the added

12–15% service charge; the former for taking away the food. In better-class establishments it is customary to leave an extra 5% to 10% for the waiter; but even in the lowliest tavern 5–10 dr. per person must be left for junior (*mikfos*) who did most of the serving *on the table* (and not on the plate on which the bill is presented and where it will be taken by the waiter). At Christmas and Easter restaurant service charges are increased to 20% for two or three weeks. In cafés and bars service is included in the price of drinks; leave an extra 5%. On cruises, cabin and dining room stewards are tipped at the rate of about 100 dr. per day.

Barbers and hairdressers expect 20 to 30%. Strangely enough one does not usually tip taxi-drivers. Check what the meter indicates (25 dr. on the clock then 15 dr. per km, minimum charge 70 dr.), and round off the amount shown to the next multiple of 10. 15 dr. are added per piece of luggage and after midnight, 15 dr. at Christmas and Easter. Porters charge according to a fixed scale, usually 15 drachmes per bag; hotel porters and bellhops expect 20 dr. per bag. Ushers at cinemas, theaters and concerts expect 5–10 dr. for showing you to your seat. Hat-check attendants expect 20 drachmes or more, depending on the type of place you are in and the number in your party. Washroom attendants receive 10 to 20 dr. according to the use you made of the facilities.

MAIL, TELEPHONES. Airmail letters within Europe, 27 dr. for 20 grams, 20 dr. for postcards. To the U.S. and Canada, 32 dr. for 20 grams, 25 dr. for postcards. A letter from England or the U.S. may reach Athens in 48 and 72 hours respectively, but might take up to a week in some out-of-the-way island.

Public telephones, coin operated, are at all the numerous newspaper kiosks. Local calls cost 2 dr., long distance calls within the country from 4 dr. to 45 dr. for three minutes. Night calls (from 9 P.M. to 5 A.M.) are slightly cheaper. To phone to New York you will have to pay 513 dr. for three minutes, and 171 dr. for each additional minute; to London 195 dr. for three minutes and 65 dr. for each additional minute. No special night rates.

The main Post Office in Athens is at Eolou 100, branch offices on Syntagma Square and Omonia subway station. Central Cable Office: 28 Oktovriou 85; Central Telephone Exchange: Stadiou 15.

CLOSING TIMES. The principal national and religious holidays are: January 1, New Year's Day; January 6, Epiphany; Shrove Monday, usually early March; March 25, Greek Revolution (1821) Memorial Day; Good Friday to Easter Monday; Whitsun Monday (50 days later); May 1, May Day; August 15, Assumption; October 28, Ochi Day; December 25–26, Christmas.

Clocks go forward one hour from the first Sunday in April to the last Sunday in September. The GNTO supplies a list of banks which remain open afternoons and Sundays. Business hours vary from season to season and from district to district; thus, Athens summer hours are as follows:

banks..................	8 A.M. to 2.30 P.M. (Mon.–Fri.)
travel agencies..........	9 A.M. to 1.30 P.M. and 4.30 to 7.30 P.M. (closed Sat. afternoons)
restaurants	noon to 3.30 P.M. and 7.30 P.M. to midnight
cafés	8 A.M. to well after midnight
nightclubs..............	9 P.M. to 3 A.M.
cinemas................	5 P.M. to midnight (open-air, 8 to midnight.)

 HINTS FOR BUSINESSMEN. Normal office hours are from 8 A.M. to 1.30 P.M. and from 4.30 to 7.30 P.M., but several large firms keep the same hours as ministries and public corporations, 7.30 A.M. to 2.30 P.M.; more in summer than in winter. Almost all offices are closed Wednesday and Saturday afternoons. The number of cups of Greek coffee served is inverse to the size of the company; sophisticated companies go in for whiskey. Punctuality is expected from the foreigner—punctual as an Englishman is constantly quoted—but not necessarily reciprocated.

Secretarial assistance can be obtained through the reception desk of the better-class hotels, where telex and cable facilities are also available.

 LAUNDRY. Relatively cheap and quick in all hotels down to C category, though ironing is often careless. Laundromats in all major towns. In Athens: *Aparámillon*, 28 Oktovriou 3; *Lux,* Tríti Septemvríou 13; *Star*, Venizélou Ave. 67, all near Omonia. Plyntex, Voukourestíou 34; *Golfinopoulos,* Kydathinéon 24, near Syntagma.

CONVENIENT CONVENIENCES. Except at air terminals and railway stations there are hardly any. The one on Syntagma Square in Athens is not signposted. You can use the facilities in the better cafés; in the simpler places it's very often of the no-seat variety.

NEWSPAPERS. English and Paris-published American papers are on sale toward late afternoon on the day of their publication. The daily English-language *Athens News* (30 dr.) is useful for happenings in town; also available is the monthly *Athenian* (100 dr.).

 PHOTOGRAPHY. Greece is the perfect f-22 country, and indeed the bright sunlight and endless color and variety of the landscape seem to cry aloud to be photographed or filmed. You can buy Ilford, Kodak, Gevaert and Agfa film in all the better photo-shops. Black and white film can be developed and printed practically everywhere in Greece. Color film and motion picture footage can also be processed in Athens but may take too long for you. There is hardly a Greek who does not wish to be immortalized in photography, and even simple country folk will strike photogenic poses.

It is somewhat less than wise to photograph to seaward on border islands, or wherever it is expressly forbidden. Care should be taken in this regard.

Don't leave already exposed film in your pockets or in any hand luggage while passing through airport X-ray machines. The process can sometimes fog the film and you may find a whole trip's photographs ruined. It is worth investing in a product called *Filmashield,* a lead-laminated pouch. It stores flat when not in use and holds quite a lot of film—or, indeed, your camera with half-used film in it. It is available in many countries and, while it is not the complete answer, it is certainly worth trying.

 MEDICAL SERVICES. The *I.A.M.A.T.* (International Assoc. for Medical Assistance to Travelers) offers you a list of approved English-speaking doctors who have had postgraduate training in the U.S., Canada or Gt. Britain. Membership is free; the scheme is world-wide with many European countries participating. For information apply in the U.S. to 736 Center St., Lewiston, N.Y. 14092; in Canada, 123 Edward St., Suite 725, Toronto, Ontario MSG 1E2; in Europe, 17 Gotthardstrasse, 6300 Zug, Switzerland. A similar service is provided by *Intermedic,* 777 Third Ave., New York, N.Y. 10017, but there is an initial membership charge of $6 per person, or $10 per family; there is a subsequent schedule of prices for house and hotel calls, etc. *Intermedic* is affiliated with Carte Blanche.

Travelers from Britain can avail themselves of the unlimited medical assistance provided by *Europ Assistance Ltd.,* 252 High Street, Croydon, Surrey. When you need help, there is a 24-hour, seven days a week (all holidays included) telephone service staffed by multilingual personnel. Medical advisors give world-wide cover and, additionally, casualty surgery specialists, plus air and road ambulances, are on call throughout Western and Eastern Europe, Turkey, Tunisia, and the Mediterranean islands, (the Canary Islands and Madeira for nonmotorists). Medical expenses insurance of up to £10,000 is also included. Worldwide cover is divided into 3 zones and both individual and group travelers are eligible at a basic price of £9.75 per person for 13 to 23 days coverage including all baggage; £2.35 for each additional week. This service is available to British residents only.

POLLUTION REPORT. Much of the long, indented coast of the mainland and the innumerable islands is unpolluted, owing to a stringent enforcement of the international conventions by spotter planes of the harbor police, which impartially impose heavy fines for any violation on Greek and foreign shipping alike. Yet, like anywhere in the Mediterranean, an occasional slick of tar, for which warships are usually blamed, is washed ashore even on the most remote beaches.

The bigger island towns, especially Corfu, pour out a seemingly disproportionate amount of sewage, luckily restricted to the town seafront. Bathing is prohibited in all the major ports—not that anyone would want to. Greater Athens' shores are washed by a chemical mixture of which H_2O is only a part. The effluent of four million people and the bulk of the country's industry give the Homeric wine dark sea a wholly new connotation. The water is considered clean when the filth at the bottom becomes visible. The same holds good for Thessaloniki, where the Aretsou beach had to be closed, and Volos. Near these industrial zones air pollution is sometimes four times what W.H.O. considers safe. Nearly half of it comes from cars. Athens is increasingly under a "chemical cloud," a euphemistic term for obnoxious pollution which is as harmful to man as it is to the antique marbles.

 SEA SPORTS. Along 9,333 miles of coastline water sports are, of course, by far the most important. Swimming is safe everywhere, there are neither currents nor tides. Organized beaches, mainly under the aegis of the GNTO, as well as all larger beach hotels, provide water skiing and wind surfing—a runaway popular pastime.

Submarine fishing without breathing apparatus is permitted, except in ports or at organized beaches.

Submarine fishing with breathing apparatus is forbidden; gogglers, however, may explore the underwater abysses for entertainment only in certain specific areas, like the Cyclades, the Ionian Islands and the Halkidiki peninsula. Check with the local GNTO or the tourist police.

Swimming and diving lessons at the *Hellenic Federation of Submarine Activities,* Agios Kosmas (8 miles from Athens), tel. 981 9961, and at several organized beaches.

Fishing tackle and boats can be hired at most coastal towns and villages. Charge for a rowing boat is about 300 dr. per hour, for a motorboat from 700 to 900 dr. *Amateur Anglers and Maritime Sports Club,* Akti Moutsopoulou, Zea Harbor, Piraeus, tel. 451 1311.

Sweetwater fishing is free all over Greece and its principal catch is the mountain trout. The best regions are: Epirus (rivers Voidomatis, Kalamas, Louros, Aoos and the artificial lakes); Central Greece (Sperhios, Tavropos and Acheloos); Peloponnese (Vouraïkos, Alfios and Ladonas).

 SAILING AND YACHTING. The jagged coasts and innumerable islands offer a unique blend of archeology, folklore, fishing, skin diving or just lazing in the sun. If possible, don't pick the months of July or August for your sea cruise. The Aegean can be a great deal rougher than most people think, especially in August when the *meltemi,* the north wind, is a regular visitor to these waters. Yachting is a year-round sport in Greece and the water is fine for swimming from May to the end of October. Zea harbor in Piraeus offers the most extensive mooring and wintering facilities. Among the remaining 100 yacht supply stations, Vouliagmeni, Gouvia (Corfu), Rhodes, Pata, Syros and Thessaloniki are best equipped.

From April through November the Royal Yacht Club of Greece organizes a series of international sailing races under the IYRU rules.

Renting a Yacht. Yacht rental agencies and travel agents have over 1,000 yachts of all sizes and at all prices for hire, but in high season it is necessary to book well in advance. Complaints are frequent, even on the luxury vessels.

In the U.S.: Best write ahead directly, but do hold on to any written confirmation you are sent.

In Great Britain: *Halsey Marine International Ltd.*, 22 Boston Place, Dorset Sq., London NW1 6HZ (tel. 01-724 1303); *Yachting Enterprises Ltd.*, 14 Oak Tree Meadow, Walton, Wakefield, W. Yorks. WF2 6TF (tel. 0924-251815); *Worldwide Yachting Holidays*, c/o Liz Fenner, 35 Fairfax Pl., London NW6 48J (tel. 01-328 1033/4).

In Greece: *Zea Marina Yacht Service Center*, Zea Marina, Piraeus.

To avoid an endless exchange of letters with an agency, it is essential to give the following information in your first letter when you write to reserve a yacht: desired date and period of charter; the number of passengers; the type of craft you want—auxiliary sailing yacht, motor yacht or caique.

What Will It Cost? There is something for every budget—on condition that your budget is not too tight! The prices quoted are only approximate, because you must also take into account the season which you choose for your trip, the age of the vessel and the facilities aboard. They cover the wages and expenses of the crew, insurance, sometimes fuel (for a maximum of eight hours sailing every day) and all other expenses connected with the charter.

Boats are available at prices varying from 10,000 to 500,000 dr. per day. Sailing boats from 24 to 75 feet long without crew from 8,000 to 50,000 dr. per day for four to ten passengers.

Motor caiques from 35 to 70 feet long, accommodating four to ten passengers, cost from 10,000 to 45,000 dr. a day.

Motor sailers from 60 to 85 feet long, accommodating six to ten passengers, from 80,000 to 120,000 dr. a day; and deluxe yachts, of over 100 feet long, accommodating eight to ten passengers, from 150,000 to 250,000 dr. a day. Yachts over 500 tons run from 250,000 to 500,000 dr. a day.

If you want to take all your meals on board, 700 to 900 dr. per person per day (for three meals) should be added. A cook can also be hired and his wages will be additional to the charges mentioned. It's hard to cook aboard a small craft where there is just about enough room to prepare breakfast and nothing else. This, however, is no serious disadvantage because nothing prevents you from going ashore at meal times to have a reasonably priced lunch or dinner at one of the tavernas you are bound to find there.

If you have two weeks or so for your cruise, then you will have no problem in planning your itinerary. But if you only have a week, the question becomes somewhat more delicate. Here we offer two alternatives, allowing, however, for only the briefest visits ashore.

	Trip No. 1.	*Trip No. 2.*
1st Day	Aegina-Ydra	Sounio-Serifos
2nd Day	Milos	Ios-Thira
3rd Day	Iraklio (Crete)	Astypalea
4th Day	Thira-Ios	Rhodes
5th Day	Paros	Kos-Kalymnos
6th Day	Delos-Mykonos	Mykonos-Delos
7th Day	Tinos-Syros	Tinos-Kythnos
8th Day	Zea-Piraeus	Zea-Piraeus

GAME SHOOTING. Permits are easily obtainable from the local Forestry Departments; 1,500 dr. for two months, 3,000 dr. for the whole shooting season from August 1 to March 31. Payment for local beaters is about 500 dr. a day. Five special hunting areas have been created, on the islands of Antipaxi (near Corfu), Atalantonisi (off Kammena Vourla), Dia (facing Iraklio, Crete), Elafonisi (in the Laconic Gulf) and Sapientza (facing Methoni). The wild mountain goat, an imposing beast, and the stags (*platykeros*) of Rhodes are protected.

Shooting season: from August to March, according to the game; there is hare, quail, partridge, waterfowl, woodcock and wild boar. *Confederation of Greek Shooting Clubs*, Koraï 2, Athens 132.

MOUNTAINEERING. *The Greek Skiing and Alpine Association*, Karageorgi Servias, 7 Athens 126, tel. 323 4555, operates some 40 mountain refuges (Olympos, Parnassos, Taygetos, White Mountains, etc.). Cost is 200 dr. per night and 150 dr. for members of foreign alpine clubs. Pack animals with guide cost around 1,500 dr. per day. Points of departure: for the Olympos range, Litohoro (sub-section of the HAC); for Mt. Vermio Seli. There are sections of the HAC at other important starting points, such as Ioanina and Iraklio (Crete). Climbers who are visiting Northern Greece should contact the Thessaloniki section, Karolou Deal 15. All guides have a rudimentary inkling of English, French or German.

SKIING. The four main ski centers in order of importance are: Mount Parnassos, Mount Vermio, Metsovo and Mount Pilio. Skilifts operate on ten other mountains.

GOLF. The 18-hole *Glifada Golf Course* is near the airport, eight miles from Athens. Entrance fee 400 dr. per day, 750 dr. weekends. Golf clubs 200 dr., pushcart 100 dr., caddy 500 dr. The courses on Corfu, Porto Carras and Rhodes are international standard. There is a 9-hole course on Skiathos.

RIDING. *Hellenic Riding Club*, Paradissou 18, Amaroussi, eight miles from Athens; *Athens Riding Club*, Yeraka, Agia Paraskevi, five miles. Non-members are admitted. *Northern Greece Riding Club*, Mikro Emvolo, Thessaloniki.

TENNIS. The large sports center of Agios Kosmas, on the coast eight miles from Athens, offers among other facilities several tennis courts. The *Athens Tennis Club*, Vassilissis Olgas 2, is nearly always booked out by members. Courts also at most resorts and organized beaches.

GAMBLING. Casinos near Athens (Mount Parnis), on Corfu, Rhodes and Porto Carras; baccarat, chemin-de-fer and roulette.

MUSEUMS AND ARCHEOLOGICAL SITES. Hardly a week passes in Greece without important archeological finds coming to light. But however thrilling pre-historic, antique or medieval foundations, potsherds and fragments may be to the expert excavator, they hold little interest for the layman. A careful selection of sites has, therefore, been made in this book, with those where there is actually something to see being chosen. Wherever local museums are attached to the site they have been mentioned. It is, of course, impossible to foresee when and for how long monuments or churches may be closed for repairs, especially after earthquakes, an ever-present fact of life. Strikes by guards occur with almost the same frequency.

Opening hours for museums are: summer (April 1 to October 15)— weekdays 8 or 9 to 4 or 5; Sundays and holidays 10 to 2 or 4. Winter— weekdays 9 to 4; Sundays and holidays 10 to 2. These are Athens times, in the provinces also Sundays 3 to 6, and holidays 2.30 to 5. Closed on Tuesdays (except Archeological and Byzantine Museums in Athens which close on Mondays), Christmas, New Year, March 25, Orthodox Easter Sunday. Admission 25 to 150 dr., free on Sundays.

Archeological sites are open from 7.30 in the summer to sunset. In winter, they open at 9. The Acropolis is also open at night at full moon.

Please note that all these times are liable to change—so be sure to check.

ARCHEOLOGICAL OUTLINE. The pre-Hellenic period is characterized by the supremacy of the Minoan civilization of the Bronze Age (2400–1200 B.C.). Minos, legendary king of Crete, built the palaces of Knossos and Phaestos which date from about 2000 B.C. Cretan hegemony spread to the mainland (Peloponnese) to be succeeded by Mycenae which became the political and cultural center of the Aegean between 1400 and 1200 B.C. after the destruction of Knossos. Mycenaean civilization disappeared with the arrival of the Dorians whose architecture was born of a combination of solemn Nordic inspiration, measured Mycenaean outlay and of Oriental influences in decoration. The Doric style predominant till the end of the fifth century B.C. was characterized by severe simplicity; the flowering of the Ionic style lasted until the period of Macedonian hegemony (338 B.C.), when it was superseded by the more florid Corinthian style of the Hellenistic and Roman domination.

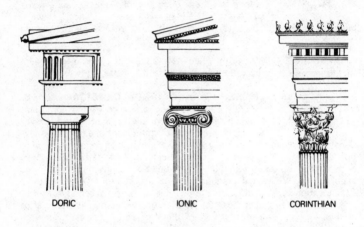

DORIC   IONIC   CORINTHIAN

Greek sculpture played an important role in the ornamentation of temples but it was also an independent art. The most important periods of its evolution were: the *archaic* (8th to 6th century B.C.), characterized by a column-like rigidity of its subjects; the *classic* period, attaining the summit of corporeal harmony (500 to 300 B.C.). The most outstanding artists of this epoch were Phidias, Praxiteles and Skopas. Alexander the Great and his armies introduced Greek art to the eastern Mediterranean and this era (300 to 150 B.C.), typified by an opulent anatomy and by Asiatic influences, is known as the *hellenistic* period.

The Greek temple, open mainly to priests but sometimes to prominent citizens, was the home of the Divinity, and more often than not it was of small proportions. A rare exception to the oblong, rectangular outlay is the *tholos,* a round temple with circular colonnade. Ictinos, Callicrates and Mnesicles were among the most outstanding architects.

Secular architecture consisted of open-air theaters, stadiums, and of the *agora,* the city's commercial and civic center. The *acropolis,* a citadel, usually enclosed all the sanctuaries. The Greek cities were surrounded by ramparts, the walls of which varied with the epoch (cyclopean, pelasgic, trapezoidal, etc.).

Important archeological work has been carried out by the American

School of Classical Studies in Athens (the Agora), in the Peloponnese (Corinth, Pylos), in Macedonia and on the island of Samothrace. British excavation work was most notable at Megalopolis (Peloponnese), in Thessaly and, of course, in Crete (Knossos, Phaestos). The French unearthed the sanctuaries of Delphi and Delos. Germany's contribution is mainly Mycenae and Olympia. In recent years, the Greeks themselves have made important finds at Brauron, Pella, Thira, and Vergina, but there are still teams of archeologists from many countries working in Greece.

Current archeological terms, with their meanings, are:

Amphora vase, jug

Apse semicircular part of an edifice

Basilica rectangular, oblong edifice

Bouleuterion senate house

Capital uppermost part of a column, usually decorated

Caryatid sculpture of maiden, replacing a column

Hieron sacred enclosure

Megaron reception hall in Mycenaean palace

Metope plain or carved panel on temple's frieze

Naos sanctuary of temple

Odeon roofed edifice for artistic performances

Peristyle inner or outer colonnade

Pinacotheca picture gallery

Plinth rectangular base of a column

Pronaos vestibule of sanctuary

Propylaea pillared gate to monumental sites

Stele upright, decorated tombstone

Stereobate substructure of a temple

Stoa roofed building, supported by frontal columns, usually a business center

Stylobate foundation platform of a temple

Traveling in Greece

BY AIR. Although Greece is quite a small country it does have a wide network of internal air services all operated by Olympic Airways. These mostly radiate from Athens although some go from Thessaloniki and there are direct flights between the larger islands. Many of the smaller islands have air services and fares on the whole are quite modest compared to other internal flights in Europe. In summer nearly 40 cities, towns and islands are linked by scheduled air services. Full details from all Olympic offices.

Internal passenger rates are reasonable: one-way from Athens to Corfu, 2,890 dr.; to Rhodes, 3,300 dr.; to Thessaloniki, 2,410 dr.; to Iraklio (Crete) 2,500 dr. Return fares are double. All are approximate; check locally.

The free baggage allowance is 15 kilos (33 lbs) per passenger. Infants 90% reduction, children from 2 to 12 years half fare.

Airports. Athens Airport is in two distinct divisions—the International Terminal served by all airlines except Olympic, and the Domestic Terminal which also serves Olympic's international flights. They are on either side of the airport. Be quite sure which terminal you want. The International Terminal is called the East Terminal and the Olympic, the West Terminal.

Buses run to and from East Terminal on Amalias Ave. 4, and West Terminal in Syngrou Ave. 96. They run every 20 minutes from around 6.30 A.M. to midnight. It takes from 30 to 50 minutes according to traffic. The fare is likely to be about 70 dr. by 1985, a taxi will run you nearer 300 dr.

International airports also at Corfu, Iraklio (Crete), Kavala, Rhodes and Thessaloniki. Duty free shops sell mainly Greek folk art, liquor and cigarettes. Olympic Airways provide buses to all provincial airports which are adequate if simple.

BY TRAIN. The Greek railway system is very basic. There is the main line from Athens to Thessaloniki, which divides there with one route going north into Yugoslavia and the other east to Turkey, with a branch on that line which turns north again into Bulgaria. There is also a secondary line running west from Thessaloniki then up into Yugoslavia.

In the Peloponnese there is a narrow gauge line which runs from Athens to Corinth, where one branch leads west to Patra, Pyrgos (Olympia) and Pylos, the other south to Argos (Nafplio) and Tripoli, both meeting at Kalamata. Trains are slow, even the diesel units, some of which provide buffet or refreshment services. But it is a most scenic system.

On the main line north to Thessaloniki from Athens there are four daytime trains and two overnight expresses (sleeping cars and couchettes). Daytime trains have either a restaurant car or refreshment services.

There is a runabout ticket called the *Greek Tourist Card* issued for 10, 20 or 30 days in 2nd class only. Giving unlimited rail travel it is also valid on the bus routes operated by the railway. The cost is amazingly cheap being around $55, $90 and $120 for 10, 20 and 30 days respectively. It can be bought through travel agencies or Greek railway offices in Athens or other main cities.

Greece is also a participant in the *Eurailpass* scheme and in *Inter Rail* for the under 26s and over 65s (women 60).

BY SHIP. A variety of steamers operated by a dozen shipping lines ply the Aegean, the Argo-Saronic and the Ionian waters, connecting Piraeus, the port of Athens, with the different islands and the coastal cities. Schedules are liable to sudden alterations. To obtain reliable, up-to-the-minute information, see your local travel agent or the daily press. Embarkation at the main harbor (or at some Attic ports) for some of the Cyclades and Euboea. Sample fares in drachmes are at present (but likely to be about 20% higher by summer 1985):

	Cars	1st	2nd	Tourist	3rd
Piraeus–Iraklio	2,512/4,285	2,233	1,763	1,309	983
Piraeus–Mykonos	2,138/3,649	1,497	—	823	688
Piraeus–Mytilini	2,889/4,918	2,183	1,634	1,213	983
Piraeus–Naxos	2,360/4,110	1,997	1,067	841	713
Piraeus–Rhodes	3,097/5,334	3,037	2,051	1,567	1,207
Piraeus–Thira	3,180/5,600	2,347	1,299	1,041	868

First class, exclusive of meals, costs about the same as airfares. Tourist and third are redolent with local atmosphere (which often means transport of livestock). Embarkation Tax: from Piraeus 41 dr.; from all other ports 28 dr. plus 5% of the fare.

 AEGEAN CRUISES. One of the treats, and the most effortless way of touring the Greek islands (but not of meeting the Greeks, as at least two-thirds of the passengers are Americans), are the cruises in the Aegean, operating mostly out of Piraeus but also out of some Adriatic ports. These cruises usually consist of full-day stopovers and conducted sightseeing at such places as Corfu, Rhodes, Crete, Mykonos (and Delos), Athens (two days); some include visits to Istanbul, Izmir, Ephesus and Halicarnassus in Turkey, others combine with a stay at attractive resorts. Occasionally Israeli or Egyptian ports are substituted for the Turkish ones on the longer cruises.

From April through October, there are many cruises of the Greek Islands out of Piraeus (Athens). Among the lines offering three, four and seven-day Greek Islands cruises (combined with Turkey or Yugoslavia) are *Blue Aegean Sea Line, Cycladic Cruises, Epirotiki, Hellenic Cruises, Hellenic Mediterranean, Karageorgis, Oceanic Sun Line*. Other cruise lines call at Piraeus and other Greek ports. They include the *Chandris, Costa Cruises, Norwegian America Cruises, Royal Viking Line* and *Royal Cruise Line*.

Fares, subject to increase, are officially quoted in U.S. dollars and range from $450 to $1,260 for a 3-day cruise; $850 to $2,200 for a 7-day cruise; shore excursions additional.

MV Saronic Star. 1-day cruise, Egina, Ydra and Poros, to be interrupted and resumed at will.

MTS Jason and *MV Jupiter*. 7-day cruise, Piraeus-Iraklio (Crete)-Thira-Kusadasi (ancient Ephesus, Turkey)-Istanbul-Delos-Mykonos-Piraeus.

MV Neptune. 4-day cruise, Piraeus-Istanbul-Izmir-Patmos-Mykonos-Piraeus. 3-day cruise, Piraeus-Ydra-Thira-Iraklio-Rhodes-Piraeus.

MTS Oceanus and *MTS Orpheus*. 4-day cruise, Piraeus-Mykonos-Delos-Iraklio-Rhodes-Kusadasi-Patmos-Piraeus. 3-day cruises, Piraeus.

MS Aquarius. 7-day cruise, Piraeus-Ydra-Thira-Iraklio-Rhodes-Izmir-Istanbul-Patmos-Delos-Mykonos-Piraeus.

TSS Orion. 7-day cruise, Piraeus-Iraklio-Thira-Rhodes-Kusadasi-Istanbul-Delos-Mykonos-Piraeus.

MV Galaxy. 4-day cruise, Piraeus-Delos-Mykonos-Kusadasi-Patmos-Rhodes-Iraklio-Thira-Piraeus. 3-day cruise, Piraeus-Delos-Mykonos-Rhodes-Iraklio-Thira-Piraeus.

MV Meltemi. 7-day cruise, by coach from Athens to embarkation in Corinth, then Corfu-Parga-Paxi-Kefalonía-Ithaki-Zákynthos-Pilos-Nafpaktos-Itea-Corinth. Return to Athens by coach.

MS Stella Solaris. 7-day cruise, Piraeus-Thira-Iraklio-Rhodes-Kusadasi-Istanbul-Delos-Mykonos-Piraeus.

MS Stella Oceanis. 3-day cruise, Piraeus-Delos-Mykonos-Rhodes-Iraklio-Thira-Piraeus. 4-day cruise, Piraeus-Thira-Iraklio-Rhodes-Kusadasi-Piraeus.

SS Sissy. 7-day cruise, Ancona (Italy)-Piraeus-Halicarnassus-Rhodes-Iraklio-Thira-Piraeus-Ancona.

Andrea C and *France C.* 8-day cruise to the Greek islands and Turkey, followed by seven nights in Athens.

SS Navarino. 14-day cruise, Venice-Corfu-Mykonos-Patmos-Rhodes-Iraklio-Thira-Venice.

TSS Regina. 15-day cruise, Venice-Katakolon-Piraeus-Rhodes-Beirut-Haifa-Iraklio-Corfu-Dubrovnik-Venice.

MV Kentavros. 4-day cruise, Piraeus-Delos-Mykonos-Kusadasi-Patmos-Rhodes-Iraklio-Thira-Piraeus.

BY BUS. In addition to the wide variety of coach tours (from a half day to a week) operated from Athens mainly by the *CHAT* company, there is a network of bus services reaching to even the smallest village. Frequencies vary and in the remoter rural areas they don't necessarily run every day. Some are owned and operated by the railway, others by private companies. Full details from many travel agents in Greece and at the main bus stations in Athens and Piraeus and from tourist information offices. Travel by bus in Greece is inexpensive (about half what it is in the U.K.), always crowded, sometimes a bit trying on the nerves—the driving can be dramatic—but usually great fun. Timetables are not always adhered to.

The Ionian islands and the cities of the mainland as well as of the Peloponnese are connected with Athens and other inland centers by overland bus routes. From Thessaloniki and Larissa lines run to Kastoria, Ioanina and Kavala. The two main overland-bus terminals in Athens are at Kifissou 100 and Liossion 260.

American Express, Syntagma Square, *CHAT,* Stadiou 4; *Hellas Tours,* Stadiou 7; *Key Tours,* Ermou 2, etc. have their own fleet of luxury buses (Pullmans) for a wide-ranging choice of tours.

BY CAR. Ordinary registration papers and an international third party insurance (green card) are required as well as a driving license (American, British or international) for those who are to drive the vehicle within Greece. A free entry card is issued, valid for four months. The car may circulate for a further eight months without payment of import duty, provided a guarantee for duty payment is given, should the stay exceed a year. Holders of a *carnet de passage en douane* do not require any guarantee. You may bring into the country an automobile rented elsewhere in Europe as easily as if it were your own car.

Current price of gasoline (petrol) is 53 dr. per liter for regular, 57 dr. for super in the main centers, slightly more in remote areas. Motor oils from 200 to 260 dr.

Car Rental. There is a well developed rental system in Athens, as well as in the major resorts. Cars are delivered to the airport, harbor or railroad station. Rates include public liability, third party, passenger and fire risks, oil and greasing. Charges are higher March 15 to October 31, ranging from 1,000 dr. per day plus 10 dr. per km. to 3,500 dr. plus 30 dr. per km. Always add 18% for tax and service. There are reductions for longer periods. *Avis,* Amalias Ave., 48; *Hellascar,* Stadiou St., 7; *Hertz,* Syngrou Ave., 12, and Vassilissis Sofias Ave. 71, Athens. All have branches in Corfu, Iráklio, Rhodes, Thessaloniki.

Transit Cars. Several firms on Syngrou Ave. and Alexandras Ave. are authorized to buy and sell cars in transit. The largest and most experienced in cutting through the red tape are *Boomerang,* Vassilissis Sofias 129, and *Kokkinos,* Syngrou Ave., 303.

Automobile Associations. The *Automobile & Touring Club of Greece* (ELPA), Athens Tower, Messogion 2, tel. 779 1615.

Rules of the Road. International road signs are in use throughout Greece. You drive on the right, pass on the left, and yield right of way to all vehicles approaching from the right (except on posted main highways). Speed limits are visibly marked, keep to 30 m.p.h. in built-up areas. Always park on the right; avoid overnight parking on main thoroughfares. In Greece appalling road manners alternate with utmost helpfulness. The use of the triangular danger warning is compulsory if you have a breakdown. Roving repair trucks, manned by skilled ELPA mechanics, patrol the major highways; services free of charge, but a commensurate tip is expected. Police are empowered to impose on-the-spot fines for offenses, but do so rarely.

Car-Ferry Services. In addition to the ferry between Brindisi, Corfu, Igoumenitsa and Patra there are several services which can shorten your journey by many hours. The local ferry boat between Corfu and Igoumenitsa runs thirteen times daily in each direction. The coastal highway leads directly to Preveza and the ferry to Aktio every half hour from 7 A.M. to 12 P.M., and via Messolongi to the Rio-Antirio ferry which connects Epirus with the NW Peloponnese; every fifteen minutes from both sides, 7 A.M. to 12 P.M.; every twenty minutes during the night. Daily ferry from Patra to Sami, Kefalonía, touching three times a week at Ithaki and Saturdays at Vassiliki, Lefkada. That island is also connected by a continuous (and in daytime free) ferry service across the narrow canal separating it from the mainland. Zákynthos can be reached four times daily from Kylini on the Western Peloponnese.

The Aegean island of Euboea is connected with the mainland: south, Rafina to Marmari and Karistos twice or three times daily; Agia Marina (Marathon) central, Oropos to Eretria and vice versa every half hour from daybreak to 11 P.M.; in the north, Arkitsa to Edipsos, seven to thirty times daily; Glifa, 8 miles off the Lamia-Volos road, to Agiokampos, north of Edipsos nine times daily; from Kymi (East Euboea) to Skyros, Alonissos, Skopelos; Skiathos, once daily. From Volos to Skiathos, Skopelos, Alonissos, twice daily. From Kavala to Thassos, fifteen times daily; more frequent on holidays.

From Piraeus to Aegina, fourteen to thirty-five times daily; to Methana, and Poros, six times daily. Piraeus to Hania or Iraklio once or twice daily; to Naxos, Paros eleven times weekly; to Siros and Samos. The shortest crossing to the Cyclades is from Rafina and Lavrio in Attica; to Gavrio on Andros, Syros and Tinos, once or twice daily. Eight times weekly; Piraeus-Kos-Rhodes; Piraeus-Hios-Lesbos. Crossings to Turkey are from Hios to Cesme; Rhodes to Marmaris; Samos to Kusadasi.

Temporary speed limits. In accordance with most European countries, in order to save petrol, the maximum speed allowed on the Patra-Corinth-Athens-Thessaloniki-Evzoni (Yugoslav border) motorway and the other toll road is 120 km (75 miles); on all other roads 100 km (63 miles) unless lower limits are indicated.

Spare Parts. These are readily available in all Greek towns, but not always on transit through Yugoslavia. Before leaving home, ask your dealer for a kit of vital spares; if you find you don't have to open it on your trip, you can usually return it. Make sure your spare wheel is in good shape. As for mechanical repairs, there are garages with competent mechanics even in the smallest towns. Most of the leading American and European automobile manufacturers have agents in the main cities of Greece. Here is a list of dealers you can contact in an emergency: *British Leyland*, Syngrou Ave., 116; *Citroën*, Syngrou Ave., 100; *Ford*, Kondellis, Plapouta 10, Argyroupolis; *General Motors, Talbot, Renault, Volvo*, Athinon Ave., 71; *Fiat*, Evdoxon, 73; *Volkswagen*, Iera Odos, 131; *Mercedes, Auto Union*, Fosteropoulos, Athinon Ave., 40. All in Athens.

Leaving Greece

CUSTOMS ON RETURNING HOME. If you propose to take on your holiday any *foreign-made* articles, such as cameras, binoculars, expensive timepieces, and the like, it is wise to put with your travel documents the receipt from the retailer or some other evidence that the item was bought in your home country. If you bought the article on a previous holiday abroad and have already paid duty on it, carry with you the receipt for this.

U.S. Residents. You may bring in $400 worth of foreign merchandise as gifts or for personal use without having to pay duty, provided they have been out of the country more than 48 hours and provided they have not claimed a similar exemption within the previous 30 days. Every member of a family is entitled to the same exemption, regardless of age, and the exemptions can be pooled.

The $400 figure is based on the fair retail value of the goods in the country where acquired. Included for travelers over the age of 21 are one liter of alcohol, 100 cigars (non-Cuban) and 200 cigarettes. Any amount in excess of those limits will be taxed at the port of entry, and may additionally be taxed in the traveler's home state. Only one bottle of perfume trademarked in the U.S. may be brought in. Unlimited amounts of goods from certain specially designated "developing" countries may also be brought in duty-free; check with U.S. Customs Service, Washington D.C. 20229. Write to the same address for information regarding importation of automobiles and/or motorcycles. You may not bring home meats, fruits, plants, soil or other agricultural items.

Gifts valued at under $40 may be mailed to friends or relatives at home, but not more than one per day (of receipt) to any one addressee. These gifts must not include perfumes costing more than $5, tobacco or liquor.

Military personnel returning from abroad should check with the nearest American Embassy for special regulations pertaining to them.

Canadian Residents. In addition to personal effects, the following articles may be brought in duty free: a maximum of 50 cigars, 200 cigarettes, 2 pounds of tobacco and 40 ounces of liquor, provided these are declared in writing to customs on arrival and accompany the traveler in hand or checked-through baggage. These are included in the basic exemption of $300 a year. Personal gifts should be mailed as "Unsolicited Gift—Value Under $40." Canadian customs regulations are strictly enforced: you are recommended to check what your allowances are and to make sure you have kept receipts for whatever you have bought abroad. For details ask for the Canada Customs brochure, "I Declare."

British Residents except those under the age of 17 years, may import duty-free from *any* country the following: 200 cigarettes or 100 cigarillos or 50 cigars or 250 grams of tobacco; 1 liter of alcoholic drink over 22% volume (i.e. whiskey and other hard liquor), *or* 2 liters of alcoholic drink under 22% vol. plus 2 liters of still table wine. Also 50 grams of perfume, ¼ liter of toilet water and £28 worth of other normally dutiable goods (not to include more than 50 liters of beer).

Returning from any *EEC country* (and remember that Greece is now in the EEC), you may, *instead* of the above exemptions, bring in the following, provided you can prove they were *not* bought in a duty-free shop: 300 cigarettes or 150 cigarillos or 75 cigars or 400 grams of tobacco; 1½ liters of alcoholic drink over 22% volume, *or* 3 liters under 22% vol. plus 4 liters of still table wine (it would be wise to check the latest position regarding wine allowance, as EEC are considering an increase); 75 grams of perfume and ⅜ liter of toilet water and £120 worth of other normally dutiable goods.

THE GREEK SCENE

THE GREEK WAY OF LIFE

"When I speak to you, you are my friend"

by

PAUL STRATHERN

Paul Strathern has twice been a resident in Greece, and has traveled widely throughout the country. Besides writing a guide to Corfu, he also has an extensive knowledge of modern Greek literature, cultural life and politics. He has written travel books on Britain, several parts of Europe and America. His most recent novel The Adventures of Spiro *was partly set in Greece.*

Who is the real Greek? The proud mustachioed Cretan in his shining riding boots; the portly Peloponnesian paterfamilias leading his overdressed wife and candy-box children to church; the Aegean fisherman in his grubby vest, sprawled in the shade of an

41

olive tree, gorging himself on watermelon; or the pushy Adonis, parading himself on the beach before the bikini-clad tourists? Is Melina Mercouri more typically Greek when she's playing the open-hearted Piraeus tart in *Never on Sunday* or when she's acting as the firebrand Socialist member of parliament for her underprivileged constituents? The answer is that they are all typically Greek. Yet what have all these disparate elements in common?

The sheer vitality of the Greeks is the first thing that strikes you on your arrival. As soon as the Athens express crosses the frontier from Yugoslavia the train is besieged by gesticulating, boisterous, unshaven characters plying soft drinks, and shouting souvenir salesmen. When you emerge from the arrivals lounge at the Athens or Iraklio airport, you will immediately find yourself overwhelmed by taxi-drivers, tourist agents and self-appointed welcomers of all kinds. The moment you step off the ship's gangplank at Corfu or Piraeus you are engulfed by a hundred helping hands all trying to help you in different directions. Yet at the heart of all this chaotic bustle and often commercially-inspired enthusiasm lies one of the deepest Greek characteristics—hospitality. Parts of Greece are now over-run with tourists, yet even there you frequently come across that spontaneous generosity and open-heartedness towards strangers that is so typically Greek. Step off the beaten track, and you'll find this hospitality difficult to avoid. Unlike so many people, for the most part the Greeks actually *like* foreigners.

Greece is no place for the reticent. Strike up a conversation in a cafe, and in no time they'll be asking you all kinds of detailed questions. Are you married? How much did your watch cost? How much do you earn? What do you think of Greece? As likely as not you'll be bought drinks, shown photos of the family, invited for a drive or a trip in their boat.

This kind of hospitality can sometimes be oppressive and embarrassing—but it's always meant in good faith. The Greeks are genuinely interested in such personal matters and see no reason for tempering their curiosity. This is particularly the case in the outlying islands and remote villages. Here you're liable to be invited home to meet the family, have a meal, join in a discussion about the political scene. And should you express interest in some knick-knack or ornament, you're quite likely to find it being pressed on you as a gift. (Though if you make the mistake of trying to pay for this gift, this will be deemed a deep insult.)

Yet don't think that these apparently simple, generous and extrovert people are in any way naive or lacking in worldly wisdom. No matter which country you come from, and no matter how remote the village or island you find yourself in, there will usually be at least one local who knows your country and a fair amount about it. I can remember stumbling across a mountain hamlet at the end of a donkey track in Samos and being taken for coffee in a tiny stone cottage. Inside turned out to be a shrine to New York—the walls covered with colored postcards of Broadway and the Manhattan skyline, crossed American and Greek flags, and even a tiny plaster effigy of the Statue of Liberty. The black-shawled old peasant woman who served the coffee had lived in New York for over thirty years—though she still only spoke half a dozen words of distinctly Brooklynese English.

Since the beginnings of history the Greeks have been travelers. For them the Hellenic world has always extended far beyond the borders of Greece itself. The Greeks, like the Jews, have had their Diaspora—largely through the necessities of trade and a long troubled history. The Black Sea coast, the coasts of Libya, Egypt, southern Italy and Sicily, southern France and even southern Spain were all colonized at some time by the Ancient Greeks. Alexandria was founded by Alexander the Great; Naples, or Napoli, comes from the Greek *nea polis* meaning new city; and even the name "Greek" was first bestowed on the Doric colonizers by the local Italians.

Nowadays, the Hellenic world extends across the globe—from the suburbs of Sydney to the Rio de la Plata in South America, from the great cities of North America to the industrial centers of Western Europe. At any given moment there's hardly a major port in the world without at least one Greek ship in dock. The nature of the Greek colonies may have changed since ancient times, but the motherland still depends on them much as before. To this day the Greek economy relies very heavily upon the incomes generated by expatriates. And, as ever, all Greek exiles dream of returning home to their native island or village. When I stayed recently on the Aegean island of Serifos, I learnt that the owner of the local beach cafe spent his winters stoking the boilers in a hospital in Britain's Southend; on stepping into a dim stable in rural Kithyra to ask directions, I was welcomed with the traditional Aussie greeting "G'day sport!", and after conversing with some Cretan fishermen in halting Greek and then informing them that I was English, a dour old salt tending his nets in the background piped up: "I kinda guessed you weren't from the States." These experiences are typical—so, no matter how pressing the questions, don't ever try to fool a Greek about who you are.

Liberty, Suspicion and Troubled Memories

Beneath all their friendliness, the Greeks are still a deeply uncertain people. They will be "your friend" within moments of meeting you, but to strike up a deep and lasting friendship with a Greek will often take years. Where their deepest sympathies are concerned the Greeks have always been a clannish people. Yet even amongst themselves there is a lasting element of division, together with a residual suspicion of strangers of any kind— whether they be from the next village or a distant continent.

Politics is one of the great Greek national pastimes. The daily papers range through the entire political spectrum—from traditional monarchist to extreme communist. Savage political cartoons and vitriolic polemics are a daily commonplace, and no *kafeneion* is complete without its political discussion group. The Greeks have a profound and sophisticated political acumen, which is deeply imbued with a suspicion of foreign interference. This is hardly surprising when we think of Greece's plight through much of this century. We tend to forget that as far as Greece was concerned the two world wars lasted from 1912–1922 and 1940–1949.

When the British sailed into Piraeus in 1944 bringing back the Greek government in exile it arrived in a land as devastated as any in Europe. The Greeks are a superstitious people, deeply conscious of their long history, and when the exile government disembarked on a Tuesday many feared the worst. Tuesday has been an unlucky day for the Greeks for half a millennium. (It was on a Tuesday in 1453 that Constantinople fell to the Turks.) Within months of the arrival of the liberation forces in 1944, fierce fighting had broken out between the local resistance forces (who were largely communist) and the government troops (supported by the British). The economy, such as it was, collapsed. The ensuing inflation surpassed even that of the pre-war German Weimar Republic. The gold sovereigns brought in by the British soon became the only acceptable currency, with an exchange rate equivalent to one gold sovereign for 170,000,000,000,000,000 drachmes. Famine and civil war spread throughout the land, and in the bitter fighting 80,000 Greeks lost their lives (more than during all the hostilities against the Italians and the Germans). At the same time, over 700,000 people (nearly 10% of the population) were forced to flee their homes. No visitor should forget that the modern easy-going Greece we see today grew out of this devastation and ruin. These events are indelibly etched in the memory of every Greek over forty years old, and play a significant part in Greek politics to this day.

Greece has a wide range of political parties, from the newly revived radical right, across the conservatives, the splintered center and the ruling socialists, to the extreme left. The communists are divided into the much larger pro-Moscow party, the only one represented in parliament, and the more independent Communists of the Interior. Together they account for about 15% of the electorate. Memories of communist atrocities committed during the Civil War are still vivid and play a decisive part in Greek politics. It's worth remembering that three of Greece's land borders are with communist states—Albania, Yugoslavia and Bulgaria. Greece's only other border is with her traditional enemy Turkey. Only nearby Italy, a hundred miles away across the Adriatic, belongs to the "friendly West"—and it's less than forty years since Italy was at war with Greece. It is not difficult to see why, for the Greeks, politics matter.

Divisions there may be on the political scene, but all Greeks profess a deep belief in Democracy. But to the delight of politicians and the confusion of the citizens, the same word also means Republic, an ambiguity skillfully used by the Colonels in the referendum overturning the monarchy. During the last decade Greece has been ruled in turn by a military junta, the Right, and the Left. It has also changed from being a monarchy to a republic. Few countries have managed such rapid transformations with such comparatively slight disturbance. Bombs have been thrown, there have been sit-ins and occasional riots—but on the whole the country has continued to function and make progress throughout.

A similar level-headedness applies towards that difficult question of foreign interference. I can remember sitting at a cafe table in Thebes listening to an old violinist who used to play with the Athens Symphony Orchestra. He described to me how he had fought in that very street alongside his resistance colleagues against "Churchill's troops." This experience, he explained, meant that his political sympathies would always be with the extreme left. He also spoke of his hatred of foreigners, who were always trying to interfere in Greek affairs. Yet to him this was a matter of politics and governments, and though we had only just met, he insisted on paying for my meal at the end of the conversation. "I am a Greek," he explained. "I will always fight for liberty. But when we speak together, you are my friend." This instinctive mistrust of larger powers has been exploited by demagogues throughout the centuries.

The Greek National Anthem is derived from the *Hymn to Liberty* by the 19th-century poet Dionysios Solomos. Loosely translated, this begins:

"I find you with the fearful blade of the sword,
I find you in the books that speak of justice on earth,
Out of the sacred bones of the Hellenes you arise valiant once more.
Hail, oh hail, Liberty!"

Watch the old men standing at the edge of a dusty village square listening to the local band playing the jaunty yet faintly melancholy music which accompanies these words, while the assembled children's choir sings under the baton of the local schoolmaster—this is what Greece means to the Greeks.

The Timeless Land, Exile and Tourism

For centuries Greece was essentially a primitive rural country, and even with the coming of modern prosperity this still remains much the case. 80% of the country is mountainous, and despite recent reclamation of swamps and lakes only 30% of the surface area is arable (an area the size of Wales or West Virginia). 150 years ago even Athens had a population of only a few thousand, and outside the main towns life remained almost medieval. The chief form of transport was the donkey, or small caiques plying between the islands, and the olive groves produced the main source of income. Tiny terraced vineyards provided the villages with wine, the herds of goats in the hills provided milk, cheese, meat and clothing, and the fishing boats harvested the sea for fish, octopus and sponges.

In the more remote villages and islands this way of life has changed little. Electrification may have brought telephones and television, and better roads may have provided bus and truck links with the local markets, but the routine of daily existence goes on much as before. At first light the cocks crow and the peasants set out to tend their fields. Throughout the long hot days of summer the village alleyways are silent, with the cats basking in the shade. A few elderly citizens congregate at the local cafe, sitting on wobbly straw-seated chairs such as Van Gogh painted, and on the doorsteps of the houses the old black-shawled crones sit peeling the vegetables for the evening meal. As the sun rises to its zenith even these signs of life disappear for the long siesta. The peasants in the fields spread out their picnics of bread, olives, *feta* (goat's cheese) and wine, and then snooze under the shade of the olive trees. Only the tinkling bells of the goats moving in the hills disturb the sun-dazed silence.

As the light fades in the late afternoon the villagers return along the tracks between the fields, driving laden donkeys and calling out to one another across the valleys. With the coming of dusk the men gather in the cafés for their evening glass of *ouzo*—an aniseed-flavored spirit which turns milky when diluted with water (the Greek equivalent of that pan-Mediterranean drink which becomes *pastis* in France, *anis* in Spain, and *raki* in the Middle East). Meanwhile the women and young girls take their traditional *volta*—another timeless Mediterranean custom, the evening stroll up and down the main street in front of the cafes. After dinner in the island villages it is time for the fishing boats to set out—the caiques with their spluttering engines drawing lines of lighted rowing boats out of the harbor. Throughout the night the darkness of the sea is pitted with tiny acetylene flares as the fishermen spear for octopus and squid in the shallow waters off the rocks. A way of life which has changed little since before Columbus set out to discover the New World.

Nowadays many of the peasants drive to work with lorries and tractors, but there are still countless hidden fields and vineyards which can only be reached by donkey track. The local cafe will probably have a TV and a fridge of ice creams, but the main topics of conversation will still be the harvest and local gossip (and, of course, politics). This is the village way of life which every Greek harks back to. Even among the tourist-block hotels of the resorts and the bustle of modern Athens, elements of this life persist. In smaller towns the locals still take their evening *volta;* while the daytime water-skiers are living it up in the discos, the fishing boats still set out with their trails of acetylene lights; and even in the back streets of the cities the workshops and garages often have trellises of vines growing over the windows and doorways. Talk to an urbanized cafe-owner in Thessaloniki or Piraeus and he will invariably tell you that he is really a Cretan or a Corfiot, giving you the name of his tiny village as "home."

Nowadays, over half the population of Greece are city dwellers. The urban sprawl of Athens and Piraeus houses almost 4 million, and the Eleusian Fields (once so beloved of Demeter) are now noisy suburbs enveloped in a haze of smog. In the summer Athens is a hot, noisy, bad-tempered city—the main consolation for the unfortunate Athenians who haven't been able to escape to their native island or village being the boisterous night life of the colorful Plaka district or an evening performance of Ancient Greek tragedy under the stars in the amphitheater beneath the Acropolis. With the coming of August the Athenians head for Piraeus, where the ferries leave day and night for the islands. Piraeus is now the third largest port in the Mediterranean (after Marseilles and Genoa), and its shipping industry is one of the main sources of Greece's new affluence. The shipping magnates, such as Niarchos and Onassis, played a major role in Greece's economic recovery after the war, and the Greek merchant navy (under both its own flag and flags of convenience) is now second only to Liberia.

Yet, despite recent advances, the Greek economy is still not self-supporting. Once again history has played its part here. Greece's first attempts at industrialization were ruined by the long wars and natural disasters which bedeviled the country through the first half of this century. Greece also suffers from the fact that it has no quality coal, just deposits of lignite, and only a limited amount of oil (though this may soon change as a result of drilling in the Aegean). For years tobacco was the country's main export, along with olive oil, sultanas and raisins. Hardly great currency earners. Even today, with its growing manufacturing industry, Greece still has to import most of its raw materials, fuel, chemical fertilizers and machinery. High rates of inflation and large-scale rural unemployment have taken their toll. Prices continue to rise sharply, accompanied by devaluation; and the drift from the land to the urban areas of Athens and Thessaloniki continues.

Without its "invisible earnings" the Greek economy could not survive. Even here the slump in world shipping has hardly helped—witness the mile-long lines of rusting tankers and freighters anchored in the lanes outside Piraeus. Remittances from American and Australian relatives still keep many families going. However, the main source of "invisible earnings" is now produced by migrant workers earning large wage packets in the industrial centers of Western Europe. Temporary emigration to West Germany, Holland, Belgium and Switzerland has now become a part of the Greek way of life. Many young men spend years in such places as Dusseldorf or Frankfurt before returning to build a house and settle down. The big idea is to build a holiday villa which can be rented to summer tourists, or enter into a partnership and put up a hotel. Tourism is now the country's second largest source of income after shipping, providing summer work in many areas of high unemployment. Unfortunately the chief benefactors here have tended to be those who need it least. Big chains of tourist hotels have been financed by the shipping firms of Chandris and Onassis. Likewise, it is the Athenian financiers who have tended to buy up and exploit the best stretches of coastline. This, too, certainly contributed to the recent victory of the Left in the elections.

From Byzantium to Bouzouki

One of the traditional pillars of Greek society is the Greek Orthodox Church. During the centuries when Greece was part of the Turkish Empire, it was the church which provided the Greek people with a national focus. The Greek Orthodox Church is the church of Byzantium, and to this day it considers Constantinople as its spiritual center. The church provided many heroes in the Greek struggles for liberty, and it still plays a distinct role in daily and political life. The Greeks saw no anomaly in Archbishop Makarios being President of Cyprus, and the village priest with his black stove-pipe hat, black robes and flowing beard is often to be seen debating matters of local import in the cafe.

The Greeks are a deeply religious people, especially in the rural areas. Few country roads are without their tiny white-washed roadside shrines, and the local saints days are always celebrated in style, with the priests donning their golden ceremonial robes to lead the processions of relics and brass bands through the streets. The main event in the Orthodox calendar is Easter. This is preceded by a widely observed Lenten Fast, culminating in a meatless week before Easter. (Though admittedly in Athens this is the week when the seafood restaurants come into their own.) Throughout the land on Easter Sunday there are processions, followed by the roasting of lambs on spits and dancing in traditional costume.

The Greeks are great believers in festivals of all kinds. At the New Year there is the "Blessing of the Sea" at Piraeus and other harbours all over the country. The summer cultural festivals at Athens and Epidaurus are not just tourist events, they are an integral part of the Greek cultural scene. And behavior at the Daphne Wine Festival would not have appeared out of place at ancient bacchanaliañ revels—Zorba lives!

Yet it's not just at wine festivals that the Greeks believe in letting their hair down. In every Greek there is a latent Zorba. The Greeks have a deep love of music and dancing, and have cultivated a music and a way of dancing that is utterly their own. In the music of the lute-like bouzouki the East blends with the West. Listen to the Cretans playing their traditional songs and you will hear distinctly Middle Eastern strains, whilst up in Kavalla the folk melodies have more than faint echoes of the music of the Steppes. In the night spots of Athens the bouzouki manages to accommodate even the wilder reaches of Western pop without losing its own distinctive quality. Bouzouki music is a living tradition absorbing many disparate elements of traditional and modern music, folk culture and poetry. The internationally renowned composer Nikos Theodorakis is as much a poet as he is a musician, and his repertoire ranges from left-wing political songs to haunting love lyrics.

The *taverna* is another pillar of the Greek way of life. Here the Greeks eat, drink, talk, play backgammon, dance, or simply watch the world go by as they linger over a glass of *ouzo*. The *taverna* occupies a place equivalent to the ancient tavern in Shakesperean England. The wine is nearly always local, and served from barrels, and the cooking will tend to be traditional. Greek cuisine is basically Middle Eastern. Indeed, according to the Turks, Greek cuisine is really Turkish cuisine mangled by bad cooks. Anyone who has had a plate of good home-made *moussaka* will know this to be a slander—though the elements of Turkish influence are undeniable. What we call Turkish coffee is punctiliously referred to as *Greek* coffee. And be sure not to ask for Shish Kebab—the Greek name for this dish is *souvlakia*.

For the Greeks, a meal in a taverna is a lively communal experience, usually turning into something of a party once the wine begins to flow and the music starts. Though once the party gets going, attention to culinary detail sometimes leaves a little to be desired. Flustered waiters besieged by waving hands and calling customers often tend to forget orders, and dishes that may well have left the stove hot have a habit of cooling down somewhat before they arrive at your table. Likewise, the bill will sometimes tend to be of a rather approximate speculative nature. Pay attention to detailed figures and miraculous reductions often ensue. However, this is not to be mistaken for outright cheating—more a hangover from the era of bargaining, when the seller felt it his right to charge whatever price he thought his customer could afford.

It's all Greek to Me

The other great focus of Greek nationalism is the Greek language. Like many aspects of this beguiling country, this, too, has elements of Byzantine complexity. For a start there are several different types of Greek, ranging from Katharevusa (or 'pure' Greek) to Demotic Greek as well as a wide range of flourishing regional dialects. But despite these confusions, Greek literature has flourished in this century. Since the war Greece has had no less than two Nobel prize-winners for literature—the poets Seferis and Elytis.

Better known are the Greeks who have achieved international recognition in the entertainment world—such as Irene Papas, Melina Mercouri, Nikos Theodorakis and Telly Savalas. These are the heroes and heroines of the modern Greek Pantheon, and their star status is treated as a matter of national pride. Now at last, the Greeks feel, they are known for something more than the antics of their millionaire shipowners. Though these, too, are still regarded with a certain respect. These are the Greeks who have "made it" in the world—and show that, despite coming from a small nation, Greeks are still capable of being in there with the best of them when it comes to making money or marrying former First Ladies.

This characteristic is also reflected in the Greek attitude towards class. A Greek will be admired by his fellow countrymen if he makes money, and often respected if he comes from one of the older families—but underneath it all he will be considered as a Greek, and just the same as any other. The successful Athenian businessman returning to his local village or native island for the summer is expected to talk as an equal to his fellows. Though naturally social divisions do exist. Urbanized and newly-rich Greeks tend to believe in showing off their possessions, which often goes down rather sourly with the less fortunate. Similarly, students returning home from the universities will often find that their "modern" behavior jars. Despite their openness and vitality, the Greeks are on the whole a deeply conservative people. In the main, families are close—and this tends to encourage a strict morality, especially in the Greek male attitude towards women. Apart from the occasional Melina Mercouri, Greek women are still largely second-class citizens. In most of Greece and especially in the rural areas, when a woman's husband dies she is expected to wear black, often for the rest of her life. Also, it's all very well for the boys to go picking up tourist girls, but when it happens the other way round all kinds of trouble are liable to ensue.

Tourist behavior, especially on the beaches, has brought a certain element of liberalization—but this remains highly selective. Tourist islands such as Mykonos and Ydra have long since come to terms with gay beaches, singles bars and the like—which would be greeted with horror in less frequented spots. A typical situation is that found on the Aegean island of Serifos, where there are two main beaches. On the village beach proprieties are strictly observed amongst the middle-aged bathers and family picnickers, whilst on the beach around the headland which can't be seen from the village anything goes amongst the young tourists and local students. As ever, the Greeks believe in making you feel at home—unless you interfere with their sacred liberty.

ARMS AND MAN

A Surfeit of History

by
PETER SHELDON

*A resident of Greece for many years and a past director of the
British School on Crete, Peter Sheldon has traveled extensively in
every part of the country. Besides lecturing on English literature,
he has written several books on Greece and contributed most of
the chapters in this volume. He is also our Area Editor for North
Africa and Turkey.*

Ancient history has been the most widely taught period in western education, for the very good reason that within one thousand
years, all possible—and several impossible—forms of government
were tried and found wanting. Tribal, feudal, absolute and constitutional monarchy; landed and commercial oligarchy; tyranny—

which was not half as bad as it sounds, being more often than not benevolent dictatorship of an ambitious aristocrat; totalitarian racism with a sprinkling of communism; democracy with its concomitant demagogic abuses; and ephemeral empires . . . all had their moments of glory and all failed in turn, less because of any inherent faults in the systems themselves, but rather because of the one weak point they all shared, the human factor.

While failure may have been inevitable when a system made its first appearance—democracy had its world première in Athens—this cycle of failures became progressively less excusable. Politicians the world over seem determined to ignore the lessons of the past, though the dreary repetition of mistakes has brought about the same dire consequences for almost three thousand years of recorded history, not to mention another millennium of pre-history, when legends tell the same tale of disasters.

From the Bull of Minos to the Trojan Horse

Europe's oldest state—as opposed to mere tribal groupings—arose in Crete. It was a theocracy founded by an Asiatic people which invaded that island before 3000 B.C., developed an astounding culture and extended its dominion over the South-Aegean islands and parts of the mainland coast, before coming to a dramatic end in about 1450 B.C. Myths and theories for its downfall abound, ranging from a devastating earthquake accompanied by a tidal wave to an Achaean invasion, perhaps from Athens.

On the mainland the original Celtic inhabitants experienced—but hardly enjoyed—successive waves of invaders, starting in about 1900 B.C. with the Pelasgians, followed by the Acheans, Aeolians and Ionians till the Dorians began to destroy the kingdoms of their precursors from 1200 B.C. on. The invaders were all Indo-European and came from the north; which is a vague enough statement to leave room for endless scientific disputes. Whether the Pelasgians were Greek or not is another favorite guessing game among academicians, but the rest certainly were, though they could hardly have differed more in appearance and mentality; the earlier tribes were remarkably short, dark, brown-eyed and quick-witted; the Dorians were somewhat taller, blond, blue-eyed and slow, a racial divergence which explains much of a thousand years of incompatibility.

Paradox is a Greek word and highly applicable to Greek history. Since the rehabilitation of Homer by Schliemann's excavations, Agamemnon, Great King of Mycenae, and his subject—when they felt like it—Achean princes, have moved from legend into history and the remote 13th century B.C. is more familiar than most of Greek happenings in better documented later periods. Not that subsequent ages were any duller, the one epithet that is utterly unsuitable in Greece, but they lacked the master-touch of the great epic poet. This is true even of the 5th century B.C., which produced the world's greatest journalist, Herodotus, and the first unbiased historian, Thucydides.

As Homer has proved so remarkably accurate in geographic descriptions, why should we spurn his poetic version that the Trojan War was caused by Helen's elopement with Paris, and insist instead that it was brought about by the economic necessity of keeping the Hellespont open for trade? The Trojans did ask a toll from passing ships and Troy was destroyed quite often enough— some eight times—to leave room for the dialectic interpretation. Be that as it may, the Trojan War was the starting point in the never-ending ding-dong match between Europe and Asia, which was to lead the Persians to Athens, Alexander the Great to India, and the Turks to Vienna, to mention only the rounds fought across the Hellespont. The first round went to Europe, but the Achean princes had little time left to enjoy their victory, as soon after the destruction of Troy in about 1220 B.C. their brilliant Bronze-Age civilization went down before the iron weapons of the barbaric Dorians.

Laying the Foundations

The Dark Ages descended, almost four hundred years of which next to nothing is known. The Greek renaissance of the 9th century B.C. was centered on the city-states of Ionia on the coast of Asia Minor, founded by the refugees from the Dorians, who had subjugated most of the Peloponnese and the mainland. The quest for better government spread more rapidly westwards across the Aegean islands than did philosophy or the arts, which remained an Ionian preserve for some 200 years. Monarchies tottered and were overthrown by the landed aristocracy, which, since Homeric times, alone possessed the horses essential for warfare. The military revolution of the 8th century heralded a thousand years of infantry predominance, first manifested in the hoplite formation, with the citizen-soldier supplying his own short spear, sword, shield and armor. This participation in defense tilted the balance of power in favor of the merchants and wealthy artisans, and broke the monopoly of the landowners. Tyrants supported by this new middle class formed the necessary link between oligarchy and democracy, and, dependent on popular support, carried out large-scale land reforms, public works and, on the whole, peaceful foreign policies. They acquired their bad present-day reputation only through Aristotle, who wrote in the 4th century about the ruthless military dictators of his own time. Semi-legendary Lycurgus laid the foundation of Spartan totalitarianism; approximately 100 years later Dracon promulgated his harsh laws in Athens, where revolution was only averted by the reforms of Solon in 593. For over 200 years Athenian public life was dominated by Europe's first political family, the Alcmaeonids.

In the 8th century B.C. the Olympic Games assumed a Pan-Hellenic character, sacred peace prevailed while they were in progress, a uniform reckoning of time was based on their quadrennial celebration, and participation meant recognition as part of Hellenism.

Threat from the East

In the middle of the 6th century Persia became the dominant near-Eastern power and, by the conquest of Lydia, the master of the Greek cities of Ionia. When these revolted in 499, Athens rashly intervened where Sparta, Greece's leading military state, feared to tread. An Athenian contingent advanced as far as Sardis, the Lydian capital, burnt it down, but was then decisively beaten and forced to sail home. A slave ruined Darius', the Great King, every dinner by reminding him of the Athenian misdeeds. The promptings bore fruit for, after a first expedition had been wrecked in a storm off Mount Athos, some 25,000 Persians sailed across the Aegean in 490.

After sacking Naxos and occupying Euboea they landed at Marathon, on the advice of Hippias, the former tyrant of Athens who accompanied the Persian force. Only 1,000 Plateans fought on the side of the 10,000 Athenians—"serves them right" seemed the consensus of Greek public opinion—but the brilliant strategy of Miltiades, one of the ten generals who took turns as field commander for one day, won a decisive victory. In gratitude the democratic but hardly efficient shared-command was abandoned and Miltiades led a punitive expedition against the island of Paros, which had aided and abetted the Persians. Miltiades failed, got entangled with a priestess of Hera, and was wounded jumping over her garden wall. Accused of mismanagement by the Alcmaeonid Xanthippus, Miltiades was condemned to an enormous fine. He was unable to pay and died in prison.

Xerxes, the new Great King, hesitated for a long time whether to avenge his father's defeat. Urged by exiles from all the leading Greek states and the rulers of some of the minor ones, he decided not on a mere punishment of Athens but on total subjugation of Greece. An alliance was concluded with Carthage, to attack the Greeks in Sicily, thus bringing about the first world war; a canal was dug across the isthmus of the Athos peninsula and the two-mile-wide Hellespont was bridged; supply depots were established in Thrace and Macedonia for the largest army Europe had ever seen, some 180,000 combatants—though hardly the five million mentioned by Herodotus.

To face that monstrous horde 31 Greek states temporarily patched up their feuds and under Spartan leadership formed an alliance, the largest since the Trojan war. But when the first natural defense barrier in the Vale of Tempe was turned early in 480 the alliance was deprived of the Thessalian cavalry. The second natural defense, the Pass of Thermopylae, was held by a totally insufficient force—the main Spartan army being once again delayed by a religious festival—exposing Sparta's chief rival, Athens. The heroic sacrifice of King Leonidas and his 300 men was in vain, and most of Boeotian defected to the Persians. The Spartans began the construction of a wall across the Isthmus of Corinth, abandoning mainland Greece to the enemy.

Themistocles

The political genius and patriotism of a great Athenian, Themistocles, foiled the Asian invader and triumphantly re-established Europe in Asia Minor. Though not above accepting a bribe from the Euboeans to defend them in the sea battle of Artemision, and sharing it with his Spartan commander-in-chief, he probably used part of the remainder to bribe the oracle of Delphi, which for once had abandoned its customary ambiguity and foretold a Persian victory. A complete reversal of so defeatist a stance would have lacked credibility, but Themistocles ingeniously used obscure references to "wooden walls would be the salvation" to persuade the Athenians to evacuate the town by ship, and "divine Salamis" as a prediction of a Greek victory. This somewhat thin religious argument was reinforced by the tactical fact that the narrow straits of Salamis provided the smaller Greek ships with the required advantage of maneuver. To this was added both the threat that the Athenian contingent would sail to Italy in case the Spartans withdrew, and even apparent treason, by advising Xerxes to bottle up the Allied fleet.

The end justified the means, the unwilling Allies won a resounding victory and Xerxes returned to Asia, but left a large army behind. Defeating the Persians proved a lesser problem than keeping the Allies together; Themistocles, for instance, was unable to destroy the demoralized Persian fleet, for fear of losing the blackmail lever of indispensable Athenian maritime power. Aware of Allied disunity, the Persians offered generous terms to Athens in a diplomatic turnabout which at last shocked the Spartans out of their prevarications. By the battle of Platea Greece was finally freed from the Asian threat.

Every Man has His Price

Sensationalism makes Herodotus place another great Allied victory, on the promontory of Mykale, on the same day in August 479. The Spartans wished to forestall involvement in a second Ionian revolt by proposing the evacuation of the entire Greek population of Asia Minor, a dramatic solution which was actually imposed some 2,400 years later in another turn of the wheel. Athens succeeded in reopening the vital Hellespont alone, which aroused Spartan jealousy sufficiently to send King Leotichydas, victor of Mykale, to Thessaly, and Pausanias, victor of Plataea, to Byzantium. The former was bribed by pro-Persian local rulers, condemned to death, but allowed to escape; the latter conspired with Xerxes to make him ''Rules of Hellas'', was recalled but only fined. He was finally stoned to death, his mother reportedly throwing the first stone, when he tried to raise the helots in revolt.

The recurrent bribery of Spartan leaders—who, though condemned to death were usually allowed to escape, remain kings and sometimes were even recalled—is matched by an equal laxity in democratic Athens, where politicians rarely escaped trial for an astounding variety of misdemeanors. Even high treason was not the end to a distinguished career, as was demonstrated by the most brilliant of the Alcmaeonids, Alcibiades, who decisively influenced the policies of Athens, Sparta and Persia, betrayed each and was condemned to death in each. Though bringing about the greatest military disaster suffered by Athens, he was wooed by all political parties, deserted the oligarchs he had just raised to power, and was given the greatest triumph ever accorded an elected commander-in-chief.

Sparta's discomfiture was Athens' finest hour. It assumed leadership of an Aegean confederacy based on Apollo's sacred island of Delos. But when the Persian danger receded, due to the brilliant victories of Miltiades' son Kimon, the Delian League was transformed into an Athenian empire, the member states were brought under Athenian jurisdiction and the treasury moved from Delos to Athens in 454. Only the deeply rooted belief in the *polis* (city) as the ideal unit of government prevented the formation of a unified Aegean state.

Kimon's foreign policy as leader of the conservatives was coexistence with Sparta and extension of the maritime dominions. After Themistocles' ostracism and death sentence—albeit passed *in absentia,* as the great man mistrusted the democracy he had saved, and fled to Persia where he was given the governorship of three towns—Kimon went too far in his basically correct limitation of spheres of influence between Greece's main maritime and territorial powers. He was ostracized in turn, though acquitted on a bribery charge brought by the Alcmaeonid Pericles, in a replica of their fathers' confrontation.

Pericles and the Golden Age

The stage was now set for the Golden Age of Pericles, who dominated Athens, and through it Greece, for some 30 years. He was exceedingly lucky in coming to the fore when Athens had been raised to the zenith of its power by the political genius of Themistocles and the military genius of Kimon. Moreover, after Kimon's ostracism and the murder of his fellow democrat, Ephialtes, Pericles was without any serious rival from the very outset of his career. A complete change of policy led to a head-on collision with Sparta, from which Pericles could only extricate himself by bribing King Pleistoanax. Condemned to death, the king found asylum in the sanctuary of Zeus in the Arcadian mountains and 19 years later was restored on the command of the Delphic oracle, to which the Athenian bribe finally passed.

War with Persia came to an end in 448. Pericles showed once again his astuteness as party politician by sending Kimon's brother-in-law as ambassador, thus forestalling any conservative criticism of a treaty which left Cyprus to the Persians, but confirmed Athenian dominance in the Aegean, from which the Persian fleet was excluded. After a royal betrayal the Spartans were always ready to conclude peace, and this rare commodity came to Greece in 445. Officially intended for 30 years—which seemed all that could be conceded—though in reality lasting only half that time, yet it was sufficient to make Athens the unrivaled cultural center and most beautiful town of antiquity, due to the most glorious misuse of public money in world history. The contributions of member states of the Delian League, by then rightly renamed "tribute of subjects", was employed in the rebuilding of the Acropolis and of temples throughout Attica.

In 435 Pericles resumed a policy of brinkmanship which, after several lucky escapes, led to the Peloponnesian War. Even his eulogist, Plutarch, could not decide if Pericles acted "inspired by the highest motives and a clear conception of Athens' advantage or whether by arrogance, contentiousness and a desire to display his own power". He died of the pest in 429, together with about one half of his fellow citizens.

But for a short interval of peace, patched up by the conservative leader Nicias and the restored Pleistoanax, the war continued amidst increasing atrocities, destructive, demoralizing, to be finally decided by Persian gold and the mistakes of Athens, where demagogues again and again prevented favorable peace. True to form, the worst of these excrescences of a decaying democracy was discovered to have evaded his military service and was executed.

Alas, too late. Athens was stripped of all its possessions, the walls were pulled down and the fleet surrendered. But the very greatness of the Spartan victory united such inveterate enemies as Athens, Corinth and Thebes in opposition. The ephemeral Spartan empire collapsed in 394 and the Greek towns of Asia Minor once more fell under Persian sway. A weak Persia, racked by dissensions and rebellions, became the arbiter of Greece, due to the judicious use of gold needed for the hiring of mercenaries.

The hitherto invincible Spartan hoplite army was shattered by the Thebans in 371 at the battle of Leuctra, but, with the death of Epaminondas in the battle of Mantinea ten years later, Theban federalism proved as impotent as Athenian and Spartan coercion had before.

Enter Alexander the Great

The power vacuum was filled by Philip II of Macedon, who was as great a diplomat as a general. The Athenian orator, Demosthenes, still championed the obsolete city-state, but in 338 Philip crushed the uncommonly united Greeks at Chaeronea. Macedonians garrisoned the main towns and at a Panhellenic congress at Isthmia, Philip was "elected" leader with full executive power and commander of a crusade against Persia in which the Greeks felt no desire to take part.

Philip's murder in 336 was joyfully received throughout Greece, but his twenty-year-old son, Alexander, showed the lightning decisiveness which was to make him master of the greatest empire the world had yet seen. He executed the rival Macedonian claimants to the throne; cowed the Greek cities—which were busy passing votes of thanks to Philip's murderers—into electing him their leader; subdued the barbaric tribes beyond the Danube as well as the Illyrians north of Epirus; marched back to Greece and razed rebellious Thebes to the ground, sparing only the house of the poet Pindar. The incipient Greek revolt collapsed.

In spring 334 Alexander crossed the Hellespont into Asia and, with some 40,000 men—of which less than a third were Hellenes—marched out of Greek history. But in the ensuing 11 years of unparalleled triumphs he spread Greek culture from the Nile to the Indus by founding 30 towns which bore his name. Passing beyond his tutor Aristotle's political philosophy, he attempted to merge the Macedonians and Persians into a new master race, but when he died in Babylon in 323 his revolutionary concept, as well as his family, were sacrificed to the unscrupulous rapacity of his generals. In the merciless struggle for the succession, Antigonus almost reconstituted the empire; his brilliant but unstable son, Demetrius Poliorketes (the Besieger) nearly established a Macedonian kingdom, which was realized on a diminished scale by the grandson, Antigonus Gonatus, in 276.

The able monarchs of the Antigonid dynasty imposed their rule on turbulent Greece in competition with the Seleucids of Syria and the Ptolemies of Egypt, both houses founded by Alexander's generals. But rebellion was endemic and once again the shifting leagues and confederacies called in a foreign power. Rome "liberated" with fire and sword, and finally annexed Macedonia as well as Greece in 146. The cultural conquest-in-reverse and the *Pax Romana* compensated for the loss of a much abused independence.

Rome's University

In the three decisive battles for the mastery of Rome the Greeks consistently backed the wrong side. In 48 Pompey's vastly superior army was annihilated by Julius Caesar at Pharsala in Thessaly. In 42 Brutus kept his fatal appointment with Caesar's ghost at Philippi in Macedonia; Brutus and Cassius committed suicide; Mark Anthony and Octavian divided the empire and prepared for the final contest. In 31 Mark Anthony abandoned his army at Actium in Epirus, breaking off the naval engagement to follow Cleopatra in her flight; Octavian became Augustus and the first Roman emperor.

Successive emperors favored their classical province which was renamed Achaia. Nero won the chariot races in all the venerable Games—which had to be celebrated in the year of his visit, A.D. 67—and also the singing competitions introduced for his benefit, though hardly that of his sophisticated audience. He also carted off hundreds of statues. Hadrian carried out a grandiose scheme of embellishment of towns and sanctuaries around A.D. 125.

The Roman jeunesse dorée studied rhetoric at the academies of Athens and Rhodes; tourists flocked to the monuments and battlefields, using Pausanias' excellent guidebook, published in the 2nd century A.D.; but Greece remained a political backwater, even after the transfer of the capital to Byzantium, renamed Constantinople, by Constantine the Great (324–337). His adoption of Christianity as the state religion, leading to the suppression of the Olympic Games and of the Delphic oracle by Theodosius the Great (379–395), started the decline which was hastened by Justinian's closure of the Academy of Philosophy in Athens in 529.

Slavs, Schisms and Serbians

Ruin was consummated by disastrous raids of Goths, Huns, Vandals and Avars. But only the Slavs settled permanently and, according to no less an authority than the Emperor Constantine Porphyrogenitus, the country districts became entirely Slavonic after the great plague of 747. The Macedonian dynasty, especially Basil II (the Bulgar-slayer, 976–1025), re-established effective imperial rule, which continued under the Comneni and Angeli dynasties (1081–1204), despite frequent raids by the Sicilian Normans.

But the schism of 1054 between the Greek and the Roman Churches was to lead to the shameful Fourth Crusade, diverted by Venetian greed and from the reconquest of the Holy Land to the occupation of the Christian bulwark against the eastern Moslems. Powerless Latin emperors from 1204 to 1261 claimed suzerainty over feudal lords, but not over the large Venetian part of the spoils, mainly islands. Marquis Bonifacio of Montferrat, King of Thessaloniki, married the widow of Isaac II Angelus in an attempt to unite Greeks and Franks. With his stepson Manuel, who had a good claim to the imperial crown, he conquered Thessaly, where he captured the ignoble Alexius III Angelus and the imperial regalia. Bestowing Athens and Thebes on the Burgundian Othon de la Roche, Bonifacio consented to the occupation of the Peloponnese by Guillaume de Champlitte and Geoffroy de Villehardouin. The threat to his capital by the Despote Michael Angelus of Epirus and Bulgarian raids called Bonifacio north. He was killed in an ambush and his severed head was sent to the Bulgarian king, who had previously imprisoned and murdered the first Latin emperor, Baldwin of Flanders. With the death of Bonifacio in 1207 all hope for a Frankish-Greek reconciliation disappeared.

From 1222 onwards, the Byzantines regained some territories at the expense of the Frankish principalities. Michael Palaeologus re-established an emaciated Byzantine Empire in Constantinople in 1261, but the Serbian Empire extended deep into Greece by the middle of the 14th century, while Catalan mercenaries no one could afford to hire established lawless soldier-republics.

Turkish Domination

By the close of the century, the Turks had occupied Macedonia and Thessaly. The dying Byzantine Empire achieved a final triumph by conquering the Frankish Peloponnese in 1430, but 30 years later the last emperor's brothers, who shared the rule of this province which had outlived the empire, quarreled and called in the Turks.

Mohammed II, the Conqueror, preserved the feudal system of military fiefs, but Turkish veterans replaced the Frankish and Greek nobles. The Greek peasants remained serfs paying, beside tithes, a poll-tax and a blood tribute of a fifth of their male children. Brought up as Moslems, the most gifted boys entered the imperial administration, especially the corps of Janissaries, the élite of the Turkish army.

The Orthodox Church remained as the sole Christian organization and the Patriarch of Constantinople became the representative of the Greek nation. Ecclesiastical tribunals judged most cases in which only Christians were involved. The parochial clergy was mainly responsible for the survival of the subject races during centuries of ruthless suppression, while the bishops assumed temporal as well as spiritual guidance.

The Struggle for Independence

War continued intermittently between the Turks and the Venetians, but though the latter lost all their Aegean possessions in the course of the 17th century, the decline of the Ottoman Empire became apparent not long after. The sultans cared little about what happened in their vast domains as long as tribute flowed into the imperial treasury. Inherited feuds, frequent rebellions and constant brigandage reduced the country to near anarchy. The enterprising sailors of the islands of Chios, Idra, Spetse and Psara benefited, however, from the breakdown of the central administration and their merchant navies played a decisive part in the War of Independence.

In 1770 Prince Orloff, favorite of Catherine the Great, attempted to establish a Greek principality, relying on the common bond of religion. The appearance of a Russian fleet was the signal for a rising in the Peloponnese, which was bloodily suppressed. Continued resistance by the outlaws in the mountains was complemented by a cultural revival in Greek communities. Literary and political societies were founded by wealthy Greek merchants in Europe, the most important being the *Philiki Hetairia* (Friendly Society), which eventually included 200,000 adherents.

Where Orloff failed, a Moslem Albanian adventurer briefly succeeded. By unscrupulous treachery combined with merciless cruelty Ali of Tepelen, Pasha of Trikala, extended his rule over the western Greek mainland and most of Albania. Yet, after his surrender in 1822, he himself fell victim to Turkish treachery and was murdered.

Turkish preoccupation with Ali Pasha provided an opportunity for revolts throughout the Balkans. Alexander Ypsilanti raised Moldavia, which his ancestors had ruled under Turkish suzerainty, but failed in 1821. On March 25 of the same year, the feast of the Annunciation, Archbishop Germanos of Patras proclaimed Greek independence at the monastery of Agia Lavra in the Peloponnese. The Turks retaliated with massacres of Greeks in Macedonia and Constantinople, where the Patriarch was hanged on Easter Sunday.

The War of Independence started with daring exploits of the *klepht* (outlaw) leaders, Botzaris and Kolokotronis on land, Kanaris and Miaoulis at sea, soon marred by fratricidal quarrels and even fighting. The intervention by an Egyptian force under Ibrahim Pasha in 1825 led to a Triple Alliance of Great Britain, France and Russia to mediate. Lord Byron's stint as Greek commander-in-chief had been too brief to change the course of the war and as he had been chosen mainly for his financial contribution and European reputation his authority was by no means generally recognized. However, the appointment of Sir Richard Church and Lord Cochrane as commanders of the insurgent army and navy added the badly needed professional touch.

In 1827 Count Capodistrias, former foreign secretary of Tsar Alexander I of Russia, was elected first President of Greece, but Ibrahim Pasha reconquered a large part of the Peloponnese and Athens fell to the Turks. An ill-advised Turkish shot precipitated the destruction of the Turkish-Egyptian fleet in the harbor of Navarino by the Allies, despite their orders to abstain from any active intervention. But in accordance with the rules of ancient tragedy it was Demetrius Ypsilanti, Alexander's brother, who defeated the Turks in the last engagement in 1829.

Jockeying for a Throne

In the same year Greek independence was recognized by the Treaty of Adrianople. The frontiers were drawn rather haphazardly from the Gulf of Arta to the Gulf of Volos by the Protocol of London in 1832. This left the majority of Greeks under Turkish rule, but the new state was guaranteed by the three main European powers. The assassination of Capodistrias by a Peloponnesian clan led to near-anarchy. In the first of the alternations between republic and monarchy, which have been so remarkably constant an element in modern Greece, the throne was offered to Prince Leopold of Saxe-Coburg, widower of Princess Charlotte, King George IV's only child. In an age when thrones and not their occupants went begging, Leopold could afford to decline, and became King of the Belgians instead.

The choice then fell on the younger son of King Ludwig I of Bavaria, seventeen-year-old Prince Otho. Neither the Bavarian Council of Regency nor the young King, who transferred the capital to Athens, showed sufficient regard for Greek nationalist feelings, trying too hard to equate Greece with a central European kingdom. The foundation of Athens University as a center of Hellenic culture only added students to the other discontented sectors of the population. The bloodless revolution of 1843 obtained a constitution and sent the multitude of Bavarian dignitaries packing. During the Crimean War the King patriotically but unwisely gave voice to the pro-Russian sympathies of his subjects. An Anglo-French fleet occupied the Piraeus, Otho lost face and Russia lost the war. Greece was beset by brigandage, bankruptcy and disaffection, Queen Amalia failed to produce an heir, and the army forced Otho's abdication in 1863.

The Protocol of London excluded dynasts of the Protecting Powers from the Greek throne. Never taking no for an answer and eager to regain British support, the Greeks voted overwhelmingly for the Duke of Edinburgh, Queen Victoria's second son, in the first in the long series of constitutional plebiscites. An ideal substitute was found in Prince William George of Denmark, who was brother-in-law to both Edward, Prince of Wales and the Russian Tsarevich Alexander. To sweeten acceptance, Great Britain ceded the Ionian Islands on the accession of the new king.

Like his predecessor George I was seventeen years old, but he soon learned to keep out of the grueling party strife by adhering to the spirit of the 1864 constitution, which restricted the royal prerogative. The adoption of the title "King of the Hellenes" signified not only willingness to follow the French and Belgian model, but also the aspiration to include the unredeemed Greeks in the kingdom.

A Cretan rebellion in 1866 nearly led to war with Turkey; British support at the Conference of Constantinople in 1881 gained Thessaly and further concessions in Crete. The Cretan revolt of 1897 led to war, Crown Prince Constantine's army was driven out of Thessaly, George I almost lost his throne and only Gladstone's intervention halted the victorious Turkish forces.

Venizelos and the First World War

In exchange for the loss of a northern Thessalian district, Crete was granted autonomy, with Prince George of Greece as High Commissioner under nominal Turkish suzerainty. In 1906 the Prince was forced to resign by the up-and-coming Cretan politician, Eleutherios Venizelos, to be succeeded by Alexander Zaïmis, who had proved his diplomatic subtlety as prime minister at the peace negotiations in 1897. His final score after 40 years in public life amounted to: High Commissioner of Crete, Governor of the Bank of Greece, ten times Prime Minister and once President of the Republic.

The defeat in the recent war brought about a Military League of some 500 officers, who forced the King to exclude the royal princes from all commands, remove the discredited politicians from office and to appoint Venizelos, who in Zaïmis' absence had proclaimed union with Greece.

After a false start with a Revisionary National Assembly, Venizelos obtained a sufficient majority to introduce badly needed administrative, agricultural and educational reforms. A British naval and a French military mission reorganized the armed forces, while for the sake of national unity Crown Prince Constantine was reinstated as Inspector-General of the Army. Venizelos' greatest achievement was, however, the formation of a Balkan League of hereditary enemies against Turkey. While the latter was resisting Italian aggression in Libya, disturbances in Macedonia led in 1912 to the First Balkan War. The League was victorious on all fronts, but dissensions quickly became apparent and Crown Prince Constantine's army occupied Thessaloniki only hours before the arrival of a Bulgarian division. George I triumphantly entered the Macedonian capital, where he was murdered by a lunatic early in 1913.

Turkey ceded all European territory to the League, and in the ensuing quarrel over the spoils Greece joined Serbia and Romania in the Second Balkan War against Bulgaria. The Turks regained eastern Thrace, Bulgaria surrendered, and the Treaty of Bucharest doubled the area of Greece. The Dodecanese was provisionally assigned to Italy and retained in violation of formal obligations.

Greek sympathies lay with the reunited Protecting Powers in the First World War. But after two bloody wars Greece desperately needed time to recover, while King Constantine, who lacked his father's political wisdom, firmly believed in the superiority of Germany, where he had received his military training. The ancient conflict between Themistocles and the conservatives, representing maritime and landed interest, was revived in the King and his Prime Minister. Queen Sophia and the pro-German General Staff prevented any reconciliation, Venizelos resigned and Zaïmis tried to preserve strict neutrality. Cyprus was refused as price of Greek support for the Allies; Venizelos formed a government in Thessaloniki in October 1916; the King was forced by the Allies to leave the country, and was succeeded by his second son Alexander.

Venizelos, once more Prime Minister of a united Greece, wholeheartedly supported the Allied army in Macedonia, where the decisive penetration of fortress Europe in September 1918 sealed the fate of the Central Powers. With the Treaty of Sèvres in 1920 the

Kingdom of the Hellenes became a reality, by assigning Thrace and the Province of Smyrna, ancient Ionia, to Greece.

In the same year King Alexander died of blood-poisoning from a monkey bite, leaving only a daughter from a morganatic marriage. A plebiscite declared overwhelmingly in favor of King Constantine, and it was Venizelos' turn in the modern form of ostracism.

Between the Wars

Turkey's revival under Mustapha Kemal was assisted by France and Italy, while Great Britain ceased to support Greece on the return of King Constantine. Initial victories hardened Greek pretensions at a time when the commander-in-chief thought himself literally possessed of a pair of glass feet, on which he lavished greater care than on the over-extended troops.

Lunacy on top of incompetence brought about disastrous defeat. The Greek army was driven back to the coast and in a typical irrational reversion of popular feeling a military Revolutionary Committee of the few efficient officers forced King Constantine's abdication in favor of his eldest son, George II. Venizelos declined to return, but represented Greece at the Lausanne Peace Conference. Even Zaïmis refused the premiership, as the army insisted on the execution of three royalist prime ministers, two ministers and the commander-in-chief of glass-feet fame.

In July 1923 Greece ceded to Turkey the Thracian districts east of the Evros river as well as all claims in Asia Minor, and agreed to a hitherto unprecedented wholesale exchange of population, almost two million Greeks against 370,000 Moslems. The resettlement of refugees numbering almost one half of the existing population led to untold misery which, however, only exacerbated petty politicking. Zaïmis failed to reconcile monarchists and republicans; King George II left the country; Venizelos resigned and the Armed Forces proclaimed the Republic on March 25, 1924, anniversary of the Revolution. By a coup within the coup General Pangalos became Premier-President, brought some order into chaos, but was laughed out of office on decreeing that women's skirts must rise no higher than a maximum 14 centimeters from the ground. The police spent a busy time on their knees with measuring rods. Pangalos was overthrown in 1926, Zaïmis formed a coalition government and Venizelos returned in 1928. He abolished proportional representation, which had made the country ungovernable, while Pangalos was imprisoned for corruption.

Thanks to English and American loans the economy recovered, brigandage was suppressed, relations with Turkey improved and involvement in the Cyprus rebellion of 1931 was avoided. The monarchists won the election of 1935, Venizelos resigned and a

97% majority voted for the King's restoration in yet another plebiscite.

George II insisted on including Venizelos in a general amnesty, but the elections in 1936 gave fifteen Communist deputies the balance of power. The old party leaders, who had been playing musical chairs far too long for the good of the nation, died opportunely though naturally, opening the way for General Metaxas to assume dictatorial powers to deal with a Communist-inspired general strike. He alone, among all contemporary Balkan regimes, changed from the execution of political opponents to the traditional Byzantine device of exile to remote islands. He also laid the basis of social welfare, and on the whole followed the example of antique paternalistic tyrants.

The Second World War and After

The Second World War found the Greeks for once united in their desire to remain neutral, despite Italy's annexation of Albania and the torpedoing of the cruiser *Helle* by an Italian submarine during the celebration of the Assumption of the Virgin at the island of Tinos. Metaxas' historic "No" was vindicated by the occupation of nearly one third of Albania by the Greek army, inferior in numbers and equipment, but brilliantly led by General Papagos according to the strategy of Metaxas, the only foreigner to graduate top ot his class in the Imperial Military Academy of pre-World-War-I Germany.

Metaxas died on January 29, 1941; on April 6 the Germans invaded Yugoslavia and Greece. Anglo-Hellenic forces fought Hitler's war machine heroically against a background of defeatism, intrigue and incipient treason till the inevitable evacuation. The determined courage of King George II after the suicide of his Prime Minister prolonged resistance sufficiently to delay the German aggression against Russia, thus probably altering the course of the war. But when the royal government had to abandon Crete for exile in Cairo, the squabbles among the politicians there equaled those within the puppet governments in Athens. Greek troops, however, participated on the side of their British allies in the campaigns of Africa and Italy.

Under the German, Italian and Bulgarian occupation famine claimed innumerable victims, while the Communist-dominated guerrilla faction soon ceased fighting the invader and prepared for a takeover. Their moment seemed to have come when the small Anglo-Hellenic force, which had entered Athens on October 13, 1944, held little less than the center of the capital and a corridor to the airport. In December the Communists massacred 10,000 hostages on their retreat to the mountains.

This retreat was due to Churchill's decisive intervention on his visit with Eden, the Foreign Secretary, when the vacillating Papandreou was dismissed and Plastiras, the surviving leader of the Revolutionary Committee of 1922, was installed as Prime Minister under the regency of Archbishop Damaskinos, who had valiantly opposed the Germans.

The plebiscite of 1946 declared overwhelmingly in favor of George II, who returned to face a second Communist rebellion, actively supported by Greece's northern neighbors. Only after Yugoslavia's break with Russia, the displacement of over 700,000 villagers, the abduction of 25,000 children to be indoctrinated behind the Iron Curtain, destruction and murder of their fellow-Greeks by the partisans far surpassing those committed by the enemy, and after the reorganization of the armed forces first by a British and then by an American military mission, did General Papagos defeat the Communists in late 1949.

King, Colonels and the Return of Democracy

On April 1, 1947 King George II died childless and was succeeded by his brother Paul. Political instability and unscrupulous jockeying for power retarded economic rehabilitation, despite massive American aid, till General Papagos' newly founded party swept the poll in 1952. Confidence returned, industrialization gathered momentum, and Greece joined NATO. Yet the gods were as jealous as ever; when it was not the politicians, Nature herself disturbed the peace. Three major earthquakes devastated the Ionian Islands, Central Thessaly and the Pelion region, before Papagos died in 1955.

Karamanlis, the popular Minister of Public Works, was appointed Prime Minister, and in the approved Greek fashion formed a new party, winning three successive elections, unparalleled in modern Greece. During this period of relative political serenity, the standard of living rose spectacularly and economic recovery culminated in acceptance as first associate member of the EEC. But in June 1963 Karamanlis resigned and went into self-imposed exile in Paris. Three caretaker governments and two elections later, Papandreous returned to the political fore and formed a government. King Paul died in March 1964 and was succeeded by his son Constantine who, however, was not called "the Second" because of the ill-defined yet inviolable pretense that the Greek kings continued the line of Byzantine emperors among which there had been eleven Constantines. The young King's popularity as winner of the sailing competition in the Olympic Games—the only gold medal ever for royalty in an international race of that prestige—was further enhanced by his marriage to Princess Anna Maria of Denmark, but the fall of the Papandreou government heralded a period of acute instability.

Governments rose and fell every few weeks till the Colonel's Revolution of April 1, 1967. On December 13 the King, supported by his Prime Minister and the army high command, attempted a counter coup, but the armed forces obeyed the colonels. The King left the country, one of the generals who had sided with the colonels was appointed regent, and Papadopoulos, who emerged as the regime's strong man, became Prime Minister and eventually also Regent.

A plebiscite in 1968 confirmed the constitutional monarchy, while another in 1973 declared for a republic. Papadopoulos became President, martial law was lifted and an elder statesman appointed Prime Minister to prepare elections.

A few days before the state visit of the Romanian President, a proof that ideological differences were no hindrance to peaceful coexistence in the Balkans, riots at the Polytechnic University were suppressed by the army with some loss of life, more among innocent bystanders than students and activists. But the Romanian state visit was canceled.

Within days the hard core of young officers staged another coup under the leadership of Brigadier Ioannides, commander of the military police which had been built up to considerable strength. Papadopoulos became a non-person, though left free, another general was appointed President, a Greek-American lawyer became Prime Minister, but real power lay with Ioannides.

Ever since 1954 the problem of Cyprus had bedeviled foreign relations, first with Great Britain, then bringing Greece, on several occasions, to the brink of war with Turkey. Never closer than in summer 1974, when a coup overthrew the Cypriot President, Archbishop Makarios, who sought refuge in the British military base. Turkish troops landed in Cyprus. Faced with war the Greek high command forced Ioannides to resign; Karamanlis returned in triumph. Makarios was reinstated but died in 1977, with the Turks still holding almost half of the island.

In the subsequent election Karamanlis' renamed party obtained the largest parliamentary majority in Europe and yet another plebiscite in December 1974 confirmed the republic by a two-to-one vote.

The constitution of 1975 is an emaciated presidential democracy, where much depends on the respective personalities of president and prime minister, by giving the former the right to appeal directly to the people. The leaders of the military regime, who had not availed themselves of the ample opportunities to leave the country, were tried but their death sentences were commuted to life imprisonment.

The restoration of democracy has been achieved conspicuously painlessly, especially when compared with the troubles elsewhere; the Karamanlis government could rightly claim that never before had Greece been more democratic and prosperous. Unemployment has remained well below the EEC average while income has risen spectacularly above the per capita threshold for developed countries. Yet the largest number of newspapers in any capital, representing every shade of political opinion—but not unbiased reporting—keeps political passions at an unhealthy fever pitch with sensational stories as lurid as they are unfounded.

Greece Today

Though Greece became a full member of the European Economic Community on January 1st, 1981, the economic problems remain reduction of inflation, still running at 25%, and of the huge deficit in the balance of payments. A host of social conflicts are apparent in a multitude of strikes.

Over-consumption is rampant. In fifteen years the number of private cars has risen by well over 1,000% to one million and a half, despite prohibitive taxes which more than double the cost. There are about 1,000 fashion boutiques in Athens, while the proliferating nightclubs and taverns are packed with customers willing to pay staggering bills.

The 1977 election reduced Karamanlis' majority to 172 of the 300 deputies in the single chamber, yet in 1980 he was elected by the required two thirds of deputies President of the Republic for a five-year term. He was succeeded as Prime Minister by George Rallis, whose father and grandfather had held the same office. Political leadership is as hereditary in modern as in ancient Greek democracy, in the Republican no less than the Royalist party, and confined to a few families, with Karamanlis being the outstanding exception. The socialist victory in the election of October 1981 brought to power the son of another former prime minister, and to continue the dynasty a grandson was elected Greece's youngest deputy. Andreas Papandreou, once a Professor at Berkeley and a U.S. citizen, has reneged on his campaign slogan of withdrawal from the EEC and NATO, but is increasingly at odds with his partners over loosening traditional ties with the West. This policy is, naturally, opposed by the main Democratic opposition, but supported by the Communists, the third party represented in Parliament.

Major banks are state-controlled, and the public sector accounts for about 30% of industrial production, much above the EEC average. Yet by far the most successful industry is privately owned, usually by one family or even one individual, those fabulous Greek shipowners. With about 3,500 ships totaling about 38 million tons, the Greek flag holds fourth place among the merchant navies, third if the seven million tons of Greek-owned vessels under flags of convenience are added. The country's second largest industry is also the second-largest foreign exchange earner, despite the continuing lay-up of millions of tons, as Greek shipping firms have ridden out the storm better than many foreign competitors. The same is true for shipyards, which are mainly repair yards, largely occupied in maintaining the aging fleets of their owners, except Niarchos' *Hellenic,* which also builds ships.

Tourism is the largest industry, earning two billion dollars from over five million visitors in 1983. But the very rapidity of totting up million upon million has created serious problems, though the country's 9,333 miles of coast are still less crowded than the western European Mediterranean shore. Hotel capacity stands at over 320,000 beds, the shipowners once again having secured the most prominent position. The Chandris group owns the largest chain, connected with its cruise operations; Carras has built the biggest and most luxurious holiday complex, even producing its own excellent wine, in the Halkidiki.

The Public Power Corporation has completed its rural electrification program and supplies 99% of the population with 18,000 million KWH, a per capita consumption of 1,780 KWH (71 KWH in 1950). 70% of the electricity is produced from indigenous lignite and waterpower, the rest from imported oil. The percentage for total energy consumption is, however, the reverse, 26% to oil's 74%, although since 1982 production from the offshore Prinos field near Thassos has covered about 10% of oil consumption. Drilling is in progress in many parts of the country, and promising uranium deposits have been discovered in Macedonia.

Agriculture still employs about 20% of the labor force, achieving self-sufficiency in cereals and exporting large quantities of fruit, olive oil and, above all, tobacco. Greece is Europe's largest cement exporter, and a well-established textile producer based on homegrown cotton and wool; other industries enjoy a five-year period for the necessary adjustments within the EEC.

WHO'S WHO ON OLYMPOS

A Yearbook of Gods and Heroes

Ancient Greece was happily free from the religious fanaticism of later ages for the Greek attitude toward their gods was remarkably eclectic and never hidebound by rigid tradition. Gods from many parts of the Ancient world were assimilated into the Olympian family. This extremely tolerant and open attitude toward their gods accounts to a very large degree for the development of the great Greek philosophic systems side by side with popular religion.

Like most Mediterraneans the original inhabitants of Greece worshipped the Great Triple Goddess. Her celestial symbol was the moon, whose three phases recalled the change from the maiden into the woman and finally into a crone. Ever since, three has remained a sacred number, playing a mystical part in religion.

In the pre-Hellenic matriarchal organization the tribes were ruled by a queen, whose annual lover was sacrificed at the end of the year and his blood sprinkled on trees and crops. His flesh was devoured by the priestesses disguised as mares, sows or bitches. The frenzied followers of Dionysos indulged in this cannibalistic practice down to the 6th century, with Orpheus as their most famous victim.

Successive invasions of Hellenic tribes undermined the authority of the terrible Great Goddess, and introduced male supremacy and succession towards the close of the 2nd millenium B.C. Yet the goddesses were never completely stripped of all influence, thanks to the great poets, especially Homer, who had clearly defined their spheres of action.

Religion was an imaginative comment on natural phenomena, without any rigid creed. As the moral consciousness developed, the notion of reward and punishment based on ethical conduct gained strength, and by the 6th century B.C. hell, purgatory and paradise had become established concepts. But the gods were not exempt from passions and faults, they simply acted on a grander scale. Even their immortality depended on the divine food and drink of ambrosia and nectar. They were conceived as an upper class of very superior nobles, above the humans, yet essentially human.

Feasts and ceremonies followed largely older local traditions, while rules were concerned with pleasing the gods, not with regulating the belief of the worshipper. Impiety was a crime only when it led to a neglect of ritual determining the daily life. This close connection makes some familiarity with mythology essential for the better understanding of the Greek mind.

Owing to the different poetical interpretations, the gods were endowed with a bewildering assortment of vices and virtues to satisfy everybody's taste. Greek sense of humor, moreover, was stronger than blind respect for the immortals. The Olympians' amorous misadventures or their far from harmonious family life were discussed with relish.

The Creation Myth

At the beginning was Chaos, from which Gaea (Earth) emerged—though how successfully has remained a point of dispute. All by herself she bore a son, Uranos (Heaven), who was ashamed of his naked mother. His tears of indignation must have been copious, as rivers and seas, flowers and trees, and even animals sprang up where they had fallen. The earth became divided into two equal parts by the Mediterranean and the Black Sea, with the river Okeanos encircling the disc. Greece occupied the central position, while far north, in the inaccessible British Isles, lived the blameless Hyperboreans in perpetual springtide. (It is pleasant to reflect that Britain once enjoyed such a reputation.) They were often visited by the gods, like their southern counterpart, the equally virtuous Ethiopians.

Incest was a practical necessity for the first gods and men alike, in both cases with singularly unprepossessing results. Heaven's union with Mother Earth produced three hundred-handed giants, followed by three hardly more attractive one-eyed Cyclopes. It is not surprising that the exasperated father flung his hideous brood into Tartaros, the remotest and gloomiest part of the underworld. Yet Uranos must have been fond of children, as he proceeded to father the seven Titans, more pleasing in appearance, but far more dangerous to their luckless progenitor. Urged on by their mother, who pined for her exiled Cyclopes, the Titans attacked their sleeping father with a flint sickle and castrated him.

The Titans divided the world among themselves under the leadership of the youngest, Kronos (Time). Mother Earth however, failed in her attempt to set the beloved Cyclopes free. After one look Kronos confined them and their hundred-handed brothers again to Tartaros; and in revenge the frustrated mother prophesied that he too would be dethroned by one of his own sons.

Kronos married his sister Rhea, but mindful of the prophecy swallowed the children his wife bore him, a parable of Time annihilating all creation. On Mother Earth's advice Rhea substituted for her sixth child a stone wrapped in swaddling clothes which Kronos promptly devoured. It says a lot for his excellent digestion that he never noticed the fraud.

The infant Zeus was hidden in the cave of Dicte in Crete, under the care of the goat Amalthea, whose milk he drank together with his foster-brother Goat-Pan. Zeus showed his gratitude to his nurse by setting her image among the stars as Capricorn. Around the infant's cradle Rhea's priests performed wild dances, clashing shields and uttering piercing screams to drown the noise of his wailing. He grew up among the shepherds of Mount Ida, and with his mother's assistance was made cupbearer to his unsuspecting father. Rhea provided Zeus with a mixture so potent that even Kronos could not stomach it. He vomited up first the stone—venerated throughout antiquity in Delphi—and then disgorged his elder children.

After deposing their father, Zeus, Poseidon and Hades drew lots for the division of the world. Zeus won the heaven, Poseidon the sea, and Hades the underworld. The earth was left common to all the gods under the vague sovereignty of Zeus, who only succeeded in controlling his quarrelsome family by the threat of the thunderbolts he alone might wield. And it was the thunderbolts—forged by the Cyclopes at last released—that give the third generation victory over those Titans who refused to acknowledge Zeus as their master. For ten years a terrible war raged in Thessaly, the rebels piling mountain upon mountain to reach the abode of the gods, before Kronos was defeated and banished to the British Isles.

According to another version, he was allowed to withdraw to Italy, where he ruled a prosperous kingdom, until in his dotage he was compensated with the Elysian Fields. Atlas, his second-in-command, was set to hold up the sky, while the lesser Titans took the Cyclopes' place in Tartaros.

Having successfully disposed of his uncles, Zeus settled down to enjoy his unlawfully obtained power. But Mother Earth changed sides, and, never averse to bringing forth a monster, now created the worst abomination of all, called Typhon.

To a hundred dragon heads spouting flames were added arms reaching a hundred leagues in either direction, while instead of legs he featured the coils of a serpent. One glance at Gaea's youngest sent the gods in headlong flight to Egypt, a favorite refuge for divinity in distress. For greater safeguard Zeus assumed the form of a ram, Hera became a cow, Artemis a cat, each god choosing the animal shape of his Egyptian counterpart.

But Zeus soon grew ashamed of his cowardice and resuming his true form pursued Typhon with thunderbolts, finally hurling Mount Aetna at him. Buried beneath the Sicilian mountain the monster still belches forth fire and flame, and when he occasionally changes his position an earthquake ensues.

The Story of Man

Prometheus (Forethought), the wisest of the Titans, had foreseen the outcome of Kronos' rebellion and loyally fought on the Olympians' side. As a reward he was entrusted with the creation of man. From a lump of clay kneaded with water Prometheus fashioned a creature in the image of the gods, and bestowed on man the supreme gift of fire, lighting a torch at the sun itself.

During the Age of Gold men lived without care and without women. After Zeus had fathered the seasons life became harder for men, who had to seek refuge from wind and cold in caves. No more could they live on fruit, milk and honey, but had to work for their food. Contrary to expectation, work and sin went hand in hand, and as punishment Zeus extinguished the fire. Prometheus once again came to the rescue and brought a torch to earth hidden in the pithy hollow of a giant fennel stalk. But the gods took a terrible vengeance on both Prometheus and mankind. The Titan was chained to a peak in the Caucasian mountains, where an eagle tore at his liver all day; and there was no end to his pain, because every night the liver grew whole again and the ghastly process was resumed the next morning.

To men was meted out a fate hardly less atrocious. Haephaestos fashioned a woman, Aphrodite taking care of the sex appeal. This gift of all the gods, Pandora, was sent to Epimetheus (Afterthought), who in spite of his brother Prometheus' warnings was enslaved by her charms. As dowry Pandora had received a jeweled box, which Zeus had exhorted her never to open, realizing full well that disobedience and curiosity would distinguish the female. Before long Pandora did indeed open the box, and out flew all the mental and bodily diseases that have plagued mankind ever since. But caught under the lid remained Hope, which alone makes men's lives bearable.

Mankind degenerated so intolerably that Zeus resolved to destroy it in a flood. But there was one righteous man, Deukalion, who with his wife Pyrrha had been warned to take refuge in an ark, which floated about for nine days, before at last coming to rest on Mount Parnassos. When the flood receded a divine voice ordered them to fling the bones of their mother behind. This they rightly interpreted as meaning the bones of Mother Earth, the rocks. Those thrown by Deukalion became men, and those by Pyrrha women. Thus humanity was renewed, though the couple also produced one son in the orthodox way. He was called Hellen, who gave his name to the Hellenic race, and his sons Aelos and Doros, and grandsons Ion and Achaius, became the ancestors of the tribes bearing their names.

The Olympians—Zeus and Hera

Having thus connected the tribes, Greek love of systematization likewise wrought the principal gods into one great family, regardless of their varied origins.

Zeus fixed the abode of the gods in Mount Olympos, whence he decreed laws and controlled the heavenly bodies. When his mother Rhea forbade him to marry, he violated her and proceeded to court his sister Hera. Unsuccessfully, until he transformed himself into a bedraggled cuckoo, which the merciful goddess warmed against her bosom. Resuming his true shape, Zeus ravished her, shaming her into marriage.

Mother, now grandmother, Earth gave Hera a tree with golden apples as a wedding present. The newly-weds spent the wedding night, lasting 300 years, on Samos, but in spite of the birth of two sons and one daughter, Ares, Hephaestos and Hebe, the marriage could hardly be called happy. There was constant bickering over Zeus' numerous infidelities, which Hera proved utterly incapable of preventing, though she occasionally took terrible revenge on her rivals or their children.

She only rarely succeeded in arousing her husband's passion, even though she sometimes borrowed Aphrodite's girdle; perhaps the wedding night had been too prolonged. Their family however, increased to 12, partly by children born in wedlock, partly through extra-marital affairs with nymphs or mortals, a yield of four supplemented by two miraculous births.

Zeus grew increasingly overbearing, and at last the Olympians revolted, binding him, as he lay asleep, with rawhide thongs tied in a hundred knots. While the gods were quarreling over his succession, the sea nymph Thetis, fearing a civil war, set one of the hundred-handed uncles to untie the knots all at once. No sooner was Zeus free than he hung Hera, the ringleader, in golden chains from heaven, with heavy anvils weighing down her ankles. She was only released after her fellow conspirators had taken an oath of loyalty.

Poseidon

Poseidon too had taken a prominent part in the rebellion, and was condemned to serve King Laomedon for one year, for whom he built with Apollo's assistance the city of Troy. He equaled his brother Zeus in dignity, though not in power, which was all for the good considering his perpetual bad temper.

In the best family tradition he raped his sister Demeter, then had a son, a most objectionable giant, by his grandmother Earth, before he began courting the sea nymph Thetis, to have a spouse who would feel at home in the depth of the sea. Zeus was his rival for Thetis' hand, but both desisted when it was prophesied that her son would outshine his father. They forthwith encouraged her to wed an innocuous mortal, King Peleus, the future father of Achilles.

Another sea nymph, Amphitrite, became his consort and though rather insignificant herself, she could rise to fits of jealousy worthy of Hera. Needless to say she had plenty of provocation. Her children were singularly undistinguished, with the exception of Triton, the dangerous and touchy merman.

Not content with the seas, Poseidon was exceedingly greedy for earthly kingdoms, quarreling fiercely with Dionysos over Naxos, with Hera over Argos, and especially with Athena over Athens.

Hestia and Demeter

Though both unmarried, these two sisters of Zeus were unlike in character. Hestia, alone of all Olympians was never connected with any scandal, and it was probably her very purity that made her lose her place to the orgiastic Dionysos. The ancient Greeks were too fond of love and intrigue to honor greatly so placid, mild and charitable a goddess as this protectress of the hearth.

Demeter, on the other hand, shared fully the stormy life of the Olympians. She did not escape Zeus' amorous advances and bore him Persephone. After a passing affair with a Titan, she was raped by brother Poseidon.

But this dallying came to a sudden stop when Hades abducted young Persephone while she was picking flowers. The disconsolate mother searched in vain, until she reached Eleusis, where the king's elder son had news of the vanished Persephone. He had seen a chariot drawn by black horses racing down a bottomless chasm. And then the earth closed again over the driver who was clasping a struggling girl. There could be no doubt as to the charioteer's identity.

Demeter instantly forbade all trees to bear fruit and all grain to grow, until life on earth was threatened with extinction. She only relented after a compromise was reached thanks to mother Rhea's intervention. Persephone was to spend the three winter months with Hades, and the rest of the year with her mother. Demeter lifted the curse, instructed the king's son in her mysteries and rewarded him with seed corn and a wooden plow to teach mankind the art of agriculture.

Aphrodite and Eros

The goddess of love rose naked from the sea. Though originally an orgiastic Oriental, her cult, if not her conduct, improved in comformity with the Greek moral code. Only in Corinth, the trading center most exposed to foreign influences, did temple harlots serve her in the Syrian fashion.

Aphrodite was exceedingly fickle and capricious, but worst of all, she hardly ever lent her magic girdle, which made its wearer irresistible. As punishment she was married off to Hephaestos, physically the least attractive Olympian. Yet this match was harder on the husband than on the wife, who had fallen for the virility of Ares. Hephaestos surprised the lovers in bed, and throwing an unbreakable net over them summoned the gods to witness their shame. The immortals were merely amused, while Poseidon and Hermes greatly appreciated Aphrodite's provocative helplessness. As reward for Hermes' flattering remarks she spent a night with him and bore double-sexed Hermaphroditos. Then she could not but do likewise with Poseidon, and, after rounding off a hectic season with Dionysos, she retired to Cyprus renewing her virginity in the sea, to the pained envy of mortals and immortals.

Woe to anyone who offended the goddess of love. Her main instrument of vengeance was her son Eros, whose progenitor could never be ascertained owing to the mother's promiscuity. Eros wantonly kindled passions with his golden arrows shot at random, yet he himself did not escape the fate he had meted out to countless victims.

Call!!
back — any
time today

Diane
627-0117

He had been instructed by his jealous mother to make Psyche (Soul) fall in love. For once handling the fateful arrows clumsily, he wounded himself, while Psyche remained untouched. Aphrodite was enraged that his own weapon had been turned against her son. She set the desperate maiden some seemingly impossible tasks which Psyche nevertheless accomplished, sustained by Eros' invisible assistance. As supreme trial she was bidden to fetch some of Persephone's beauty from the underworld, as Aphrodite had lost some of hers tending her love-sick son. Psyche was on her way back with the priceless gift wrapped in a box, when she bethought herself that a touch of divine beauty might not come amiss to restore any possible ravages caused by her sorrow. Pandora's heritage of disobedience and curiosity undid Psyche for a second time. Yet thanks to the power of love and Eros' fervent pleading, Psyche was made immortal and married her lover. Spiritual and bodily love were united and blessed with a child called Delight.

Athena

Some cannibalistic tendencies still persisted among the gods, especially within the close family circle. After having got his aunt, the wise Titaness Metis, with child, Zeus swallowed her. Surprisingly enough this did not cause indigestion, but a raging headache. As a drastic, though unusual remedy Zeus ordered Hephaestos to cleave his skull open with an axe. The fruit of this heroic midwifery was Athena, who sprang full-grown and fully armed from her father's head.

Though excelling in the domestic arts, she was a formidable warrior, but only supported just causes and, unlike Ares, did not love war for its own sake. She inherited her luckless mother's wisdom, which kept her from the petty jealousies so common on Olympos. Only once did the boast of Princess Arachne (Spider) that she wove more skillfully than the goddess, drive Athena to cruel revenge. Defeated in a competition, Arachne hanged herself and was changed into a spider weaving for all eternity.

Apollo

Leto was vainly seeking for a place to bear Zeus' child, abandoned by her lover to his wife's vindictiveness. Hera forbade Mother Earth to grant Leto hospitality and sent a monstrous serpent, Python, in pursuit. At last Poseidon took pity, and on the floating island of Delos, Leto gave birth to a son and a daughter. In the land of the Hyperboreans Apollo grew into a skillful archer, ready to avenge his mother on the Python, who had been rewarded with the guardianship of the sacred cave in Delphi. To commemorate his slaying of the monster, Apollo instituted the Pythian games, culminating in a race from Delphi to Thessaly—what a pleasant stroll the Marathon seems in comparison!

The victor returned crowned with laurels, which recalled one of Apollo's many misadventures. In spite of his great beauty he was singularly unlucky in love, as Eros was determined to prove the superiority of his own bow and arrow: Apollo chased Daphne, Peneus' daughter, through the forest. In answer to the terrified maiden's prayers, Peneus, a river god, changed her into a laurel tree on the banks of his stream. In his grief Apollo decreed that laurel wreaths should thenceforward be the reward of athletes and artists.

A flower, too, bears witness to the god's misfortune. He loved a handsome youth named Hyacinthos, who was also coveted by Zephiros, god of the west wind. Apollo and the boy were throwing the discus at Amyclae, near Sparta, when Zephiros blew Apollo's discus so violently aside that it wounded Hyacinthos mortally. The drops of blood were changed into a cluster of hyacinths.

Apollo usurped the place of the sun god Helios whose statue, the famous Colossus, stood astride the harbor of Rhodes. Heralded by his attendant Eos (Dawn), Helios drove the sun chariot daily from his splendid palace in the east to the far western sea. After pasturing his horses in the Fortunate Isles, he sailed back on the ocean stream which encircles the world. Because of the similarity of attributes and youthful beauty, Helios became identified with Phoebus Apollo, and the myths attaching to them merged into one cycle.

Artemis

Like her twin brother Apollo, Artemis usurped the place of the older goddess Selene, mistress of the moon. Artemis was a great huntress, and, when she had finished driving the moon chariot she spent the rest of the night in the woods with her attendant nymphs. From a silver bow she shot her unfailing arrows indiscriminately at beasts and those unlucky huntsmen who accidentally saw her bathing in the nude. Her inordinate irritability and morbid insistence on chastity make her an obvious case of acute frustration. Yet there were ugly rumors in connection with a handsome shepherd, Endymion, whom Zeus put to perpetual sleep for the sake of his daughter's reputation. Even more serious was her infatuation with Orion, a fellow-hunter. Apollo, aware that amorous Eros had already fallen for Orion's charms, thought it necessary to intervene. Playing on his sister's prejudice, he tricked her into shooting the object of her affection. That he was subsequently placed with his faithful dog Sirius among the stars seemed but little consolation.

Ares, Hephaestos and Hebe

The impetuous god of war was exceedingly unpopular on Olympos, even with is own parents, though his mother Hera often used him for her own ends. Always spoiling for a fight he was not consistently victorious. Athena twice worsted him in battle, and Heracles sent him running back to Olympos. Ares was among the numerous claimants to paternity of Eros, but his ascertained progeny was hardly less formidable: Eris (Discord), Phobos (Fear) and Pallor (Terror).

His brother Hephaestos presented a startling contrast to the general run of Olympian good looks. He was such an ugly baby that his disgusted mother dropped him from Olympos and forgot all about him. Kind Thetis brought him up, and the child became exceedingly clever with his hands. It was only when Hera inquired where Thetis' lovely jewelry came from that she learned of her son's matchless skill and promptly fetched him home. Hephaestos was of a forgiving nature and became strongly attached to his mother. He even dared to draw up the chains by which she was hanging in punishment for her abortive rebellion. It was now Zeus' turn to hurl his son from heaven. Striking the earth at the island of Lemnos he broke both his legs and was permanently lamed. Zeus became reconciled to Hera, but neither thought of recalling Hephaestos.

Hebe, the third legitimate child and personification of youth, was never admitted into the inner council of the big twelve. She was her father's cup-bearer, until she was ousted even from this minor position by Ganymede. Zeus had taken a passionate fancy to the boy and abducted him in the disguise of an eagle. Despite Hera's violent protests, Ganymede was constantly at Zeus' side. Hebe was married off to Heracles.

Hermes

One of Zeus' innumerable extra-marital relations was with Maia, Atlas' daughter. Luckier than Leto, she met with no particular difficulty in bringing Hermes into the world in an Arcadian cave. No sooner had the mother turned her back than the child prodigy left his cradle, strangled a tortoise and from its shell made the first lyre, with which he lulled Maia to sleep. He then went in search of adventures to Macedonia, stole 50 cows belonging to Apollo and drove them backwards to Pylos, so that their hoofmarks pointed in the opposite direction. He made sacrifice to the twelve Olympians, among whom he modestly included himself, and returned to his cradle. When Apollo came looking for his cattle, Maia indignantly pointed at the child still wrapped in swaddling bands and feigning sleep. But Apollo was not deceived and hauled the culprit before their father, who was rather proud of his youngest's cunning and bade them be reconciled. This was effected by exchanging the lyre against the cattle, and the two half-brothers became friends.

For his ingenuity Hermes was chosen the herald and messenger of the gods. His duties included the making of treaties, the promotion of commerce and the protection of travelers. But in memory of his promising beginnings he was also the god of thieves, and it must have happened many a time that a robber and his victim both invoked Hermes' help for opposite ends.

Dionysos

Semele, daughter of King Cadmus of Thebes, was proud of Zeus' love. Rumors reached Hera, who assumed the shape of Semele's old nurse and pretended to doubt the lover's divine nature. So Semele pestered Zeus to reveal himself in all his splendor, but when he finally consented she had a miscarriage and died. The infant was sewn up in the father's thigh and delivered three months later. That is why Dionysos was called twice-born and became immortal. When he grew up he discovered how to make wine, and went roaming about the world, accompanied by a wild army of Satyrs and Maenads.

Dionysos propagated the cult of the vine, and the resistance to this innovation is the clue to his bitter struggles from Asia Minor to India. The new intoxicant met with particularly strong opposition in Thrace, where beer had long been established as the national drink. Only after the Thracian king had gone mad and believing his son to be a vine, started pruning the poor boy's nose, ears and fingers, did Dionysos triumph.

No better fate awaited the king of Thebes, who wanted to arrest his cousin for disorderly conduct. The raving Maenads rent the king limb from limb, led by his own mother who wrenched off his head. The constant recurrence of the madness theme in these myths shows the devastating effect of wine at its first appearance.

When all Boetia had acknowledged Dionysos' divinity, he made a tour of the Aegean islands, during which he was kidnapped by pirates. But his bonds fell off, vine and ivy grew about the mast and rigging and to the sound of flutes, lions and tigers played round the god's feet. The terrified pirates leaped overboard and were turned into dolphins. Dionysos steered the ship to Naxos, where he married Cretan Ariadne, abandoned by Theseus.

The Underworld

To Hades, Kronos' eldest son, had been alloted the underworld, a gloomy, though vague concept trying to reconcile conflicting views of the afterlife.

The souls of the dead were ferried across the river Styx by Charon, who demanded the coin laid under their tongue before the burial. Yet why they should be so anxious to enter the underworld, instead of dallying with the penniless souls on the near bank, is hard to understand. The three-headed dog Kerberos guarded the entrance to the Asphodel Fields, a kind of purgatory for minor transgressions. In front of Hades' palace lay the twin pools of Forgetfulness and Memory, from which the souls might drink at their choice.

Though Hades only rarely visited the upperworld, being less amorous than his brothers, he delegated the judgment of the souls to the wise kings Minos, Radamanthys and Aeakos; the second was competent for Asiatics, the third for Europeans, while Minos held a court of appeal. The evil-doers were sent to Tartaros to undergo eternal punishment, as for instance Sisyphos, who had to roll a heavy stone up a hill only to see it crash down again.

Virtuous souls were allowed to enter the Elysian Fields, over which Hades had no power, but which formed the domain of old Kronos. In that paradise there was constant feasting, games, music and dancing. Yet one grade superior were the Fortunate Isles, reserved for the privileged though undeserving few, like Achilles and Helen of Troy, who just failed to make Olympos.

Minor Deities

But there were also several divinities who never attained Olympian status. Zeus' foster-brother, goat-footed Pan, was content to live in Arcadia. When he was not guarding his numerous flocks, he was busy seducing nymphs, and boasted of having possessed all the drunken Maenads. An unusually chaste nymph preferred turning into a reed to his embrace. Unable to distinguish her from all the rest, he cut several reeds at random and made them into a pan-pipe, which was afterwards copied by Hermes and claimed as his own invention.

The Thessalian Princess Koronis was with child by Apollo. The correct behavior for a mortal pregnant by a god was to remain faithful till the child was born. But Koronis did not comply with this reasonable rule of conduct. Artemis avenged this insult by killing her with an arrow, but as she lay on the funeral pyre Apollo rescued the unborn baby and entrusted it to Chiron, the wise Centaur.

Under his tuition young Asklepios grew marvelously proficient in medicine, so that he not only cured the sick, but even restored a dead man to life. Zeus was annoyed at this interference with the normal course of events and hurled a thunderbolt at the culprit. Yet later Zeus himself repeated Asklepios' transgression and resurrected him as god of healing. Asklepios became increasingly popular, and at his shrines, especially at Epidaurus, medical science came into being.

Aeolos ruled the seven islands in the Tyrrhenian sea, which bore his name. Hera had entrusted him with the guardianship over the Winds, which were confined in deep caverns. At his own discretion or at the request of some Olympian, Aeolos would thrust his spear into the cliff and the appropriate wind would stream out of the hole, until he sealed it again.

Halfway between the Aeolian islands and the underworld lay the kingdom of Hypnos (Sleep), surrounded by the waters of Lethe (Oblivion). Round the entrance to his palace grew poppies and other plants that induce dreams.

The relationship between Zeus and the Moirai (Fates) always remained uncertain. Some held that Zeus determined destiny, while others believed that Zeus himself was subject to the Fates. The three sisters assigned to each newborn child his lot by spinning, measuring and cutting the thread of life.

Apollo as patron of the arts was assisted by the nine Muses, the daughters of Zeus and Mnemosyne, goddess of memory. Each presided over a separate artistic or scientific sector, but they met regularly in the divinely inspired academy on Mount Helicon, to discuss the latest intellectual movement.

The Heroic Legends

The great cycles of legends which originated in Mycenaean times were grouped principally round two families: the descendants of Tantalos, and those of Io.

King Tantalos of Phrygia was the progenitor of the most intolerably tragic family ever known, each generation adding new, hateful crimes and punishments to an unparalleled record. Tantalos had been favored by the Olympians and even been admitted to their banquets. Yet in return he set before the gods the roasted flesh of his own son Pelops, as a test of their omniscience. The immortals were not deceived; only Demeter, distraught with grief over the loss of Persephone, helped herself to a tender shoulder.

Tantalos was thrown into the underworld, eternally thirsting for the water in which he stood up to his neck, while Pelops was restored to life, complete with a miraculous ivory shoulder that healed all disease at a touch.

Unlike his sister Niobe, Pelops prospered and became Poseidon's lover. He left his native country for that part of Greece which was named after him, the Peloponnese, and with the god's help won the daughter of Oenomaos, king of Pisa. Oenomaos, who was in control of the Olympic games, had been forewarned that his son-in-law would cause his death. Confident in his superb horses, he stipulated that every suitor should compete with him in a chariot race, and pay with his life if defeated. Thirteen princes had already suffered this fate when Pelops appeared in a golden chariot, drawn by Poseidon's own horses. Yet Pelops did not rely entirely on his divine protector, but to be on the safe side bribed the king's charioteer to replace the linch-pins of his master's chariot with wax. The wheels fell off, the king was killed, and so was the charioteer on claiming his reward.

But not before he had cursed Pelops and his sons, Atreus and Thyestes, who later led the Achaeans to the conquest of Mycenae. Atreus succeeded to the dynasty founded by Perseus, but the gruesome family habits did not improve. Thyestes seduced his brother's wife, and in revenge Atreus followed their grandfather's example by serving up Thyestes' children at a banquet. One son however escaped, Aegisthos, who was instrumental in fulfilling the old curses, while becoming the cause of new blood-guilt. Atreus' son Agamemnon extended his hegemony over the entire Peloponnese, and was thus the natural leader of the Greek expedition against Troy, to recover his brother Menelaus' wife, Helen.

An adverse wind kept the fleet at Aulis, and Artemis demanded the sacrifice of Iphigenia, Agamemnon's daughter. Iphigenia and her mother Clytemnestra were lured to Aulis under the pretext of the girl's betrothal to Achilles, the most attractive of the Greek heroes. Clytemnestra never forgave her husband, even though the goddess relented in the last moment and substituted a hind for the victim kneeling at the altar. The inconsolable mother withdrew to Mycenae, where Aegisthos became her lover. On Agamemnon's return from Troy ten years later, she murdered her victorious husband in his bath.

Their daughter Electra, in her turn, nagged her brother Orestes into avenging the beloved father. For his matricide Orestes was pursued by the Furies, till he rescued Iphigenia from Artemis' sanctuary in savage Tauris. The ancient curses were at last lifted and a double marriage provided an unexpected happy end; Electra to Pylades, her brother's companion in the Taurian adventure, and

Orestes to his cousin Hermione, daughter of Menelaos and Helen. Their descendants ruled over Mycenae till the coming of the Dorians in the 12th century B.C.

Menelaos was king of Sparta, but his main claim to fame was his marriage with Helen. She and her brother Polydeuces (Pollux) were Leda's children by Zeus, disguised as a swan, while Castor and Clytemnestra were fathered by Tyndareus, the lawful husband.

Helen's incomparable beauty attracted numerous suitors. To avoid quarrels Tyndareus made them swear to respect Helen's choice and to champion the cause of her future husband. She chose Menelaos, and when she eloped with Paris the rejected suitors kept their oath and followed Agamemnon to the war against Troy.

The Loves of Zeus

A considerable share of Zeus's amorous intrigues fell to one mortal family, which not only produced a corresponding number of heroes, but was also singularly geographically minded, naming seas, continents and countries.

It all started with Io, daughter of the river god Inarchos of Argos. Although Zeus changed her into a heifer at the approach of his jealous spouse, long and bitter experience had made Hera distrustful and she set hundred-eyed Argos to watch over the suspect. Hermes lulled Argos to sleep and slew him. Thereupon Hera placed her faithful servant's eyes in the tail of the peacock, and sent a gadfly to sting poor Io, who, maddened by pain, plunged into the sea, later called in her honor the Ionian Sea. After what must have been a record swim for a cow, Io came ashore in Egypt where Zeus, by a touch, restored her to human form. She bore him a son, Epaphos (him of the touch), whose daughter Libya became by Poseidon the mother of Agenor and Belos, the biblical Baal.

Zeus now lusted for Agenor's daughter Europa and approached her in the form of a gentle white bull. The misguided maiden jumped upon his broad back, to be carried away to Crete, where she gave birth to Minos, Rhadamanthys and Sarpedon. Minos founded the Cretan dynasty and after his death became, together with his second brother, judge in the underworld. The love for bulls was pathological in the family and Minos' queen, Pasiphae, followed in Europa's footsteps but with less satisfying results, as her offspring, the Minotaur, was a most unprepossessing monster.

Agenor sent his sons Phoenix, Cilix and Cadmos in search of their sister. Far and wide did they travel, until Phoenix and Cilix, weary of the hopeless quest, settled in the fertile countries they had reached named Phoenicia and Cilicia respectively. Cadmos consulted the Delphic oracle, and following a cow as bidden, built the Theban Acropolis, the Cadmea, where the beast lay down. He married Harmonia, daughter of Ares and Aphrodite, and one of their children was Semele. Oedipos likewise traced his descent from Cadmos.

Neither did Belus lack in progeny. His eldest, Pygmalion, fell in love with the statue he had fashioned and prayed to Aphrodite to make the smooth marble come to life. The goddess gladly acquiesced as Pygmalion had hitherto not been among her devotees. Galatea proved even more enchanting as a woman than she had been as a work of art.

The younger twins Aegyptos and Danaus quarreled over their inheritance, and the latter fled with his 50 daughters to Argos, which accepted him as king. The 50 sons of Aegyptos followed their cousins, and Danaus feigned agreement to a mass marriage, but secretly advised the brides to kill their husbands on the wedding night. All obeyed except Hypermnestra, who helped her husband to escape. He later returned, slew Danaus, and became the ancestor of a line of famous Argive kings. The murderous 49 Danaids were condemned to eternal frustration in Tartaros, carrying water in sieves to fill a cask with a hole in the bottom.

Hypermnestra's grandson Acrisios had been warned that his own grandson was fated to kill him. To prevent this he imprisoned his only daughter Danaë in a tower of bronze, a vain precaution against Zeus, who came upon the maiden as a shower of gold. When the distraught king was told of the birth of a grandson, he locked Danaë and the infant Perseus into a chest, which was cast into the sea. Washed ashore at the island of Seriphos, they were kindly received by King Polydectes, who fell in love with the appealing outcast. Wanting to rid himself of the brawny youth, he cajoled Perseus into fetching the head of the Gorgon Medusa, whose glance turned every living creature to stone. Medusa was the only mortal of three wildly unattractive sisters, who featured snakes instead of hair, and had faces to match.

Never could Perseus hope to carry out his rash enterprise unaided, but the gods gave a helping hand. Hades lent his helmet of invisibility, Hermes his winged sandals, and Athena her brightly polished shield, so that Perseus might cut off Medusa's head, looking at her reflection.

Triumphantly holding his hideous booty, Perseus on his return flight turned the inhospitable Titan Atlas into a mountain. Somewhat off his course, he saw the Ethiopian Princess Andromeda chained to a rock, waiting to be devoured by a sea monster. A display of the head, and Perseus was at leisure to cut Andromeda's chains and take her back to Seriphos. There was more work for Medusa's head, as Polydectes had been bothering Danaë. The king and his courtiers were promptly turned to stone; the circle of boulders is still shown on the island.

Perseus returned the magic objects to their kind owners, trimming Athena's shield with the fatal head. Soon afterwards he fulfilled the prophecy by accidentally killing his grandfather with a discus. Ashamed to succeed his victim at Argos, the hero founded Mycenae and a new royal line.

Untiring Heracles

It was now his granddaughter Alcmene's turn to be favored by Zeus, who showed great constancy in his inconstancies. Their son Heracles gave from his birth undeniable proof that he was destined to grow into the greatest of all the heroes, but also the object of Hera's unrelenting hatred. Not unnaturally the Queen of Heaven wanted at last to get even with the family that had caused her so much matrimonial unhappiness. She sent two huge serpents, but the amazing child in the cradle strangled them. Brought up like all the best people by the wise Centaur Chiron—tutor of Asklepios, Jason and Achilles, to name but three—Heracles married the Theban Princess Megara, whom he killed together with their children in a fit of madness. To expiate the crime, the Delphic oracle decreed that Heracles should perform twelve labors for his uncle Euristheus, king of Mycenae.

These labors included some useful work, as for example the killing of the Nemean lion and the Lernean Hydra, and above all the cleansing of the Augean stables by diverting the river Alpheus. But there were also some utterly futile enterprises, like the abduction of the hellbound Kerberos.

On that visit to the underworld, Heracles had to compete with the river god Achelous, who assumed the form of a bull. One of his horns was broken off and was presented by the victor to the goddess of plenty. Filled with fruits and grain, it is known as Cornucopia, the fabled Horn of Abundance.

Zeus caught him up to Olympos, where he was received among the immortals. Even Hera at last relented and gave the hero her daughter Hebe in marriage and the couple lived happily ever after. . . .

Divine IDs

The twelve chief gods formed the elite of Olympos. Each represented one of the forces of nature and also a human characteristic, interpreted by sculptors in their statues of the gods. They also had attributes, by which they can often be identified. The Romans, influenced by the arts and letters of Greece, often identified their own gods with those of Greece, with the result that Greek gods had Latin names as well, by which they are known today.

| Name | | Natural and human | Attributes |
Greek	Latin	characteristics	
Zeus	Jupiter	sky, supreme god	scepter, thunder
Hera	Juno	sky, queen, marriage	peacock
Athena	Minerva	wisdom	owl, olive
Artemis	Diana	moon, chastity	stag
Aphrodite	Venus	love, beauty	dove
Demeter	Ceres	earth, fecundity	sheaf, sickle
Hestia	Vesta	hearth, domestic virtues	eternal fire
Apollo	Phoebus	sun, music and poetry	bow, lyre
Ares	Mars	tumult, war	spear, helmet
Hephaestos	Vulcan	fire, industry	hammer, anvil
Hermes	Mercury	trade, eloquence	caduceus, wings
Poseidon	Neptune	sea, earthquake	trident

PROMETHEUS UNBOUND

The Spring of Western Civilization

In *Prometheus Bound* Aeschylus dramatized the legend of the defiant titan, the first symbol of revolution, who stole fire from the gods and taught men the crafts of Athena and Hephaestos, thus giving them wisdom to stay alive. For this act he was terribly punished by Zeus.

But according to the philosopher Protagoras the creator of tragedy conceived a happy ending in a sequel, the lost play *Prometheus Unbound,* in which Zeus became reconciled to Prometheus and added political wisdom, justice and reverence, so that man might lead a civilized life. Yet progress was man's own task.

This progress reached its first European flowering in Minoan Crete, where, by the middle of the 2nd Millennium B.C., rudimentary Egyptian elements had been developed to sophisticated perfection. This splendor was reflected, but not equaled, by the Mycenean Bronze-Age civilization, which perished in the Dorian invasion of the 12th century B.C.

Dawn in the East

The Greek awakening dawned on the shores of Asia Minor and the nearby islands, to which numerous Ionians had fled during the Dark Ages. Phoenician traders taught the humble refugee settlements the alphabet and commerce, which enabled them to turn from the crude struggle for survival to things spiritual.

The offshore island of Chios claimed Homer and the wandering minstrels of the 9th and 8th centuries B.C., who celebrated in epic strains a cycle of stories revolving round the Siege of Thebes, the Trojan War and the return of the heroes. Homer fashioned gods in the likeness of man in two great epic poems, the *Iliad* and the *Odyssey*—if indeed both were composed by the same poet or either by one man. By depicting gods endowed with the virtues and vices of mankind, the Greeks stressed man's responsibility and dignity, thus putting man in the center of the universe where the Israelites had placed God. Despite the cogent unity in Achilles' impulsive emotionalism and Odysseus' continuous low cunning, some literary experts insist that these epics must have been conceived in the Greeks' exuberant youth, but completed only in full artistic maturity. Yet during all the centuries in which they constituted the basis of education in Greece and Rome, they were ascribed to one Homer.

Hesiod was born around 700 B.C. in Asia Minor where his father had traded before returning to a farm in Boeotia. His *Works and Days* is an impassioned appeal for divine and human justice against being cheated out of his farm inheritance by his brothers, besides enumerating all the favorable and unfavorable omens for agriculture. Homer praised the glory of heroic death, while Hesiod extolled the joys of simple life. His *Theogeny* remained the standard genealogy of the Olympians.

In the 7th and 6th centuries the Aeolians substituted varied metrical forms for the epic hexameter. In short songs, accompanied by a lyre or flute, the gods and heroes were abandoned for the passions the poets felt and the deeds of their contemporaries. Time and Christian prejudice destroyed most of this lyric poetry which, however, immortalized an aristocratic society in rare fragments.

Alcaeus of Lesbos showed his disdain for the rising merchant class and delighted in the pleasures of wine. Another Lesbian, Burning Sappho, brought lyric poetry to its passionate perfection. Priestess of a sanctuary of Aphrodite, the goddess of love seems to have inspired her violent and searing poems addressed to various girls, which connects Lesbos forever with a particular form of love.

Abandoning his native Ionia for the courts of Polycrates at Samos and of Hipparchus at Athens, Anacreon described his love for boys in no uncertain words. Nor could his epitaph, composed by no less a poet than Simonides, be called squeamish.

The last of these lyric poets belongs to Greece-in-Europe, Pindar of Thebes, who wrote odes for tyrants and nobles, or glorified the victors at the great Panhellenic games.

The Nature of Man

Greece-in-Asia likewise gave birth to philosophy, which originated in a cosmic mythology. Yet Greek creativeness was no less impressive for incorporating alien ideas and achievements. Thales of Miletus, most ancient of the sages, answered in about 600 the question "What is God?" by "That which has no beginning and no end", thus taking the decisive step from myth to rational thought. His disciples Anaximander and Anaximenes were astoundingly modern in their attempt to reduce the material world to a common principle in a philosophical system where the infinite, animated and eternal, albeit impersonal, was none other than the One God. The Greek version of the universal tradition of the Great Flood— where Deukalion, cast in the role of Noah but landing in considerably more places, created a new race of men from rocks and dragon's teeth—was elaborated into a scientific theory of origin from the wet element. Spontaneous generation, caused by the action of warmth on mud, produced thin womb-like membranes from which life emerged.

Pythagoras (c. 530 B.C.) associated philosophy with strict moral rules and mathematics; a curious though by no means inexplicable combination. Stating that "the body is a tomb" led to such peculiar prohibitions as beans, bed linen and white cocks. Leaving the brilliant court of the Tyrant Polycrates on his native Samos, Pythagoras was one of the rare foreigners ever to be initiated into the Egyptian mysteries before founding and governing Croton in southern Italy.

Heracleitus of Ephesus (c. 500) started the unphilosophical but very common contempt for his predecessors and contemporaries, yet he found enthusiastic admirers from the Stoics to Nietzsche. He believed in a governing principle of the universe, yet also in eternal change, summed up in his famous saying: "All is in flux, nothing abides". Harmony is the final aim, but it consists in the union of opposites. That is why "War is the father of all things".

Hecataeus from Miletus provided history and geography with a rational basis, being the first to use *historia* in the meaning of "research". Hellanicus of Lesbos reconstructed early history through chronological lists of kings and officials, to which later historians are indebted.

Another significant attempt at rational thinking was in the field of medicine, where the human individual was the object to be treated. Hippocrates was born in about 460 into the family of the Asklepiads, whose name indicates a connection with the god of healing, but more as practitioners of medicine than as priests of Asklepius. Hippocrates freed medicine from magic and founded a medical school on his native island of Kos. Clinical observation was collected in the 58 books of the *Corpus Hippocraticum*, but the outstanding document is the Hippocratic oath, a code of behavior of very high ethical standards.

In a mere 150 years the Asian Greeks advanced from primitive simplicity to mature awareness and even disillusionment before the Persian conquest scattered philosophers, poets, musicians and artists westwards to teach their tardier European brothers profounder thought and greater perfection.

Go West, Young Man

Anaxagoras, Protagoras and Herodotus provide the link with Athens where all the beauty and wisdom of antiquity was to gather. Anaxagoras of Clazomenae (c. 500–c. 428) deserted from Xerxes' army and became a resident of Athens, where he was chosen as Pericles' tutor and evolved the doctrine that *nous*, the mind, dominated the universe. Pericles' political opponents accused him of impiety for stating that the sun was a ball of fire and there were mountains in the moon. Pericles could not obtain his acquittal, but arranged his escape to Lampsacus on the Hellespont, where an altar was set up to Mind and Truth, flanked by the phallic pillars of Priapus, who possessed many devotees in that versatile community.

The sophists were not a school of philosophy but individual teachers giving lessons for pay to the sons of the wealthy. Man was the central subject of their teaching, which consisted mainly of political education, with special emphasis on rhetoric as essential in a democracy. The earliest and greatest of the sophists was Protagoras of Abdera (c. 485–c. 415), who repeatedly visited Athens where he was admitted to Pericles' inner circle. His "Man is the measure of all things" and "As to the gods, I have no possibility of knowing that they are, nor that they are not" brilliantly summed up the scepticism of his time.

What Herodotus of Halicarnassus (c. 484–c. 420) had observed or heard on his extensive travels he described in his *History* in an astonishing blend of the supernatural, sensationalism and common sense. Ranging from Babylon to Egypt, his main theme is the Persian empire under Xerxes, who had committed *hubris*, excessive pride inevitably punished by the jealous gods.

The School of Hellas

By the middle of the 5th century B.C., Athens had become the leading cultural center of Greece, attracting the great names in philosophy and literature from abroad. Then suddenly there happened a flowering of native talent in every field of intellect and art as has never been surpassed and only once been equaled, though more diffused, in the Italy of the Renaissance.

While Herodotus described with exuberant optimism the victory of freedom, Thucydides witnessed with profound disillusionment the decay of freedom into demagogy and licentiousness. Born in Athens in 471, he served in the siege of Samos in 442, together with Herodotus, Sophocles and Socrates under the command of Pericles, who then made the deeply melancholic remark: "The spring has gone out of the year". It was indeed high-summer for Athens, and though the creative genius outlasted military and political disaster, the youthful zest had gone forever. Exiled for failing to relieve Amphipolis, to which the fleet he commanded was ordered too late, Thucydides records with admirable impartiality the decline into brutality and treachery in his *History of the Peloponnesian War*, which ends with the folly of the Sicilian campaign.

Xenophon continues in his *Hellenica* the tragic history of Greek dissent to the battle of Mantinea in 362 in which his son was killed. His inevitable exile by the decaying Athenian democracy had embittered him sufficiently to write with a strong pro-Spartan bias, which is particularly noticeable in his praise of Lycurgus in the *Republic of the Lacedaimonians*. On the country estate near Olympia which his former commander, King Agesilaus of Sparta, had put at his disposal, Xenophon was at leisure to recount in the *Anabasis* his own brilliant exploits as leader of 10,000 Greek mercenaries on their retreat across Asia Minor. Not only had he played a prominent part in the rebellion of Cyrus the Younger against his brother King Artaxerxes but, like so many Greek intellectuals, Xenophon was fascinated by the great power in the east, whose origin he traces in *The Education of Cyrus*. Beside this historical romance, he ventured into economics in his *Ways and Means*, in which he advocated income tax, a nationalized merchant-fleet and hotels. In his *Memorabilia*, Socrates is depicted as a virtuous and rather commonplace philistine.

The Aim of Man

Socrates, the greatest and yet least known among the intellectual giants of that unique period, was born in 470 son of a stone mason, a profession he followed in a somewhat lackadaisical man-

ner. Much more consistently he practised his mother's calling,
midwifery, by bringing men's hidden thoughts to life. He soon
turned to teaching, but unlike the sophists he charged no fee, to the
vitriolic chagrin of his wife Xanthippe. He founded no school or
philosophical system, yet changed the direction of human thought
by simply talking to pupils and opponents in a city he never left
except on military service. His didactic method has been immortalized in a series of dialogues by his most famous disciple, Plato.
But, as they were written several years after Socrates' death, it
can never be established where the master ends and Plato begins.
Aristotle ascribes to him inductive reasoning and universal defini-
tion.

In a head-on collision with the sophists, Socrates derided their
endeavor of "making the weaker case the stronger one". He declared rhetoric a useless study, because "if a case has merit it does
not require artful advocacy, and if it has not such art may prove
harmful", a prophetic warning, as demagogues have all too often
brought disaster on Greece. Not that his views were popular in the
restored Athenian democracy. His outspoken criticism as well as
his contempt for public opinion led inevitably to the time-honored
accusation of impiety coupled with an up-to-date one of corrupting
youth.

In a typical Socratic cross-examination he embroiled the official
accuser in contradictory charges of atheism and of introducing
new gods. Condemned to death by a majority of 60 from the 501
angry judges, he was, according to Athenian law, entitled to propose an alternative penalty. Instead of an acceptable sentence of
exile, Socrates suggested free meals at state expense. Refusing to
escape and stressing his loyalty to the laws of the state, he drank
the cup of hemlock. A people's court put to death the man who
taught the freedom of the individual.

Despairing of the excesses of democracy, Plato (428–347) jour-
neyed three times to Syracuse in Sicily to make the young tyrant
Dionysius II into the philosopher-king of his *Republic*, a dismal
failure ending in flight. Unable to turn a ruler into a philosopher,
Plato taught philosophers how to rule—or at least to advise
rulers—in the Academy, established in a grove sacred to the hero
Academus outside Athens in 387. Plato emphasized the importance of the soul, incorporeal and immortal, which from previous
incarnations retains memories mistakenly thought to be new discoveries hitherto unknown. Though the creator of idealist philosophy, Plato remained concerned with practical political and moral
problems, and his pupils spread his theories throughout distraught
Hellas.

None with greater success than Aristotle of Stagiros (384–322),
who studied and taught at the Academy from 366 to Plato's death,

but failed to be appointed the latter's successor. Instead he became tutor of young Alexander of Macedonia, in another attempt at forming a philosopher-king, in accordance with the *Treatise on Monarchy*. On his return to Athens in 336, Aristotle founded a rival to the Academy, the Lyceum, complete with an extensive library and a museum. In an unparalleled universality of research, he created the sciences of meteorology, zoology, embryology and botany, beside teaching literature and eloquence in his *Poetics* and *Rhetorics*, establishing a new terminology in the *Physics*, expounding the theoretical sciences in the *Metaphysics*, moral and political theories in the *Nichomachean Ethics* and the *Politics*, and, most important, providing in the *Organon* a system of thought which dominated the Middle Ages down to St. Thomas Aquinas.

Charged with impiety in 323, Aristotle fled to Chalkis, declaring that "he would not allow Athens to sin twice against philosophy". The probably apocryphal story of his suicide the following year for failing to discover the cause of the Euripus' constantly changing current is, nevertheless, well in keeping with an inquisitive mind irked beyond endurance by an inexplicable phenomenon.

Spontaneous originality had discovered everything that was worth knowing and the philosophers, poets, scientists and artists of the Hellenistic Age only elaborated what had already been created.

The Birth of Dramatic Art

The Greek theater was constructed under the open sky. Its tiers of seats were laid out in the shape of an enormous fan. On the stage an all-male cast struggled in vain against an inexorable destiny. For tragedy as for comedy the actors wore masks with a mouthpiece of copper designed to amplify the voice.

Before the appearance of the great tragic Athenian poets, there were a few obscure playwrights. It was apparently the success of the resistance against the Persians which gave the stimulus necessary for changing from the religious spectacle of choral singing and dancing with interspersed speeches into true drama, where the suffering of man became that of an individual hero.

Aeschylus endowed Greek tragedy with its classic form and instituted its major theme: the conflict between thought which strives to liberate itself, and traditional belief. The *Oresteia* trilogy, which dates from 450 B.C., is the masterpiece of the Greek theater and perhaps of all times. The chorus pleads in favor of a new belief, one which knows forgiveness. Religious feeling has profound overtones with Aeschylus, who was a thinker as well as a great poet. The qualities which characterize his 90 or so tragedies—imaginative power, amplitude of dramatic development, depth of characterization, beauty of style—are not found in combination again until the time of Shakespeare. Yet contrary to Elizabethan custom, the *Persians* present Xerxes' insolent pride and his punishment by the Greeks far from the scene of battle and action. With mysterious fate playing so prominent a part, it is not unfitting that Aeschylus' death seems to have been caused by a tortoise dropped on his bald head by an eagle searching for a rock to crack the shell.

Of 125 plays written by Sophocles, 24 won first prize, but only seven are extant today. With this poet, tragic language takes on a more natural tone. His psychological perspicacity makes him seem like a relative of our modern dramatists. He opposes hope to fatality: if the moral order of the world is too subtle for us to understand it, it exists nonetheless, and justice will triumph in the end. In his Theban trilogy, *Oedipus Rex, Oedipus at Colonus* and *Antigone*, Aristotle's dictum that "the function of tragedy is to rouse pity and fear" is most closely realized as Oedipus moves with heroic grandeur to his tragic death at Colonus, Sophocles' own birthplace in 495.

Aeschylus had shown the way and fixed the form of tragedy in austere verses which express his grave philosophy. Sophocles models his art with proportion, harmony and serene wisdom. Euripides completes antique tragedy in works that overflow with pathos and passionate feeling. One can compare Aeschylus to a preacher as rigorous as the prophets of Israel: Sophocles to a classic artist. As for Euripides, he never wrote a perfect tragedy because of the irregularity of his dramatic action and the length of his philosophical tirades, but of the three he is the most human. He also surpasses the others in the depiction of characters and in psychological skill. He represents that generation which scoffed at the old myths and cherished the dream of a new order in which man would not be exploited by man and all men by the state. Certain of his plays have modern accents, and the battle of the sexes is brought up, as in the plays of Ibsen. In the *Trojan Women* he exposed the ignominy of revenge and the hollowness of victory, an unequivocal condemnation of contemporary Athenian atrocities. In the *Bacchae* he shows the evil of excessive emotionalism; while *Medea* is equally critical of the barbarian lacking the restraint of Greek civilization as of the prim husband Jason. No wonder that only four of his 90 plays won him first prize.

Comedy originated in fertility rites, which accounts for obscenity being an integral part of the plays, which first flourished in the Greek towns of Sicily. But ancient comedy has become synonymous with the work of the Athenian Aristophanes.

He was still a young man at the outbreak of the Peloponnesian War in 431, a conflict which provided him with bitter raw material for his work. Denouncing this hateful internecine war and the Greeks who massacred each other, he turned his comedies into spirited pleas for peace. In *Lysistrata* the wives refuse their matrimonial duties to blackmail their menfolk into stopping the struggle; in the *Peace* a clown rides on a beetle to Olympus to ask Zeus to stop the war which only politicians and profiteers still desired; in the *Birds* an exemplary citizen leaves Athens to escape from politics and violence; the anti-hero makes its first appearance with the god Dionysos disguised as Heracles in the *Frogs,* which is a sly attack on Euripides; while the *Clouds* ridiculed Socrates so effectively that it permanently prejudiced the Athenians.

For him the weakened state of public life in Athens came from two evils: the decadence of democracy and the irreligious spirit. His art is a mixture of wisdom, poetic fantasy and scurrilous language. He let himself go to such an extent in lampooning his contemporaries that a law was passed forbidding all satire aimed at living persons. Subsequent playwrights like Menander and Philemon had to play it safer; their comedies of manners and imagination, known as the New Comedy, are more concerned with elaborate plots and happy endings than with social criticism.

The Cult of Harmony

Greek art did not spring in a blinding flash like Athena fully modeled from the brain of Zeus. The earliest ceramic cup, said by legend to have been moulded after the breast of Helen of Troy, is a libel on that siren's reputation; it is coarse, clumsy and rough. The late Minoans developed an astonishing variety of superb pottery, the Mycenaeans introduced realism in vase painting, which in the 8th century was superseded by the abstract designs of the geometric style. Subsequent centuries saw the perfection of the black-figured, red-figured and polychrome vases, with all of which Athens achieved supreme artistry.

Before attacking stone, Greek sculptors worked in wood. The earliest temples were made of wood and brick; the use of stone only developed as the country prospered. The architectural concepts are an exact reflection of the personality of the peoples who composed the Greek world. Thus the Doric order is all mathematics; the Ionian and Corinthian, all poetry. The first is northern; the others are essentially southern and Oriental. The first expresses the proud reserve, massive strength and severe simplicity of the Dorians. The other two represent suppleness, sensitivity, elegance and a love of fine detail. No matter what the order, however, the Greek column exerted such a sway over all subsequent architecture that even the modern architect has difficulty in freeing himself from it. This phenomenon is explained by the fact that Greek art is the absolute incarnation of reason in form. The tradition asserts itself everywhere: in the logic of a line in painting, in the cult of symmetry in sculpture, in the geometric harmony of architecture. The Greeks did not propose to represent reality with its clutter of uncoordinated details; their aim was to seize the essence of things and let its light shine forth. And here again Athens achieved the architectural masterpiece, the Acropolis, where the most perfect Doric and Ionic temples stand side by side.

But it would be false to conclude, as certain romantic spirits have done, that the Greeks were effeminate aesthetes, lost in ecstasy before abstract beauty and subordinating their lives to it. Quite the reverse; it was the art of living which, for the Greeks, was the supreme art. A healthy utilitarian inclination combined with their worship of beauty to such an extent that art within their homes was not an idle ornament, but had a functional quality related to everyday life. Nourished by such a society, the artist was not an isolated man expressing himself in a language incomprehensible to the ordinary citizen.

The Inheritors

By the time Alexander the Great began the conquest of Asia, the magnificent outburst of creative genius had worn itself out after 150 triumphant years. Greek art spread to India, where statues of strange gods were draped in the Greek manner. Painting still advanced, but in sculpture as well as in architecture size was more appreciated than beauty. The luxurious courts of Alexandria and Antioch took the place of Athens, which gradually assumed the role of a university town where the rulers of the empires of the world sent their sons to study the precepts of the greater empire of the spirit.

Thanks to the diffusion of Greek as a common language, a cultural unity was established which lasted in the eastern Mediterranean for nearly a thousand years. Eleven hundred Hellenistic writers wrote for a public impregnated by Greek art and thought. In the library of Alexandria toward the end of the reign of Ptolemy Philadelphus in the 3rd century before Christ, there were no less than 532,000 scrolls, the equivalent of 100,000 modern books. Among those drawn to the court of this king, a patron of the arts, was Theocritus, creator of pastoral poetry.

But in the older Greek centers, research and discovery continued. Aristarchus of Samos even formulated the hypothesis that the earth revolved around the sun and that the sun was the center of the system to which the earth belonged. It took mankind 17 centuries to rediscover this explanation of the world, in the time of Copernicus. Euclid formulated the first principles of plane geometry. Hipparchus of Nicaea created the science of trigonometry. Apollonius anticipated analytical geometry, made possible the theory of projectiles, and exerted incalculable influence on mechanics, navigation and astronomy. Archimedes, without knowing the decimal system, conceived infinitesimal calculi and opened immense horizons to physics and mechanics by finding the means of determining the specific gravity of bodies. Eratosthenes measured the surface of the earth and drew the first map. Philosophical Schools flourished. Pyrrho, first of the sceptics, declared that all certainty is impossible, that all is relative, a pattern of thinking very congenial to the 20th century. Epicure based his doctrine of moderation and good sense on the enjoyment of life, while the stoics preached austerity.

The last of the great historians, Plutarch, was born at historical Chaeronea in A.D. 46. In appreciation for his *Lives*, a biographical comparison of eminent Greeks and Romans, he was given priesthood at Delphi as a sinecure, though he mostly resided in Rome.

The ancient Greeks, by virtue of having cultivated science and the science of ideas to their highest point, continued, long after the decline of their civilization, to be the teachers of the world. Among the problems which occupy us today, there are hardly any which they did not tackle with freedom of spirit and matchless ardor, and it is to their language, two thousand years after the fall of Athens, that scientists of all countries turn to designate the instruments and the ideas of a new world.

The Greek Message

The classical culture which was the grandeur of the Greek world no longer exists. It died, for civilizations are mortal. But it left indelible marks in all domains, bearing witness to its universal radiance. Through the intermediary of Rome, it was spread throughout the world. The Roman state took over the laws of Greek cities as a basis for its own legislation. The writers of Rome pillaged the literature of Greece, helping themselves to an inexhaustible treasure of lyric poetry, odes, stories, essays, orations, biographies, and above all of tragedy and comedy. Plautus and Terence borrowed plots from Menander and Philemon, thus making them accessible centuries later to Ben Jonson and Molière, who found in them the source material for their comic masterpieces.

From the cultural point of view Roman expansion is nothing more than the propagation throughout Europe of the Greek intellectual inheritance. Greek thought was concentrated in Byzantium, the adopted daughter of antique Greece. From this city the great ideas which form the basis of our civilization were dispersed throughout the world. Greek works, translated into Latin, were the sparks that lit the fires of the Italian Renaissance. From then on, schools, universities, theaters and stadiums are marked with the seal of Greece. Classic architecture lives again in public buildings, palaces and academies which rise in the greatest cities of Europe and America. The basis of our musical scale and many of our instruments are bequests from ancient Greece. Modern mathematics would be inconceivable without reference to Pythagoras and Euclid. And even our daily vocabulary, from atom to zoology, from psychoanalysis to stratosphere, is a lexicon of Greek words.

Why does this ancient civilization continue to correspond to our daily needs? Why does its universality continue to encompass our epoch, dominated as it is by a technical progress unimaginable in antique Greece? The answer is simple: while the sages of Egypt and Babylon evolved empirical formulas, the Greek masterminds extracted pure science from the formulas. Eager to explain everything—nature, society, the soul—the Greek genius represented, in all domains and for the first time, the liberation of the human spirit.

As ancient Greek literature achieved a last, if somewhat decadent, flowering in the Alexandria of the Macedonian Ptolemies, it is a remarkable conformity with Aristotelian canons that the first internationally recognized modern Greek literary figure should have been Kavafis, an Alexandrian poet influenced by the cosmopolitan decadence prevailing under another dynasty originating in Macedonia.

With George Seferis and Odysseus Elytis, Literature Nobel Prize winners in 1963 and 1980, poetry returned to its European homeland.

FOOD AND DRINK

Greece "à la Carte"

Although the cuisines of Greece and Britain are so very different, a number of generalizations will apply to them both. In neither country would a gourmet travel for the sake of the food, as he might in France or parts of Italy; the general level of cooking is undistinguished, and there can hardly be said to be any significant regional differences between one province and another. In both countries, the food has been exaggeratedly condemned by travelers who have had bad luck, or have not known what to order; in Greece it has also been patriotically or romantically overpraised by nationals or foreigners. Overpraise is, ultimately, as much a disservice as exaggerated condemnation. A balanced verdict on Greece would be this: the food is never good enough to travel for, and not bad enough to keep anyone away. A prudent traveler will not expect "European" food (at least, he will not expect it to be excellent) outside deluxe establishments, and he will be well advised to avoid second-rate imitations in the provinces. He will eat the dishes of the country, or he will order a plain grill or fried eggs; if he shows a little interest, the restaurateur is more likely to think him worth pleasing, and he should not fare too badly—he may even have an occasional pleasant surprise.

Now for the specific character of Greek food. It is a variant of the food of the Eastern Mediterranean, found all over those countries (Turkey, Syria and Egypt) which once formed part of the Ottoman Empire. It will probably never be known if any dishes were specifically Greek, what dishes were introduced by the Turks, and what came from further east—for Persia influenced both Byzantium and the Ottoman Turks. Olive oil is its basis, nearly always well-refined, but in the cheaper eating-places, there is simply too much of it, more often than not as a lukewarm, oily tomato sauce; stick to boiled or grilled food. Those who are unused to eating food cooked in oil will do well to take some simple precautions against the slight upsets which may result from the change in diet.

Luncheon can generally be obtained from one o'clock, or even a little earlier, dinner from about eight o'clock, though the Greeks prefer to have their evening meal considerably later. In private houses, the Greeks will generally have their midday meal often as late as three o'clock, and they will sup when they like, off odds and ends. Peasants are frugal and live cheerfully for days on little more than bread, sheep's cheese, tomatoes and olives, but on a feast-day, they put away quantities of food (such as sheep's heads and roast pork) that would astonish a western visitor. The "nothing too much" of the ancients is not the rule.

It is a great convenience for the traveler—especially if he does not know the language—that it is a habit in all *tavernas,* and in most provincial restaurants, for the customer to go into the kitchen and look into the pots, rather than to choose his food from a menu. You know what you are getting, and what you can face. If the eye is sometimes deceived by the brightness of the colors, the nose may be relied on as a guide.

Apéritifs and Appetizers

The usual apéritif is *oúzo,* a spirit with an aniseed flavor. In the provinces it is generally served neat in thimblefuls; in the towns you get larger quantities, and most people prefer to add water, which clouds it. There are good Greek vermouths, but you will be rather lucky if one is served to you in a café. Another apértif, sweeter and more scented than *oúzo,* is *mastíka,* and in the islands you may sometimes find *cítro* (sweet, and with a citrus flavor), which is made in Naxos.

They are usually accompanied by *mezé,* some form of appetizer. In the simplest form this will consist of a small bit of cheese and an olive, and a slice of tomato or cucumber, but it can be very elaborate indeed. In a good restaurant, or at a party, you may get a small canapé spread with *brik* (red caviar) or with *taramasaláta* (a delicious preparation of fish roes). Other good appetizers are *dzadzíki* (cucumber with yoghourt and garlic), or small *keftédes* or *dolmádes.* Olives of various sorts may be sampled, green or black (the oval olive of Delphi, or the pointed olive of Kalamata). If you are sitting at a café pedlars will probably pass and you can supplement your *mezé* by buying pistachio nuts or almonds. A more substantial snack is the *tyrópitta* or cheese pie. This may be filled with egg and cheese, or with just a piece of dryish white cheese. In the country, made of local cheese and marjoram, it can be very tasty.

There are two main types of soup: a chicken broth thickened with rice and eggs and flavored with lemon (*avgolémono*), or a fish broth, (*psarósoupa*) generally served with pieces of boiled fish and vegetables in it.

Seafood

Fish is a staple diet in the islands and round all the coasts of Greece, and standards for freshness of fish are high; inland, it is of the frozen variety, often even dried Atlantic cod. It is usually eaten for the main course of a meal—(indeed, outside tourist hotels, Greece knows nothing of the table d'hôte; one or two dishes are ordered à la carte, and are served in generous portions). However, although fish is excellent, especially if eaten along the shore, it *is* expensive. Pollution and overfishing have between them reduced the availability of fish in the Mediterranean and consequently forced prices up.

Of shellfish and their like: prawns (*garídes*), langoustines (*karavídes*) and crayfish, frequently misnamed lobster (*astakó*), are usually served boiled, with a simple sauce of oil and lemon juice (one of the three sauces of Greece). On the islands you will enjoy *garídes piláffi,* freshly prepared with a new catch of shrimps or prawns.

Octopus (*oktapódi*) and squid (*soupiá*), which may be new to many Western visitors are often stewed in wine; they have an interesting and individual flavor, but are apt to be tough. A greater favorite with foreigners is the young cuttlefish (*kalamarákia*); if very small and crisply fried, they seldom fail to please.

Of the larger fishes, slices of sea bass (*synagrída*) are served fried or grilled, and squares of swordfish (*xiphiós*) are grilled on skewers with tomato, onion and bayleaf between the pieces—a delicious dish. Other fish is fried or grilled whole, and simply served with a piece of lemon, and perhaps a salad. Red mullet (*barboúnia*) and sea bream (*lithrínia*) are generally very good, and sometimes one gets an excellent sole. Fish should be chosen personally, and it will be gladly brought out for your inspection. Whitebait (*marídes*) are good in season, but are not worth eating once they are too large.

Meat Courses

Meat is of poorer quality, but there are two honorable exceptions. Lamb (*arnáki*) is killed very young in the spring, and sucking-pigs (*gourounópoulo*) in the late summer; both of these are best when roasted whole over charcoal. At any time of the year, lamb cutlets are safe, and pork (*chirinó*) is lean yet tender; veal and beef are less recommended outside expensive restaurants. A favorite dish in any sort of eating-place is *souvlákia,* kebabs of meat grilled on a skewer, and often dusted with marjoram. *Giuvetsi* (roast lamb with pasta) is a specialty of many an Athens taverna, cooked and served in an earthenware dish.

Dishes made of minced meat are better avoided in a restaurant in which you have little confidence, though they are excellent when conscientiously prepared, and of good materials. They include *keftédes* (meat-balls); *souzoukákia* (balls of meat and rice, served in tomato or in egg and lemon sauce); *moussaká* (a pie made of minced meat and aubergines); and a number of dishes made of stuffed vegetables, such as tomatoes, courgettes, green peppers and aubergines, or *dolmádes* (vine or cabbage leaves, folded round a stuffing of mince and rice). Rice, which is generally well cooked in Greece, occurs in combination with minced meat, in the above-mentioned dishes; one may also find stuffed vegetables served cold in oil (*laderá*) where the meat is replaced by currants, pine nut kernels and herbs. These are often excellent—the *dolmádes* of vine leaves (*yaprák dolmádes*) are specially to be commended. Moreover a rice pilaff is a wholesome and satisfying dish, whether served with a tomato sauce, or with one of the many possible garnishes, such as prawns (very good in Salonica), glazed tomatoes—a Smyrniot touch—or kidneys. Macaroni is often overboiled.

Ragouts are best inspected in their pots. There are many stews of meat and vegetables, in tomato or in egg-and-lemon sauce, which, while they lack subtlety, can be excellent if well prepared, and make a welcome change in a limited diet. In spring, the fricassée of lamb with lettuce or with artichokes, or of pork with celery can be delicious, and at any time of the year *styphádo* a stew of Italian origin, made of veal or tongue or (best) of hare, with oil and wine and small onions, is often very good indeed. The ubiquity of tomato sauce, fresh in summer and preserved in winter, is apt to be monotonous: try and manage not to have too much of it.

In season, game is good, especially hare, woodcock and wild pigeons; poultry is tasty, as rarely battery-bred; try chicken (*kotópoulo*) grilled, or stuffed (with rice and cheese, or currants and pine nut kernels) and roasted on a spit over charcoal. Turkeys, stuffed with chestnuts and raisins or olives (*galópoulo yemistó*) are also very good in winter.

Restaurants make good use of the vegetables in season; in spring one finds peas (*bisélia*), cabbage (*láchano*), French beans (*fasólia fréska*) and broccoli (*prókola*) on the menu. Artichokes (*agináres*) and broad beans (*gígantes*), mixed or separate, make an excellent dish served cold in oil, with a touch of dill and lemon. Small pumpkins (*kilokíthia*) and eggplants (*melintzánes*), the main vegetables in summer, are good when sliced and fried; they can be eaten—by those who can put up with the smell—with a strong garlic sauce (*skordaliá*). Eggplant stuffed with tomato and onion must have been the Turkish clergy's favorite, judging by its name: *imám bayildí* ("the priest fainted"). Dandelions (*vlíta*), and other wild and often bitter mountain leaves (*radíkia*) are boiled, and served cold with oil and lemon.

Desserts

Fruit is plentiful and good all the year round, from the first strawberries (*fráoules*) and cherries (*kerássia*) to the last oranges (*portokália*) in April. Specially to be commended are the yellow peaches (*yarmádes*), nectarines (*milorodákina*), yellow-fleshed melons (*pepónia*) of Argos, and the small seedless grapes (*stafída*), black or white.

There is little variety in local cheeses; *kaséri*, a hard cheese, and *féta*, a soft cheese made of sheep's milk, are the most popular and good when not too salty. But the white soft cheeses, the Cretan goat's cheese, *manóuri* and *myzíthra* are very good in the spring; they are sometimes eaten with honey. Féta, mashed with butter sauce and baked makes a tasty cheese pie called *tyrópitta*. Don't miss yoghourt (*yaoúrti*), but insist on *próveio*, made from sheep's milk; with honey it is one of the highlights of the Greek menu.

The universal favorite in restaurants of all types is crème caramel, but most also serve the sticky Turkish cakes, made of flaky pastry, honey and nuts combined in various ways—such are *baklavá*, *cadaíf* and *galaktoboúreko* (with a custard filling), and *co-*

penhái (so called because created in honor of the election of Prince William of Denmark as George I of Greece). These are eaten at confectioners' shops (*patissería*) or the numerous dairies (*galaktopoulía*) and are all called *glyká toú tapsióu* (sweets of the dish or pan, for they are baked in large shallow pans, and afterwards cut up).

Cafés, except the with-it western-style establishments, provide what used to be known as Turkish, but has chauvinistically been renamed Greek coffee, served in tiny cups, (*skéto*—without sugar; *métrio*—with a moderate amount of sugar; *glykó*—sweet: and these distinctions may be further qualified by *vrastó*—well boiled, or *varý*—heavy) or a "sweet of the spoon" (*glykó tóu koutalióu*), a spoonful of syrupy jam dissolved in water, or a preserved fruit; *vísina* (black cherries); *nerántzi* (tiny green oranges); *fráoula* (strawberry-flavored grapes); *ypovrýchion* (a spoonful of white mastic jam, served in a glass of water); *ánthos* (lemon blossom); *triantáfillo* (rose petal); *melintzanáki* (a tiny eggplant) and many more. In the country they are a symbol of the proverbial Greek hospitality: the stranger is immediately offered a spoonful of preserved fruit and a glass of cold water.

Drinks

Beer is served well-iced; *Fix Hellas, Henninger* and *Amstel,* light lagers, are best. Coca-Cola and Pepsi-Cola are available everywhere. Other soft drinks include *visináda* (a syrup made of black cherries, diluted with water), and a wide choice of orangeades and lemonades, nearly always too sweet to quench the thirst. There are a number of good mineral waters: *Loutráki, Nigríta, Sáriza* and others.

Many tourists are at first taken aback by the most characteristic wines of Greece, those rugged white wines mixed with resin (*retsína*), an inheritance from the ancients. *Kokkinéli* (rosé) generally contains less resin, and is more palatable to those who have not got used to the taste. *Retsína,* though a few like it from the first, is an acquired taste, except that most never acquire it. There is, of course, retsina and retsina—the best from the barrels of one of the taverns in the plain of Attica, or, if bottled, *Hyméttos* or *Kourtákis*. An addition of mineral water is refreshing, but does not reduce the taste of the resin.

The better restaurants have their own unresinated wine on draught (red or white), but everywhere bottled unresinated wine is available. The best red, rosé and white is *Porto Carras* from the Halkidiki; red and white *Mirabello* from Crete, where *Minos* is also quite drinkable. Likewise recommended are the white Attic

Kava Camba, Cellar, Elisar, Pallini, Viliza, Amalia and *Gold of Attica; St. Helena,* from the Peloponnese; and *Chevalier de Rhodes* from Rhodes. *Petit Château* is an excellent red; the pleasant, full-bodied red wine from Macedonia is named after its place of origin, *Náoussa.* The ubiquitous *Demestica* lacks character, both red and white.

Several Athenian taverns specialize in the products of the various regions; the very drinkable red and white wines are kept in the barrel. A discerning Athenian friend may guide you to these; the directions would be too complicated to give here—nor are the wines so good as to justify it. It may be said, however, that good, light, drinkable wine is nearly everywhere obtainable.

Sweet wines are those of Achaia (*Mavrodáphne*), Santorini (*Vino Santo*) and the *Moscháto* of Samos (Byron: "Fill high the bowl with Samian wine!"). In those islands, and in Patra, these wines may be had at their best; a glass brought to you in Athens may well be disappointing. *Cinzano* vermouth is locally produced, and *Botrys* is deservedly popular. Brandy, if you take what a provincial café will give you, may easily taste of hair oil or cheap scent; but goodish Greek brandy exists, and if you order a *Metaxá* you will find it enjoyable but different from what you have been accustomed to. Greek liqueurs, based on synthetic fruit syrups, delight the eye by their deep and unconvincing colors, but hardly please the palate with their cloying sweetness.

It is safe to drink the water; in Athens, it is purified by an unpleasant surfeit of chloride of lime. In the country, especially in the mountains, the water can be exceptionally pure and delicious. The Castalian spring of Delphi has, rightly, been famous since ancient times.

In Athens and Thessaloniki *Floka's Cafés* and the *Brazilian Coffee Shops* provide the best continental breakfasts with French *croissants* or *brioches.* White bread is generally without taste—brown bread is better, but is not often obtainable—and butter is indifferent. Fortunately Nescafé is provided everywhere and is much more palatable than the attempts made at French coffee, or than the Greek coffee served with hot milk. Honey is always delicious—that of Mount Hymettus is very likely the best in the world. Honey will, if you ask for it, be served with a hotel breakfast, and in many places in the provinces you will find a café that advertises "Butter and honey" (*voútyro-méli*).

THE FACE OF GREECE

ANCIENT ATHENS

Birthplace of Democracy

It was called "the violet-crowned" by the ancients because, just before sunset, the flanks of Ymitós (Mt. Hymettus), running like a backbone between the Attic plain and the vine country of the Mesógeio, often glow with a curiously warm violet-tinted light which is reflected on the buildings of the city below. Then, suddenly, as though a switch had been worked by the unseen hand of some Olympian deity, everything turns dun-grey and Athens and its encircling mountains are engulfed in the shadows. This remarkable sight may now be observed only by courtesy of the north wind, blowing away the noxious mixture of carbon monoxide, sulphur dioxide and lead particles, forming the notorious chemical cloud, and temporarily restoring the unrivalled clarity and brilliance of the Athenian atmosphere.

Many millennia ago, according to the legend, Kekrops, a Phoenician, came to Attica, where he founded a city on the great rock near the sea. Two of the most powerful gods of Olympos, Poseidon and Athena, contended for the patronage of the new strategically-placed city, ringed round by a semicircle of protective mountains and possessing the excellent harbors of the Saronic Gulf at the seaward end of the plain. Poseidon, to prove the justice of his claim to divine overlordship struck the earth with his trident, and instantly a magnificent horse sprang forth, symbolising all the manly qualities for which the marine god was famous. But the astute Athena, goddess of wisdom, in her attempt to outbid Poseidon, merely produced an olive tree from the ground. This, she explained, represented the qualities of peace and prosperity which would serve mankind to better purpose than the arts of war personified by Poseidon's fiery steed. The council of gods decided in her favor, and the city of Kekrops, where European culture was destined to be born, was accordingly named Athens. Henceforth its inhabitants regarded the goddess of wisdom as their tutelary deity.

Handicapped by the natural aridity of the soil—little else but the vine and the olive have ever been successfully cultivated in Attica—Athens is nevertheless admirably situated; and the practical convenience of its position marks it out as the obvious capital of the country. Facing the Saronic Gulf, with its good anchorages, on the main trade routes between Italy and the coast of Asia Minor on the one hand, and the Black Sea and the Straits of Gibraltar on the other, the modern city is built around the Acropolis (as the ancient one was) and the pinnacled crag of Mt. Lycabettus, which the goddess Athena was said to have dropped on a spot north-east of the Acropolis, where it could serve as a bulwark to defend the city. With the increase in population and building activity since the late 1950s, the suburbs have covered the barren plain in all directions, in some places actually climbing the foothills of the mountains.

A Leader in Political Fashion

The historical origins are, of course, enveloped in the mists of mythology. Built by Kekrops in the remote Pelasgian Age, the city was enlarged by Erechtheus, who, half-man, half-serpent, was buried in a temple on the Acropolis afterwards known as the Erechtheion. Later, the legendary hero, Theseus, united the independent states of Attica into a single body, making Athens the capital of the state.

In the age of recorded history, what Athens did one day Greece did the next and Europe did two and a half millennia later. In 593 B.C., the ruling oligarchy appointed Solon, one of the Seven Wise Men of Antiquity, to carry out the necessary reforms to stave off tyranny, which had been prevented in 628 B.C. only by the decisive, if sacrilegious, action of the Alcmaeonid Megacles. Solon cancelled all debts, freed citizens enslaved for debts and prohibited future enslavement, bought back those sold abroad at state expense, limited landholdings, gave citizenship to foreign artisans, introduced pensions for war widows and orphans, introduced trial by jury and changed the coinage. But by basing himself on the maxim, "nothing in excess" he displeased all the social classes and there ensued fifty years of civil strife, till a successful general, Peisistratus, firmly established tyranny and the tradition of military interference in politics.

In a typical Greek paradox, he imposed the Solonian reforms, which had been intended as preventing tyranny. A sound economist and administrator, he raised Athens from the status of a country town to that of a city of international importance. He also erected temples and public buildings, and encouraged the development of poetry and drama, which revived public interest in the epics of Homer.

His son and successor Hippias, appointed his brother Hipparchos as a singularly successful Minister of Culture. To Athens flocked all the great names in Ionian intelligentsia till Hipparchos' murder in 514 B.C.

The first political family in Europe, the Alcmaeonids, in exile for the third time and experts in propaganda, turned a lovers' quarrel into the heroic deed of tyrannicides. But they failed to rouse the Athenians and had to use their influence over the Delphic oracle to bring about the overthrow of Hippias by Spartan intervention in 510 B.C. The Alcmaeonid Cleisthenes completed the Solonian reforms by what is generally termed the "first democratic constitution in world history", which retained sufficient checks and balances to make it workable.

Athenian intervention in the Ionian Revolt in 499 B.C. had made Persian retaliation inevitable. The campaigns of 490 and 480 B.C., culminating in the defeat of the Persian invaders at Marathon, Salamis and Plataea, inaugurated a new era in the history of Athens which had been reduced to ashes by Xerxes, the Persian king, on the eve of the destruction of his own fleet at Salamis. The prestige of Athens which had resisted and routed the Asiatic hordes, now naturally stood very high in the Greek world. Under Themistocles, celebrated for his unrivalled statesmanship in keeping the Greek alliance together, the security of the city was ensured by surrounding it with fortified walls, and its chief port was transferred from the open roadstead of Phaleron to the security of the admirable harbors of the Piraeus. The process of construction and embellishment continued under Kimon.

The Golden Age

For its architectural splendor, however, Athens is chiefly indebted to Pericles. It was indeed in the golden Periclean age of Athenian democracy that the Parthenon, the Erechtheion and the Propylaea of the Acropolis were built. The rapid development of Athens as a maritime power, begun under Themistocles, continued, and a virtual Athenian empire was soon established over the Aegean.

The Peloponnesian War, in which Athens and Sparta fought for the supremacy of Greece, and in which Athens was finally defeated in 404 B.C., brought an end to the Classical Age. But during those miraculous years, the little state had produced an unparalleled succession of geniuses. To name only a few: statesmen such as Themistocles, Pericles and the glamorous though utterly unscrupulous Alcibiades; Aeschylus, Sophocles and Euripides among the dramatists, and Pheidias and Myron, masters of the art of sculpture; historians of the calibre of Herodotus, Thucydides and Xenophon; as well as an entire galaxy of architects, poets and comic writers. As for the philosophers—Socrates, Plato and Aristotle, above all—their teachings have never ceased to influence Western thought and civilization to this day.

Little more than ten years after the defeat of Athens, however, a naval victory over the Spartans off Cnidos, by the Athenian admiral Conon, turned commander of the Persian navy in one of those kaleidoscopic changes of alliance so frequent in Greece, enabled the Athenians to turn their thoughts once more to the improvement of their city. Persian gold started the rebuilding of the fortifications and the theater of Dionysus and the Stadium were eventually completed.

In the second half of the 4th century B.C., the Macedonians, led by Philip, invaded Greece, and Athens and its allies suffered a crushing defeat at the battle of Chaironeia. This spelt the end of Greek democracy, for Philip, and his son, Alexander the Great, who succeeded him, imposed a rigid rule over the conquered city states. After two hundred years of uneasy acquiescence to Macedonian overlordship, the stage was set for the Roman conquest. Materially Athens suffered disastrously when Sulla, the Roman general, captured the city in 86 B.C., after which commerce and maritime power declined rapidly.

The Romans, Goths and Turks

Nevertheless, under the Romans, Athens continued to be the cultural capital of the Graeco-Roman world, and was much frequented by Romans as a seat of learning and refinement, becoming, in fact, a kind of "finishing school" for elegant and educated patricians. Numerous public buildings were erected and embellishments made by the Roman emperors, especially by Hadrian. During the reign of the Antonines, imperial munificence was emulated by a rich banker, Herodes Atticus, the first of many public benefactors to whom Athens, even in modern times, owes much of its municipal architecture.

The city remained intact until the 4th century A.D., after which public buildings fell into disrepair and a general decay set in. Paganism was now gradually being stamped out and Christianity beginning to flourish triumphantly in Constantinople, the new capital of the civilized world.

The curtain had thus come down on the violet-crowned city. At the end of the 4th century Greece suffered the appalling visitation of Alaric and his Goths. Athens was sacked, ravaged, and henceforth left to moulder away in total insignificance. In the 13th century, when the great feudal barons of Western Europe, descending upon the eastern Mediterranean on the pretext of liberating the Holy City from the Infidel, began to carve out principalities for themselves out of the Christian Byzantine Empire, Athens came under the suzerainty of Florentine bankers, the Acciajuolis. In 1455, two years after the fall of Constantinople, the city was captured by a general of the triumphant Turkish Sultan, and henceforth remained, for nearly two centuries, little more than a dilapidated oriental village, a group of houses clustered round the dismantled Acropolis.

One episode during the dark centuries of Ottoman occupation is, however, worth recording. In 1687, the Venetians, under Francesco Morosini, the subsequent Doge, tried to wrest Athens from the Turks. The Acropolis underwent a sustained bombardment, and a Venetian shell, bursting on the Parthenon, where the Turks had placed their gunpowder magazine, caused a terrific explosion which reduced a considerable part of the temple to a heap of ruins. It was largely from the debris left by this explosion that Lord Elgin later recovered several statues and fragments of the frieze and metopes, now in the British Museum.

Exploring Ancient Athens

Although Athens, together with its suburbs and port, the Piraeus, sprawls across the plain for more than 150 square miles, most of the ancient monuments gravitate round the Acropolis, which rises like a massive sentinel, white and beautiful, out of the center of the city. Sightseeing is therefore confined to a fairly limited area and is not likely to prove too tiring. Nor do the Byzantine churches of the Middle Ages lie far off.

The history of Athens falls into three sharply defined chronological periods—ancient, Byzantine and modern: a fact naturally reflected in the existing monuments, most of which actually belong to the first and most famous of these periods. The gap of nearly four hundred years of Ottoman domination, between the Byzantine and modern eras, when the "dead hand of the Turk" lay heavy on the Greek lands, has left no architectural legacy worth speaking of.

The Acropolis—The Glory that was Greece

In mountainous Greece, most ancient towns were backed up by an acropolis, an easily defensible upper town (which is what the word means), but when spelt with a capital "A" it can only refer to antiquity's most splendid group of buildings—the Acropolis of Athens.

The square precipitous rock of limestone, 886 feet at its greatest length and 512 feet broad, rising over 200 feet above the surrounding plain, served both as a fortress and as the sacred sanctuary of Athena, its tutelary goddess, whose festival, the Panthenaea, was celebrated every four years when an embroidered crocus-colored robe, woven by the upper-class maidens of Athens, was carried in great pomp to the holiest of her shrines in the Erechtheion. Today it is crowned by the ruins of three temples and an entrance way, the architectural perfection of which has not been surpassed in two and a half thousand years.

Despite the efforts of UNESCO and the Greek government to protect monuments from pollution, especially from rains acid with sulphur, an international symposium of archeologists and architects has despairingly concluded that among all known methods for the protection of marbles, there exists none harmless and efficient enough that they could recommend. During the restorations, the equilibrium of the monuments was strengthened and the iron clamps of the previous major works dating from the turn of the century and the 30s, which held the teetering marble blocks together, were replaced by titanium; the buildings have been closed to the thousands of daily visitors; but all these measures are mere palliatives.

Starting from Syntagma (Constitution) Square, center of modern Athens and following Amalias and Dionysiou Areopagitou Avenues, the approaches to the Acropolis are reached in about five minutes by car or fifteen on foot. The first ancient monument on the southern slope of the Acropolis is Peisistratus' 6th-century B.C. theater of Dionysus. Here, for several days in the early summer of

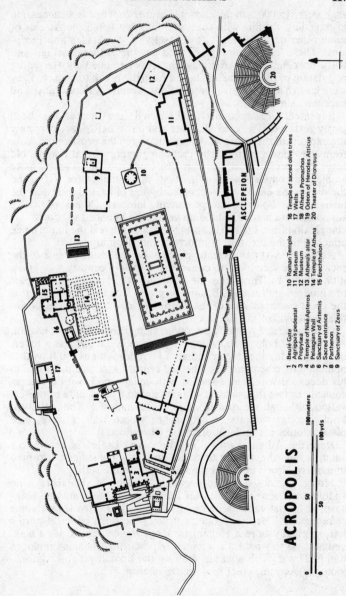

ACROPOLIS

0   50   100 meters
0   50   100 yds

1 Beulé Gate
2 Agrippa's pedestal
3 Propylaea
4 Temple of Niké Apteros
5 Pelasgian Wall
6 Sanctuary of Artemis
7 Sacred entrance
8 Parthenon
9 Sanctuary of Zeus

10 Roman Temple
11 Museum
12 Museum
13 Athena's altar
14 Temple of Athena
15 Erechtheion

16 Temple of sacred olive trees
17 Walls
18 Athena Promachos
19 Odeon of Herodes Atticus
20 Theater of Dionysus

ASCLEPEION

each year, 15,000 Athenians would gather to witness a succession of tragedies, dealing with the awful fate that befell the Atreids or some other doomed family, by Aeschylus, Sophocles and Euripides. These performances, livened by the satirical sallies and witty obscenities of Aristophanes, were attended by the entire population of the capital and lasted from daybreak to sunset. They were known as the festival of the Dionysia and combined plays and bacchanalian feasts.

Repeatedly enlarged and embellished, the theater has been partly restored. The circular stage and bas-relief frieze, depicting the exploits of the winegod, which supported the proscenium, date from the Roman period. The crouching figure of that famous old satyr, Silenus, is worth noting. The front row of 67 seats, more ample and comfortable than the rest, was intended for VIPs, and the one in the center was occupied by the officiating priest at the festival. The holes in the pavement, indicating the spot where supports were placed to hold up an awning intended to protect his complexion from the bright spring sunshine, reveal the importance attached to the creature-comforts of this dignitary.

Above the last tier of seats, perched on the southern side of the rock, will be seen a grotto converted in the 4th century B.C. into a little temple by Thrasyllus the Choragus (the ancient counterpart of a modern impresario). Beside the grotto, and immediately below the great southern wall of the Acropolis, rise two delicate Corinthian columns of the Roman period.

Continuing in a westerly direction, along Dionysiou Areopagitou Avenue, and below the ruins of a colonnade intended as a foyer, one reaches another theater: that of Herodes Atticus, built by that opulent public benefactor of the 2nd century A.D. as a memorial to his deceased wife. Once roofed with cedar wood, with a seating capacity of five thousand, it still remains in a good state of preservation, although the roof has long since vanished. The mellowed brick facade, with its arched niches where statues were once placed, looks particularly dramatic when floodlit.

Here the Athens Festival of Music and Drama is held every summer, and the ancient tragedies and Attic comedies performed in modern Greek in their original incomparable setting.

Motor coaches disgorge unending streams of sightseers, who should wear sensible shoes for the ascent of the ramp and staircase. A tourist canteen below the ticket office provides welcome refreshment. The first monument, a 27-foot-high pedestal on the left, originally bore a Hellenistic king. Never ones to let a good pedestal go to waste, the eminently practical Athenians replaced him in 27 B.C. with a statue showing the Roman general Agrippa, victor of Actium, erect in a bronze chariot.

The Propylaea, one of the masterpieces of classical architecture, serves as a magnificent entrance way to the buildings of the "upper city". With the defeat of the Persian fleet at Salamis and the decisive Greek victory at Plataea in the following year, the Persian menace had been finally removed, and Athens, under Kimon and Pericles rose to the heights of power and creative achievement. The adornment of the Acropolis with imperishable works of art was one of the main preoccupations of Pericles. He entrusted the building of the Propylaea to Mnesicles, a fashionable architect of the time, who completed it in five years. Built entirely of Pentelic marble, it extends 150 feet across the whole western front of the Acropolis, which was, and still is, the only means of access to the summit. It thus formed a vestibule to the five gates through which the Acropolis was entered, and the marks of the chariot wheels may still be seen on the age-worn rock. The porticos consist of six massive fluted Doric columns on the outside, doubled by graceful Ionic inside; the large north wing, the *Pinakotheke*, where pictures, mostly by Polygnatus, were exhibited, became the residence of the Orthodox archbishops, and later of the Frankish dukes, when a huge fortified tower was added. The Acciajuoli dynasty was replaced by the Turkish commander, who kept his powder dry in the portico till it was struck by lightning in 1645. The Turks placed their guns in the shattered walls. The German archeologist Schliemann paid for the removal of the Frankish tower in the 19th century, when the successful reconstruction, even of parts of the roof with its marble beams and decorated coffers, was begun.

The one room of the south wing might have served as a waiting room for the adjoining temple of Athena Nike, sometimes called Nike Apteros (Wingless Victory), because the crafty Athenians depicted Nike wingless, to prevent Nike from flying away. This little temple (only 27 feet long and 18 broad), its eight delicate Ionic columns glistening in the sun, stands on a western bastion of the Acropolis, commanding a superb prospect of the plain, sea and islands of the Saronic Gulf, with the backcloth of the crenellated ridges of the Methana peninsula and the mountains of the Peloponnese beyond. To the south-west, Egáleo tapers off into the sea, where the hump of the Kastella headland and the sprawling conglomeration of houses, docks and smoking factories of the Piraeus extend against the background of the off-shore island of Salamis.

According to legend, King Aegeus flung himself from this bastion into the sea—no mean achievement considering the six-mile distance—to which he has given his name. His son, Theseus, had forgotten to hoist the white sails proclaiming his slaying of the Minotaur, a strange omission as he had also rid himself of his protectress, Ariadne, and on seeing the black sails, the aggrieved father committed the somewhat acrobatic suicide. The bas-reliefs of the Frieze of Victories on the surrounding parapet, now closed to the public, must have been of exceptional workmanship, judging from "Nike unfastening her sandal" in the Acropolis museum.

The temple of Nike Apteros was built to commemorate the Greek victories over the Persians in the 5th century B.C. Completely demolished by the Turks in order to provide building material for a gun battery, the fragments were reconstructed during the 19th century into a perfect replica of the original. After this temporary respite for victorious Athena, the foundations gave way in 1936 because of unsuspected Turkish cisterns. The strengthening of the base led to the discovery of the foundations of Peisistratus' temple of Artemis, below the once again rebuilt home of Victory. The frieze, extending all 86 feet round the building, represented scenes from mythology and battles.

The Parthenon

Returning to the Propylaea, and passing through one of its five gates onto a rocky plateau, one is confronted with a staggering view of the western front of the Parthenon, its honey-colored columns of Pentelic marble rising from a massive limestone base which extends across the highest part of the Acropolis. The Sacred Way from the Propylaea to the Parthenon was once lined with statues, ex-votos and foundations of more ancient temples. Here, too, was Pheidias's colossal statue of Athena Promachos (all traces of which have now vanished), whose raised spear and plumed helmet could be seen flashing in the sunlight by sailors approaching the coast. Today the approach to the Parthenon, littered with slabs of marble and broken drums, is crowded with sightseers talking a dozen different languages, with garrulous guides and leech-like photographers. But neither they, nor all the evidence of the wanton destruction caused as much by man and his rapacity as by time and the elements, can detract from the awe felt at that first prospect of the ruins of the Parthenon. But the hard marble is slowly being dissolved by the sulphuric acid in the polluted air, which has stripped off the age-old patina and exposed new white stone.

The Parthenon, the "Virgin's Chamber", was built on the site of earlier temples also dedicated to the worship of the virgin goddess, Athena. Standing on the highest part of the plateau, its base was on a level with the roof of the Propylaea. It was under construction for nine years, and the design was drawn up by Ictinus, while Pheidias, the greatest sculptor of the age was entrusted with the sculptural decoration. But both Ictinus and Pheidias were responsible to Pericles, who took a keen personal interest in the completion of what was destined to be the most perfect example of Doric architecture in existence.

The temple had eight fluted columns at either end and 17 on each side, and was entirely built of Pentelic marble, which, with age, has taken on a warm golden tint of astonishing beauty. The genius of Ictinus and his collaborators is revealed in the fact that the structure does not possess a single straight line of any length, the shafts of the columns inclining slightly inwards, the lines of the cornices of the gables being oblique, and the entablature rising gradually to a point three inches higher in the middle: all these gentle deflections creating an unusually pleasing and tranquil effect. The subtle convexity of the columns can be seen best from either end of the two great colonnades. At every point, moreover, the simplicity, grandeur and complete harmony of design and execution astonishes and delights.

The exterior sculptural decorations, all of which were originally brightly colored, and commemorated the history of the goddess Athena, were of a fabulous quality and richness—92 sculptured metopes, 44 statues ornamenting the gables, and a frieze 523 feet long: all the work of Pheidias and his pupils. Most of the sculptural ornaments which escaped destruction from the Venetian siege of 1687 were taken down in 1801 by Lord Elgin, British Ambassador in Constantinople and, with the Sultan's permission, shipped to England, where they now form one of the showpieces of the British Museum. Those remaining became so badly damaged by pollution that they had to be removed to the Acropolis Museum.

In the eminently practical way of the Athenians, the Parthenon was a place of worship and, at the same time, a national treasury. It contained bullion as well as priceless ornaments and it stood as a symbol of Athenian imperialistic pride. Even Pheidias' huge chryselephantine statue of the goddess Athena, in her detachable dress of solid gold formed part of the bullion reserve. When the sculptor was charged with embezzlement, the robe was found to weigh the full 40 talents' worth of gold. Pheidias had to be acquitted only to be rearrested on a charge of impiety, in the relentless way with which the Athenian democracy persecuted all its great men, as he had depicted himself and Pericles upon Athena's shield. He either died in prison or, helped by Pericles to escape, was killed in an anti-Athenian riot at Olympia. The spot occupied by the statue can be identified by a paving of dark-colored limestone.

The subsequent history of the Parthenon is eventful. Alexander the Great dedicated the gilded shields taken from the Persians to Athena, but one of his successors, Demetrius Poliorketes, installed his mistress in the Virgin's Chamber. Athena eventually took her revenge when Demetrius came to a bad end, but could not prevent the removal of her jewels when the Athenian commander absconded with the temple treasure during Demetrius' siege of Athens in 298 B.C. Pheidias' statue was taken to Constantinople by the Emperor Theodosius II in 426 A.D., when the Parthenon became the church of Holy Wisdom. Some hundred years later, the Emperor Justinian dedicated the church to the Virgin of another faith, perhaps because he resented so glorious a rival to his own Saint Sophia. In 1206, the Franks changed the rite but kept the patroness and Saint Marie of Athens was worshipped till the conversion into a mosque in 1460. A minaret was attached, but nothing could prevent the Turks from storing ammunition in inappropriate places, with the obvious disastrous consequences.

The hazards of war were resumed in 1944, when British paratroops chased the Communists out of besieged Athens, after siting their bazookas between the Parthenon's columns. Since then, a more insidious enemy has been added to 2,400 years of warfare—pollution—so that intense effort, time and money has now to be devoted to preservation.

The Erechtheion

More than any other ancient monument, the Erechtheion, which lies north of the Parthenon, has its roots in the legendary origins of Athens. Here it was that the contest between Poseidon and Athena took place for the possession of the city. Here grew the olive tree which Athena had called forth from the ground, and the fountain, which had sprung up where Poseidon struck the earth with his trident, trickled. Here was buried Kekrops, the founder of Athens, and Erechtheus, Athena's ward, after whom the shrine was named, and at the first sight of whose serpent tail some of the royal attendants went mad with fright and hurled themselves from the top of the Acropolis. And here finally was venerated the ancient olive-wood statue of Athena Polias, which was said to have fallen from heaven.

Burnt by the Persians on the eve of the battle of Salamis, the Erechtheion was rebuilt on its original site after the outbreak of the Peloponnesian War. If the Parthenon is the masterpiece of Doric architecture, the Erechtheion is undoubtedly that of the more graceful and feminine Ionic order. A considerably smaller edifice than the Parthenon, for sheer elegance and refinement of design and execution, it cannot be matched by any other monument of antiquity. Extensively restored, the sanctuary of Athena, Poseidon and Erechtheus is easily recognizable by its complete difference in style from any other known Greek temple. Irregular in shape and built on different levels, it has three porticos of different dimensions. The six slender columns of the exquisitely proportioned northern portico framed the richly ornamented doorway which led into the chamber of Erechtheus. The southern portico, equally famous though less beautiful, is that of the Caryatids—six larger-than-lifesize maidens (replaced by cement casts, while five of the originals are in the Acropolis Museum and one in the British Museum), supporting a heavy roof of over two tons of Pentelic marble. Taking into account the enormous burden which these impassive maidens are carrying, their uniformly complacent, almost simpering expressions seem a little out of place.

If, during the Turkish occupation, the Parthenon suffered the indignity of being converted into a gunpowder dump, a fate of a quite different kind befell the Erechtheion. For here, in these holiest of ancient Athenian precincts, the Turkish governor, who himself resided in the Propylaea, housed the plump oriental beauties of his extensive harem.

East of the Erechtheion, there is a belvedere from which the white blocks of flats of the modern city can be seen washing like foam round the sides of Lycabettus and the suburban plain rolling eastwards towards the foothills of Mt. Hymettus.

The contents of the Acropolis Museum—a new building is planned below the rock—are described in the section on museums.

If asked what is the best time to see the Acropolis, one might be hard put to find an answer. Such is the beauty of the monuments and the grandeur of the setting that a visit in all weathers and at all hours is rewarding. The moonlight visit is of course the most romantic. But in winter if there are clouds trailing across the mountains, and shafts of sun occasionally lighting up the marble columns, which glisten with added brilliance after a shower of rain or a thunderstorm, the setting takes on an even more dramatic quality. In summer the heat is blistering at noontime, and the reflection of the light thrown back by the rock and marble ruins almost blinding; morning and late afternoon are preferable.

Sites near the Acropolis

After the Acropolis all will at first seem to be an anti-climax. But there is still much that is well worth seeing, especially the sites on the periphery of the Acropolis. A few low hills face its main entrance. The hill of the Muses is crowned with the funeral monument of Philopappos, the last descendant of the Commagene kings (Asia Minor), who was an important personage in the Roman administration. In the central upper niche of the ruined marble memorial, erected in about A.D. 116, are the remains of the statue of Philopappos.

This hill, now a favorite haunt of couples at sundown, is honeycombed with caves, one of which is commonly known as (but not proved to be) the prison of Socrates. And here, it is said, the greatest of ancient philosophers, condemned for the alleged corruption of Athenian youth by his advanced ideas on religion, drained the fatal cup of hemlock as the sun set fierily behind Salamis, its last rays liquefying the columns of the Parthenon into gold.

North-west of the hill of Philopappos rises the low, rocky Pnyx. The semi-circular terrace on its summit was the place of assembly of the Athenian people; and in the middle of a wall of rock projects a solid rectangular block, identified as the tribune from which the great orators of antiquity—Solon, Themistocles, Pericles, Aristides and Demosthenes—addressed the national assemblies. It must have been an ideal spot on which to arouse patriotic fervor, with the imposing entrance way of the Propylaea above, and the city below studded with all the public edifices attesting to the glory of Athens.

Every evening (Apr.–Oct.) audiences gather on the Pnyx to watch the impressive floodlighting effects on the rock and temples of the Acropolis, accompanied by sound effects and commentaries in English, French and German in one of the most effective Sound and Light performances in the world.

North-east of the Pnyx is the Areopagus, the "hill of Ares", so-called because it was here that the god of war was brought to trial before the council of gods by Poseidon for the willful killing of one of his sons. Being the first judgment ever to be pronounced in a murder trial, it made legal history and after a distinguished record of some thousand years in antiquity the name Areopagus was revived for the Supreme Court of modern Greece.

The Areopagus has two other associations: one mythological and the other historical. A dark cavern in a chasm of the rock corresponds to the sanctuary of the Eumenides, the restless Furies who hounded Orestes from the Lion Gate of Mycenae to Delphi and Athens. On the Areopagus too St. Paul made his famous sermon to the Athenians, in the course of which the senator Dionysus was converted to Christianity and subsequently canonized by the Orthodox Church for being the first Athenian to adopt the Christian faith. As St. Denis the Areopagite he was declared patron saint of the city; but the veneration which the Athenians once felt for their pagan tutelary deity does not seem to have been extended to her Christian successor, who remains a worthy but dim figure in the annals of Athenian history.

Between the Pnyx and the Areopagus, Apostolou Pavlou Street descends gently, leaving the hill of the Nymphs, crowned by a modern observatory on the left, into a wide flat area, below the north-western bastions of the Acropolis. Dotted with the ruins of numerous ancient edifices, this quarter once constituted the commercial hub of the city.

On the right of Apostolou Pavlou Street is the Hephaestion, the best-preserved temple in Greece, which has erroneously been styled the Theseion for many centuries, because the sculptures of the frieze depict the exploits of Theseus and Heracles. It was, however, dedicated to Hephaestus, the god of artisans and black-smiths, whose shops and forges, from antiquity to the present day, have echoed with the hammering of metal on anvil in this part of the town.

Designed by Ictinus, the architect of the Parthenon, it is, like-wise, a Doric temple, surrounded by 34 columns, and 104 feet in length. The porticos were once filled with sculptures, but today the only remaining adornment is the mutilated frieze and a few met-opes. These, like those of the Parthenon, were painted, and still preserve remains of the colors when carefully examined.

The Theseion's chief claim to fame rests in its excellent state of preservation. Although conceived and executed in the best of 5th century B.C. workmanship, it is likely to leave the spectator rather cold, and even to recall some of those commonplace replicas of Doric temples much favored by municipal architecture in Western Europe during the 19th century. The reason for the failure of the Theseion to create an impact similar to that made by the Parthenon or the Propylaea may also be due to the fact that it lacks a noble site. Its ample enclosure is surrounded by the houses of a poorish, densely-populated quarter, criss-crossed with crowded suburban bus routes to the Piraeus and the Athens-Piraeus electric railway line.

The Agora, Commercial Hub of Ancient Athens

The remains of the ancient Agora, the marketplace, extend south-eastwards, dominated by the restored Stoa of Attalus. The classical scholar and archeologist may well find the exploration of the Agora and the identification of the ancient municipal build-ings—thoroughly destroyed by successive invaders—an occupa-tion of absorbing interest. The scene, however, as it strikes the layman, is one of sprawling confusion, since none of the buildings are standing, and it is not always easy to identify the foundations among the rubble of stones and broken slabs of marble.

The Agora was the center of public life, and all the principal urban roads and country highways traversed it. The procession of the great Panathenaea Festival, composed of chariots, magis-trates, virgins, priests and sacrificial animals, also crossed the Ag-ora on its way from the Dipylon gate to the Acropolis. Six stoas, long colonnades closed on three sides, offered shade in summer and protection from rain in winter to the throng of people who transacted the day-to-day business of the city; but also to a succes-sion of philosophers, so that one school, Zeno's exposition of serene endurance, was even named stoicism; several centuries later, St. Paul went about his missionary task. It was indeed the heart of the city and a general meeting place, where news was exchanged and bargains transacted, alive with all the rumors and gossip of the market place.

In 1981 the American School of Classical Studies celebrated its centenary and the 50th anniversary of the Agora excavations, a major archeological event, by the discovery of the Stoa Poikile (Painted Stoa). A whole quarter had to be torn down to remove layer after layer of older buildings, finally revealing the antique foundations. The northwest corner was only recently expropriated, so that the first important building to rise from the ashes of the Persian invasion of 480 B.C. was the last to come to light. The Stoa Poikile received its name from the murals depicting mythical and historical battles, executed by the greatest painters of around 460 B.C.; it served thus as an art gallery as well as a war memorial.

The foundations of some of the main buildings which may be most easily distinguished include the Tholos, the principal seat of executive power in the city, the Bouleuterion, where the four hundred senators met, the Metroon, a vast building of complicated structure, in which the state archives were kept, and the Stoa of Zeus, where Socrates lectured and incited the youth of Athens to adopt his progressive ideas on morality.

The reconstructed Stoa of Attalus, which cost the Rockefeller Foundation $1,500,000 in the 1950s, is of course the showpiece of the Agora. The two superimposed colonnades of 134 columns, of which the lower are Doric and the upper Ionic, gleam white and all too obviously new above the ruins of the Agora. The original Stoa, built by Attalus, King of Pergamum, in the 2nd century B.C., as a tribute and memorial to Greek culture, was lined with statues and expensive shops, and soon became the favorite strolling ground of fashionable Athenians. In the principal hall of the reconstructed Stoa may be seen the vases and sculptures found on the site. Two statues, a headless Apollo and a Winged Victory, have been placed on either side of the Stoa.

Keramikos Cemetery

Leaving the Theseion on the right and continuing along Apostolou Pavlou Street, the Keramikos is reached. This, from the 7th century B.C. onwards, was the smart cemetery of ancient Athens. During succeeding ages cemeteries were superimposed on the ancient one until the latter was discovered in 1861 during the construction of Piraeus Street, the main road linking the capital with its port.

Situated in one of the noisiest and shoddiest parts of modern

Athens, the setting of the Keramikos is not inspiring although the gasworks that have for a century deposited soot on this archeological site are being replaced by a park. An alley bordered by sculptured memorials to the dead includes several 6th-century B.C. bas-reliefs of exceptional artistic value, depicting horsemen and wild animals. Some are in the small museum on the site, but the finest *steles* (funerary tablets) have been taken to the National Archeological Museum. Beyond the Sacred Gate, a hotchpotch of masonry of successive periods, is the Dipylon, built in the 4th century B.C. into a section of Themistokles' earlier wall. This rectangular court with two gateways facing north-west and south-east (hence the name Dipylon: the two doors), led from the inner into the outer Keramikos and was the most used of all the city's gates. It was also the favorite hunting-ground of prostitutes of antiquity, who lurked in its shadow, offering the solace of their charms to the weary traveler entering Athens.

The Tower of the Winds

In a line east of the Stoa, and past the remains of the Roman Agora, the little Tower of the Winds is situated in an open space surrounded by a cluster of old houses on the western slope of the Acropolis.

This edifice—more precisely, an hydraulic clock—was built in the shape of an octagonal tower in the 1st century B.C. in order to serve as a public clock and weather-vane. Its eight sides face the direction of the eight winds into which the compass was divided. The weathercock, long since vanished, consisted of a bronze Triton turning on a pivot on the summit of the tower. The frieze is sculptured with the inscriptions and figures of the eight winds.

Below the Tower of the Winds, a glance at the few remaining columns of the library of the Emperor Hadrian, once a vast quadrilateral edifice, with 100 Corinthian columns, will complete the tour of the periphery of the Acropolis.

The City of Hadrian

Starting from Syntagma Square, Amalias Avenue skirts the National Gardens until the Arch of Hadrian, a conspicuous landmark, is reached. Built by the Emperor Hadrian to define the limits of the original "city of Theseus"—all that lay beyond was the "city of Hadrian"—this monument consists of a Roman archway, with a Greek superstructure of Corinthian pilasters topped by an architrave and pediment. The combination of Greek and Roman styles, superimposing one another, succeeds in producing a rather ungainly effect.

Turning from Hadrian's Arch into Lysikratou Street, opposite, the Choragic Monument of Lysicrates appears below the eastern walls of the Acropolis. A small circular marble edifice, covered by a cupola, supported by six Corinthian columns, it dates from the 4th century B.C. and has a delightfully elegant appearance. The frieze depicts the rout of the Tyrrhenian pirates by Dionysus. It was elevated in honor of a group of young musicians who won a contest at the neighboring theater of Dionysus. The adjacent street of the Tripods (Tripodon Street) was once bordered by a series of similar monuments, surmounted by bronze tripods awarded as prizes to contestants in the Dionysiac festivals.

At the end of the 17th century, the monument of Lysicrates was incorporated in the grounds of a French Capuchin monastery and formed part of the monk's library. Here Byron stayed during his first visit to Athens, and met Theresa Makris, the "Maid of Athens" of his famous poem, who lived in a house overlooking the monastery garden where the English lord would sometimes amuse himself by joining in the games of a group of convent-reared boys.

Returning to the Arch of Hadrian, one enters the vast precincts of the temple of Olympian Zeus. This famous temple, begun by Peisistratus in the 6th century B.C., was only completed 700 years, and two styles, later. Exceeding in magnitude all other temples in Greece, Aristotle, who could only have seen the incomplete Ionic version, described it as being in the same class as the Pyramids of Egypt. It was finally consecrated, in the Corinthian style, by the Emperor Hadrian, who had already done so much to embellish Athens. Beside the statue of Zeus, father of the gods, he placed one of himself and probably one of his ubiquitous favorite, Antinous, whose subsequent death by drowning in the Nile caused the grief-stricken Emperor to enrol him among the gods. The destruction of the temple dates from the invasion of Alaric's Goths, and during the Middle Ages its massive masonry and the drums of its columns, the largest of any marble temple of antiquity in Europe, supplied the Athenians and their successive conquerors with building materials. During this period also a Byzantine anchorite perched his eyrie on a piece of lonely architrave above two columns which had been completely detached from the rest.

Although inferior in conception and execution to the temples of the Acropolis, the immense scale of the temple's design (it is 354 feet long and 135 broad) and the majesty of the towering sun-browned columns, with their decorative acanthus leaf capitals, makes a deep impression. It is thrilling also, when approaching Athens from the sea (and the airport), to see two of the sixteen remaining columns standing like sentinels on either side of Syngrou Avenue before it curves round by the Arch of Hadrian into the center of the town.

The Stadium

From the temple of Olympian Zeus, Queen Olga Avenue, flanked on one side by the Zappeion Gardens, leads to the last important monument of ancient Athens, the Stadium, now completely restored, and situated in a fold of the pineclad Ardittos Hill. Laid out in the 4th century B.C., it was embellished by the public-spirited Herodes Atticus four centuries later, and completely restored by George Averoff, a 20th century Herodes Atticus, among whose various other works of public benefaction was the defrayment of the cost of a battleship to the nation.

The Stadium, when completed in 1896, was the scene of the revived Olympic Games. A vast structure of white Pentelic marble, set against the surrounding green of dwarf-pines, it is an accurate replica of the ancient Roman stadium, and can seat 70,000 spectators, but the track area is too restricted for large international sporting events, which are held in the Olympic Stadium in the northern Kalogresa suburb. The tunnel of rock at the end of the arena may have been used, it is thought, as an exodus for animals in the course of wild beast shows during Roman times.

Byzantine Athens: Decay and Oblivion

During the thousand years of the Byzantine Empire, Athens declined in power and influence in inverse ratio to the growth and development of Constantinople as the capital of the Greek world. The paucity and modest proportions of such Byzantine monuments as may now be seen in Athens are proof of the insignificant status to which the city of Pericles had been reduced.

At no point, and at no time, does Athens, with its ruined classical temples, and its present feverish tempo of life, conjure up any of the usual concepts associated with Byzantium. The word "Byzantine" recalls an atmosphere of slow-moving, semi-Eastern ritual, redolent of incense, echoing with solemn liturgies chanted in chapels glowing with elaborate frescos. The beauty of Athens lies in the open—in the sun: that of Byzantium in dim mysterious interiors. Athens is Europe; Constantinople is already the Orient—or, at least, the beginning of it.

Three Byzantine churches, architectural gems of their kind, however, will be found tucked away in one of the busiest quarters of the modern town. Small in size, built in the traditional Greek Cross plan of "cross in square", their exteriors (brickwork in the case of the first two and marble in that of the third), crowned by a dome resting on the arches of an octagonal drum, are very arresting.

The oldest and best preserved is that of Agii Theodori, which may be seen from Stadiou Street, surrounded on three sides by tall buildings, at the lower righthand corner of Klafthmonos Square ("square of weeping"), so called because it was here that a group of dismissed civil servants once assembled to bemoan their fate; this, it seems, they did so loudly and persistently that the authorities were compelled to rescind their decision and restore them to their former jobs.

Not far off, in the middle of a minute square, halfway down the incline of crowded Ermou Street, is the coquettish little Kapnikarea, hemmed in by drapers' shops. Turning to the left into Mitropoleos Square, the smallest and loveliest of these churches of the 12th and 13th centuries, the Old Metropolis, nestles below the vast structure of the 19th-century cathedral of Athens. This is an incongruous mixture of non-styles constructed from the debris of 70 churches to furnish an object-lesson in the decline of good taste in the course of six centuries!

The Old Metropolis, built of Pentelic marble which has matured to a warm ochre hue, is distinguished by an exterior decoration of exquisite variety and refinement. All four sides are embellished with bas-reliefs of symbolic beasts, as well as with ancient fragments of classical friezes depicting the principal feasts of the calendar, and various heraldic or purely ornamental designs, all of extreme elegance.

Wandering in the tortuous ways of the Plaka—the little that is left of the 19th-century Athens which Byron knew—on the northern slope of the Acropolis, one does occasionally stumble upon a pretty little chapel. These, although probably of later construction than the three churches already described, present some of the best qualities of Byzantine church architecture in miniature.

Of the strange interlude of Frankish occupation, which resulted from that most sordid of all politico-religious mockeries, the Fourth Crusade, no architectural trace remains. The brief sojourn of the feudal barons of the West, who virtually ruled Athens from Thebes, left no mark on the city. Their rapacity and chivalry, their jousting and heraldry seem strangely out of place under the blazing sky of Attica. As for the four long centuries of Ottoman domination, so low had the fortunes of Athens then sunk that only one mosque was constructed, in 1759, by an Athenian Moslem governor, who obtained good lime by burning a marble column of the temple of Olympian Zeus. Now the Museum of Greek Handicrafts, but badly in need of repairs, it adds an oriental touch to Monastiráki Square.

MODERN ATHINA

Progress and the Pick-Axe

The recent change from the prehistoric name *Athine* to demotic *Athina* stresses the lack of historical continuity, more apparent than in any other important European capital. After the sack of the city by the Goths no building of importance was erected, with the exception of a few Byzantine shrines, until it became the capital of the new kingdom in 1834, when it was little more than an oriental village.

The first sovereign of the independent state, the Bavarian King Otho, brought with him in the second quarter of the 19th century, a group of German architects, who planned and built much of the city which existed until the 1950s. Othonian Athens was of course planned as the modest capital of a small Mediterranean state, whose main thoroughfares had only to accommodate horse-drawn traffic and pedestrian strollers (Greek pedestrians prefer to walk in the middle of the street, whether bent on business or pleasure).

Long after most of the imported German architects had left Greece or died, Othonian architecture continued to flourish as the domestic style: rows of stuccoed facades, heavy wrought-iron balconies, ornamental balustrades, little porches of Ionic columns. Now it has all—or practically all—been engulfed in the maw of Progress.

The pick-axe has done its work, and the cement mixer has engendered the Athens-Piraeus conurbation, a vast capital city—choked with traffic—of apartment buildings up to 24 stories high. But there is hardly a monument to attest to the city's history for the past eighteen centuries.

The centuries of decay, neglect and even oblivion reduced Athens to a village of 5,000 souls centered on a group of marble columns. But after the Greek War of Independence against the Turks (1821–30) and the choice of Athens as the capital of the independent state, the village rapidly became the focus of all the reawakened social, political and commercial forces in the country. In 1834, the population of Athens, together with its port, the Piraeus, was under 10,000. It has now risen to over four millions, including the outlying suburbs, which fill the entire plain from the sea to the mountains. After the evacuation of Asia Minor in 1922 and during the Communist rebellion of 1946–49, waves of refugees swamped the city resulting in the emergence of large new quarters.

Since the rapid industrialization of the 60s and 70s, some 100,000 country people have been settling annually in the ever-increasing circle of unplanned suburbs adding to the general overcrowding and stifling pollution.

Exploring Modern Athens

Modern Athens is centered around the twin hills of the Acropolis and Lykavitós (Lycabettus). Skirting their bases, it spreads untidily in every direction, but the center and heart of the city is Sýntagma (Constitution) Square, about midway between the two. Built on an incline, bordered with hotels and travel agencies, the central expanse of asphalt is brightened by orange trees, a fountain and several cafés, where customers sit till late at night.

Above the square are the marble and bronze bas-reliefs of the dignified Tomb of the Unknown Warrior on the marble ramp leading to a large 19th-century building, sometimes likened to a barracks: the former palace of the kings of Greece, built by Bavarian architects for King Otho. It was paid for by his father, King Ludwig I of Bavaria, who luckily vetoed the plans for a royal residence on the Acropolis, using one end of the Parthenon as the entrance and blowing up the rest. The palace was finished just in time for Otho to grant the constitution of 1843, which gave the name to the square. After the revolution of 1923, the palace served as shelter for refugees from Asia Minor, and since 1933 has housed the parliament or some substitute.

The Heart of the City

Though traffic is one way in the center of Athens, 800,000 cars plus a startling number of buses, emitting the blackest diesel smoke imaginable, cause horrendous traffic jams, and parking is as difficult as driving. A former Minister of Communications recently pronounced that 75% of females had lost their sexual ardor as a result of air pollution in the capital. He failed to state how he arrived at this depressing conclusion, or why males have apparently been spared.

The two chief thoroughfares of the city, Stadíou, the main shopping street, and Venizélou, more often called by its former name, Panepistimíou (University), run north-westwards, and parallel to each other, from Syntagma Square. Both streets terminate in Omonia Square, a bedlam of touts, pedlars and newsboys centered by a pool and fountain which spouts water above the underground station of the Piraeus-Athens-Kifissia electric railway.

Half way down Venizelou, an imposing group of marble buildings conjures up an illusion of classical antiquity. They consist of the 19th-century neo-classic structures of the Academy, adorned with a colonnade and pediment, the University, which has a colored colonnade, and the National Library, faced with a Doric portico. Statues of Athena and Apollo, on tall columns, flank either side of the Academy. Paid for by the Austro-Greek Baron Sina, the Academy is a copy of the Parliament in Vienna. The architects were the Danish Hansen brothers, who also designed the neo-Byzantine Eye Hospital next door, adjoining the Catholic Cathedral of St. Denis. The German archeologist Schliemann's mansion, distinguished by a loggia, is being transformed into a Museum of Ancient Coins. The graceful Othonian building behind the University houses the Theater Museum.

North of Omonia Square extends a residential area on either side of 28 Oktovríou Street, formerly Patissíon, leading to the Patíssia district, below the distant barrier of Párnitha (Mt. Parnis). Past the neo-classic Polytechnic and Archeological Museum, at the junction with Leoforos Alexandras, is a large park, resounding in summer to the tunes played by the band of a popular cabaret of distinctive *Merry Widow* flavor. One of the alleys is bordered by marble busts of the heroes of the War of Independence, and above the wispy eucalyptus treetops, rises a memorial to British Commonwealth servicemen killed in Greece in the last war, consisting of a helmeted Britannia precariously placed on top of a column, at

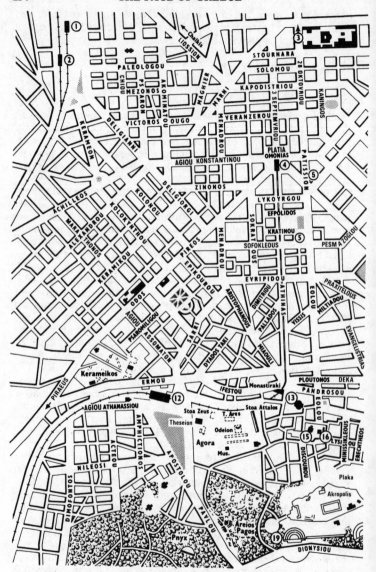

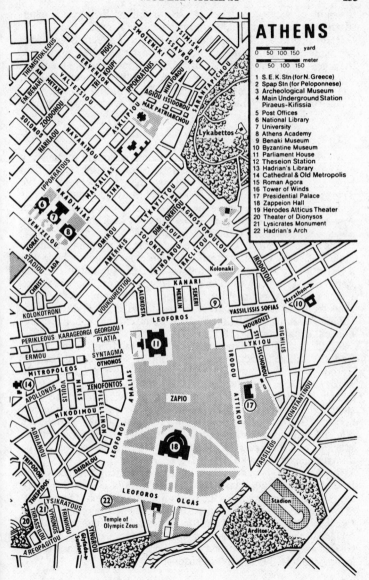

ATHENS

yard
0   50 100 150

meter
0   50 100 150

1 S.E.K. Stn (for N. Greece)
2 Spap Stn (for Peloponnese)
3 Archeological Museum
4 Main Underground Station
   Piraeus-Kifissia
5 Post Offices
6 National Library
7 University
8 Athens Academy
9 Benaki Museum
10 Byzantine Museum
11 Parliament House
12 Theseion Station
13 Hadrian's Library
14 Cathedral & Old Metropolis
15 Roman Agora
16 Tower of Winds
17 Presidential Palace
18 Zappeion Hall
19 Herodes Atticus Theater
20 Theater of Dionysos
21 Lysicrates Monument
22 Hadrian's Arch

the foot of which crouches the British lion. Britannia's hand, struck and severed by lightning, has been replaced.

Returning to Syntagma Square, Vassilíssis (Queen) Sofías Avenue, known as millionaires' row, leads past embassies, museums, the long-unfinished concert hall and the Venizelos monument to the Olympic Stadium, inaugurated for the 1982 European Games, and the northern residential suburbs of Psihikó, Filothéi and Kifissia at the foot of Pentéli, whose sides are scarred with marble quarries, both ancient and modern.

An Oasis of Parks

Amalias Avenue runs south from Syntagma Square to the Arch of Hadrian. Immediately on the left, after passing Parliament House, extend the National Gardens: an oasis of green in the desert of cement and marble. This delightfully informal park was laid out by a German landscape gardener at the request of Queen Amalia, in the middle of the 19th century. Its cool shady alleys are a welcome refuge from the glare and bustle of the main streets.

The National Gardens adjoin the wide walks of the Zapio Gardens, named after the benefactor who built the semi-circular edifice with a Corinthian portico. Renovated for the EEC summit in 1983, the Zapio has since been used as a conference center. There is a good view of the Acropolis and the columns of the temple of Olympian Zeus from the gardens, a favorite strolling ground of Athenians on summer evenings when the cafe next to the exhibition hall presents musical programs.

South-east of the Zapio lies the Stadium, from which shady Irodou Attikou Street (not to be confused with the theater of Herodes Atticus situated at the foot of the Acropolis) runs northward, with the National Gardens on the left. On the right the pseudo-Renaissance palace built for the first Crown Prince Constantine in the 1880s became the royal residence after the restoration in 1935: it is now used by the President of the Republic for official functions; outside the gates the colorful kilted Evzones (the Presidential Guard) stand on duty: sturdy and impassive, as the tourists' cameras click.

The Evzones barracks are being reconstructed at the corner of Irodou Attikou and Vassilíssis Sofías Avenue; across the latter, the Benaki Museum marks the beginning of Kolonaki, the fashionable residential quarter situated on the northern slope of Mount Lycabettus. Here, apart from the new blocks of flats which have replaced the old town houses of well-to-do families, are some embassies and, further up the slope, the British and American archeological schools, set in pretty gardens.

A Fine Panorama

The ascent of Mt. Lycabettus, nearly three times the height of the Acropolis, can be made by funicular railway. The summit of this precipitous crag, rising sheer out of the center of the city, is crowned by the little chapel of St. George and a restaurant, but the open-air theater in a crater below is accessible by car. The view from the terrace of the chapel not only embraces all Athens filling the plain of Attica, but may include, pollution permitting, Aegina, Salamis and the distant mountains of the Peloponnese in the west.

The last remains of 19th-century Athens are in the Plaka, a quarter climbing the northern slope of the Acropolis. This maze of narrow, winding streets and steps, small, color-washed houses with upper wooden stories, miniature Byzantine chapels, dank cellars filled with wine vats, narrow stairways lined with tavernas, and occasionally a court or tiny garden, has been partly restored. Numerous small shops display antiques, most of doubtful provenance, tourist souvenirs of equally doubtful taste and handicrafts and leather work along the pedestrian zone. Only the quieter nightspots have survived the recent clean up.

The Piraeus: Yachts, Wharves and Factories

Pireas (The Piraeus), separated from the center of Athens by six miles of suburbia, is at once one of the great emporiums of the Levant and the main port and industrial center of Greece. The port and famous Long Walls were constructed by Themistocles, the victor of Salamis and creator of Athenian maritime power, in the second quarter of the 5th century B.C. Completely destroyed by the Romans more than 300 years later, the Piraeus never fully recovered until after the establishment of the Greek kingdom in the 19th century.

This vast, densely populated port spreads its wharves and dockyards, mills, factories and foundries from the sea to the barren ridge of Mount Egáleo. The main harbor, one of the busiest in the Mediterranean, is crowded with ships flying the flags of all nations; from the central quay, the numerous island ferries bound for the different archipelagos, sail at all hours of the day. On Epiphany, January 6, the "Blessing of the Waters" is celebrated by the Archbishop of Athens and All Greece in the presence of the government with great solemnity. Church bells clang and sirens hoot deafeningly as the cross is thrown into the sea, more often than not to be hauled up by a rope as on a cold day youths no longer dive after it into the chilly waters.

But the small vessels of antiquity anchored in the infinitely more attractive two semi-circular basins facing south towards Aegina. The larger is the well-equipped port of Zea, with mooring and wintering facilities for yachts; the small pool is crowded and the adjoining beach is badly polluted. The crescent-shaped waterfront is bordered with open-air cafés, extending to the Naval Museum at the western end below the meager remains of a Hellenistic theater next to the Archeological Museum. The steep headland of Kastélla on the eastern end is topped by the Bowling Center and the Veákio open-air amphitheater which greatly improves on the ancient models by providing backrests, so that the performances of ancient dramas and folk dances can be enjoyed to the full against the superb backdrop of the Saronikos Gulf and Mount Hymettus.

In repairing a sewer, workmen discovered a number of ancient statues of great archeological value imbedded in the soil. Among these were a superb *kouros* (young man) in perfect condition, a bronze helmeted Athena in a beautifully draped full-length robe, an Artemis with quiver and bolt, and a handsome Hellenistic maiden. These statues were probably stored by the Romans after Sulla's sack of Athens in 86 B.C., with the intention of shipping them to Rome. Why the shipment was never made can only remain a matter of conjecture.

In Greece the past is omnipresent. When a bus hit the olive tree under which Plato supposedly lectured at his academy on the sacred way to Eleusis, the Greek atomic commission obligingly certified the tree's age by carbon dating as 2,500 years. The remaining roots sprouted a new olive bush beside the mangled trunk. After this propitious reanimation, the Academy grounds were made into a park.

PRACTICAL INFORMATION FOR ATHENS

WHEN TO COME. As in most places, spring and early fall are best. In May, when it is warm without being too hot, Athens is at its best; the beaches are not yet overcrowded and the countryside around the city has not yet been parched by months of blazing sunshine. But October and early November are also good, with days of mellow sunshine, and are an ideal period for sightseeing. July-August-September is the peak of the tourist season. The heat is sometimes intense, and the nearer bathing beaches are always overcrowded and often badly polluted. In winter, though the rains rarely last more than a few days and snow makes only one or two appearances, the city has less appeal than in the other seasons. There is opera at the Olympia Theater, Akadimias 59, but it is of very uneven quality. Numerous small theaters have plays and shows to offer, but they are in Greek of course. There are symphony concerts every Monday evening (in the ancient open air theater of Herodes Atticus in summer).

From the start of April through October the National Tourist Organization presents a Sound and Light pageant in the setting of the Acropolis. The public on the Pnyx may watch the alternate lighting of the monuments while listening to historical texts accompanied by music and sound effects. Every night a performance in English is given, at 9 to 9.45 P.M. Seats cost 150 dr. To reach the Pnyx you take the Thission-Thon bus—or a taxi. Flower festivals at Patissia and Kifissia on May 1.

The Athens Festival of Music and Drama is held each year from July to September in the theater of Herodes Atticus, the ochre-colored Roman building which glows in a brilliant floodlight scene that includes the Acropolis, the monument of Philopappos and the temple of Olympian Zeus. The festival is a revival of the Dionysia instituted by the tyrant Peisistratus in the 6th century B.C. The programs include symphony concerts by the Athens State Orchestra, as well as by foreign orchestras. There are also performances of opera and ballet by Greek and foreign companies.

One of the highlights of the festival is the cycle of ancient Greek tragedies and Attic comedies put on by the National Theater. In an incomparable setting at the foot of the Acropolis, these productions have done much to revive interest in ancient drama. The familiar old legends, as retold in the noble verse of Aeschylus, the brilliant plots of Sophocles or the moving choruses of Euripides, no longer seem to bear any relation to the realm of mythology. The performances are all in modern Greek. Ancient drama and other performances are also presented at the Lycabettus theater, while the Philopappos theater is given over to folk dancing from May through September. Tickets for the festival should be obtained in advance from the ticket office on Spirou Miliou Arcade, off Stadiou 4 (tel. 322 1459), 150–1,200 dr. In keeping with the Dionysian origin, a Wine Festival is held from mid-July to early September at the Byzantine monastery of Daphni. Entrance 100 dr., plus a small sum for a glass and a carafe you can take home.

Easter is the most solemnly observed of all Greek religious holidays. It also falls at one of the loveliest times of the year. Nobody should miss the Good Friday procession, in the course of which a bier, supporting an effigy of the body of Christ, is borne through the streets between 9 and 10 P.M. The procession is followed by the Archbishop of Athens and all Greece and other high dignitaries of the Church in colorful robes, by members of the government and contingents of the Army, Navy and Air Force, while military bands crash out solemn funeral marches. At the conclusion of the Resurrection service on the following night, church bells toll and pious churchgoers finally wind their way home, carrying lighted candles cupped in their hands. The fairylike procession of candles zigzagging down the path from the chapel of St. George on the top of Mt. Lycabettus is something worth seeing.

HOW TO GET ABOUT. By Taxi. To complicate getting one of the 13,000 yellow taxis, their signs are illuminated when occupied, switched off when empty. For utter frustration try for one in the rush hours, which seem to stretch longer and longer, or when it rains. Drivers appear to have arrived in town simultaneously with the tourists, judging by their ignorance of any but the main streets, which, to add to the confusion, are renamed more frequently than seems justifiable. Insist on having the car radio turned off, unless you really enjoy long speeches in Greek or weird music. A show of authority might even get you to your destination by a less round-about route. Fare from the airport or Piraeus harbor to the town center about 300 dr.

By Electric Train, Bus and Trolleybus. Buses, and the more comfortable yellow trolleybuses, run until midnight; at rush hours they are dangerously overcrowded and one has literally to fight one's way through a seething crowd. All suburbs and beaches of the southern coast are connected with buses from the center of the city. An electric service connects Omonia Square via Monastiraki and the Thesio with Piraeus; and via the northern suburbs with the resort of Kifissia.

There are conducted motor coach tours of the city by day and night, organized by *American Express,* Syntagma Square, *CHAT,* Stadiou 4 and *Key Tours,* Ermou 2, among others.

HOTELS. Athens hotels generally offer good value in all price ranges, but remember that the Greek word for hotel is *xenodochion,* meaning container for strangers. And, with some notable exceptions, this is exactly what they are; adequate for a rest and a wash, but not to spend any time in. The Greeks are an outdoor people and they rarely spend much time at home, let alone in an hotel. Where there are public rooms, besides restaurants and mini-bars, they are dark and forbidding.

Try to avoid rooms fronting the street, as they tend to be noisy. Go instead for those overlooking the courtyard. Reserve well in advance, especially from June to September.

In our lists below, you'll find that all Moderate hotels have restaurants and are airconditioned, unless otherwise stated, but that there is otherwise very little to distinguish one from another other than location. Inexpensive hotels do not have either restaurants or airconditioning unless stated.

Deluxe

Athenaeum Intercontinental, Syngrou 89 (tel. 922 5950). 580 rooms, 20 suites. Somewhat off-center; French and Greek restaurants, disco and *Kava Bar* till 2 A.M.; roofgarden pool.

Athens Hilton, Vassilissis Sofias 46 (tel. 722 1201/10). 480 rooms, 30 suites. Slightly away from the center in luxurious residential district near the U.S. Embassy. Oldest of the international chain hotels, but holding its own. *Ta Nissia* downstairs is pretty much what the folks back home think an island taverna should look like; very fancy indeed. *Byzantine Cafe,* buffet at the large pool and roofgarden with *Supper Club* (dancing to live bands to 2 A.M., closed Mon.).

Caravel, Vassileos Alexandrou 2 (tel. 729 0721/9). 416 rooms, 55 suites. Earthquake-proofed hotel near the Hilton. Italian restaurant, bouzouki tavern; piano bar and roofgarden pool.

Grande Bretagne, Syntagma (tel. 323 0251/10). Maintains its great tradition in enlarged and modernized premises in the heart of the city. The restaurant and bar are favorite meeting places.

Holiday Inn, Mihalakopoulou 50 (tel. 724 8322/9). 190 rooms, 8 suites. Near the Hilton, with bowling alley and disco. *Le Bistro* is a creditably French restaurant.

Ledra Marriott, Syngrou 113 (tel. 952 5211). 250 rooms, 20 suites. Newest of the internationals, a little far out. *Kona Kai* Polynesian restaurant, complete with waterfall; *Bali Lounge, Crystal Lounge, Ledra Grill, Zephyros Cafe*; roofgarden pool.

N.J.V. Meridien, Syntagma (tel. 325 5301/9). 170 rooms, 12 suites. A member of the French luxury chain, so special attention is paid to the original *Brasserie des Arts* and *The Athenian Bistro.* Same fine view as its neighbor, the Grande Bretagne.

Expensive

Astor, Karageorgi Servias 16 (tel. 325 5555). 133 rooms, 3 suites. Just off Syntagma; with roofgarden restaurant.

Delice, Vassileos Alexandrou 3 (tel. 723 8311/3). Service flats, next to Caravel Hotel; 20 suites.

Divani Zafolia Alexandras, Leoforos Alexandras 87 (tel. 692 5111/4). 191 rooms, 8 suites. A little far from the center, but good value; roofgarden pool and minigolf.

Divani Zafolia Palace, Parthenonos 19 (tel. 922 2945/5). 193 rooms. Near the Plaka district; pool.

Electra, Ermou 5 (tel. 322 3222/7). 110 rooms. In noisy shopping street very close to Syntagma.

Electra Palace, Nikodimou 18 (tel. 324 1401/10). 106 rooms, 5 suites. On the quiet fringe of the Plaka and same management as the above; good value; roofgarden pool.

Golden Age, Mihalakopoulou 57 (tel. 724 0861/9). 122 rooms. More than adequate hotel near the Holiday Inn; disco.

Herodion, Rovertou Galli 4 (tel. 923 6832/6). 90 rooms. Closest hotel to the Acropolis.

President, Kifissias 43 (tel. 692 4600). 513 rooms. Largest and furthest from the center in this category, but in good residential district; night club, roofgarden, pool.

Riva, Mihalakopoulou 114 (tel. 770 6611/5). 50 suites. Outstanding restaurant that is worth visiting; near the Hilton.

Moderate

Alexandros, Timoleontos Vassou 8 (tel. 643 0464). 96 rooms. Near the U.S. Embassy; garage.

Alfa, Halkokondyli 17 (tel. 552 1253/5). 88 rooms. Near Omonia Square.

Arethusa, Mitropoleos 6 (tel. 322 9431/9). 87 rooms. Just off Syntagma; roofgarden.

Athens Gate, Leoforos Syngrou 10 (tel. 522 6110). 106 rooms. Opposite Hadrian's Arch, but the price for the fine view is the noise from the major thoroughfare, though back rooms are quiet.

Athinaïs, Vassilissis Sofias 99 (tel. 643 1133). 84 rooms. Conveniently-placed near the U.S. Embassy.

Candia, Deliyanni 40 (tel. 524 6112/7). 142 rooms. Near Omonia Square; small roofgarden pool.

Christina, Petmeza 15 (tel. 921 5353). 93 rooms. Fairly near the Acropolis.

Dorian Inn, Pireos 15 (tel. 523 9782). 146 rooms. Small roofgarden pool; near Omonia Square.

Eretria, Halkokondyli 12 (tel. 363 5311/20). 63 rooms. Near Omonia Square.

Galaxy, Akadimias 22 (tel. 363 2831/9). 102 rooms. On the fringe of the elegant Kolonaki district.

Lycabette, Valaoritou 6 (tel. 363 3514/8). 39 rooms. Only hotel in the tiny, quiet pedestrian zone off Leoforos Venizelou, with good view from the topfloor rooms with balconies; no restaurant.

Marathon, Karolou 23 (tel. 523 1865/8). 93 rooms. Near Omonia Square.

Minoa, Karolou 12 (tel. 523 4622/4). 42 rooms. Near Omonia Square; no restaurant.

Oscar, Samou 25 (tel. 883 4215/9). 78 rooms. Near railway station; disco, roofgarden.

Pan, Mitropleos 11 (tel. 323 7816/9). 48 rooms. Near Syntagma; no restaurant.

Stanley, Platia Karaiskaki (tel. 524 1611/8). 395 rooms. Near Omonia Square; small roofgarden pool.

Titania, Venizelou 52 (tel. 360 9611/9). 398 rooms. Near Omonia; roofgarden.

Inexpensive

Alkistis, Platia Theatrou 18 (tel. 321 9811/9). 120 rooms. Near Omonia Square; roofgarden restaurant.

Amaryllis, Veranzerou 45 (tel. 523 8738). 57 rooms. Near Omonia.

Aphrodite, Apollonos 21 (tel. 323 4357/9). 84 rooms. Central. Airconditioned; roofgarden.

Aristides, Sokratous 50 (tel. 522 3940). 90 rooms. Near Omonia.

Aristoteles, Aharnon 15 (tel. 522 8126/7). 60 rooms. Restaurant.

Capri, Psaromilingou 6 (tel. 325 2085). 44 rooms. Airconditioned roofgarden restaurant.

Economy, Klisthenous 5 (tel. 522 0520/2). 56 rooms. Airconditioned.

Erechthion, Flammarion 8 (tel. 345 9606). 22 rooms. Near the Acropolis.

Filoxenia, Aharnon 50 (tel. 882 8611/3). 51 rooms. Airconditioned, restaurant.

Iniohos, Veranzerou 26 (tel. 523 0811). 134 rooms. Airconditioned, restaurant.

Kalypso, Epikourou 34 (tel. 325 1451/2). 35 rooms. Airconditioned.

King Jason, Kolonou 26 (tel. 523 4721). 114 rooms. Restaurant.

Museum, Bouboulinas 16 (tel. 360 5611/3). 58 rooms. Near the Archeological Museum.

Omonia, Platia Omonias 4 (tel. 523 7210/20). 260 rooms. Restaurant, bar.

Paradise Hostel, Mezonos 28 (tel. 522 0084). Rooms with 2 to 6 beds. Close to railroad station.

Theoxenia, Gladstonos 6 (tel. 360 0250). 59 rooms. Restaurant.

In Piraeus

Moderate

Cavo d'Oro, Vassileos Pavlou 19 (tel. 411 3742). 74 rooms. On the Kastella headland with a lovely view over the Saronic Gulf, but above a very polluted beach; disco and roofgarden.

Diogenis, Vassileos Georgiou 27 (tel. 412 5471/5). 78 rooms. Disco and small roofgarden pool; near harbor.

Omiridion, Harliaou Trikoupi 32 (tel. 451 9811/5). 59 rooms. Disco and roofgarden; near harbor.

Park, Kolokotroni 103 (tel. 452 4611/5). 80 rooms. Disco and roofgarden; near harbor.

Savoy, Vassileos Konstantinou 93 (tel. 413 1102/8). 71 rooms. Near harbor.

Inexpensive

Anemoni, Karaoli Dimitriou 65 (tel. 411 1768). 45 rooms.

Arion, Vassileos Pavlou 109 (tel. 412 1425). 36 rooms. On the Kastella headland, fine view.

Atlantis, Notara 138 (tel. 452 6871/4). 54 rooms.

Capitol, Filonos 147 (tel. 452 4911/4). 56 rooms.

Cavo, Filonos 79 (tel. 411 6134). 47 rooms. Near harbor.

Diana, Filellinon 11 (tel. 452 5020). 41 rooms.

Lilia, Zeas 131 (tel. 417 9108). 17 rooms. Facing the yacht harbor.

RESTAURANTS. There is plenty to write home about on the subject of Athens restaurants, but rarely anything favorable (seafood restaurants are an honorable, if expensive, exception). Though food here is reasonably tasty, it is never outstanding and *specialités de la maison* are rare.

Outside the deluxe hotels, the international restaurants are grouped around the Hilton Hotel, Syntagma Square or the central Kolonaki quarter. The Plaka district below the Acropolis hill features the largest number of tavernas listed separately below. And on the coast between Piraeus and Vouliagmeni, and on Syngrou Avenue, which connects Athens with the sea, there are a number of seafood restaurants (also listed separately below).

Expensive

Abreuvoir, Xenokratus 51 (tel. 722 9061). One of the most popular French restaurants in Kolonaki; closed Mon.

Act One, Academy 18 (tel. 360 2492). International and Greek cuisine, piano at night; very central.

Angelo's Corner, Athanasiou Diakou 17 (tel. 922 7417). Good choice; opposite Temple of Olympian Zeus; closed Sun.

The Annex, Eginitou 6 (tel. 723 7221). Like most of the international eating spots in Athens, it complements its international fare with some Greek dishes; soft background music, cocktail bar; closed Sun.

Avancé, Xenokratous 43 (tel. 723 0151). Speciality avocados with prawns; piano at night.

Chang's House, Doiranis 15 (tel. 723 3200). Same management as the *China*.

Le Calvados, Alkmanos 5 (tel. 722 6291). Another French effort; closed Sun.

China, Efroniou 72 (tel. 723 3200). Probably the best of several Chinese spots in town.

Al Convento, Anapiron Polemou 4 (tel. 723 9163). Good Italian spot; closed Sun.

Da Walter, adjoining above, same management but more expensive (tel. 724 8726).

Dionyssos, Robertou Galli 43 (tel. 923 3182). Fine view of the Acropolis opposite. Moderate-priced version on Lycabettus.

Escargot, Ventiri 9 (tel. 723 0340). Leading French restaurant, dinner accompanied by piano music.

Fatsios, Efroniou 5 (tel. 721 7421). Good selection of Greek and Middle East specialties; lunch only.

Le Foyer, Antoniros 36 (tel. 724 6287). French and Greek cuisine to musical accompaniment; closed Sun.

Gerofinikas, Pindarou 10 (tel. 362 2719). Slightly pretentious restaurant skillfully hidden; selection of Greek and Turkish specialties.

Grande Bretagne Corner, Grande Bretagne Hotel (tel. 322 8361). Outstanding for atmosphere and service at very reasonable prices; less a part of the hotel than the other restaurants due to its direct entrance from Venizelou.

Je Reviens, Xenokratus 49 (tel. 721 1174). Good French restaurant in Kolonaki, with piano music.

Kyoto, Garibaldi 5 (tel. 923 2047). Reasonable Japanese restaurant, made somewhat incongruous by its Japanese architecture and its location on the Philopappos hill opposite the Acropolis; closed Sun.

Maralinas, Vrassida 11 (tel. 723 5425). Lebanese specialties with an Oriental *plat du jour*.

Michiko, Kidathineon 27 (tel. 322 0980). Unusual but nonetheless pleasantly situated Japanese restaurant in the largest surviving mansion in the Plaka, with small garden; closed Sun.

Papakia, Iridanou 11 (tel. 721 2421). Specialty here (as the name, duckling, indicates) is duck, *aux olives* or *à l'orange*; but there are the usual Greek dishes as well. Pleasant atmosphere in converted old house with small garden, one of the very few left in this area.

Prunier, Ipsilantou 63 (tel. 722 7379). No connection with its famous Parisian namesake, but still fairly French; closed Sun.

Stage Coach, Loukianou 6 (tel. 724 3955). Next to the British Embassy but decidedly American flavor with T-bone steaks in Wild West setting.

Stage Door, Voukourestiou 14 (tel. 361 2801). More select offspring of above; very central.

Steak Room, Eginitou 6 (tel. 721 7445). The best of the steak houses, excellent meat from own supply; charcoal broils and genuine French snails; closed Sun.

Tabula, Pondou 40 (tel. 779 3072). Behind the Riva Hotel, and with a wide choice and well-stocked bar; closed Sun.

Vengera, Aristippou 34 (tel. 724 4327). Good variety and near the funicular; closed Sun.

Moderate

Corfu, Kriezotou 6 (tel. 361 3011). Just off Venizelou; menu varied by some Greek specialties. Excellent quality.

Delfi, Nikis 13 (tel. 323 4869). Good value for the price, and therefore very crowded.

Dionyssos, on top of Lycabettus (tel. 722 6374). Cheaper version of the one opposite the Acropolis. Reached by funicular railway starting on top of Ploutarhou. Commands sweeping view of the whole town. Cafe and snack bar beside restaurant open 9 A.M. to 11.45 P.M.

Flame Steak House, Hatziyanni Mexi 9 (tel. 723 8540). Charcoal broiled steaks and chops; bar.

Ideal, Venizelou 46 (tel. 361 4604). Exceptionally large menu and popular with students from the nearby University.

Jimmy's Cooking, Loukianou 36 (tel. 724 7271). Outstanding for the price.

McMilton's, Adrianou 91 (tel. 324 9129). Very American among the Plaka taverns, with hamburgers and apple pie, but some Greek dishes.

Mike's Saloon, Vassileos Alexandrou 5 (tel. 729 1689). Bar, snacks and full-course meals; closed Sun. evening.

Othello's, Mihalakopoulou 45 (tel. 729 1481). Speciality is prawns with bacon and Beef Stroganoff.

Ploughman, Iridanou 26 (tel. 721 2623). English food; dartboard.

Le Quartier, Kolonaki Sq., (tel. 360 4765). A cafe-restaurant with tables on the square to watch the world go by.

Remezzo, Haritos 6 (tel. 722 8950). Dining area, bar and lounge; nightly from 8.

Syntrivani, Filellinon 5. Offers a good choice of dishes at very reasonable prices in small garden.

Tourist Tavernas. Concentrated in the Plaka, many of these places boast some species of local color, but it is mostly of an obviously artificial kind. They are fairly expensive nightclubs with floor shows but call themselves tavernas nonetheless (and indeed stress their Greekness not only in the nature of their shows but in their very indifferent food). Among the best are:

Dionyssos, Lysiou 7 (tel. 322 7589).

Kalokerinou, Kekropos 10 (tel. 323 2054).

Lito, Tripodon 1 (tel. 322 0388).

Mostrou, Mnisikleous 22 (tel. 322 5558). Also included in the *Athens by Night* tours.

Palia Athena, Flessa 4 (tel. 322 2000). The closest of all to a cabaret, and the most expensive.

Vrahos, Adrianou 101 (tel. 324 7575).

Seafood Restaurants. Though there are hundreds of fish taverns, most of them expensive, along the Attic coasts, in Piraeus they are mostly concentrated on Akti Koumoundourou in the picturesque fishing port of Mikrolímaño below the Yacht Club. For much of the year food is served on the water's edge, especially at lunch time. They can be very crowded on summer evenings, particularly at weekends.

Aglamair, Akti Koumoundourou 54 (tel. 411 5511). The most expensive of the bunch, with the accent on lobsters.

Bouillabaisse, Zisimopoulou 28 (tel. 941 9082). Behind the Planetarium on Syngrou Ave., but any resemblance to the Marseilles original is purely accidental; nonetheless good fresh fish and shell fish.

El Greco, Akti Koumoundourou 24 (tel. 412 7324). Excellent shrimps.

Kaplanis, Akti Koumoundourou 50 (tel. 411 1623). Recommended.

Kranai, Akti Koumoundourou 34 (tel. 417 0156). Also good.

Red Boat, Akti Koumoundourou 18 (tel. 417 5853). One of the oldest and still fairly reasonable.

Zorbas, Akti Koumoundourou 14 (tel. 412 5501). Stuffed mussels.

Tavernas. The more genuinely Greek tavernas the tourist is likely to sample are crowded together in the Plaka. Among such a large number, the choice is necessarily arbitrary. An orchestra of three guitarists is usual; without them the food improves. In winter they are frequented by Greeks, but in the summer the small gardens and tables on the pavements are almost entirely taken over by tourists. If, like the Athenians, you don't mind braving the chaotic traffic, drive to the openair tavernas and night-clubs stretching along the coast from Faliro to Sounio. But you will need a car as the buses in the evening are infrequent and crowded.

Bakaliarakia, Kydathineon 41 (tel. 332 5084). Specializes in cod, as the name indicates, best with garlic mash; in the classical Plaka basement.

Kostoyannis, Zaimi 37 (tel. 822 0624). Best of the lot, standing in splendid isolation behind the Archeological Museum. Excellent selection, from *mezedes* to desserts; closed Sun.

O Platanos, Diogenous 4 (tel. 322 0666). One of the oldest Plaka Tavernas; no music so prices are low for what is offered in the large garden.

Palia Taverna Kritikou, Mnisikleous 24 (tel. 322 2809). Room for tourists to indulge in Greek dances to the amusement of the few Greek customers.

Psarra, Erehtheos 16 (tel. 325 0285). Specialty here is swordfish kebab; customers are invited to play the guitar themselves.

Strefis, Irinis Athineas 5 (tel. 882 0780). Tasty jugged rabbit.

Theophilos, Vakhou 1 (tel. 322 3901). Above average food and good open rosé; closed Sun.

Thespis, Thespidos 18 (tel. 323 8242). Roofgarden with a view of the Acropolis.

Vassilena, Etolikou 72 (tel. 461 2457). The only fish tavern to be highly recommended; in Piraeus (to the right facing the main harbor). You don't order, but are served some 20 seafood *hors d'oeuvres* before soup, chicken and fruit, with unlimited retsina; and all for an astoundingly low price. Perhaps the cheapest meal in town for quality and quantity.

Xynou, Angelou Geronta 4 (tel. 322 1065). Large but fairly quiet and perhaps the best truly Greek taverna in Athens, thus Greek customers all the year round. It's a little difficult to find, but worth asking the way.

Zafiris, Thespidos 4 (tel. 322 5460). *The* place for game (chosen from colorful cards presented by the owner) and unchanged since 1918, and hence deceptively simple. Reservations essential; closed Sun.

Fast Food. The largest concentration is on Leoforos Alexandras: **Jolly Hamburgers, Tammy's Burgers** and **White Spot** at numbers 122, 175 and 152 respectively. Closer to the center are **Fry Up,** Ippokratous 31, and **Goody's,** Solonos 108, behind the University. All open from about 9 A.M. to past midnight.

Psistaria (charcoal grills) abound in the side streets around Omonia Square. No, you won't get a steak—which in any case should only be ordered in top-grade establishments—but try *doner kebab*, a huge hunk of pressed and seasoned meat turning outside on a spit. Also available in grillrooms are chicken, *souvlakia, keftedakia* (usually with salad) and *tiri feta* (goat's cheese) which is tasty but salty. Choose the least dusty of these ephemeral establishments.

A useful standby are the numerous *Galaktopolia* (milk shops), a very distant cousin of the milk bar. They specialize in milk products such as yogurt from sheep's milk, *yaóurti próvio*, or the slightly cheaper *yaóurti agieládas*, which is made from cow's milk and served with or without honey; *rizógallo* (rice pudding), *kréma* (custard), *bougátsa* (Semolina) as well as other oriental sweets. They also offer plain *bóutyro mé méli* (butter with honey) and sometimes *avgá tiganitá*. Quality and price in these places are almost identical.

American Coffee Shop, Karageorgi Servias 1. Among the better snack bars around Syntagma Square; the others mostly seem to charge for the location rather than for what they serve.

Bretannia, Platia Omonias. Fried eggs at sunrise, yogurt with honey in the wee hours.

Eden, Flessa 3, Plaka. Imaginative vegetarian dishes in old house with rooftop garden.

Kostas Souvlaki Shop, Platia Lyssikratous, Plaka. Best souvlakia in the district.

Seven, Filellinon 7. Off Syntagma Square and reasonably good value.

YWCA (HEN), Amerikis 11. Canteen food.

Cafes, Sweetshops. Though still the social center of remoter villages, the traditional *kafenío,* in which a goodly proportion of the male population spent hours over tiny cups of Turkish (now Greek) coffee, playing backgammon or more often just lounging about, has vanished from the towns. Its place has been taken by western-style cafes or *zaharoplastia* (sweetshops), which, wherever possible, extend over the sidewalk or take up entire squares. Athenians keep late hours, sitting over ices and rich cream cakes summer and winter alike. Most cafes and sweetshops fall into the Moderate price range.

Syntagma Square and Kolonaki Square are lined with cafes and sweetshops, the two big names being **Floka's** and **Zonar's,** both with (E) restaurants, at Venizelou 9, the former with branches in Athens and Thessaloniki, the latter assuming the appelation **Dionyssos** in the two restaurants and the cafe on Syntagma. Next to the latter, serving snacks, beer and aperitifs from quite early in the morning to 2 A.M., is **Papaspyrou,** in front of the American Express office on Syntagma Square. Popular from breakfast to late supper is the Hilton's **Byzantine Cafe.** The outdoor **Mousio,** in front of the Archeological Museum, operates only in the warm season with a pre-war vintage orchestra at night. **Möven Pick,** Akadimias 28, and **Everyday,** Stadiou 4, are conveniently central.

Ouzerí. These drinking establishments, named after the national aperitif, are the only genuine local bars, but there are very few anywhere in the country as drinking is nearly always accompanied by a meal (which helps account for the remarkably small number of drunks).

Apotsos, Venizelou 10 (tel. 363 7046). The capital's oldest and most original *ouzeri,* with amusing old posters, and a favorite of resident Anglo Saxons. Wide selection of ouzo from all over Greece accompanied by appropriate mezedes.

Asteria, Kratinou 7, off Kotzia Square (tel. 321 6727). A colorful small establishment frequented by the neighborhood wholesalers; also offers a wide variety of mezedes.

Athinaikon, Santaroza 8, off Venizelou (tel. 322 0118). A regular with judges and lawyers; mezedes includes seafood.

Orfanides, Venizelou 7 (tel. 323 0184). In the same block as the *Grande Bretagne Hotel*; pavement tables.

Bars and Pubs. These are newcomers on the Athens scene, mostly catering to foreigners, or Greeks who would like to be mistaken as such. Though some feature dartboards and other Anglo-American paraphernalia, these self-proclaimed pubs could also be classified as piano-bars, discos, snackbars or just plain restaurants, at least in parts. Pub-crawling bar-hopping presents no problems, given the geography of the main concentrations, which are around the Hilton and Kolonaki.

Athenian Inn, Haritos 22 (tel. 723 8097). The quiet, Tudor-style bar of this unassuming little hotel; downstairs, foreign jazz groups perform nightly after 9.

Dewar's Club, Dexameni Square (tel. 721 5412). Candle-lit bistro with a spacious bar.

Entre Nous, Alopekis 9 (tel. 729 1669). Piano bar.

Fame Club, Levendi 3 (tel. 723 0507). Drinks and snacks.

Montparnasse, Harites 32 (tel. 729 0746). Three-level bar restaurant favored by the theatre crowd.

Prince of Wales, Sinopis 14 (tel. 777 8008). Doubles as a steak house, with soft music and soft lights; business dinners and lunches.

Star, Holiday Inn, Mihalakopoulou 50 (tel. 724 8322). American-style bar.

NIGHTLIFE. To conserve energy, 2 A.M. closing in all nightspots has been decreed, though it is not always observed, especially in summer when the scene moves to the coast. Classification of the various establishments is not easy as several nightclubs double their dance orchestras with bouzoukia orchestras, or alternatively might suddenly restrict themselves to one of the two, or even convert themselves to discos or cabarets. Staying power and consistency of individual spots must, therefore, be a decisive factor in the determination of our listings.

Cabarets. Unlike the Tourist Tavernas in the Plaka, the main accent, in Athens cabaret spots, is on the international as opposed to the local. They are all expensive, though fairly cheap in every other respect by western standards. All are in the center.

Among them are:

Copacabana, Kallirois 4, opposite the Temple of Olympian Zeus (tel. 923 2648). Striptease, among the other pleasures offered.

Coronet, Venizelou 4 (tel. 361 7397). Has one of the better programs at the moment, but might at any time revert to a disco-restaurant.

Maxim, Othonos 6, Syntagma (tel. 323 4831). More striptease.

Bouzoukia. Greece's contribution to nightlife was introduced in the 1920s by refugees from Asia Minor, who danced to a large clanging Oriental version of the mandoline in numerous humble taverns in the suburbs, especially in the Piraeus area. In the '50s, the wailing airs of this popular music were taken up by the Athenian smart set as the true expression of Greek entertainment, displaying a fine disregard of its obvious Anatolian and Balkan influences. It thus became established as the genuine local noise; tourists should have one go, few will desire a second. Food in the *bouzoukia* is sinfully expensive for what is offered, and if you have fruit only you don't get away with paying any less. In the larger *bouzoukia*, orchestras often feature a female vocalist generously amplified by loud-speakers.

Unlike the tourist tavernas, the dances are not performed by professionals but by the customers. The nostalgic *zeimbékiko* is a solo dance for men, with the dancer bending down to run his hand piously across the ground. Likewise dealing with exile, the faithlessness of women, death and similar popular themes, the *hassápiko*, the butcher's dance, originated in Constantinople. It is performed by two or three people, and increasingly by women these days—hissing and snapping their fingers to a rhythm clearly marked by footbeats. The steps are precise and intricate, with graceful bending and stretching of the knees. The only joyful tunes and refrains are those that accompany the *sérviko*, which, as its name declares, is of Serbian antecedence, quick, lively, almost acrobatic. The *tsiftetéli* is a debased oriental belly dance performed by men. Because of the noise and shouting, several of the most popular are along the motorway, out of reach for the average tourist. Closest to the center are:

Lido, Zoodohou Pigis 3 (tel. 362 3933).

Monseigneur, Mithimnis 41 (tel. 865 3216). The most fashionable, largest and loudest are on Leoforos Syngrou:

Athina, 165 (tel. 934 3485).

Diogenes, 255 (tel. 942 4267). Currently tops and thus the most expensive.

Regina, 40 (tel. 922 8902). The cheapest. Closed Sunday. More are scattered along Leoforos Posidonos, the coastal road of Neo Faliro.

Athinia, 63 (tel. 942 3089). Highly prized and priced.

Hryse Vareli, 33 (tel. 942 2858). Closed Thursday.

La Cité, 65 (tel. 942 3028). Closed Thursday.

Sou-Mou, Iera Odos 160 (tel. 346 7687).

Boites. Out of fashion since the closing of numerous low-ceilinged, dark, smoky and rather claustrophobic nightspots in the Plaka. Some folk and revolutionary songs are still strummed out, mainly in the Exarhia district; the one common feature is the high mortality rate (strangely enough not among the revellers, though boredom must take its toll). The (M) admission price includes one drink.

Ah Maria, Solomou 20 (tel. 363 9217). Closed Monday.

Klotho, Ippokratous 56 (tel. 360 5790). No cultural claptrap.

Snob, Anapiron Polemou 10, Kolonaki (tel. 721 492 9). Closed Tuesday.

Discos. Very much "in." They are divided here, but not very strictly, into **disco restaurants** (E) and plain **discos** (M), with cold plates and drinks. It's difficult to say which come and go more rapidly. Among the disco restaurants:

Athens Athens, Leoforos Syngrou 253 (tel. 942 5601). Half way to the sea; upstairs bar overlooking the dance floor and pop art decor; prides itself on being particularly American; airconditioned, closed Tues.

Athinea, Venizelou 6 (tel. 362 0777). Conveniently central; continues long tradition at present with dinner dances and cabaret, but might easily resume its earlier disco incarnation; closed Sun.

Barbarella, Leoforos Syngrou 253 (tel. 942 5602). Three dance floors. Barbarella girls.

9 + 9, (Ennea Syn Ennea), Platia Stadiou 5 (tel. 722 2258). Right next to the Stadium, so grand that it doesn't even advertise its name as everyone is supposed to know and, judging by the attendance, does; good restaurant; closed July–August.

Papagayo, Patriarhou Ioakim 37, Kolonaki (tel. 724 0736). Dining on ground floor, dancing in basement.

Among the discos:

A.B.C., Patission 177 (tel. 861 7922).

Atheneum, Mihalakopoulou 39 (tel. 724 1418).

Bla-Bla, Athens Tower, Sinopis 6 (tel. 778 9092). New Wave.

Disco 14, Kolonaki Square 14 (tel. 724 5938). For the younger generation.

Make Up, Venizelou 10 (tel. 364 2160). Most central.

Beware of the several "Nightclub open all day" clubs in Nikis, off Syntagma Square. These clip joints do indeed open before midday, but they are not subject to any price controls. But if the hostesses that loom there and, with even less inhibition though also less expensively, in some bars around Omonia Square, should leave any doubts as to their hospitable intentions, these doubts vanish in the cabarets (using the term very loosely, that is) in those clubs near the main port in Piraeus, where neither prices nor holds are barred.

MUSEUMS

For details of opening times, see Museums in *Facts at Your Fingertips* (page 29).

Acropolis Museum, (tel. 323 6665). Full of rare objects of Attic art found on the Acropolis. Its showpiece is the unrivaled collection of archaic statues of women of the 6th century B.C., notable for the delicacy and intricacy of their head-dress, their enigmatic expressions and faintly mocking smiles. These young women, known as *korai*, are strangely impersonal, though they most likely represent priestesses. Here also are the Caryatids, who had to carry the Erechtheion too long; acid rain had reduced them to leprous anonymity before they were lodged in a special room. Noteworthy are the sculptures of a bull devoured by a lion, the struggle of Heracles against the Triton (a monster with three bodies), the famous statue of a man carrying a calf across his shoulders, and the bas-relief of Athena leaning on her lance.

Archeological Museum of Piraeus, Harilaou Trikoupi. 31 (tel. 452 1598). Exhibits of local finds mainly, but also has a fine Hermes from Kifissia.

Benaki Museum, Koumbari 1 (tel. 361 1617). Well-arranged and interesting museum, containing a hotch-potch of objects from different countries and periods, acquired largely from private collections. There are Byzantine icons and a rare collection of Byzantine jewelry as well as Ottoman ceramics, Coptic textiles and, above all and not to be missed, a stunning collection of genuine Greek national costumes, remarkable for their color, variety and opulence.

Byzantine and Christian Museum, Vassilissis Sofias 22 (tel. 721 1027). Housed in the attractive 19th-century town residence of the Duchesse de Plaisance, who lived in Athens during the reign of King Otho. A visit to this museum gives one an idea of what to expect at the principal Byzantine sites outside Athens; Daphni, Ossios Loukas and Mystras. There are exhibits of early Byzantine decorative sculpture and a large collection of icons. The most beautiful single exhibit is the famous Epitaphios of Thessaloniki, a masterpiece of 14th-century Byzantine embroidery in gold, silver, yellow and green. It represents the body of Christ laid out on a bier.

Center for Folk Art and Traditions, Iperidou 18, Plaka (tel. 324 3987). What its name implies. Open 9–1, 5–8; closed Sun. afternoon and Mon. Admission free.

Epigraphical Museum, (tel. 821 7637). Attached to the Archeological Museum; an extensive collection of valuable historical inscriptions (of interest mainly to scholars).

Goulandris Natural History Museum, Levidou 13, Kifisia (tel. 801 5870). Combines botanical, zoological and palaeontological exhibits.

Historical and Ethnological Museum, in the Old Parliament, Stadiou (tel. 323 7617). Items from 1453 to World War II, with main emphasis on the Greek War of Independence.

Jewish Museum, Melidoni 5 (tel. 325 2823). Art and artifacts from local Jewish communities. Closed Tues. and Sat.

Kanellopoulos Museum, corner of Theorias and Panos (tel. 321 2313). In the Plaka, a private collection of pre-Christian and later exhibits, including some remarkable Tanagra figurines and Byzantine icons and jewelry.

Keramikos Museum, Ermou 148 (tel. 346 3552). Finds from the ancient cemetery.

Museum of Greek Popular Art, Kydathineon 17 (tel. 321 3018). Contains 6,000 examples of traditional folk art, a collection of pottery from Rhodes, clerical robes, costumes and embroideries. Admission free.

Museum of the City of Athens, Paparigopoulou 7 (tel. 324 6164). King Otho's first Athenian residence; still has most of the original furniture and a number of interesting contemporary prints. Admission free; Mon., Wed., Fri. 9 to 1.30 only.

National Archeological Museum, Tossitsa 1, off 28 Oktovriou (tel. 821 7717). By far the most important museum in Athens. The well-arranged exhibits illustrate every period of ancient Greek civilization, complemented by an interesting Byzantine collection. New finds are constantly added, though on occasion they remain only till the construction of a local museum.

But by far the most sensational finds are those made by Schliemann in the course of his excavations of the royal tombs on the Homeric site of Mycenae in the 1870s. This treasure-trove has thrown a new light on the hitherto unsuspected standard of artistic refinement achieved in the pre-historic Bronze Age. There are priceless gold vessels, exquisitely designed gold dishes, gold balances and masks of gold which covered the faces of the dead. Many of the gold ornaments are based on maritime subjects, such as shellfish and seaweed, and the bases are beautifully shaped and ornamented. Further treasures found in another series of royal tombs, including gold cups, diadems and a delightful crystal bowl with a handle shaped like a duck's head are also on display, as are the superb 15th-century B.C. frescos unearthed in 1972–3 on the island of Thira.

Other exhibits of later periods, particularly the classical period, which should not be missed, include the enormous head of a *kouros* (young man) found in the Keramikos; a 5th-century tombstone depicting a young man followed by his servitor; the famous Eleusinian bas-relief of Demeter, goddess of plenty, handing the first ear of corn to the youthful Triptolemus, the inventor of the plough; and the tombstone of a young hunter, his father at his side and his little servant at his feet. The latter is believed to be the work of Scopas.

The most famous individual statues are: Kalamis' majestic bronze Poseidon about to throw a trident (surely one of the greatest statues in the world), a colossal archaic Apollo, a lovely marble head of the goddess Hygenia, also attributed to Scopas, and the bronze jockey boy (a masterpiece of movement). These, and other magnificent bronze statues, were, for the most part, found in the sea off the coasts and islands of Greece. The museum also contains numerous painted vases and the delightful little statuettes from Tanagra.

National Picture Gallery, Vassileos Konstantinou 50 (tel. 721 1010). Contains some works by El Greco, but the bulk of the collection is of 19th-century Greek pictures. Admission free.

Numismatic Museum, same building as the National Archeological Museum (tel. 821 7769). Contains 250,000 ancient Greek, Hellenistic, Roman and Byzantine coins. The most interesting and unique are those from the Ptolemaic period.

Piraeus Maritime Museum, Akti Themistokleous (tel. 451 6822). Model ships from ancient to modern times and naval memorabilia. Admission free Tues. and Fri.; closed August.

Stoa of Attalos Museum, (tel. 321 0185). At the ancient Agora; displays the excavation finds of the American School of Classical Studies.

War Museum, Vassilissis Sofias 24 (tel. 723 9560). Weapons, flags and uniforms; admission free.

 SHOPPING. Though the *National Organization of Greek Handicrafts*, the leading jewelers and top boutiques have branches in the main tourist centers, while souvenir shops are all-too-prevalent wherever a tourist might venture, Athens still overshadows the rest of the country for a serious shopping spree. We start, therefore, with an indication of where to look for what in the capital. This is no great problem, as the two main shopping streets branch off central Syntagma Square.

Stadíou is the more elegant street, ending in bigger, though not necessarily better, stores near Omónia Square; some shops are also located in parallel Venizélou Ave., beyond which innumerable boutiques crowd up the slopes of Mount Lycabettus, especially in that part of Voukourestiou which in 1979 became a pedestrian zone, to chic Platía Filikís Etairías (Kolonaki Square).

More popular Ermóu runs west to Monastiráki Square, where, despite all price labeling and other modern business procedures, a lot of purchasing is based on bargaining. It is difficult to explain where bargaining is in place, but roughly, the further you proceed from Syntagma Square, the more you come into bargaining areas. The heart of haggledom is Monastiráki Square and its vicinity. Food and commercial products, imported as well as local, are usually dealt with by the fixed-price system; antiques, second-hand objects and handicrafts by the bargaining system. It must be left very much to the individual's flair to know where he can play the pleasurable game of bargaining, so as to acquire some handsome object at a reasonable price.

Antiquities and Handicrafts. Antiques and local handicrafts are the items that are special to Greece and you can buy them at a commensurate price. Antique dealers are concentrated in the Monastiráki area, with the top echelon in Pandróssou, running parallel to lower Ermóu.

Remember that antiquities are governed by special laws. Customs officers will prevent you from taking out of Greece any object from the Greco-Roman and Byzantine period, but will, instead, take you to jail, unless you have a written permission from the Greek Ministry of Culture. Any antique dealer will tell you how to obtain one.

The shopkeepers usually know some English, but their willingness to bargain stands in inverse ratio to their knowledge. If, however, you are not an expert, or accompanied by one, you may easily be buying a fake at too high a price. Admittedly this is a real problem, but considering that a permanent flow of genuine old pottery and ancient coins finds its way into Pandróssou, falsification, in many instances, would just not pay.

Articles belonging from all periods can be found in the many antique shops in Pandróssou, among them: *Martinos* (no. 50), the most reliable and expensive, with the biggest choice; *Adam's* (no. 40); *Zarakovitis* (no. 49); *Vitalis* (no. 75). Equally interesting are *Antika,* Amalias Ave. 4 and in the Kolonaki district, *Haritakis Antiques,* Valaoritou 7; *Rodi,* Iraklitou 17; *Vasiliadis,* Voukourestiou 36; *Zoumboulakis,* Kriezotou 7 and Kolonaki Square 20.

On the shadier side (no mean achievement) of Monastiráki Square, next to the underground train station, is Ifestou (Hephaestos Street). The name is most fitting, for here are the picturesque workshops of many copper- and blacksmiths, interspersed with some of the more dubious antique shops.

The Athens Flea Market functions only on Sunday mornings. All along Ifestou you can get anything from a used toothbrush to broken auto spare parts and from old pants to an obsolete dentist's chair. Shops are closed, but the sellers spread out all their wares on the ground and an occasional villager will sell an ancient copper jug, or a nicely-worked ring, a rug, or some other object of local handicraft.

If you have not the time and occasion to travel all over the country, a representative selection of this type of work can be found in Athens itself. The widest variety can be found in the *Arts and Crafts* shops of the National Welfare Organization, Karageorgi Servias 8, Voukourestiou 24 and the Hilton. Equally rewarding is a visit to the *Greek Lyceum,* Dimokritou 17, *Hellenic Artisan Trades Cooperative,* Amalias Ave. 56, and the show-rooms of the *Y.W.C.A.,* Amerikis 11, Kifissias Ave. 299.

Laces and embroidery are featured by the *Greek Women's Institution,* Voukourestíou 13; china may be bought at *Kerameikos,* no. 19; *Pandora* and *Mati* are opposite at nos. 12 and 20. The *National Organization of*

Greek Handicrafts displays miscellaneous products, but only sells carpets and rugs on several floors at Mitropoleos 9.

You might also try the *Plaka Art House*, Lysiou 10, an old Athenian house arranged as a curiosity shop; and *Miki*, Anagnostopoulou 16. *Flokati* and *Kokkinos,* both Mitropoleos 3, specialize in traditional rugs. Pottery is on striking display in numerous shops along Kifissías Avenue, in the suburb of Paradissou-Amaroussion.

Objects of Greek craftsmanship will also be found in many tourist shops. They should, however, be strictly distinguished from the products of the souvenir industry which, despite any merits they may or may not have, are certainly not representative of Greek handicraft, especially not the very fancy "national costumes" no Greek woman has ever been seen in, nor is likely to. These tourist shops, often just called that, crowd the streets off Syntagma Square, especially Stadiou: *Knossos,* one of several at no. 4 (also in the passage), *Greek Arts* at 7, *Diakosmitiki* at 8, *Kalokerinou* at 3, and more in the passage leading to *Kambouropoulos* in Karageorgi Servias 4 and *Delphi* at 7; *Parthenon,* Nikis 2; *Greek Arts,* Venizelou Ave. 6; *Kalokairinos,* Venizelou Ave. 3a and Voukourestíou 8; *Athens Design Center,* 4 Valaoritou.

In the passage off Valaoritou St. is a gallery of modern Greek art, *Nées Morphes,* with paintings, ceramics, sculpture and other signed items by leading contemporary artists.

The famous fur coats from Kastoria consist of every imaginable kind of fur scraps, including mink, sent to that picturesque old town in Macedonia from all over the world. They are pieced and put together by workers with a skill acquired through a centuries-old tradition and made up into rolls like woven textiles and eventually into somewhat heavy coats. Still, this is a chance to buy a fur coat at a price lower-income brackets can afford. Naturally, you can also get coats made of whole skins.

The most important furriers in Athens are: *Sistovaris,* Nikis 4, Voulis St. 14, and Venizelou Ave. 9 and at the Hilton; *Mary's Furs* and *Fur House,* Filellinon 4 and 7; *Arnocouros, Voula Mitsakou* and *D. Naoum,* Mitropoleos 3, 7 and 27; several more at no. 12; *Canada Furs* and *Papathoma Bros.,* Karagéorgi Servías 1 and 7.

Street Corner Kiosks. The little *períptero* (kiosks) at street corners are open from morning to night. In addition to cigarettes, matches, periodicals and newspapers from all over the world, you will be able to buy aspirins, batteries, shoe laces and almost anything you might urgently need.

Should you need something more complicated than an aspirin, try one of the following chemists' shops, at all of which English is spoken: *Pitsinos,* Mitropoleos 14; *Bakakos,* Omonia Square; *Marinopoulos,* corner of Patission and Venizelou Ave. and at Kanaris 23; *Vyzas,* Kanaris 10c (Kolonaki); *Damvergis,* Venizelou Ave. 39.

Discs and Books. For records of Greek music, *bouzoukia* and others, visit *Orphanides,* Kolokotroni Square and Korai 2: *Discophile,* Voukourestiou 17; *Ikaros,* Voulis 4; *Music Box,* Nikis 2; *Neodisk,* Stadiou 23 and Venizelou Ave. 25.

A great many books on all aspects of ancient and modern Greece have been published in several languages. You will find the greatest selection, but also modern novels, at *Eleftheroudakis*, Nikis 4, *Pantelides*, Amerikis 9 (passage) and 11, *American* at no. 21 and *Kaufmann*, Stadiou 28 and Voukourestiou 11.

Helpful Hints. The National Tourist Organization card pasted on some shop windows indicates membership of the Foreign Visitors Service organization and affords a certain guarantee as to quality and price.

But what is the good of knowing all about shopping in Athens if you find the shops closed? Opening hours are very intricate indeed: from June 1 to September 30 shops are open from 8.30 A.M. to 1.30 P.M., and from 5 to 8 P.M. on Tuesdays, Thursdays and Fridays, opening and closing half an hour earlier in the afternoons the remainder of the year. Most shops open from 8 A.M. to 2.30 P.M. only, on Mondays, Wednesdays and Saturdays. Food stores, barbers, hairdressers and beauty parlors close later, open Saturday afternoon with variations between 4 and 10 P.M., but remain shut on Friday afternoons. Better check, as these times are liable to alteration.

Major hotels are entitled to change money. Some U.K. and U.S. banks have branches near Syntagma Square, but only some Greek banks in the same area stay open on Saturdays, Sunday mornings and holidays to exchange money and travelers' checks.

SPORTS. Swimming. The west and east coasts of Attica are fringed with beaches and coves, with pine trees often stretching down to the water's edge. Nearer to Athens on the southeast coast are the popular GNTO (Greek National Tourist Office) beaches at Voula, Vouliagmeni and Varkiza (rather exclusive). All are well under an hour's drive from Athens. However, they become very crowded on Sundays. Vouliagmeni in particular is an enchanting spot, with a deeply indented shore, red cliffs, pine trees, a freshwater lake with mineral baths and, apart from the GNTO beach, another more exclusive one (the Astir beach), which, like the other Astir beach at Glifada (a little nearer to Athens) is well provided with bars, restaurants and sports facilities.

Closer still to Athens is another GNTO beach at Alimos, near the Agios Kosmas Athletic Club, which provides swimming and diving instruction, but is badly polluted and cannot be recommended. Another diving school operates at Vouliagmeni.

There are windsurfing and water skiing centers at Vouliagmeni and three sailing clubs at Mikrolimano in Piraeus.

Tennis. There are tennis courts at all the GNTO beaches, as well as at the Glyfada Athletic Club and the Agios Kosmas Athletic Club. There is also a tennis club (the Athens Tennis Club) at Vassilissis Olgas 2.

Riding. There are riding clubs at Paradissou 18, Maroussi, and Gerakas, Agia Paraskevi. Both some miles outside Athens. There are horse races at the Faliro Race Course every Wednesday and Saturday.

Golf. There is an 18-hole golf course at Glyfada, near the airport.

Winter Sports. While Greece is hardly renowned for its winter sports, there is nonetheless skiing to be had on Mount Parnís, little more than an hour's drive from the capital. However, it is limited to January and February, and then only if the weather is cold enough.

 USEFUL ADDRESSES. Consulates. *Australia*, Messogion 15 (tel. 360 4611/5); *Canadian*, Ioannou Gennadiou 4 (tel. 723 9511); *Great Britain*, Ploutarhou 1 (tel. 723 6211); *Ireland,* Vassileos Konstantinou 7 (tel. 723 2771); *United States,* Vassilissis Sofias 91 (tel. 721 8561).

Tourist Services. *American Express*, Syntagma Square and at the Hilton; *Wagon Lits/Cooks*, Karageorgi Servias 2; *Automobile & Touring Club of Greece*, Tower of Athens Mesogeion 2 (tel. 779 1615); road assistance, tel. 104; tourist guidance 174.

The terminals of all the major airlines are on or near Syntagma Square, as is the ticket office of *Olympic Airways* (tel. 929 2555), the Greek national airline. Their terminal, however, is at Syngrou Avenue 96.

Tourist Information Office, Karageorgi Servias 2 (tel. 322 2545); at Elleniko airport (tel. 979 9500); at Piraeus, Vassilissis Sofias 105 (tel. 412 1400). *Tourist Police,* tel. 171.

Car Hire. *Hertz,* Syngrou Avenue 12, and Vassilissis Sofias 71; *Avis,* Amalias Avenue 48; *Hellas Cars,* Stadiou 7.

Emergencies. City Police, tel. 100; Suburban Police, tel. 109; First aid Center, tel. 166.

Churches. St. Paul's Anglican Church is at Filellinon 29; St. Andrew's (Interdenominational) Church at Sina 66. The Roman Catholic Cathedral of St. Denis is at 24 Venizelou Ave. There is a Synagogue at Meldoni 6.

ATTICA

Industry, Antiquity and Beaches

The history of Attikí (Attica) is the history of Athens: a mountainous country, bounded on three sides by sea and an indented coastline fringed with beaches. On the stony foothills the soil is so poor that only a few pungently aromatic shrubs grow: thyme, myrtle and lentisk. Higher up, the feathery pine of Attica is supplanted by dark fir trees. The plains yield little but the olive and the grape. But the immemorial beehives of Ymitós (Hymettus) still produce a clear highly-scented honey; and from the quarries of Mt. Penteli there has never ceased to be extracted a special quality of marble that weathers to a warm golden tint. The remoter parts are still blessed with the purest of lights, sharply delineating the exquisite configuration of mountains, sea and plain, though not the capital, round which most of the Greek industry is concentrated. If anything was ever truly classical, it is the landscape of Attica.

Exploring Attica

The bare undulating foothills of Hymettus, the closest to the capital of the mountains ringed round Athens, are dotted with Byzantine shrines. Four miles east of Athens, beyond the working-class suburb of Kessarianí (Kaisariani), is the charming monastery of Kaisariani, built on a sanctuary of Aphrodite, and partly restored on the tree-planted slope of the mountain. The spring, shaded by a large plane tree, is reputed to have retained its remarkable powers of fertility, despite the change of religion.

The church, parts of which date from the 11th century, is in the best Byzantine style of architecture, and some of the decorative work indicates a harmonious blending of different classical styles. The frescos date from the 16th and 17th centuries. Worth noting are those of the Virgin seated between the Archangels in the apse, and the portraits of the Apostles on the north wall of the narthex. The monastery, with its shady trees and spring, is a favorite haunt of holiday-makers on Sundays.

From Kaisariani the road winds up to the airforce installations on the bleak summit of Hymettus, from which there is an incomparable view of the whole of Attica, the Saronic Gulf, southern Euboea and some of the Cyclades in the east. About half way between the monastery of Kaisariani and the saddle of Hymettus, the Byzantine chapel of Asteri may be seen from the road.

Along the lower foothills, covered with bushes of thyme and origan—in early spring they are carpeted with delicate pink, white and mauve anemones—one can easily spot the church of St. John the Theologian, and, on a ridge farther north, that of St. John the Hunter. The urban periphery has crept ominously close to this rolling, shrub-scented heathland, under the shadow of violet Hymettus.

The Monastery of Dafní (Daphni)

The main exit from Athens to the west and the Peloponnese is by Leoforos Athinas, a broad highway running roughly parallel to the ancient Sacred Way from Athens to Elefsína (Eleusis). After mounting the rocky slopes of Mt. Egáleo, the road enters a wide pass, long barred by the Emperor Justinian's fortified monastery of Daphni, enclosed within tall battlemented walls.

In turn sacked by Crusaders, reconsecrated by Cistercian monks and desecrated by Turks, Daphni remains one of the most splendid Byzantine monuments in Greece. Dating from the 11th century, the Golden Age of Byzantine art, the church contains a series of mosaics without parallel in the legacy of Byzantium: portraits of austere prophets, venerable saints and ephebe-like archangels, as well as compositions of scenes from the life of Christ, colored in the loveliest of pinks, greens and blues against gold backgrounds. In the dome lowers the great Christ Pantocrator: a formidable Messiah, with eyes that transfix and with the power to inspire terror. Note the long index finger crooked over the jeweled Book of Judgment; and the thin-lipped almost predatory mouth turning down at the sides. This is a Christ of Nemesis; all the austerity of Byzantium, the death-fixation of Greek folk songs, the savage dirge-like measures of Greek popular music, are represented in this astonishing portrait. The last Acciajuoli Duke strangled his usurping aunt before the altar, which led Sultan Mohammed II to occupy Athens, murder the Duke and drive out the Cistercians. The ducal sarcophagi with their fleurs-de-lis and Latin crosses still stand in the Gothic cloister.

Close to the monastery, a wine festival is held every summer. The produce of all the winegrowers in the country is displayed; the stalls are designed by well-known Athenian painters, and wine, of which one may drink unlimited quantities for the price of a modest entrance fee, is served by girls in national costume.

The Shores of the Saronikós

From Daphni, the road descends towards the Bay of Eleusis, where many laid-up ships reflect the world recession. Beyond is the island of Salamis, and in the narrow straits to the left occurred the momentous sea battle in 480 B.C. which decided the fate of Europe. To the right, the road runs between the sea and the dammed up salt springs of Rheiti, sacred to Demeter, and across the Thriasian plain, where, according to legend, corn was grown for the first time. At the end of the plain lies Eleusis, now a center of heavy industry and thus the least attractive of Greece's ancient sites. Hemmed in by factories are the marble blocks of the Great Propylaea, a gift of Antoninus Pius, one of the eight Roman emperors to be initiated; the foundations of a temple of Demeter, once the largest in Greece; and of the Telesterium, the great Hall of the Mysteries, where the most famous of all ancient religious rites was celebrated annually. What actually occurred is shrouded in mystery (the initiates were bound by a strict oath of secrecy), but it is fairly certain that the story of Demeter, the goddess of fertility, and of Persephone, the offspring of her incestuous relationship with her brother Zeus, was reproduced. The performance of the Mysteries was accompanied by orgiastic dances, the singing of obscene songs on the fertility theme, (no doubt to relieve emotional tension) and spectacular torchlight processions which proceeded from the Hall of the Mysteries to the temples of Demeter and Persephone.

The toll motorway by-passes Eleusis. The branch to the right just beyond the town is the old road to Thebes and Delphi, while the highway links up with the Thessaloniki-Athens motorway and continues along the coast of the Saronikos (Saronic Gulf), scarred by shipyards and refineries, parallel to the island of Salamis, towards Corinth and the Peloponnese.

After by-passing Megara—a quiet country town—Salamis and a group of islets seemingly floating on the sea and guarding the western entrance to the narrow bay, are lost to sight. The scenery becomes more spectacular and the Scironian Rocks, once the lair of Sciron, a mythological bandit who used to compel travelers to halt and wash his feet on the brink of the precipice, rise sheer out of the aquamarine-colored sea. While his unfortunate victims were obeying his orders, he would kick them over into the depths below, where a gigantic turtle lurked in readiness to devour them. Theseus alone, on his way from Trizína (Troezene) to Athens defied Sciron and hurled him into the sea, where he too was swallowed up in the maw of the omnivorous turtle. The descent from the Scironian Rocks leads to a wooded coastal belt with a strand of fine shingle several miles long, fringed with pines. The whole of this shore, known as Kinetta, is dotted with roadhouses and taverns, and is a favorite resort of campers and picnickers. The sea, owing to a number of cross-currents, is always cool, with a sparkling quality, even on the hottest day of August.

Beyond the by-passed village of Agii Theodori extends the isthmus of Corinth, a bleak and windswept stretch of land. Here Theseus slew that other dreaded scourge, Sinis the pine-bender, whose favorite pastime was to bend the top of two pine trees until they met, tie the arms of innocent travelers to each and then loosen his hold, thus causing the victims to be ripped asunder as the trees were released. Before reaching the bridge that spans the canal, a branch road leads to the spa of Loutraki—a string of hotels and thermal stations.

Eight miles west Perahóra was destroyed in the devastating earthquake of February 1981, which hit Corinth, Kiato, Megara and Thebes. Beyond the pine-fringed inlet, the tip of a rocky headland divides the Gulf of Corinth from the sweep of the Halcyonic Gulf. Little remains of the buildings of the archaic Sanctuary of Hera, the Iréo, except foundations. But there is a feeling of magnificent isolation, with the snowcapped peaks of Zíria towering above the wooded Achaian coast and the waters of the inland sea lit at night by the beams of the lighthouse above the Sacred Harbor. Near Hera's shrine stood the sanctuary in memory of the children of Medea, whom the Colchian sorceress slaughtered with her own hands in order to spite their faithless father, Jason.

Returning along the enchanting lagoon-like inlet, where restaurants and taverns serve equally indifferent food, continue up through the village of Perahóra to Píssia. From there it is four miles through an idyllic pine forest down to the deep Halcyonic Gulf and two lovely, lonely beaches, which amply compensate for the rough drive. The taverns at the Ágios Sotíris beach have good fresh fish. This excursion is far off the beaten tourist track, and offers moreover some particularly fine scenery.

Cape Sounio

Another excursion along the shores of the Saronikos Gulf is in the opposite direction, south-east of Athens. From the extreme tip of the Piraeus promontory, a coastal road runs parallel to the ancient Long Walls of Themistocles and winds round the headland of Kastella, above the little harbor of Mikrolimano, crowded with fish restaurants and sailing craft. It then skirts the fill-in on the shores of the wide Bay of Fáliro, past the Palais de Sport opened in 1984 in New Fáliro, the blocks of flats of Old Fáliro, the British and Commonwealth War Cemetery and the Ellinikó airport to Glyfáda, with its 18-hole, 150-acre golf course, the smart Asteria beach and nightclub.

Beyond Glyfáda, where the foothills of Hymettus descend gently to the sea, the road passes the pine-clad promontories of Kavouri and Vouliagmeni, with their villas, beaches and red rocks, the grey cliffs enclosing the warm mineral waters of Lake Vouliagmeni, until it reaches a long strand of white sand at Alianthos, behind which lie the rolling vineyards of the Messógia. A corniche winds in and out of rush-bordered coves and strips of sand and shingle, fringed with islets shimmering in the sun-dazzled sea. Beyond the sweep of the bay of Anavyssos rises the rocky promontory of Sounio, the southernmost tip of Attica. A 5th-century B.C. temple of Poseidon, of which twelve Doric columns remain erect, crowns the cliff rising perpendicularly from the sea. The circuit of ancient walls can still be traced and on one of the slender columns, whose gleaming whiteness stands out like a beacon to ships approaching the Saronikos Gulf, Byron carved his ubiquitous signature. The panorama of sea and islands from this airy platform on Attica's southernmost cape is spectacular. At the foot of the temple is a tourist pavilion, plus a hotel and several taverns on the beach below.

After Sounio the road follows the coast north beneath curiously metallic-colored hills facing Makroníssi (Long Island), where communist rebels were exiled during the Civil War 1946–49. At

Laύrio, a shoddy little town celebrated in antiquity for its silver mines, huge slag heaps point to the continued exploitation of the local metallurgical deposits. At Thόriko, antiquity's only purely industrial town, an ancient theater is being restored. The road turns inland through rolling vineyards, olive orchards and rich red earth, known as the Messόgia (Middle Land), dotted with archaic necropolises and numerous villages. From Keratea it is five miles east to the convent of the *Palaioemerologitae* (followers of the Julian calendar) looking like the stage set for a Russian ballet, high above the beach of Kakί Thάlassa. The most interesting of several prosperous villages is Peanía, birthplace of Demosthenes, because of the Vorres Museum and a church painted with frescos, in the best derivative Byzantine style, by Kontoglou, a fashionable contemporary painter. Two miles along the eastern slope of Mt. Hymettus is the large stalactite Koutόuki cave, open from 10 to 6. At the road fork four miles north, the right prong leads to the Marathon coast, the left back to Athens, five miles distant.

The Marathon Coast

A series of pine-girt beaches, reached from the various villages of the Messόgia, dotted with remains of Mycenaean castles, beehive tombs, archaic and classical shrines, Hellenistic fortresses and Frankish towers, extends along the east coast of Attica. The coastal road begins at Porto Ráfti, where the entrance to the bay is guarded by a gaunt islet in the shape of a pyramid, crowned with the remains of a Roman statue representing a seated man, alleged to be a tailor: hence the name Porto Ráfti, "the port of the tailor". At Vraόna, ancient Brauron, divine confusion reigned, after the local divinity of fertility, Iphigenia, became somewhat surprisingly identified with the most determined of virgins, Artemis. The plot thickened when another Iphigenia, supposedly sacrificed to Artemis at Aulis, further up the coast, but, in fact, spirited away to savage Taurus in the Crimea, landed with her brother Orestes at Brauron. She became High Priestess and was deified. The good women of Athens, who walked every fourth year in solemn procession all the 23 miles from town, might well have wondered whom they were asking for fertility, especially as the curious bear cult belonged to the first, only dimly remembered, Iphigenia.

The well-arranged local museum houses the bas-reliefs, statues, jewels and unique wooden vases dug out of the mud of the Erasinos. The large temple of Artemis has been partly reconstructed, but only foundations remain of the 5th-century B.C. stoa, where the daughters of the best Athenian families were initiated in the complicated ritual dances. Close by are the foundations of an early

Christian basilica and, about halfway between Vraóna and the village of Markópoulo, a Frankish tower stands sentinel on a lonely eminence, dominating the rolling vine country.

Beyond the pine-shaded sandy shore of Loutsa and the small port of Rafina extend more beaches and coves until the crescent-shaped bay of Marathon is reached. Here, in 490 B.C., took place the famous battle in which the greatly outnumbered Athenian *hoplites* broke the onslaught of the Persian hordes in the swampy ground between the sea and Mt. Penteli. From the shepherd god Pan's intervention on the side of the Greeks derives the word panic, while the runner who expired after having announced the news of the victory added the term, a "Marathon race" (a test of endurance). Amid fields and orchards of almond trees rises the 39-foot high tumulus erected over the ashes of the 192 Athenians who fell in battle. Some three miles inland, the graves of their only allies, the Plataeans, can be seen within a recently discovered mound on the actual battlefield. Nearby are a museum and a pre-historic graveyard of tiny men and horses protected by a concrete shell.

Just before the village of Marathónas (Marathon), a road branches right to the lovely beach of Shinias, then turns north through a sparse, barren plain to ancient Ramnoús, facing the majestic mountain chain of Euboea across the channel. In this secluded spot rise the platforms of two Doric temples, supported by marble walls. The smaller 6th-century B.C. temple of Themis, the blindfolded goddess of justice, having been destroyed when the Persians attacked a nearby Athenian fortress, the larger one was erected in honor of Nemesis, goddess of divine vengeance, who took revenge on the barbarians on the field of Marathon. Though the London Society of Dilettanti shipped part of the goddess' head to the British Museum in the early 19th century, the innumerable fragments of the marble statue by Agorakritos—Phidias' favorite pupil—have just been put together into the only surviving cult statue of the golden age.

The whole place has an atmosphere of awe and desolation, well suited to a sanctuary of the most implacable of ancient deities. A path lined by monumental tombs leads to the white marble walls of the Acropolis, choked in undergrowth; below is the port that guarded the entrance to the Euboean Channel. After Marathónas the road rises, affording splendid views over the bay; at Kapandriti it joins the Kalamos branch from the motorway.

In the Interior

About a third of the way up Mt. Pentéli, the most symmetrical of the mountains surrounding the Attic plain, there is a large prosperous monastery, enclosed within white-washed walls and shaded with poplars and plane trees under which cool streams trickle. The monastery contains the skull, enriched with jewels, of its 16th-century founder. A little higher up is a former residence of the royal family, the modernized Gothic country house built by the eccentric French philhellene, the Duchesse de Plaisance, in the mid-19th century. This eccentric daughter of a French diplomat (who negotiated the Louisiana Purchase) and of an American mother, became tired of the sophisticated life of Parisian literary and political salons, left her husband and settled in Greece. She preferred the friendship of semi-literate but colorful revolutionary leaders to that of the aristocratic Regent of the country, John Capodistrias. Nearby is the tomb of her daughter, surrounded by cypresses. A strange relationship, alternating between extremes of affection and rivalry, apparently existed between mother and daughter, both of whom entertained the tenderest feelings for a bandit dwelling in a neighboring cave supposedly connected by an underground passage with the Duchesse's residence. A rough road climbs to the summit of the mountain, past disused marble quarries inhabited by herds of baleful-eyed goats. The view from the summit embraces the whole of Attica, the sea on three sides and the distant Cyclades.

At the foot of Mt. Pentéli lies the summer resort of Kifíssia, birthplace of Menander, the ancient comic writer. Kifíssia and Ekali, a mile further on, provide the easiest, though not quickest, access to the motorway north, which converges on Mount Pentéli with four widely-spaced branch roads to the right. The first leads to Diónyssos, at the foot of huge marble quarries: the site of ancient Icaria, where Dionysus, the god of wine, when visiting Attica for the first time, was entertained by Icarius whom he afterwards instructed to spread the blessings of the grape to mankind. The second branch leads to the Marathon dam, an artificial lake for Athens' water supply. The dam, entirely faced with marble, was completed in the late 1920s by a firm of American engineers and serves as a barrage against the escape of waters through a deep glen into the Marathonian plain. The reservoir is fed by pipelines from Lake Ylíki and since 1980 from the Mornos River, over a hundred miles northwest.

The third branch runs between gently undulating hills to the fishing village of Ágii Apóstoli and the Amfiáraio, bright with oleanders, above the Euboean channel. The sheltered sanctuary is dedicated to Amphiáraos, a prophet-general, who was swallowed up by the earth together with his chariot. An interpreter of dreams, he was raised to divinity and his sanctuary became a popular dream-oracle. Close to a stream said to possess curative properties, there are ruins of a theater, Doric temple, a large hospital and the 120-yard-long portico, in which pilgrims, lying on the skin of a sacrificial ram, were visited by revelatory dreams. A final branch leads to the little port of Oropós, whence there is a half-hourly ferry boat across the blue streak of the channel to Eretria, on the opposite coast of Euboea. A secondary road hugs the mainland coast from Oropos to Halkída, passing Avlída, where Iphigenia was sacrificed to secure favorable winds for the Greek expedition against Troy. The motorway by-passes Avlóna which has a museum of embroideries, and Tanagra with a small museum of antiquities, then skirts Lake Ylíki, the main reservoir of Athens, before turning again to the sea.

On Mt. Parnis

West of Mt. Pentéli, the barrier of Párnitha (Mt. Parnis), the highest mountain in Attica, extends across the plain. After the military airport, the road climbs the foothills of Dekelia through luxuriant woods to the private estate of the royal family. The lovely park with the royal tombs, including those of the Duke of Edinburgh's parents, can be entered just below the Leonidas Restaurant at Varybobi; no signpost. The drive continues to Ágios Merkóuris, whence a very rough road descends through the scattered oak forests to the motorway at the Oropós branch.

Another road, leading through the village of Aharnés whose farmlands were constantly ravaged during the Peloponnesian War by the Spartan infantry entrenched in the fortified camp of Dekélia—climbs Mt. Parnis in a long series of hairpin bends. Towards the top, fir trees replace the eternal pines of Attica and the air becomes more alpine and rarified. A funicular railway provides an easier approach, rising in four minutes to the hotel casino at 3,000 ft, with a splendid view over the Attic plain. The road continues past several restaurants to the military installations shortly before the summit.

A third road leads through the village of Fýli to the convent of Moní Klistón (Our Lady of the Defile) into an austere mountain landscape gashed with precipitous defiles and spiky crevasses. The branch left leads to the ruins of the 4th-century B.C. fortress of Phyle, one round and two square towers dramatically perched on a little plateau guarding the shortest route into Attica from Thebes.

The Byzantine monastery of Ossios Melétis in the northwestern foothills is reached by turning right at Inoï, 30 miles along the inland road to Thebes from Athens. Scattered pines and fir trees cling to the slate-grey mountain sides—in ancient times a preserve of wild boar, lions and wolves. Just before entering the pass between Attica and Boeotia, a road branches left, passes the village of Vília, shaded with plane trees, and descends from the impressive bare uplands and passes through deserted pine groves and olive orchards into a placid inlet of the Halcyonic Gulf. Here rise the ruins of towers and posterns, as well as a massive enceinte of walls, of the 4th-century B.C. fortress of Egósthena. On the shingle beach of Pórto Germenó are several taverns and, in late summer, plagues of horse-flies. Except at week-ends, the beach is practically deserted, and the sun shimmers beatifically on the pellucid sheet of water.

PRACTICAL INFORMATION FOR ATTICA

WHEN TO COME. Preferably in spring, early summer or fall. In spring an extraordinary variety of wild flowers carpet the arid hillsides of Attica (particularly around Hymettus, Parnís and the Marathonian plain and hills leading to Ramnous). The beaches, of course, are most enjoyable in high summer; but then you have to put up with the crowds. The smartest are the Astir beaches at Glyfáda and Vougliameni. Sailing continues all year round.

HOW TO GET ABOUT. Preferably by car. All the beaches and villages mentioned, but not all archeological sites, can be reached by bus. As terminals are constantly changing, enquiries should be made at the hotel. The roads are all paved, except the last stretch below the summit of Mt. Pentéli, to Phyle, and beyond Agios Merkouris on Mt. Parnís. There is a funicular railway to the Casino on Mount Parnís.

HOTELS. The southeast coast from Faliro to Sounio is studded with hotels on or facing the sea. Deluxe, Expensive and Moderate hotels in our listings are all airconditioned, unless otherwise stated. Most charge halfboard. Distances in miles from Athens are shown in brackets after the name of the town or resort.

Southeast Coast

ALIANTHOS (20). All across the busy coastal road from the large GNTO beach; none airconditioned. *Glaros* (E), tel. 897 1217. 48 rooms, roofgarden. *Varkiza* (M), tel. 897 0927. 30 rooms. *Holidays* (I), tel. 897 0915. 34 rooms.

ANAVYSSOS (31). *Alexander Beach* (E), tel. 53 461. 105 rooms, disco, pool. *Apollo Beach* (M), tel. 36 493. 91 rooms, disco. *Eden Beach* (M), tel. 52 761/5. 286 rooms, disco, pool, minigolf, roofgarden, no airconditioning. *Silver Beach* (I), 28 rooms.

GLYFÁDA (11). Largest concentration of hotels, despite proximity to noisy airport; marina. *Astir* (E), tel. 894 6461/6. 128 aging deluxe bungalows, pool, tennis, minigolf, nightclub; the only one with private beach, but sea not as clean as it should be. *Atrium* (E), tel. 894 0971/5. 56 rooms, roofgarden. *Congo Palace* (E), tel. 894 6711/5. 91 rooms, roofgarden, pool and tennis nearby. *Palace* (E), tel. 894 1611/4. 75 rooms. Among several rather unjustifiably expensive furnished apartments are *Filissia* (E), tel. 895 3214. 15 suites; *Oasis* (E), tel. 894 1662. 70 suites, pool.

Emmantina (M), tel. 893 2111/5. 80 rooms, roofgarden. *Fenix* (M), tel. 894 7229. 139 rooms, roofgarden, disco, pool, but further from beach. *London* (M), tel. 894 5634. 75 rooms. *Regina Maris* (M), tel. 895 5118. 72 rooms, pool. *Sea View* (M), tel. 895 1311/4. 74 rooms, pool nearby. *Beau Rivage* (I), tel. 894 9292. 82 rooms, roofgarden, airconditioned. *Glyfada* (I), tel. 894 6833. 52 rooms, pool, tennis. *Oceanis* (I), tel. 894 4038. 73 rooms, pool.

Restaurants. Visiting celebrities are entertained at the Astir's *Asteria* (E), tel. 894 5675. Emphasis on seafood; dancing to live orchestra. *Antonopoulos* (E), tel. 894 5636, and *Psaropoulos* (E), tel. 894 5677, are renowned seafood restaurants opposite the marina. Slightly less expensive are *Churrasco*, tel. 895 9107, elaborate steak tartare; and *Quo Vadis*, tel. 894 0673, French and German cuisine. All (M) are: *Antonis*, tel. 894 7423, shrimp ragout and wild boar; *Dovinos*, tel. 894 4249; and *El Greco*, tel. 899 4249, both strong on baked and grilled fish. *L'Arcobaleno*, tel. 894 2564; and *La Boussola*, tel. 894 2605, both specializing in scampi and other Italian dishes. *Mayfair*, tel. 894 7204, singer accompanied by discreet piano. All open evenings and lunch Sunday. Both (I) are: *Barba Petros*, tel. 891 4937, cheesepies, kid, grills; and *Kanatakia*, tel. 895 1843, pies and short orders, wine from the barrel.

Entertainment. Nightspots are as numerous as restaurants. *Dilina* (E), tel. 894 02 05. Features well-known names in Greek and international show biz; closed Monday. Fashionable (M) discos are: *B.B.G. Disco*, tel. 893 1933; *Esperides*, tel. 894 8179; and *Olympic House*, tel. 894 2141, also meals.

KALAMAKI (8). Next to the airport. *Marina Alimos* (E), tel. 982 8911/8. 29 suites, no restaurant. *Albatros* (M), tel. 982 4981/4. 80 rooms, beach across the coastal road. *Galaxy* (I), tel. 981 8603. 44 rooms. *Hellenikon* (I), tel. 981 7227. 52 rooms, minigolf. *Tropical* (I), tel. 981 3993. 46 rooms, minigolf. All airconditioned, and on coastal road, with restaurants.

Restaurants. *Bosphoros* (M), tel. 981 2873. Constantinopolitan dishes to music; closed Sunday evening. *Château* (M), tel. 981 3375. Greek and foreign specialties. *Sta Kavourakia* (M), tel. 981 0093. Specializes, as its name indicates, in crabs, but also offers other seafood. All on coastal road.

Entertainment. *Neraida*, tel. 981 2004, and *Stork*, tel. 982 9865, present moderately good shows based on *bouzouki* music in a very lively atmosphere. *Anabella* (M), tel. 981 1124. Dinner dancing.

KAVOURI (13). *Apollon Palace* (L), tel. 895 1401/10. 286 rooms, 7 suites in 10-story building, the highest on the coast; own beach, pool, tennis. *Cavouri* (E). 114 rooms, beach, pool, disco. *Pine Hill* (M). 100 yds. from beach, 83 rooms, roofgarden, tennis.

Restaurant. *Panorama* (M), tel. 895 1289. Seafood.

LAGONISSI (24). *Xenia Lagonissi* (E), tel. 83 911/25. 357 rooms and deluxe bungalows, several restaurants, nightclub, cinema, 2 pools, tennis, minigolf.

LEGRENA (40). *Minos,* tel. 39 321/3. 38 rooms.

PALEO (Old Faliro, 5). Sea too polluted for bathing. *Coral* (M), tel. 981 6441. 89 rooms, not airconditioned, minigolf. *Possidon* (M), tel. 982 2086. 90 rooms. Both on noisy coastal road, plus pools, roofgardens.

Restaurants. *Bistrot 1900* (E), tel. 981 6245. Successfully nostalgic. *Gaskon Toma* (M), tel. 982 1114. Evenings only, with music. *Il Fungo* (M), tel. 981 6765. Pizzas and pastas, evenings only, except for Sunday lunch. *Kapri* (M), tel. 981 6379, cafeteria. All on coastal road.

SARONIDA (30). *Saronic Gate* (E), tel. 53 711/5. 105 rooms, beach, pool, tennis.

SOUNIO (44). *Cape Sounion Beach* (E), tel. 39 391/4. 152 bungalows, pool. *Egeon* (E), tel. 39 200. On beach below temple. Neither airconditioned, but not really necessary as very windy. *Surf Beach Club* (M), tel. 22 363/4. 265 rooms in central block and bungalows, pool, tennis, disco.

VOULA (11). *Voula Beach* (E), tel. 895 3851/4. 54 rooms, not airconditioned, beach, disco. *Noufara* (M), tel. 895 3450, 22 rooms.

Restaurants. *Alkyoni,* tel. 895 4479. International cuisine to piano music in the evening. *Isabella,* tel. 895 2103. At Alipedou B GNTO beach, piano and harp play Latin American music at dinner time; attached cafeteria also opens midday. At Alipedou A GNTO beach, *San Lorenzo,* a popular disco restaurant.

VOULIAGMENI (16). *Astir Palace* (L), tel. 896 0211/9. 404 rooms in two hotels and 77 bungalows, on a pine-clad promontory with private beach, pool, tennis, minigolf, several restaurants, nightclub. *Greek Coast* (E), tel. 896 0401. 55 rooms, pool, roofgarden. *Margi House* (E), tel. 896 2061/5. 100 rooms, roofgarden. *Blue Spell* (M), tel. 896 0131/2. 38 rooms, pool, roofgarden. *Strand* (M), tel. 896 0705/7. 72 rooms, disco.

Restaurants. The Astir Palace's *Club House* (E), lunches and dinners, coffee bar; and the equally international *Mooring's* (E), tel. 896 1113, above Greece's most elegant marina, are both good. Three excellent seafood restaurants are: *Lambros* (E), tel. 896 0144, on the sea opposite the lake, *Leonidas* (E), tel. 896 0110, behind the coastal road and *Psarofili* (M), tel. 896 1887, before the Astir beach. *Oceanis* (E), tel. 896 1133, on the

GNTO beach, for French cuisine. *Toscana* (M), tel. 896 2497. Italian cuisine, further inland. Several Moderate adequate fish taverns near the lake frequently change owner and name. *Vouliagmeni* (M) is the largest.

East Coast

AGII APOSTOLI (31). *Kalamos Beach* (M), tel. 81 465/7. 177 rooms, not airconditioned, pool, tennis, minigolf, disco. *The Dolphins* (I), tel. 81 202. 138 rooms, pool, roofgarden, disco. Numerous Moderate fish taverns.

MARATHON (26). Near the tumulus. *Golden Coast* (M), tel. 92 102. 241 rooms, pool, tennis, minigolf, disco. The coast is anything but golden till the Shinas beach half a mile away.

MATI (19). *Costa Rica* (E), tel. 71 103. 60 rooms, 12 suites. *Mati* (E), tel. 71 511. 70 rooms, 5 suites, disco. Both on beach, with pools, roofgarden. *Attica Beach* (M), tel. 71 711. 94 rooms, pool. *Myrto* (I), tel. 71 431. Far from beach.

NEA MAKRI (21). *Marathon Beach* (M), tel. 91 255. 166 rooms. *Zouberi* (M), tel. 71 920/4. 128 rooms, roofgarden. Both on beach, pools, discos. *Nereus* (I), tel. 91 214. 127 rooms, close to beach.
Restaurant. *Limanaki* (M), tel. 91 330. Fresh fish.

OROPOS (33). *Alkyonis* (I), tel. 32 490, 91 rooms. *Flisvos* (I), tel. 32 480. 60 rooms, disco. Both on waterfront and close to not very inviting beach. Numerous Moderate fish taverns in town.

PORTO RAFTI (24). *Korali* (I), tel. 72 602. 16 rooms; close to fish taverns and beach.

RAFINA (19). *Avra* (I), tel. 22 781. 96 rooms. *Ina Marina* (I), tel. 22 215. 79 rooms. Outstanding town for seafood, no good for bathing.

VRAÓNA (23). *Vraóna Bay* (E), tel. 82 591/5. 352 rooms in large central block and bungalows on small beach, pool, minigolf, tennis, disco.

West Coast

AGII THEODORI (46). *Hanikian Beach* (E), tel. 67 151/60. 221 rooms, on beach, minigolf, tennis, exceptionally well-run. *Siagas Beach* (M), tel. 67 501/3. 101 rooms, near beach, minigolf, disco.

KINETTA (36). *Kinetta Beach* (E), tel. 62 512/4. 192 bungalows on beach. *Sun* (M), tel. 62 243. 51 rooms, near beach.

NEA PERAMOS (21). *Megalo Pefko* (I), tel. 33 205. 70 rooms. A number of Moderate fish taverns on the seafront, but poor beach.

On Gulf of Corinth

LOUTRAKI (54). Though some hotels collapsed in the devastating earthquake of 1981, some 40 are still ranged along the seafront and round the springs in Greece's most popular spa. In accordance with our practice to list only establishments where all rooms have private baths or showers, relatively few can be mentioned, even in the Expensive class. For the most part, they are frequented by Greek rather than foreign visitors. None is airconditioned, except the one indicated.

Paolo (E), tel. 48 742. 80 rooms, close to mediocre beach. *Park* (E), tel. 42 270. 64 rooms. Both with roofgardens. *Excelsior* (M), tel. 42 254. 33 rooms, no restaurant. *Marinos* (M), tel. 42 575. 51 rooms, pool, roofgarden, disco. *Pappas* (M), tel. 43 936/8, 84 rooms, disco. *Galaxy* (I), tel. 48 282. On the town fringe. *Marion* (I), tel. 42 346. 45 rooms, disco. *Mitzithra* (I), tel. 42 316. 43 rooms, and the only one airconditioned. All with the locally much-appreciated roofgardens.

Most hotels operate their own restaurants, but they are as indifferent as the few in the main street.

A little further west are the comfortable bungalows of *Club Poseidon* (M). (See under *Holiday Villages*, p. 22).

PORTO GERMENO (33). *Egosthenion* (I), tel. 41 226. 80 rooms, roofgarden, 300 yards from shingle beach. Several Moderate fish taverns on seafront.

Inland

Though most villages possess at least one Inexpensive hotel, mostly quite modern, only a very few are likely to be suitable for tourists.

HALANDRI (6). *Acropole* (I), 55 rooms.

KAPANDRITI (18). At the motorway toll gate, *Golden Horse Motel* (M), 15 rooms.

KIFISSIA (10). Garden suburb of Athens. As in Loutraki, the numerous hotels cater mainly to a Greek clientele, and only a few have all rooms with private baths or showers. Because of the relative coolness, none is airconditioned.

Kostis Dimitrakopoulos (E), tel. 801 2546. 27 double rooms. *Semiramis* (E), tel. 801 2587. 42 rooms, nightclub, pool, roofgarden; halfboard only. *Katerina* (M), tel. 801 8495. 47 rooms. *Nafsika* (M), tel. 801 3255. 17 rooms. *Des Roses* (M), tel. 801 9952. 37 rooms.

Restaurants. *Blue Pine* (E), tel. 801 2969. Fine assortment of hors d'oeuvres and charcoal broils, dinners only and country-club atmosphere with discreet music. *La Belle Hélène* (E), tel. 801 4776. French cuisine, trout selected from the pond. *Lotofagos* (E), tel. 801 3201. Outstanding; dinners only; closed Tues. *Symposium House* (E), tel. 801 6707. International cuisine. *Bokaris* (M), tel. 801 2589. Just below the electric train station, unusually large selection, rabbit stew, wild boar, wine from the barrel. *Moustakas* (M), tel. 801 4584. Baked kid with oil and origan, shrimp sauce, guitars in the evening, open Sunday lunch. *O Nikos* (M), tel. 801 5537. Likewise kid with oil and origan, evenings and Sunday lunch. *Ponderossa* (M), tel. 801 2356. Near train station, Corfu specialties in a converted old house, dinners only, closed Sun.

MOUNT PARNÍS (20). Reached by road or funicular. *Mont Parnes* (L), tel. 246 9111/5. 106 double rooms, 16 suites, casino, nightclub, pool, tennis, spectacular view when the pollution over Athens lifts.

Several Inexpensive taverns at the fringe of the fir forest.

VARYBOBÍ (12). *Auberge Tatoï* (L), tel. 801 4537. 9 rooms, tennis, the only reason to stay in the not particularly attractive surroundings is the excellent food.

Restaurants. Just above the entrance to the royal estate, *Leonidas* (M), tel. 801 0000. Perhaps the best restaurant in Attica for the price; large outside terrace, but insufficient for the week-end crowd.

Among the numerous taverns along the roads through the wine villages of the Mesogia is *Old Stables Barbecue* (E), tel. 664 3320, 1 mile past Koropi. With old stables transformed into restaurant, bar and nightclub with a tourist village atmosphere; food adequate, but *retsina* outstanding; open from 9 P.M., closed Monday. *Glaros* (M), tel. 664 2546. Veal in wine sauce, kid in lemon sauce, washed down with rosé retsina in a pleasant garden; dinners and Sunday lunches. *Lagos* (M), tel. 664 2740. Not only hare, as the name indicates, but quail, woodcock and all kind of game. Both at Peania. Best-known for game *Tou Skorda to Hani* (M) (The Garlic Inn), tel. 667 7240. Opposite the Pikermi bus stop; daily 1 P.M. to 2 A.M.

 MUSEUMS. *Vorres Museum,* at Peania, three restored village houses and a stable accommodate the Greek-Canadian collector's folkloric items. In a striking modern wing is the largest collection of contemporary Greek art, over 300 paintings and 60 sculptures, donated to the nation. Open Sat. and Sun. 10 A.M. to 2 P.M.

On Mount Penteli, the Mansion of the Duchess of Plaisance is not open to the public, but the courtyard is the setting for a *Chamber Music Festival* for three weeks in July.

DELPHI AND THE PARNASSÓS

"Navel of the Earth"

The "Parnassós (Parnassus) Country" is a term frequently applied to the area on either side of the spine of mountains extending northwest from the borders of Attica. Rising between the Boeotian plains and the sparsely inhabited northern shores of the Gulf of Corinth, most of this highland region is rich in mythological and historical allusion. One of the great courtesans of ancient times, Phryne—mistress of statesmen and soldiers—was born here. The rugged slopes of Kitherónas (Mt. Kitheron) are associated with the haunts of Pan, the god of shepherds, and his goat-like satyrs; and the sacred grove where the nine muses dwelt, lay in a secluded valley of Elikónas (Mt. Helikon). The caves and crevasses of Parnassós itself, towering above its neighbors, were the scene of five-yearly bacchanalian revels and nocturnal dances performed by Boeotian women dressed in animal skins; and, clinging to the side of one of its spurs, Delphi, the most celebrated oracle of antiquity, rose, terrace upon terrace, above what the ancients called the "navel of the earth".

Recorded history begins with the growth of the towns in the plains of Boeotia. The most important of these was Thebes, which, according to legend, was founded by Cadmus and subsequently ruled by the Labdacides, one of whom, the luckless Oedipus, was destined to kill his father and marry his mother. During the Persian Wars, Thebes, out of jealousy of Athens, allied itself to the Persians, whose decisive defeat at Plataea it shared in 479 B.C. Yet a 100 years later, the Thebans were allied to the Athenians and for a brief ten years, from 371 to 362 B.C., dominated Greece due to the introduction of a revolutionary fighting formation, the phalanx. Young Philip of Macedon, in those years a hostage in Thebes, later perfected the phalanx sufficiently to crush the Thebans and Athenians at Chaironeia in 338 B.C. In the Middle Ages, Thebes was successively overrun by Bulgars, Normans, Franks and Lombards, and the Turkish conquerors finally moved the seat of the capital of Boeotia to Livadiá. The latter, situated at the foot of Mt. Helikon, had grown in importance and the Catalans built a castle, the ruins of which still dominate the town. Under Turkish rule, Livadiá became the second town of Greece after Athens.

Beyond Parnassos, at the foot of the mountainous mass of the Panetolikó and Vardóussia, lies the port of Náfpaktos on the northern shore of the Gulf of Corinth. Náfpaktos, like Livadiá, only gained prominence in the Middle Ages, and its possession was keenly disputed by Venetians and Turks, both of whom understood the strategic importance of its position guarding the narrows of the Gulf of Corinth. It was known as Lepanto when the Turkish fleet sailed out to be decisively defeated by a Spanish-Italian fleet under Don Juan of Austria in 1571. This was the end of Turkish naval supremacy in the Mediterranean and the turning point in Turkish history.

About midway between Thebes in the east and Náfpaktos in the west, lies Delphi: in the very heart of the Parnassos country. The origins of the history of Delphi go back to the first mysterious exhalations which issued out of a cave below the giant cliffs of the Phaedriades. At first the spot was dedicated to the cult of the earth-goddess, but, in time, Apollo came to be regarded as the presiding deity, worshipped in the guise of a dolphin (*delphos*). The mysterious prophecies of a pythoness were associated with the earth's exhalations, and a sacred city grew up around the oracle. Games, dedicated to the worship of the Pythian Apollo, were held in the stadium, and the oracular pronouncements, now made through the lips of a priestess, not only gained renown throughout the ancient world, but influenced the actions of great politicians as well as humble people who flocked to Delphi to consult the oracle. Her utterances decided the fate of men and nations.

Greek art and literature are steeped in the legend of the oracle, and there are few tragedies of Aeschylus, Sophocles and Euripides, the plot of which does not hinge on some dramatic and often ambiguous pronouncement of the priestess.

Exploring the Parnassós Country

The quickest approach is by the motorway, from which Thíva (Thebes) is visible on a slight eminence in the center of the Boeotian plain to the west. The equidistant (44 miles) mountainous inland road enters the narrow pass separating Attica from Boeotia just after the branch to Vilia, passing below the ruins of the 4th-century B.C. fortress of Elefthére, with its seven gateways and several two-storey towers. The road rises till a panoramic view is obtained of the Boeotian plains, with the mountain chain of the island of Euboea in the north. To the west stretches the backbone of Kitheron, the crenellated range of Helikon with the towering mass of Parnassos (often capped with snow until May or even June).

In the plain below, the first village is Erithrés, from where a branch road left (four miles) leads to the battlefield of Plataea. Within the considerable remains of triple ramparts stand the ruins of Hera's temple and the Katagogion, a hostel built for the pilgrims after the destruction of the ancient town in 427 B.C.

After the death of its two great statesmen and generals, Epaminondas and Pelopidas, Thebes lost its ephemeral pre-eminence and in 336 B.C. was razed to the ground by Alexander the Great, who spared only the temples and the house of the poet Pindar. Though regaining some prosperity in the later Middle Ages under Frankish dukes, the modern small town holds little interest. There are a large, frescoed Mycenaean tomb, some scanty remains of ancient gateways of the palace of Cadmus and a museum containing, among various archaic, classical and Roman fragments, three rather remarkable *steles* in black stone, with bas-reliefs, and paintings representing Boeotian warriors of the 5th century B.C. Close to the museum there is a squat Frankish tower: a reminder of the annexation of Thebes to the Duchy of Athens by the de la Roche family in the 13th century.

Beyond Thebes, both road and rail traverse what was once the

Kopaic lake: the unsalubrious marshy plain was drained by a British company at the end of the 19th century to become a main cotton producing region.

Twenty-eight miles west of Thebes lies Livadiá, whose chief industry consists of hand-made blankets, brightly colored examples of which may be seen drying on old Turkish bridges spanning the Hercyna, a legendary stream on whose banks the oracle of Trophonius, a Boeotian divinity, was situated.

The Hercyna emerges out of a gloomy gorge at the foot of the medieval castle built by a band of Catalan mercenaries who ravaged and occupied several parts of central Greece during the 14th century. Two springs have been identified as those of Lethe (Oblivion) and Mnemosyne (Remembrance). Niches for votive offering are hewn out of the rock above the springs, and in one of them—the largest—the Turkish governors of Livadiá used to retire during the heat of the day to snooze and smoke their *narghilés*. Today the site is shaded by plane trees, with little cafés along the stream.

At Livadiá the road divides, the left prong leading to Delphi, the other skirting the base of Parnassos in a north-westerly direction. Eight miles off the latter route is Orhomenós, according to Homer one of the oldest and wealthiest cities of prehistoric Greece. Enthusiasts might be tempted to the acropolis on the hilltop, but of greater interest and less painful is the Mycenaean bee-hive tomb of Minyas, excavated by Schliemann in the 1880s. Nearby a 5th-century B.C. theater was dug out in the early 1970s; across the road, there is a very fine Byzantine church (the Dormition of the Virgin), the earliest example of a church in the Greek cross plan in the country.

Further west the road traverses the site of the battle of Chaironeia (Heronía), where, in 338 B.C., Philip of Macedon defeated the armies of Athens and Thebes, which defended the antiquated concept of the city state against northern monarchy. A large marble statue of a lion, which originally rested on a monument dedicated to the Boeotians who fell in the battle, may be seen from the road.

Three miles beyond Heronía a side road leads to the village of Davlía: the ancient Daulis, where the wife of Tereus, the King of Thrace, revenged herself against her husband's violation of her sister by serving up the flesh of their own little son for him to eat. The ruins, in themselves unimpressive, are romantically situated on a spur of Parnassós which falls away in sheer precipices into a deep and luxuriant valley.

At Bralos village, at the foot of the pass, a 39-mile branch left (west) leads through a spectacular gorge via Amfissa to Delphi, making possible a circular tour of Parnassos.

The Sacred Way

The direct route to Delfi (Delphi) is the 28-mile stretch from Livadiá cutting out the hairpin bends of the Sacred Way of the ancients through the desolate uninhabited region between the massifs of Elikonas and Parnassós.

Almost exactly half way between Livadiá and Delphi is the famous junction of roads, the Triple Way, as it was known by the ancients, where the roads from Delphi, Daulis and Livadiá (and Thebes and Athens beyond) meet. It is a lonely spot, at the beginning of the long, narrow and deep valley leading to Delphi; and it is here, according to legend, and so described by Sophocles in *Oedipus Rex,* that Oedipus, returning on foot from Delphi, met his father, Laius, King of Thebes. The latter, having struck Oedipus with his whip in order to make room for his chariot to pass, was in turn attacked and accidentally killed by the enraged young man, who did not recognize his father. It was after this unintentional murder that Oedipus, who had been brought up in Corinth and had not seen his parents since his birth, returned to his native town of Thebes and answered the riddle of the deadly Sphinx that had held the Thebans in the grip of fear. He then ascended the throne of Thebes and unknowingly married his mother, Jocasta, thus fulfilling the prophecy that had caused his parents to abandon him at birth.

Close by, a side road leads into a fertile cup-shaped valley among the foothills of Elikonas, after passing through the village of Dístomo, the scene of a savage Nazi act of reprisal in 1943, when one male member of each family was taken out and publicly shot. On a flank of the hillside, amid orchards of almond trees, is situated the monastery of Óssios Loukás, one of the most important Byzantine monuments in the country.

At first a hermitage, a shrine was subsequently founded on the spot by an orthodox ascetic, Luke the Stiriote (not to be confused with St. Luke) in the 10th century. Luke possessed prophetic powers, and his shrine gained such renown that, after his death, it became a place of pilgrimage and his disciples decided to construct a fitting monument to his memory. Architects and mosaic workers, under the patronage of the beautiful and notorious Empress Theophano, were despatched to this lonely spot from Constantinople. When the Emperor Romanus II died, however, and Theophano married his successor, Nicephorus Phocas, the project had to be abandoned for the new emperor was a dour and stingy soldier, little given to lavish expenditure in the furtherance of the arts. But, on the accession of the Emperor Basil II, an intelligent monarch and redoubtable general, known as the Bulgar-slayer, work on the church of Óssios Loukas was resumed in 1019, at the new emperor's express orders.

Of the two churches (there is also a crypt and monastic cells), the larger, dedicated to Blessed Luke himself, is now a museum. Of exquisite proportions, constructed in the classic Greek cross plan (cross-in-square), with multi-colored marble paving-stones and overhanging balconies, it constitutes one of the finest extant examples of a great Byzantine shrine of the 11th century. Its supreme glory rests, however, in its mosaics. Although none have the inspirational force or exquisite mastery of execution of the mosaics of Daphni, they possess an austerity and hieratic formality which makes a powerful impression. Particularly impressive are the gaunt saints and warriors in the dome and the Nativity and Baptism in the pendentives. Some of the mosaics have been restored at different dates from the 16th century. The smaller church, dedicated to the Virgin, no longer bears any traces of mosaics or frescos; but it contains some fine stone carvings (see the capitals of the four columns supporting the dome and the cornice of the iconostasis). Outside the church, there is a large terrace, shady with plane trees, overlooking the cup-shaped valley. The simple tourist pavilion is situated here.

Beyond the fork to Óssios Loukas, the Sacred Way continues the long and lonely ascent towards Delphi. The air becomes more rarefied, the scenery more awesome. The road passes the narrow mainstreet of dizzily perched Arahova, noted for its woolen handicrafts and red wine. From this mountain village a comfortable crossing of Mt. Parnassós through dense fir forests passes between the Fterólaka and Kellária ski centers, within easy climbing distance of the summit (8,040 ft.). After descending to the village of Eptálofos you can join the Livadiá-Lamia road at Amfiklia (26 miles). Back on the Delphi road the gorge of Pleistos opens out into what seems to be a sea of olive trees below the great cliffs of the Phaedriades.

Delphi—Grandeur and Mystery

After the Acropolis of Athens, the site of Delphi leaves the most powerful and lasting impression. The scene, both from the ruins of the sanctuary and from any one of the hotels or terraced village houses, is of the greatest possible grandeur. Down below in the gorge, the bed of the Pleistos winds between a narrow strip of olive trees flanked by precipitous cliffs, opening out into the Sacred Plain where the sea of olives, probably the finest grove in all Greece, ends in the calm aquamarine waters of the seemingly landlocked Bay of Itea. In the far horizon, across the Gulf of Corinth, to the south, tower the mountains of the Peloponnese—Zíria, Helmós and Panaháiko—while in the west the massif of Vardóussia inclines gently towards the sea.

Above the ruined sanctuary rise the cliffs of the Phaedriades cleft by a narrow but deep chasm, at the foot of which gushes the Kastalian Spring. At sunset the sides of the cliff glow red with the reflection of the sun's rays and the whole ravine of the Pleistos and the steep terraced vineyards round Arahova are bathed in a warm deep purple light. Overhead, occasionally, an eagle soars.

The modern village of Delphi, overhanging the gorge of the Pleistos, is traversed by a single main street, lined with hotels, restaurants and souvenir shops, filled with postcards, thick woolen rugs and bags from Arahova with bright-colored patterns, and other products of the local crafts. The entrance to the sanctuary can be reached from almost any point in the village, in anything from five to ten minutes walk. At night the street is alive with the strains of jazz music, which the local inhabitants imagine tourists prefer to the melancholy folk music of the Parnassós country, from numerous radios and gramophones in the cafés. Some of these have terraces overhanging the gorge, the plain and the gulf beyond.

The village originally extended over the site of the sanctuary and had to be completely expropriated and demolished in order to permit the excavations to be undertaken. The villagers were indemnified by the French Treasury and their houses rebuilt on the present site. The excavations by the French School of Archeology in Athens were begun in 1892 under the direction of Theophile Homolle and continued for over ten years. In a faint reflection of antique prestige, the Cultural Council of Europe holds congresses here in a modernistic building.

The ruins of Delphi can actually be seen in one day. This means, however, that the visit will be a hurried and very exhausting one, for the monuments of the sanctuary and the temples of the Marmaria are built on steep terraces, involving a considerable amount of climbing. A stay of at least a day and a half is recommended in order to see the sights comfortably. Thus the first afternoon could be devoted to the visit of the sanctuary, the following morning (during the heat of the day) to the museum, which contains some of the glories of Greek sculpture, and the last afternoon to a tour of the Marmaria, below the Kastalian spring.

The traveler with time on his hands may, however, prolong his stay with profit: not only to examine the ruins in detail and explore the surrounding Parnassós country, but also, perhaps, to sense that extraordinary atmosphere of grandeur and mystery which haunts the place. At few other ancient sites do legend and reality,

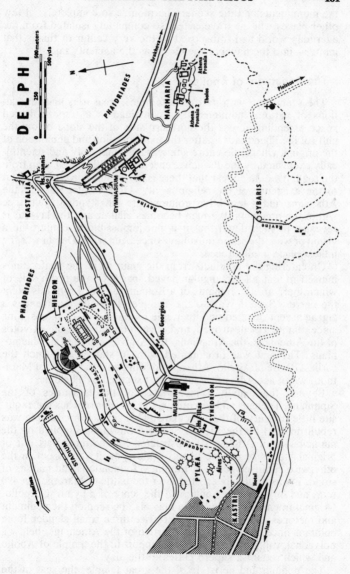

the monuments and the scenery harmonize so completely; at few other places will the traveler feel so completely isolated from the everyday world and transposed to the very center of things that matter—into the navel of the earth, as the ancients said.

The Sanctuary of Apollo

The sanctuary, with its ruined temples, treasuries and foundations of various monuments, is contained in a trapeze-shaped space extending across the northern side of the slope below the cliffs of the Phaedriades. After the expropriation and demolition of the original village the entire site was systematically and scientifically excavated by the French archeologists. When first seen from the road, it would appear that there is hardly anything left to attest to the existence of the religious city. Only the treasury of the Athenians and a few other columns are left standing; but once within the precincts, the plan becomes clearer and the lay-out is revealed in such detail that it is not impossible to conjure up a vision of what the scene must have once been when Delphi was the holiest place in all Greece.

On entering the precincts from the main road, the visitor finds himself in a small rectangular paved space, on the north side of which there are the remains of a Roman portico. From this point the narrow Sacred Way to the Temple of Apollo commences a zigzag ascent, flanked on either side by the bases of statues, long since removed or destroyed, and of such buildings as the ex-votos of the Athenians, the Arcadians, the Argives and the Lacedaemonians. The first was ornamented with 16 statues, of which the earliest (those of Apollo, Athena and Miltiades, the victor of Marathon) were, according to Pausanias, executed by Pheidias.

Beyond the equally ruined bases of the treasuries of the Siphnians, Thebans and Boeotians, the traveler reaches the exquisite little treasury of the Athenians. This small Doric temple was rebuilt in 1904 by the French School from funds supplied by the municipality of Athens. Reconstructed for the most part out of original blocks of marble lying on the spot, it stands out in the otherwise confused scene of trenches, foundations and masses of stone. It was originally erected after the battle of Marathon in 490 B.C., and on its walls is engraved the score of a hymn to Apollo. Original fragments of sculpture may also be seen on the pediment and metopes. Beyond the treasury rise three small slender Ionic columns once belonging to the portico of the Athenians, below a polygonal wall which served as a support to the temple of Apollo and which retains a superb patina to this day.

The podium and peristyle of the great temple, the seat of the oracle, in the very center and heart of the shrine, where Apollo slew the python and established the worship of his cult, are complete and several Doric columns have been replaced in their original position. From the platform of the temple, it is easy to understand the layout of the sanctuary.

It was from a deep subterranean fissure on the site of the temple that the mysterious exhalations originally emanated. Before each prophecy, the priestess, who was always a woman of over 50 (to ensure her chastity), would be purified with water from the adjacent Kastalian spring. In historical times, the subterranean gases had ceased, probably after an earthquake, and the priestess would chew equally poisonous laurel leaves and seat herself in full ceremonial robes on a tripod above the crevasse. Then followed the sacrifice of an animal, whose entrails were carefully examined. Questions relating to the fate of a war, journey, marriage or business enterprise would finally be put to the priestess, who, having now gone off into a trance, would make strange incoherent utterances which were interpreted to the anxious and puzzled consultant by a "prophet". Inscribed on the temple was the wisest and most famous of all Greek maxims: "Know thyself"—a maxim, alas, not always heeded by those who came, and still come, to Delphi.

Divine Doubletalk

Although ambiguity was, as often as not, the keynote of the prophecies, the effect nevertheless made on men's destinies by their interpretation cannot be exaggerated.

For instance, when the inhabitants of Megara were told to "settle opposite the city of the blind", they did not hesitate to emigrate to the coast facing Chalcedon, where the Chalcidians "blinded" by the attractions of the fertile soil of the Asiatic shore of the Bosphorus, had already established themselves. But the Megarans, led by Byzas, and confident in the oracle's advice, built their city on the seemingly less attractive shore: and thus founded Byzantium.

During the Persian Wars the oracle was alarmist, even defeatist. It did not, however, rule out the possibility of a Greek victory and enigmatically declared that the "sons of men" would be "devoured" at sea. The Persians—"sons of men" indeed—suffered a crushing defeat in the naval battle of Salamis in 480 B.C., and the tide of conquest by the Asiatic hordes was halted.

In the subsequent war between the principal Hellenic city states (Athens, Sparta, Argos, Thebes, etc.) the oracle's good name suffered as a result of its prophecies, many of which were inspired by obviously venal motives. The treasuries offered by the city states were frequently pillaged by victorious generals of the contending states, and earthquakes added to the destruction. But the oracle continued to be a more or less vital factor in Greek life until growing religious indifference set in and undermined its hold over the popular imagination. An attempt was made by the Roman emperors to restore the cult of the oracle, but Nero did not help by removing 500 statues from the sanctuary. It was now evident that the attack against the oracle's prestige by sceptical philosophers was irresistible, and the final blow came when paganism was proscribed throughout the Roman world by the Christian Emperor Theodosius I in 381 A.D.

Theater and Stadium

Above the temple rises the 4th-century B.C. theater restored during the Roman epoch. Although considerably smaller than the theater at Epidaurus, it remains in a good state of preservation, and its position, dominating the terrace of the temple of Apollo and the whole sanctuary, is extremely impressive. From a sun-warmed seat on the last tier, the visitor may obtain a panoramic bird's-eye view of the sanctuary and the convulsed landscape that encloses it. At sunset, when the Phaedriades glow coral pink and the soft blue light spreads over the valley and the mountains opposite, the silence, if a pullman car has not just disgorged a load of polyglot tourists, is almost complete. It is here that the feeling of isolation is at its most complete, and the circular configuration of the mountains seems best to justify the description of Delphi as the navel of the earth.

In this theater ancient tragedies are produced from time to time, performed in the late afternoon. Sophocles' *Oedipus Rex,* for instance, is so timed that when Oedipus gouges out his eyes with his own hands after being convinced of his crimes of parricide and incest, the glow fades from the Phaedriades and the warm blue, pink and mauve tints on the sides of the enclosing hills turn dun-grey.

Still higher up, on a final bastion of the cliff, as though perched midway between sky and earth, extend the well-preserved ruins of the Stadium, where the Pythian games were held. Two hundred and twenty yards long, its 12 tiers of seats still more or less intact, the stadium could hold 7,000 spectators. The decorative marbles ornamenting the judge's rostrum, the gift of Herodes Atticus, the famous Athenian benefactor of the 2nd century A.D., have, however, long since disappeared. Three columns of a Roman triumphal arch, through which the contestants entered the stadium, are still standing.

The Pythian games were held at the beginning of September of every fourth year, under the direction of the Amphyctionic Council, a religious body, including representatives of all the principal

Greek states, which administered the affairs of the shrine and its oracle. The games also included the performance of a sacred drama describing Apollo's victory over the python, a musical competition and a chariot race held in the hippodrome down below in the Sacred Plain.

The Marmaria

The term Marmaria (the Marbles) is applied to a group of ruins situated below the main road, little more than five minutes walk from the sanctuary of Apollo. These are actually the first vestiges of ancient Delphi seen by the traveler approaching from Arahova.

Midway between the sanctuary and the Marmaria, the Kastalian spring gushes out of the narrow chasm between the twin Phaedriades. It was from the summit of these cliffs, where the eagles soared in the rarefied mountain air, that criminals were hurled headlong into the valley below by the Delphians: a fate reserved for Aesop, the fable-teller of the 6th century B.C., who, as ambassador of Croesus, had fallen out with Delphi's governing body over the distribution of certain monies donated by the Lydian king. This was before Croesus, complaining about the oracle: "If you cross the river Halys you will destroy a great empire", was scolded for neglecting to inquire further as to which empire and thus losing his own. A visit to the Kastalian spring, which was supposed to have purifying properties, was considered an essential preliminary to a pilgrim's visit to the oracle. The stream, clear and ice-cold, now trickles from a basin surrounded with niches into a modern cistern, where hot and exhausted passers-by may refresh themselves with deep draughts of water. Several cafés are situated under the large plane trees.

A path leads down among the olive trees to the terraced enclosure of the Marmaria, dedicated to the worship of Athena. The archaic temple of Athena was destroyed in the 5th century B.C. by several rocks crashing down on it from the top of the Phaedriades during a violent storm. The second temple of Athena, built to replace the earlier one, was constructed on a spot less exposed to the mercy of avalanches.

The treasury of Marseille, situated between the two temples of Athena, and of which little remains today, was one of the earliest examples of a building in the Ionic order (6th century B.C.). Elegant mouldings surround the base of the treasury, and its columns, none of which are any longer standing, are crowned with capitals ringed with a design of palm leaves. Close by, the Tholos, a round Doric temple, the exact purpose of which is unknown, is one of the purest and most exquisite monuments of antiquity still to be seen at Delphi. Theodoros, its architect, wrote a treatise on his work:

an indication in itself of the exceptional architectural quality of the monument. The circular base of the temple is complete, and several columns have been judiciously restored.

On another terrace of the Marmaria, a little further to the west, extend the ruins of the Gymnasium. Built in the 4th century and considerably added to by the Romans, the gymnasium served as a training ground and meeting-place for the athletes participating in the Pythian games. Only mere traces of the large swimming-bath survive.

The setting of the Marmaria, among olive trees and tall bushes on terraced slopes, is more gentle and bucolic than that of the sanctuary, nor is the view so panoramic and awe-inspiring. Across the Pleistos gorge, the perpendicular sides of Mt. Kirfis may be discerned, with a mule-track zigzagging up to a bare upland plateau.

Down below, among the olive groves on the northern flank of the gorge, the pit of the Sybaris lies not far from the riverbed of the Pleistos. A mule-track, starting at the eastern extremity of the village leads in a walk or ride of about an hour to the pit, where a spring, situated among a chaos of huge boulders, rises. The Sybaris was a terrible monster which lay concealed in a cavern, emerging only to devastate the surrounding countryside. The monster finally found its match in a local youth, Eurybatos, who hurled it down into the ravine. Thereupon a spring gushed forth where the monster struck the earth. More modern folklore, however, has it that a shepherdess, the wife of a *pappas* (priest), met her death here for having taken her flock to pasture by the spring on a Sunday. Hence the name Pappadia is often applied to the spring and sometimes to the whole ravine.

The Museum

The museum, a partly-screened modern eyesore, is all too conspicuously placed on the main road between the village and the sanctuary. The most famous of its exhibits is the bronze statue of a charioteer, believed to have stood on a terrace wall above the temple of Apollo, near which it was found in 1896. It is not established who executed the work, although the donor was a well-known patron of chariot-racing, Gelon, the Tyrant of Syracuse. The statue commemorates a victory in the Pythian games at the beginning of the 5th century B.C. Most striking is the severe classical simplicity of the execution which does not detract from the intensely natural and life-like aspect of the young man holding the reins. Equally impressive are the eyes, which are inlaid with a white substance resembling enamel, the pupils consisting of two concentric onyx rings of different colors. The sculpture of the feet and of the hair clinging to the nape of the neck is perfect in detail.

The earliest example of ancient Greek sculpture in the museum is a pair of Caryatids from the treasury of Knidos (Asia Minor). Of a slightly later period are the Caryatids from the treasury of the island of Siphnos. Other fragments from the frieze of this treasury depict such scenes as the Judgement of Paris, the Battle of the Giants and the Contest of Greeks and Trojans before the gods. The admirable sculpture of the groups of horses deserves particular attention. A completely restored replica of the treasury of Siphnos gives the visitor an idea of what these elaborately adorned little temples flanking the Sacred Way of the sanctuary, must have looked like in the 5th century B.C. There are also fragments from the metopes of the treasury of Sicyon and of the temple of Apollo depicting the Rape of Europa, the Caledonian Boar, Castor and Pollux and the Sons of Aphareus, etc.

An impressive example of archaic sculpture is to be found in the Winged Sphinx of the Naxians, found near the column of the Naxians, on the top of which it is believed to have been originally mounted.

Fourth-century B.C. art is represented by the column of the Dancing Girls, held to be the work of an Athenian sculptor of the school of Praxiteles. It represents three dancing girls grouped round a support, and the high acanthus column on which it stood in front of the ex-voto of the Syracusans, was of Parian marble. The draperies of the figures are not only naturalistic but extremely graceful.

The Roman period is represented by a fine nude of the Greek youth, Antinous, the favorite of the Emperor Hadrian. The museum also contains numerous other sculptural fragments, statues, sherds, terracottas, vases, ceramics, etc. All the exhibits were found either in the sanctuary and the Marmaria or in the immediately adjacent neighborhood.

The Olive Country

From Delphi to Náfpaktos the distance is 78 miles inland, 70 miles along the sea. The road climbs down the last bastions of Parnassós into the plain of huge gnarled olive trees, some of which are said to be centuries old, the olives which they produce—large, bluish and fleshy—known as "Amfissa olives", being among the best in Greece. The branch left (south) leads four miles south to Itea, where cruise ships often call.

On the tapering western arm of the Bay of Itea lies the port of Galaxidi, whose Byzantine church of the Savior dates from the

13th century. From here the scenic coastal road skirts the Corinthian Gulf via Eratini to Náfpaktos.

The narrower, winding inland road leads in a westerly direction to Amfissa (14 miles from Delphi), situated on the slope of a hill crowned with a medieval castle built by the Franks and Catalans in the 13th and 14th centuries, when the town was known as Salona. The ruins of the castle include some quadrangular and polygonal walls, two watch towers, two gateways, a cistern, a circular dungeon and the remains of a Frankish and a Byzantine church.

At Amfissa one road leads through the gorge of Gravia and over the Bralos pass to Lamia or the motorway near Thermopylae. The east-west branch continues 68 miles to Náfpaktos; after Amfissa there is a steep climb up the massif of Vardoussia in a series of hairpin bends. Magnificent views are obtained of Delphi, Parnassós, the gorge of the Pleistos and the olive groves of the Sacred Plain. After the village of Lidoriki, the partly unpaved road hugs the scenically magnificent vast artificial lake created by the damming up of the Mórnos River. On the walled acropolis of antique Kallion, on a rock still rising above the waters that cover the lower town, the largest collection of 4th-century B.C. clay seals was discovered. The lake supplies 2 million cubic meters of water daily through pipelines to Lake Ylíki in Boeotia, thence to Lake Marathon, to quench the thirst of Athens 120 miles away. The road crosses the dam and follows the trickle of water in the original bed of the river between steep green banks until it reaches the sea near Náfpaktos.

From here, the road runs along a short flat coastal strip to Antírio, from where the ferry can be taken across the narrows of the Gulf of Corinth to Rio and the northern shore of the Peloponnese. Westward the motorway bypasses Messolongi and then turns north to Epirus.

A visit to Náfpaktos and even an overnight stay, is recommended, despite the indifferent accommodation. Situated on a fertile coastal strip washed by tributary streams of the Mórnos, the little harbor faces the peaks of the Panahaïko in the Peloponnese. The bathing beaches are adequate, and there is an air of friendliness about the little town. Luxuriant bushes of oleanders, bright in summer with red, pink and white blooms, line the banks of the streams, and the flowers and comparatively lush vegetation present a strong contrast to the austere grandeur of the Parnassós country.

The hill behind the town is dotted with scattered blocks of masonry, choked in undergrowth, of a vast rambling Venetian castle (some of the walls and bastions are still intact), through which it is pleasant to wander and obtain glimpses of the blue waters of the channel between the mainland and the Peloponnese. It is hardly less agreeable to sit in the evening at one of the cafés in the little semi-circular fortified harbor and watch the caiques chugging in and out between the two miniature medieval towers guarding the entrance into the port, while the lights begin to twinkle in the villages strung out along the opposite shore of the Peloponnese.

PRACTICAL INFORMATION FOR DELPHI

AND THE PARNASSÓS

WHEN TO COME. Most of the Parnassós country can be seen in the course of a visit to and from Delphi. The Boeotian plains are very hot and dusty in the summer months. So the best time of the year for a visit is April–May and October–November. But the grandeur of the scenery at Delphi is such, however, that a profound impression will be made on the visitor in all weathers. Dramatic storms are frequent in autumn.

A visit of the ruins involves much climbing which is exhausting during the middle of the day in the summer when the motorcoaches disgorge vast hoards of sightseers. In spring the countryside is comparatively green; a variety of wild flowers grow on the hillside, and the fields around Thebes are carpeted with red tulips. The *Vláhikos Gámos,* a mock-highland wedding, brings large crowds to Thebes on Shrove Monday. Náfpaktos has pleasant beaches.

Mountaineers will find the ascent of Parnassós most practicable in July, August and September. But you can also drive to the ski centers.

HOW TO GET ABOUT. One can go to Thebes and Livadiá by bus or rail from Athens. Orhomenos, Chaironeia and Davlia may be visited from Livadiá. The visit to Ossiós Loukas, lying eight miles off the main Livadiá to Delphi road, is almost invariably combined with the Delphi tour from Athens. The distance is under 100 miles, whether you take the mountainous inland road or the motorway, which goes as far as Thebes. Continuing from Delphi via Amfissa over the western shoulder, or crossing the main range of Parnassós from Arahova between the ski centers of Fterolaka and Gerontovrahos to Eptalofos, both connecting over the Bralos pass with the motorway at either Thermopylae or Lamía, make possible a circular detour on the way from Athens to Thessaloniki.

One-day and two-day coach tours to Delphi are operated daily by various coach companies in Athens. Longer coach tours lasting four or five days and visiting the main archeological sites always take in Delphi.

Náfpaktos can be reached by car from Delphi by the spectacular coastal road via Ítea and Galaxidi (70 miles) or inland via Amfissa and the Mornos valley (78 miles); and from Athens on the toll motorway via Corinth and the northern shore of the Peloponnese. There is a car ferry three times daily from Egio to Agios Nikolaos (5 miles from Eratini) and half-hourly across the narrows between Rio and Antirio. There is also a hydrofoil between Patra and Náfpaktos.

 HOTELS AND RESTAURANTS. You are best off eating at your hotel. But in cheaper hotels, where there is no restaurant, the owner will recommend the most suitable restaurant or tavern, where you will at least be able to get a simple meal. The red wine from Arahova is rough but drinkable. Try the large juicy olives from Amfissa; they are among the best in the country.

AMFIKLIA. *Leonidas* (I), tel. 22 544. 14 rooms, no restaurant.

AMFISSA. *Stallion* (I), tel. 28 330. 24 rooms, no restaurant.

ANTIKYRA. *Galini* (I), tel. 41 319. 16 rooms, no restaurant.

ARAHOVA. *Anemolia* (M), tel. 31 640/4. 42 rooms, airconditioned, disco; on slopes of Mt. Parnassos. *Xenia* (M), tel. 31 230/2. 43 double rooms; in the village but equally splendid view over the Pleistos gorge.

DELPHI. *Amalia* (E), tel. 82 101/5. 185 rooms, airconditioned; for once large is best, though hardly beautiful. *Vouzas* (E), tel. 82 232/4. 60 rooms, closest to the ruins, overhanging the Pleistos gorge; most remarkable for the unremarkable food, yet halfboard only. *Xenia* (E), tel. 82 151/2. 44 rooms, higher up the village. *Europa* (M), tel. 82 353. 46 double rooms, next to the Cultural Center of Europe. *King Iniohos* (M), tel. 82 701/3. 40 rooms, airconditioned. *Zeus* (M), tel. 82 691/4, 28 rooms. All insist on halfboard.

Numerous cheaper modern hotels line the main street, called after King Paul and Queen Friederika. Only those with restaurant terraces looking over the gorge down to the gulf of Itea are listed, but the view has to compensate for the largely uninteresting food. *Hermes* (I), tel. 82 318. 24 rooms. *Iniohos* (I), tel. 82 316. 15 rooms. *Parnassos* (I), tel. 82 321. 23 rooms. *Pythia* (I) tel. 82 328. 27 rooms.

Restaurants. *Though* (M), better than some of the (E) hotel dining rooms. *Asteras,* food and view. *Challet Maniati,* big garden opposite the Xenia hotel. *Symposium,* reliable, tennis court.

ERATINI. *Delphi Beach* (M), tel. 31 237/8. 177 rooms, halfboard, airconditioned, pool, tennis, disco.

GALAXIDI. *Ta Adelfia* (I), tel. 41 110. 5 rooms.

ITEA. *Galini* (M), tel. 32 278. 30 double rooms, roofgarden. *Kalafati* (M), tel. 32 294. 37 rooms, no restaurant. *Panorama* (M), tel. 33 161. 27 rooms, no restaurant, closest to the muddy beach.

LIVADIÁ. *Livadiá* (M), tel. 23 611/5.51 rooms, no restaurant. *Philippos* (I), tel. 24 931. 50 rooms, restaurant.

NÁFPAKTOS. *Xenia* (M), tel. 22 301, 48 double rooms, beach. The other recommendable ones, but without restaurants, are at the opposite ends of the town, across the road from the beaches. At Psani, *Lido* (M), tel. 22 501. 15 rooms, airconditioned, disco. At Gribovo *Akti* (M), tel. 28 464. 60 rooms.

Restaurant. *Fisherman's Boat* (M), an American-Greek couple serves good seafood.

PLATANITIS. *Kalydon Beach* (I), tel. 28 645. 40 rooms.

THEBES. *Dionyssion Melathron* (I), tel. 27 855. Most of the 30 rooms with showers. *Meletiou* (I), tel. 27 333. 34 rooms.

SKI CENTERS AND MOUNTAIN REFUGES. Fterolaka and Kellária on the Parnassós are Greece's largest ski centers. No hotel, but snack bar and self-service restaurant. Twelve skilifts up to 2,200 m; reached by 17 miles paved road from Arahova to parking at Kondókedro for 800 cars. Main refuge at Sarantari, 1900m.

THE PELOPONNESE

Four Millennia of History

Hanging like a large leaf from the stem of the Corinthian Isthmus, the Pelopónissos (Peloponnese) has also been called Morea, which means mulberry leaf. This slight botanical variance is nothing compared to the bewildering variety of imposing ruins, situated in equally varied and beautiful scenery. 4,000 years of history are more fully and comprehensibly illustrated on this peninsula of a mere 8,287 square miles than anywhere else in Europe. A gap of a 100 years in the stately cavalcade of temples, palaces, churches, Crusader castles and mosques is a rare exception, due to catastrophic barbarian invasions, like that of the Dorians in the 11th century B.C., or of the Turks in the 15th century A.D.

The Peloponnese, the isle of Pelops, is named after the son of Tantalus, whose intolerably tragic descendants dominate the half-legendary Mycenaean centuries. This was the area's golden age, but it was to intervene prominently in world affairs three further times: when Sparta contributed decisively to Persia's defeat in the 5th century B.C., and gained after the Peloponnesian War a brief ascendancy over the other Greek cities; when the Frankish principalities of the Morea formed the cornerstone of Latin power in the Levant in the 13th and 14th centuries; and when the bishop of Patras raised the standard of revolt against Turkish domination in 1821. But more important than that is the peaceful contest the Peloponnese has given mankind: the Olympic Games.

Exploring the Peloponnese

Unless landing off a cruise, Athens is the most likely start for a tour of the seven provinces: Corinthia, Achaia, Elis, Arcadia, Messinia, Laconia and Argolis. The toll highway leading south from the capital roughly follows the coast for 50 miles to Corinth, over the same stretch of country along which Theseus met and defeated numerous robbers and giants.

The Canal of Corinth is 6,939 yards long and 75 feet wide. Completed between 1882 and 1893, it is spanned by a road and a railway bridge. The concept of connecting the Ionian with the Aegean sea originated with the tyrant Periander of Corinth, one of the Seven Wise Men of antiquity, in the 7th century B.C. and was toyed with by Alexander, Julius Caesar and Caligula. But only Nero proceeded actively with the tremendous task, the emperor himself striking the first blow with a golden pickaxe, thus setting a fashion for royalty. Vespasian, who had offended his imperial master by falling asleep during a song recital, supplied a labor force of 6,000 Jewish prisoners of war; work was far progressed when the rebellions of 68 A.D. stopped the excavations. But Periander had constructed a paved road and up to the 13th century ships were dragged on rollers across the Isthmus.

The remains of the Isthmian wall stretch across the narrow neck of land behind the bridges. The foundations of the original fortifications, which failed to keep out the Dorians in about 1200 B.C., have been unearthed by an American archeological team in continuing excavations. The wall was restored on the occasions of subsequent invasions, against the Persians in 480 B.C. and by the Emperor Justinian against the Avars in the sixth century. Rebuilt on a grand scale by the Emperor Manuel II in 1415, it proved incapable of withstanding the Turkish onslaught 43 years later.

Little remains of the Isthmian sanctuary to the south, at the head of the Saronikos gulf, as it was pillaged for stone to build the wall. Celebrated in honor of Poseidon, the biennial games were second only to the Olympic festival, and the scene of important historic events. In 481 B.C. the Panhellenic League of 31 states decided on the defense against the Persians; in 338 Philip of Macedonia and in 336 B.C. Alexander the Great, forced their elections as *hegemons* (leaders) on the reluctant Greeks; and in the same Isthmian stadium the victorious Roman general Flaminius proclaimed the independence of Greece from Macedonian rule in 196 B.C., to swallow it up all the better 50 years later. An early Christian basilica has been partly restored. Among the local finds in the small museum are unique Egyptian glass mosaics, raised from a ship that foundered in the harbor about A.D. 400.

New Kórinthos (Corinth), built on the present site after a devastating earthquake in 1858, was in its turn destroyed in 1928. The toll road to Patra and the road to Argos bypass the modern town, which, despite its lovely position, could at best be called innocuous.

Old Corinth, the Frivolous City

Along the Patra road, which branches off to the left, the ruins of ancient Corinth are reached after a five-mile drive through vineyards. One of the oldest towns of Greece, it underwent in antiquity the customary changes from subjection to the kings of Mycenae to government by the Dorian aristocracy, replaced by enlightened tyrants, a title which in antiquity did not necessarily evoke the same feelings as nowadays. Under these tyrants Corinth became the leading commercial city in Greece, which it remained for a while after the restoration of oligarchy. But trade had dampened the belligerent spirit of old, and Corinth's main contribution to the Persian wars were the prayers for victory, offered piously by its celebrated courtesans.

The rising commercial power of Athens led to constant frictions, which finally culminated in the Peloponnesian War. Corinth regained supremacy and became the largest city in Greece. Its vast, luxury-loving wealth brought about pillage and total destruction by the Romans in 146 B.C. All men were killed, women and children sold into slavery, and the site remained uninhabited until the foundation of a Roman colony by order of Julius Caesar in 44 B.C. This explains why there is only one Greek ruin, the seven Doric columns of the 6th-century temple of Apollo, dominating the well-preserved remains of the Roman town. On both sides of the Lechaeon road, the chief artery leading to the port, and on the market-place, the ruins of public and private buildings are adequate to give a comprehensive picture of the frivolous capital of Roman Greece, which soon regained its former prosperity, due to its position between Italy and Asia, besides controlling all trade between the mainland and the Peloponnese. The well-arranged museum contains finds from the whole of Corinthia, but because of the destruction, little of the Greek town, except a fine collection of pottery and the unique stoup of holy water from Poseidon's temple at Isthmia. Outstanding among the Roman statuary is the archaic sphinx, recently discovered in the antique cemetery.

In 51 A.D., Saint Paul fulminated against immorality, caused a riot, but was acquitted by the Roman proconsul Gallio. The earthquake of 375 A.D. and Alaric's Goths 20 years later, drove the survivors up to the top of Acrocorinth, behind the ancient town. On the highest point stood the temple of Aphrodite, with no less than a thousand sacred prostitutes dedicated to the service of the goddess. An awesome proof of the ancients' lustfulness and vigor to satisfy the carnal and financial exigencies after such a climb. In the Middle Ages, deploying heroism in different ways, Acrocorinth became a fortress town. Strengthened and enlarged by Byzantines, Crusaders, Venetians and Turks in turn, the two miles of crenellated walls enclosing 60 acres of the summit are the most imposing medieval monument in Greece. Cars can drive up to the triple gate, and the superb view over the Saronikos and Corinthian gulfs, framed by the mountains of the Peloponnese and the mainland, should on no account be missed.

It is 83 miles to Patra, through a narrow, fertile plain, delightfully green with vineyards and olive trees even in the height of summer. Road and rail run close to the blue waters of the Corinthian gulf, while the motorway higher up along the gentle pine- and cypress-clad Peloponnesian foothills bypasses the coastal villages of Vraháti, Kokkóni and Kiato, from where a road leads to the ruins of Sikyon, now Sikyóna, four miles inland. The scene of particularly bloody struggles between the Dorian aristocracy and non-Dorian tyrants, it was destroyed in 303 B.C. by Demetrius Poliorcetes, then rebuilt and named Demetrias. The theater, the gymnasium, the council chamber and a lovely fountain all belong to the Hellenistic town. The museum is in a partly rebuilt Roman bath.

Twenty-five miles of mountain road, turning inland after the Kiato bridge, lead to Stymfalía (Stymphalia), where Heracles accomplished his 6th labor by killing the man-eating birds. Now there is only some less exciting duck-shooting on the reedy shores of the lake, graced by some uninspiring ruins of small temples and ramparts. A further eight miles climb steeply to the hotel at Kastania and extensive fir forests round Goura (3,100 ft.). Another scenic road branches east below the lake to Nemea and thence to the Corinth-Argos highway.

Ahaïa (Achaia)

This province begins eight miles after Kiato, at Xylókastro, a popular summer resort with a magnificent view over the Parnassós and Elikonas range from the pine-girt beach. Xylókastro stands on the site of one of the 12 cities founded in the northwestern Peloponnese by the Achaians after their expulsion from Argos.

Another scenic road zigzags up the mountains to Trikala, which belongs to Corinthia. Only 20 miles from the heat of the Mediterranean one finds relief in the cool freshness of three tiny villages strung out in a fine Alpine setting. The cave where Hermes was born is near the lower of the Hellenic Alpine Club's two refuges on Mount Ziria (7,900 ft.), snowcovered till June above the green valley. A skilift leads into this main skiing center of the south.

The next branch inland from the orange groves of the coast climbs the verdant slopes affording a superb view over the sea and distant mountains framed by perpendicular cliffs, past the monastery of Méga Spíleo to Kalávryta (2,500 ft.). Another approach is from Diakoftó, by the rack and pinion railway through the wild magnificence of the Vouraïkos gorge. The line precariously overhangs the madly churning stream, shaded by a profusion of trees and bushes. From Zahlorou station half-way up, the road mounts to the monastery of Méga Spíleo, a white elephant of the first magnitude. The old monastery burnt down in 1934, and as it happened to be one of the richest in Greece was rebuilt on a grandiose scale, though without reference to any recognizable style. Moreover, no account was taken of the constantly diminishing number of monks, who now huddle together in one wing during the long cold winter. Central heating was installed, but never functioned, because of the expense of bringing up the fuel. The electrical switches are likewise purely ornamental, and one wonders with what feelings the icon of Our Lady looks on this vain modernity. Following a vision, St. Symeon and St. Theodore discovered the miraculous icon, painted by St. Luke, in the large cave behind the church, whence the name of Méga Spíleo. Despite repeated fires, there are still some lovely 10th-century illuminated gospels, relics, silver crosses and pretentious Russian jewelry, gifts of Catherine the Great.

Kalávryta was burnt by the Germans in 1943, and over a thousand of its inhabitants massacred. The magnificent plane trees, the cool streams, and the ruined Frankish castle on a rock, lend some distinction to the ugly modern village. The falls of the Styx are imposing, but the excursion to this river of the underworld is exhausting and requires a guide. The Agia Lavra Monastery, also burnt down, has been rebuilt on the same prominent hill, which overlooks the Kalávryta plain. It is commonly believed that Bishop Germanos of Patra raised here the banner of revolt against the Turks on March 25, 1821. The longer (48 miles) road from Patra to Kalávryta runs through superb mountain scenery and links up after 20 miles with the Patra-Tripoli road. The branch right (west) 13 miles after Kalávryta goes via Tripótama to Olympia by the shortest, loveliest and most difficult (no signposts) route, 56 miles through the fastness of Mt. Erýmanthos, where Heracles slew the Erymanthian boar, and remainders of the vast oak forests that once covered the entire interior.

Eight miles past Diakoftó is Égio, prettily situated on three levels rising from the sea. Río, the Castle of the Morea, was built by Sultan Bayazid II in 1499, and together with Antírio, the Castle of Roumeli on the opposite shore, guarded the narrow entrance to the Corinthian gulf. Between the two fortresses is the car ferry on the main road to Epirus.

Pátra is the third town of Greece and its main western port where currants, dried Corinth raisins—so much prized in Anglo-Saxon cakes—are dispatched by the shipload. There is a Roman theater and the usual Frankish castle, but more distinctive are the arcaded streets, equally beneficial in the hot summer and the rainy winter. St. Andrew was crucified here and became the city's patron saint. His relics, however, met with even greater adventures than the apostle in his lifetime. The Emperor Constantine had them conveyed to Constantinople, except for one shoulder, three fingers, a bone and sundry teeth, which St. Regulus, bishop of Pátra, spirited away to Scotland, where they were received with due respect. In the 9th century the head was returned to Pátra, later returned to Rome, and finally, in the present ecumenical spirit, Pope Paul VI returned the head once again in 1965, to, one hopes, permanent rest in the cathedral.

Ilída (Elis)

After Káto Ahaía the road turns into the plain of Elis, dominated by Castel Tornese rising above the village of Kástro. A circular branch right (west) either from Lehena or Andravida skirts the castle hill, descends to the largest beach hotel in the Peloponnese and rejoins the main road via Loutra Kylínis, Greece's most up-to-date spa for respiratory diseases, at Gastouni. From here a branch left (east) follows the Piniós River to Ilída, ancient Elis, where the Austrian Archeological School is bringing to light the agora and theater of Olympia's protecting power.

Built by Villehardouin in 1219, hexagonal Castel Tornese remains an outstanding example of Frankish medieval architecture in the Levant, the bailey, keep and vaulted gallery still intact. Originally called Clairmont, the castle's later name derived from the Tournois coined there by the Frankish mint. Despite the formidable walls Castel Tornese failed in its main task: to protect the greater port of the Morea, Clarenza, of which little remains after its destruction by Constantine Palaeologus, the last Byzantine emperor. His later misfortunes were believed to have originated in a curse he incurred for his treatment of Clarenza. Railway and road branches terminate at Kylíni (not to be confused with Loutra Kylínis, about 12 miles south), whence it is less than two hours by ferry boat to the island of Zákynthos.

Andréville, now Andravida, on the main road, was the capital of the Frankish principality. The sad remains of the Gothic cathedral of St. Sophia are rather depressing. Pýrgos, a few miles from the fine Katákolo and Spiatza beaches, is a road and rail junction. The southern branch of the railway, as well as the coastal road, pass Kaiafas, another watering place, this time for skin diseases, on an island in a lake and near a splendid, lonely beach. There, according to local tradition, the High Priest Kaiaphas was shipwrecked on his way to Rome after the Crucifixion. Washing off the salt in the hot springs he transmitted to them his evil sulphurous smell, which has persisted ever since. The line continues along the gulf of Arcadia to Kyparissía, 40 miles through particularly beautiful scenery, which loses none of its charm all the way south to Methoni.

The first branch road east leads to Krestena, where it is joined by the seven-mile shortcut across the Alfios river from Olympia. The 28 miles up through idyllic hills to Andritsena make possible the inclusion of the temple of Bassae in the excursion to Olympia and a return inland via Karítena, Megalópoli and Trípoli. The second branch, 22 miles, connects with the Megalópoli-Kalamata road.

Olympia, Center of the Panhellenic Games

Thirteen miles east of Pýrgos lies Olympia, terminus of the railway, among over 5,000 acres of the *Grove of the Sacred Altis*, revived as a national park in 1976. Quadrennial games were held here from time immemorial, first in honor of Hera, then of Zeus. Greek chronology was based on the Olympiads beginning with the festival of 776 B.C. and until A.D. 393 athletes from as far apart as Sicily and Asia Minor competed under the protection of a sacred truce. Apollo and Heracles were reputed among the early winners, while Nero was certainly the most quixotic, falling twice off his chariot, as he had difficulties in controlling his team of ten horses (all other competitors had to content themselves with four), yet, not surprisingly, coming first. He likewise won the singing contest, specially introduced to display his talents, whereupon he helped himself, as he had in Delphi, to some 500 statues.

Women were excluded under penalty of death. One mother, however, accompanied her boy disguised as a trainer. Betraying herself in her joy over his victory, her life was spared because she was the sister and mother of Olympic victors. Increasing honors were heaped on the winners, their statues were erected in the Altis—which must have been a forest of statuary—as well as in their home towns, and great poets glorified their successes. There were usually 14 contests, extending over four days, culminating in the prize-giving ceremony and a feast on the fifth.

The almost rectangular Altis sanctuary is bounded by the Alfiós and Kladéos rivers, which both changed their courses in the Middle Ages, and on the north side by steep pyramidical Mount Kronion, which contributed with repeated landslides to the sanctuary's obliteration by 20 feet of mud and pebbles.

The chariot races took place in the hippodrome which, though partly washed away, was the first to be rediscovered in the 18th century. From 1875 on, systematic excavations were undertaken by Professor Curtius under the active patronage of the German Crown Prince Frederick. Quite likely, it was Hitler's wish to emulate the imperial family that was responsible for his personal order to the reluctant archeologists to dig up the stadium during the German occupation in World War II. Below the repeatedly raised earth embankments, which finally accommodated some 20,000 spectators, the largest of its kind, a great number of ex-votos was discovered, including Miltiades' helmet, dedicated after his victory at Marathon, now a prize exhibit in the museum.

The move from the old building across the Kladeos Bridge, donated by Kaiser Wilhelm II, to the earthquake-proof museum below Mount Kronion was completed in 1982. The two pediments of Zeus' temple are among the most brilliant examples of ancient sculpture. The front pediment commemorates Pelop's chariot race, with Zeus standing in the middle; the other, artistically even superior, depicts the favorite theme of the fight between the drunken Centaurs and the Lapiths with Apollo trying to restore order. His serene nobility is perhaps more moving than the flashy beauty of Praxiteles' Hermes, the famous statue found near Hera's temple, Olympia's oldest, of which two columns still stand in the shade of pine-clad Kronion. The metopes of the temple representing Heracles' Labors, the Victory of Paeonios flying down from the sky, the terracotta Zeus and Ganymede, a head of Hera and a head of Antinous are among the few masterpieces that remain from the wealth of beauty that once filled the Altis.

The ruins of the religious and secular monuments in the Altis are well marked, so it is necessary to mention only the most outstanding. The great Doric temple of Zeus still dominates the sanctuary as it has since the 5th century B.C., though the broken columns lie scattered under the trees. The sacred flame burnt within a rough circle of stone about ten feet in diameter, where the Olympic oracle spoke through the crackling of the sacrificial bull's skin. The flame was relit every spring by a "spark from heaven", unfortunately no more to be relied upon when runners convey the flame to wherever the Games may be held. The god's ivory and gold statue by Phidias, one of the Seven Wonders of Antiquity, was taken to Constantinople by the Emperor Theodosius, and perished in a fire. The arched passage leading to the stadium, the portico of the gymnasium, Phidias' workshop, and the house of Nero to the east of the sanctuary precincts, are particularly interesting for their intrinsic charm or their historical associations.

No need to identify every piece of Greek or Roman foundation; just enjoy the enchanting landscape and be grateful to the German archeologists who have made the Altis a grove again; the aging pines they planted are gradually replaced by the olive trees of antiquity. If Olympia is chosen as the permanent site of the Olympics, hopefully the huge installations needed will be built at a sufficient distance to preserve the idyllic setting.

Arkadia (Arcadia)

The road east passes the International Olympic Academy and the Museum of the Olympic Games to follow the Alfios river through a valley charmingly Arcadian in the romantic 18th-century tradition, though actually still in Elis. The wild Arcadian mountains further on have nothing of the idyllic quality the word acquired for the Romantics. In antiquity Arcadia was renowned for its backwardness and cruelty, only imperfectly counterbalanced by compulsory musical instruction.

Along the Ládonas river the scenery changes from bucolic to Alpine. A bridge on the right after five miles leads to the rudimentary spa called just that, in Greek Loutra. Five miles further along the Ládonas a road forks left (north) to Trópea and a large, artificial lake created by damming the Ládonas. The water rushes underground for six miles to the hydroelectric plant. The winding lake is enclosed by steep, pine-clad mountains, and is strangely reminiscent of a Norwegian Fjord. The road forking right eight miles after the picturesque mountain village of Langadia leads via Dimitsána to Karítena. In spite of the hair-raising sheer drop of 1,000 ft. after Ipsoúnda the rough road is sufficiently wide to permit full enjoyment of the surrounding peaks and summits, snow-covered from November to May. Another narrower road from Tripolis via Davia links up at this scenic spot, but though running through magnificent fir forests, only those young in heart and car should attempt this splendid remoteness. Both roads provide, however, an adventurous contrast to the usual approach leading up from Megalopoli through vast olive groves to Karítena, which crowds up a precipitous rock to an imposing Frankish castle. This was the fitting abode for its builder, Geoffrey de Bruyères, a model of chivalry, and one of the few feudal lords trying to reconcile his Greek subjects to Frankish domination. The main road continues straight on (east) through rugged wooded mountains before turning south, down to the plain of Tripoli.

The capital of Arcadia is an uninteresting market town, as it was razed to the ground by Ibrahim Pasha during the War of Independence. And there is little to see of the great temple of Athena at Tegea to the south. Nothing now stands higher than the second drum of the columns, and the stones have been taken to rebuild Tripoli. Nicli, important in Byzantine times and seat of the High Court of the Frankish principality, suffered a similar fate.

Nor is Mantinía, eight miles to the north, of particular interest, except to the historian and archeologist. Mantinía, like Messíni and Megalopoli, was intended by Epaminondas to keep down the defeated Spartans. But, unlike at his two other foundations, little now remains of the strong wall, with its ten gates and 126 towers, and the theater is only partly uncovered. Battlefields are notoriously difficult to trace in Greece, but somewhere nearby, Epaminondas died in a cavalry engagement in 363 B.C.

The road from Olympia to Tripoli is chosen by those in a hurry to reach Sparta or to return to Athens via Argos. But then the better part of Arcadia comprising the outstanding temple at Vasses (Bassae), is missed. The easiest approach is from Megalopoli over the vertiginous Alfiós bridge at Karítena, whose castle remains in sight for mile after winding mile. Andritsena is a well-shaded village clambering up a mountain slope and the final seven miles to Bassae open up ever more grandiose vistas. On a narrow platform, 3,700 feet above sea level, stands the second best preserved temple in Greece. But even more impressive than the severe beauty of the long, unbroken Doric colonnades is the contrast between this masterpiece of man, and the wild, unspoilt nature. The time for a visit is early morning or late afternoon, when the stark granite mountains are aglow with rich pink and violet hues, and the awe-inspiring solitude is unlikely to be disturbed by crowds of tourists. Dedicated to Apollo Epikouros (the Succorer), the temple was designed by Iktinos, the architect of the Parthenon, and erected in about 418 B.C. by the Phygalians in gratitude for saving them from a pestilence.

South of Tripoli beyond the first mountain barrier, stretches a rolling, oak-grown plain round Epaminondas' most ambitious creation, Megalopolis. The walls were 5½ miles long, and the theater, cut into a hill, the largest in Greece. The ruins bear witness to the ancient greatness, but not the modern town, badly polluted by a large thermo-electric plant. Shortly after Paradisia (don't be misled by the name) a highway branches right (west) to Kyparissía (25 miles), roughly following the railway line.

Messinia

The province is entered by rail or coastal highway from Pýrgos. Epaminondas built Kyparissía as Messini's harbor, but after a chequered career it is now a sleepy little town with dilapidated Turkish houses climbing the rock to the Byzantine castle. An idyllic, little-known corner of the Peloponnese stretches south, like a huge park with olive and cypress groves, through which one catches glimpses of the sea. Shepherds tend their flocks, and the occasional villages do not detract from the serenity of a perfectly enchanting landscape.

The road roughly follows the shore till Gargaliani which perches on a rock-shelf above the fertile coastal plain. It then turns inland to Hóra, where the museum contains the finds from Nestor's palace. The royal tombs are so poorly indicated that no one's conscience will be ruffled by missing out on this series of rock tombs, whose chronology is anyway disputed (1500–1100 B.C.). After Hóra the road converges on the sea at Nestor's palace. A corrugated iron roof shelters walls still standing about a foot high over a considerable area. Ancient Pylos provides a fascinating example of Mycenaean palace architecture, centered on the large open hearth in the throne room. Main curiosity is a 13th-century B.C. bathtub of painted clay. The bones in the sarcophagus found in the well-preserved beehive tomb 80 yards north are commonly believed to be those of Nestor, but are more likely to belong to an earlier king. Superfluous to say that the view is superb. This was the first consideration for the ancient Greeks before choosing the site for a temple or palace.

Modern Pýlos (Navarino to the Venetians) stands at the southern horn of the large, landlocked bay in which the allied fleets of Great Britain, France and Russia destroyed the Turco-Egyptian forces in 1827, and thus made Greek independence a reality. The rocky island of Sfaktiría (Sphacteria) which almost blocks the harbor, was the scene of another famous engagement. In 425 B.C. an Athenian expeditionary corps forced the Spartan garrison to surrender after a memorable siege lasting 72 days. The huge Venetian castle dominating Pýlos is well worth a visit, but does not compare with the splendor of Methoni in the south.

Methoni's fortifications are a perfect model of the military architecture of the period. Together with Koroni on the other side of the western prong of the Peloponnese it was the first Venetian foothold on the Greek mainland, and the two fortresses were called "the eyes of the Republic". Koroni is less impressive with the peaceful convent of St. John the Baptist within the castle walls. But it commands an incomparable view across the Messinian gulf to the Taÿgetos and the mountains of the Mani. Koroni is 18 miles south via the simple bathing beaches of Ágios Avgoustínos, Petalidi and Ágios Andréas from the main Pýlos-Kalamata road (33 miles). The direct, mainly coastal 18 miles from Methoni via Finikoúndas to Koroni, though lovely, are hard going in parts.

Dreary, modern Messini bears no relation to its antique namesake and no comparison with its offspring in Sicily. The enormous walls of the ancient town, Epaminondas' third foundation, climb and descend the mountain a mile beyond the village of Arsinoë. The turn-off from the Kalamata-Tripoli highway is clearly indicated and a paved road passes through the splendid masonry of the broken towers. Far below, among extensive olive groves, are the ruins of temples and the agora; closer inspection necessitates a steep descent. Mount Ithómi, 2,650 feet above the sea, was the last refuge of the earlier Messinians during their 300 years of war and rebellion against the Spartan invaders, to whom it fell at last in 459 B.C. The view from the deserted monastery on the top over the Messinian plain and gulf rewards the intrepid climber.

Kalamata, constructed by the French in 1829 as capital of Messinia, has succumbed to concrete anonymity which has even submerged the small ancient theater within the very ruined Frankish castle on a low hill; the tiny Byzantine Church of the Twelve Apostles is at least quaint, but the sad little museum only features second-rate Roman miscellany. Of greater interest to the practical-minded are the astoundingly cheap products of the local Levi-Strauss factory, the tasty black olives, and silk handkerchiefs handmade and sold by the nuns in the convent off the cathedral square.

Orange and lemon orchards extend for two miles to the sea, and along the eastern beach is a string of restaurants where music and movement continue till a late hour in summer. Five miles south on the road into the Mani, lies the popular resort of Almyró, followed by Mikra Mantinia. The road turns inland to Kampos, to rejoin the sea at Kardámili (26 miles). Stop on the bridge to enjoy a perfect landscape.

Lakonia—Where Wordiness was a Disgrace

Abruptly, the lush vegetation gives place to the lunar landscape of the Inner Mani, refuge of the last Spartans fleeing before the Slav invaders. Organized in clans, they maintained their independence in fortified towerhouses, necessitated by the constant blood-feuds arising from quarrels over the scarce soil.

Opposite Ítylo is the imposing fortress of Keléfa, conquered from the Turks by the Venetian Morosini in 1685. Ítylo beach seems like an oasis before climbing to the rocky waste of Areópoli (51 miles), the principal village and junction with the road from Gýthio (16 miles). The two large stalactite caves of Glyfáda and Alepótripa are six miles through Pýrgos Dírou on the west coast. The former, electrically lit and easily accessible by specially constructed motorboats might well turn out to be the largest seacave ever discovered, as so far only three miles of splendid chambers and halls have been explored, with corridors and passages extending into a mysterious distance, in antiquity reputedly one of the entrances to the Underworld. In the latter, cave paintings, stone implements and even a primitive pottery workshop of paleolithic man have been found. (*Closed for further excavations.*)

A branch left (east) leads to Kotronas (9 miles) on the solitary east coast, while the main road continues due south through the fishing village of Gerolimín to Vathiá, where several of the characteristic towers have been restored as a traditional settlement, overlooking Cape Ténaro, the southernmost point of continental Europe except for Tarifa in Spain.

The circuit of the Mani, though most rewarding, requires at least a half, but better a full day. No less spectacular, and much shorter, is the direct Kalamata-Sparta road (37 miles) following the Nedon gorge, before climbing through fir forests to the Taÿgetos pass at 3,300 feet.

The descent through the Langada gorge on a good but rather narrow road cut into the solid rock affords fine views over the sea of olive trees in the plain of surprisingly un-Spartan Spárti (Sparta), bisected by a wide, tree-lined avenue where 19th-century neo-classical houses maintain provincial respectability among recent cement blocks of manageable proportions. Water from the broad Évrotas (Eurotas) screened by pleasant orchards, flows into a swimming pool among the trees, and though icy, it offers welcome refreshment in the hot summer. Fortunately there is no need to emulate the luckless boys of antiquity who had to swim the Eurotas in winter in a desperate quest for physical fitness. Yet the hour of Sparta's greatness was shorter than that of cultured Athens, and pleasure-loving Corinth outlasted both. Except for the foundations of Artemis' sanctuary, of Athena's Brazen House, where two kings were starved to death, and the Menelaio to the east, the shrine of deified Menelaus and Helen, as well as some fragments of Apollo's temple at Amýkles, where hyacinths still bloom in spring from his lover Hyacinthus' drops of blood, nothing remains of ancient Sparta, which was a mere conglomeration of five villages. For hundreds of years it relied on the martial superiority of its warrior caste, and only in its decline were fortifications hurriedly constructed in 369 B.C. The Romans built a theater facing the temple of Artemis, the better to gloat over the scourging of the young Spartans before the goddess' statue.

Half-legendary Lykourgos organized Sparta on a warlike basis sometime between 900 and 600 B.C., his laws being interpreted ever more stringently with the passing of time. Its worst features were the oppression of the earlier Achaean inhabitants, once ruled by Menelaus and Helen of Troy, now serfs known as Helots, by an all-powerful secret police. But even membership of the Dorian aristocracy was a mixed blessing. Boys were taken at the age of seven from their parents and submitted to a training without parallel in history for ruthlessness, their only consolation being a lover undergoing similar sufferings. Stealing was encouraged as it sharpened the wit, but being caught out was cruelly punished. Speech was reduced to laconic brevity and trade impeded by an iron coinage—not accepted outside Spartan territory—intended to enforce contempt of wealth and luxury. As a result Spartan kings and generals became notoriously rapacious, and increasingly open to bribes. In short, Sparta presented all the hateful characteristics of a totalitarian state. But Lykourgos received his punishment at long last: in front of the large, modern cathedral stands what might easily qualify as the most hideous statue in the Peloponnese. And to add insult to injury it bears only the sculptor's, but not the lawgiver's name.

Perhaps the paucity of sunshine contributed to Spartan austerity. The sun rises late over the Parnónas range and sets early behind Taÿgetos. Yet in Roman times life became more civilized, as witnessed by several mosaics, the finest presenting Europa and the Bull. The museum's showpiece is an archaic pyramidal *stele* depicting Agamemnon, his wife and in-laws.

Byzantine Mystras

The prosperity of Byzantine Sparta continued under its first Frankish lord. But his son, William de Villehardouin, moved his chivalrous court in 1249 to Mystras, a great castle on top of the steep hill, *Mezythra* (Goatcheese), three miles west, at the foot of Taÿgetos. For ten years young nobles from the greatest kingdoms in Christendom were initiated into the art of chivalry in that splendid medieval setting, which Goethe chose for Faust's symbolic union with Helen, German mysticism and Greek classicism. Taken prisoner by the Emperor Michael Palaeologus, at the battle of Pelagonia, William had to cede Mystras as part of his ransom, and soon a town grew under the protection of the Byzantine fortress.

Mystras is thus essentially Byzantine, and for over a 100 years was the capital of a despotate, governed by sons and brothers of the emperors. Constantine Palaeologus reigned here, from 1443 to 1449, before becoming the last emperor, and under his brothers the despotate survived the fall of Constantinople for seven years. Mystras had then over 40,000 inhabitants and remained a populous town till the abortive revolt of 1770, when it was burnt by the Sultan's Albanian troops. Abandoned, in a reversal of fortune for Sparta, the empty shell of the city still stands as a great monument to the Byzantine Renaissance. Visiting the ruins of the Frankish castle on the summit necessitates a strenuous climb with few compensations. Yet, the winding road to the castle gate should be taken, as the easiest way to see the restored churches scattered throughout the town.

The monastery of the Perivleptos in the lower town is partly hollowed out of the rock, and possesses some fine frescos, particularly the Transfiguration, and the Divine Liturgy, celebrated by Christ, in the vestment of a Byzantine patriarch. Though a tiny museum occupies the bishop's palace attached to the 13th-century Metropolis, it is the view, opening north over the Eurotas valley, that holds the attention. The Aphendiko is architecturally the most interesting church, while the Pantanassa's frescos are considered the supreme manifestation of late Byzantine art. Particularly striking is the raising of Lazarus, where strawberry pink buildings blend with a honey-colored landscape under a navy-blue sky, in a singularly daring use of color in medieval religious painting. The nuns of the Pantanassa convent are the faithful guardians of all the deserted churches, and the only inhabitants of this ghost town. The vast arched hall in the despot's palace, though open to the sky, with crumbling walls and staring windows, still conveys something of past grandeur.

Gýthio, Sparta's port, lies 28 miles south, on the gulf of Laconia. Squeezed between the sea and a steep hill crowned by a castle, this small ancient town is well worth a visit, mainly for the pleasant situation, bathing, and as a starting point for excursions into the Mani. A causeway leads to the island of Kranaí, where Paris and Helen spent the first night after their elopement in Aphrodite's sanctuary. Gýthio is the port of embarkation—in no way resembling Watteau's famous painting—for Kýthira (Cythera), a harsh, dry island and a curious choice for Aphrodite to make her first appearance.

Though historically joined to the Seven Ionian Islands, Kýthira belongs geographically to Lakonia. There is an air connection with Athens and a sea connection with Piraeus. The hydrofoil calls at a number of eastern Peloponnesian ports including Monemvassía before ending up at the island's two harbors of Agía Pelagía, on a good beach, and Kapsáli (two miles from the capital), which rises like an amphitheater to the Venetian castle on an imposing cliff. Displayed in the castle museum are interesting finds from several archeological sites, mostly accessible by an adequate road network. More impressive than the ruins of Aphrodite's temple at Paleokastro is the monastery of Agia Elessa, Kýthira's present patron saint.

Monemvassía is roughly 60 miles from either Gýthio or Sparta and connected to Piraeus by hydrofoil and boat. Malvoisie to the Franks, Malmsey to the English, its vineyards were famous for centuries—until the arrival of the Turks. Legend has it that the Duke of Clarence was drowned by his brother, Richard Crookback, soon to be Richard III, in a butt of malmsey. The great rock with the impregnable Byzantine and Venetian fortifications, that for a while owed allegiance to the Pope, towers above the causeway leading to the walled but sadly diminished town, in which only the restored 12th-century churches retain something of the former splendor. A few of the 16th-century houses are again inhabited.

For the scenically loveliest return, branch north via Agios Dimitrios to Géraki, among whose medieval churches the best preserved is the 13th-century basilica of Agios Georgios within the Bronze-Age walls, successively restored by Franks, Venetians and Turks. Continue northeast at the crossroads through fine mountain forests to the Elóna Monastery, seemingly suspended from the sky. The road descends through a dramatic gorge to Leonídio. A very scenic road then follows the coast all the way to Argos (56 miles), past many inviting beaches, of which the best is at Paralía Ástros. A difficult but interesting branch leads northwest to Tripoli (44 miles) via Melígou, Agios Petros and the prosperous mountain village of Agios Nikolaos.

Flanked by Taÿgetos and Parnónas, the 37 miles from Sparta to Tripoli are as varied as the 35 miles descent from Tripoli to Argos.

Argolida (Argolis)

The first village on the gulf is Mýli, ancient Lerna, where Heracles killed the nine-headed serpent, Hydra; a team from Cincinnati University has unearthed a large terracotta-tiled Bronze Age building dating from 2200 B.C. 6 miles north is Argos, Hera's city, and the most ancient continuously occupied site in Greece. Here the 50 daughters of Danaus killed their bridegrooms, except one, the ancestor of Perseus, founder of Mycenae. Another of their descendants was Heracles, the reputed ancestor of the kings of Sparta as well as of Argos. Under the Heraclids the latter became increasingly powerful, until a decisive defeat by the Spartans in 520 B.C. Despite the Athenian alliance Argos declined. The modern town curves round a hill crowned by a Frankish citadel. The theater is cut into the hillside, flanked by the crumbling walls of the 1st-century B.C. Roman baths, later converted into a monastery. Some interesting mosaics of the same period are across the street. At nearby Kokla a 23-yard passage leads to the unique wall-engravings on the facade of a 1500 B.C. beehive-tomb, accidentally discovered in 1981.

A little more than half the 7 miles to Náfplio is Tíryntha (Tirynth), Heracles' birthplace. To the left of the road rises a low mound, on which a palace stood as early as 3000 B.C. The Cyclopean walls were built with enormous blocks of stone in about 1800 B.C. and the impressive vaulted galleries were added some 300 years later. According to German archeologists, who are continuing excavations of a religious center with Mycenaean frescos among the houses of the settlement, the fortress was finally abandoned in the 13th century B.C. following an earthquake.

Náfplio (Nauplia) is an unusually well-preserved Venetian town, beautifully situated overlooking a lovely bay. It offers a choice of good hotels and taverns, besides being ideal for excursions. Nothing remains of the town founded by Nauplius, son of Poseidon and one of the Danaids. His son Palamedes invented dice, arithmetic, some of the letters of the Greek alphabet and gave his name to the higher hill, on which solid, yet graceful Venetian walls until recently enclosed the modest house where Otho, first king of Greece, held court from 1833 to 1834. The National Assembly ratified his election in the Church of the Annunciation after the first President, Capodistrias, had been assassinated at the steps of the Church of Agios Spiridon by the Mavromichalis clan. Otho's unfortunate ministers and courtiers had to climb the 999 steps from the town. A road now winds up to the back entrance of the vast compound or, for the sound in wind and limb, a vertiginous flight of steps climbs up from the town park. Within the restored walls encircling the lower hill of Acronáfplio are two excellent hotels. Boúrdzi, a picturesque Venetian fort built on an islet in the bay, once the hangman's residence, now scheduled to become a tourist pavilion, merits the pleasant boat ride. The Venetian naval arsenal on the town square houses the museum, crowded with Mycenaean finds. The Peloponnesian Folkloric Foundation displays its collections in a neo-classical house on Vassileos Alexandrou. The larger of the two disaffected mosques, now a cinema, housed the first Greek parliament. The fountain in the garden of Agia Moni on the outskirts, founded in 1144, has been identified with ancient Kanathos, where Hera bathed once a year to regain her virginity.

The sanctuary of Asklepios is at Epídavros (Epidauros) 18 miles north-west. At this shrine of the god of healing revolting superstitions, like being licked by the sacred serpents, were slowly replaced by medical treatment, based on diet, fresh air, medicaments and even surgery. The health-giving smell of thyme and pines still lingers, but only foundations remain of the vast establishments, which included the earliest hospital ward. Models in the museum convey a picture of what Epídavros must have looked like at the height of its fame in the 5th and 4th centuries B.C. The theater is the best preserved in Greece and seats 14,000 spectators. The acoustics are so perfect that even from the last of the 55 tiers every word can be heard during the annual festival of Greek drama. Twelve miles away, at Palea (Old) Epídavros, the ruins of the antique town of 70,000 inhabitants can be discerned beneath the transparent sea in a skin-diver's paradise. The scenic coastal road linking Epídavros via the beaches of Almyrí, Loutró Elénis, Paleó Kalamáki and Isthmia to Corinth (37 miles), makes a one-day round trip through the Argolida from Athens easy.

A lovely circuit can be made by continuing 38 miles from Epídavros to Galatás, opposite the island of Poros. The view from the height at Ano Fanári over the islands of the Saronic Gulf is one of the finest in Greece. After descending into the orange and lemon groves of the coastal strip there is a choice of interesting places to visit: the spa of Methana (eight miles to the left), the ruins of Trizina (2 miles right), Theseus' inheritance from his mother, and the setting of the tragedy of Phaedra, immortalized by Euripides and Racine. The road continues beyond Galatás through orange and lemon groves for 20 miles along the coast facing Ydra island to the pleasant fishing village of Ermióni, where Roman mosaic pavements have been uncovered, beside an idyllic bay. 7 miles southeast is the beach of Kósta, opposite Spetses island. 3 miles northeast, Portohéli has grown into the Peloponnese's largest beach resort, with the added attractions of the ruins of ancient Halieis submerged in the shallow sea; and bones and stone tools of Mesolithic Period around 25,000 B.C. discovered in the nearby Franhthí cave, which was still inhabited in 8,000 B.C. as witnessed by chips of black volcanic glass imported from Milos, the earliest evidence of maritime trade. The return inland via Kranídi leads back to Epídavros. Shortly before the road forks at Trahiá, a branch is under construction to the beaches of Drépano and Toló, as well as the prehistoric acropolis, Mycenaean cemetery and Hellenistic remains of Assíani, all easily accessible just south of Náfplio.

In Agamemnon's Realm

The two hills concealing Mykines (Mycenae) stand at the northwestern confines of the Argive plain. It is only three miles from the Argos-Corinth highway to the gloomy, grey ruins, hardly distinguishable from the rock beneath. In their uncompromising severity they provide a fitting background to the horrors perpetrated by three generations of the hateful family of Atreus.

History is difficult to disentangle from legend, but his belief in Homer was triumphantly vindicated by Schliemann, when he discovered the royal towns of Troy and Mycenae, where the great poet had indicated them. The astounding beehive tombs are outside the reconstructed walls. The largest is called Treasury of Atreus or Tomb of Agamemnon—though it was neither—belonging to an earlier period. A forty-yard-long passage cut into the hill leads to a soaring, vaulted circular chamber of exquisite masonry, opening on to another, smaller burial chamber. The so-called Tomb of Clytemnestra is closer to the citadel.

The Acropolis of Mycenae is entered by the famous Lion Gate. A Cyclopean lintel supports a triangular slab, on which two lionesses are depicted standing on their legs, their forepaws resting on a column. Within the walls are the six shaft graves, where the gold masks and other treasures were found, which are now in the Mycenaean room in the Archeological Museum of Athens. Continuing excavations by British archeologists have brought to light some of the most important finds in recent years.

The palace stood on a narrow platform on the top of the hill, commanding a sweeping view of the plain. Visitors who can spend the time to take this site at a slower rate than the quick tours will allow, will find that it repays effort. There is a deep sense of the past here, it is one of the numinous places where history lies just out of reach, lurking below the surface. The gentle valleys that lead from the back of the excavations lead also into another world.

(*We advise that you carry a torch light when exploring the tombs on your own.*)

Slightly south, closer to Argos, an ancient shrine of the Great Goddess was for once not usurped by a male god but devolved to Hera. At the Iréo, the Argive Heraion, Agamemnon was elected to lead the Achaeans against Troy at a shrine predating by 500 years the 8th-century B.C. temple on a terrace supported by Cyclopean walls, the oldest identifiable sanctuary in Greece. It was burnt down through the carelessness of a priestess in 423 B.C. and replaced by another temple of which likewise only the foundations remain.

From the Corinth road four miles left (west) lead to the ruins of Nemea. Here that untiring young hero, Heracles, performed yet another of his labors by strangling the Nemean lion. Yet the Nemean Games, one of the four great Panhellenic competitions, were held bi-annually in memory of Prince Opheltes, put near a well by his nurse and bitten by a dragon. American archeologists have uncovered the baby's tomb, the foundations of the stadium, of the athletes' bathing installations and of an archaic temple burnt in the 5th century. Of the 4th-century Doric temple, dedicated to Zeus, three columns are still standing. The local finds are in a disproportionally large museum.

PRACTICAL INFORMATION FOR THE PELOPONNESE

 WHEN TO COME. The great variety of scenery makes a visit rewarding all the year round, with the possible exception of February, usually the worst month in Greece, though March too can be cold and rainy. The halcyon days of January are very suitable for sightseeing involving a fair amount of climbing, as at Mystras or Messini. But spring is the best season, when mountains and meadows are all covered with wild flowers. The sea breeze and bathing make the coast enjoyable in summer, but mountains and plains inland are baked dry. Flies and mosquitoes have reappeared on some beaches.

The great event of the Peloponnese is the festival of Greek drama at Epidauros on weekends in July and August. The Patra Carnival, though famous throughout Greece, is disappointing in comparison with similar events in other countries. The *Paleologia* celebrations at Mystras in late May commemorate the Byzantine Renaissance.

 HOW TO GET ABOUT. There are organized tours to all the main archeological sites. Those not wishing to be tied to a schedule will find it easy enough to move about by the frequent, regular buses. The diesel train follows the circular road, not including the Messenian circle, and without touching at Sparta. There are daily planes from Athens to Kalamata, Kýthira and Sparta. The 160-seat hydrofoils connect Zea harbor (Piraeus) via Poros and Spetses with all eastern Peloponnesian ports and Kýthira, also Patra with Zakynthos and Nafpaktos; most services all year round, more frequent in summer; ferry boats from Piraeus to most ports; once a week between Gýthio and Kissamos in Crete.

 MOTORING. The Peloponnese is a region where a car will provide maximum enjoyment, as every few miles there is something to see and worth stopping for. The circular tour can be combined with an excursion to Delphi, by taking the ferry boat between Egío and Ágios Nikolaos (Eratini) or Rio and Antirio. The Athens-Corinth toll motorway continues along the coast to Patra, and as a lesser road turns south to Pyrgós and Olympia, for the first night. The new 76-mile Patra–Olympia highway is due to open by 1985. Returning to Pyrgós you follow the spectacular road to Kyparissía. Don't miss the Messenian circle including Pýlos, Methoni and Kalamata, scenically very rewarding. The second night might be spent at Kalamata, leaving for Sparta on the following day, with the third night at Tripoli. On the fourth day Náfplio, Epidauros, Mycenae and return to Corinth. A road along the coast links Epidauros directly with Corinth. Four days are an absolute minimum for the complete tour. For a shorter trip you can cut across the peninsula from Olympia via Andritsena and the temple of Bassae in the Arcadian mountains to Megalopoli, Tripoli and Náfplio.

 HOTELS AND RESTAURANTS. Modern hotels exist at all places of interest while rooms in private houses, though not quite warranting the furnished apartment sign, are clean and cheap. Seaside taverns offer fresh fish, but display little imagination as to preparation. Young artichokes—*angináres*—from the Patra region make a good entrée. Corinth is known for its grapes and Kalamata for its olives.

AGIOS ANDREAS. *Akroyali* (I), tel. 31 266, 15 double rooms. *Angelos* (I), tel. 31 268, 13 double rooms. Both basic, on shingle beach, with very simple restaurants.

AGIOS AVGOUSTINOS. *San Agostino Beach* (M), tel. 22 150/7. 330 rooms and bungalows on beach, pool, minigolf, tennis, disco.

AKRATA. *Helena Beach* (I), tel. 31 663. 34 rooms.

ALAGONIA. *Taÿgetos* (I), tel. 76 236. Motel in the fir forest on the Sparta-Kalamata road; 14 rooms.

ALMYRÍ. *Almyri Beach* (M), tel. 33 301. 48 rooms; tennis.

ALMYRÓ. *Messinian Bay* (M), tel. 41 251. 45 rooms; beach, minigolf.

AMALIADA. *Olympic Inn* (I), tel. 28 632. 42 airconditioned rooms, roofgarden.

ANDRITSENA. Inadequate accommodation; book well ahead in summer. *Theoxenia* (M), tel. 22 219. Fine view over the mountains, but only half of the 17 rooms with baths. *Pan* (I), tel. 22 213. 6 double rooms with showers; no restaurant.

ARAHOVITIKA. 6 miles east of Patra. *Alexander Beach* (M), tel. 93 1262/3. 114 rooms and bungalows; pool, minigolf, disco, roofgarden.

AREOPOLI. *Pyrgos Kapetanaki* (M), tel. 51 233. 6 rooms in a converted tower; quaint, no restaurant. *Mani* (I), tel. 51 269. Most of the 16 rooms with showers; restaurant.

ARGOS. Only if nearby Náfplio is booked out. *Mycenae* (I), tel. 28 569. Most of the 24 rooms with showers. *Telessila* (I), tel. 28 351. Some of the 32 rooms with showers; no restaurants.

Restaurants. The food in the restaurants on the main square ranges from dreary to awful.

ASTROS PARALIA. *Chryssi Akti* (I), tel. 51 294. Unlike its name, Golden Coast. Some of the 23 rooms with showers. *Georgakakis* (I), tel. 51 298. 20 rooms. Both on good beach.

CORINTH. *Kypselos* (I), tel. 22 451. 18 rooms, no restaurant. *Acropolis* (I), tel. 26 568. 27 rooms, no restaurant. *Ephira* (I), tel. 22 434. 45 rooms, no restaurant. *Korinthos* (I), tel. 26 701. 34 rooms, no restaurant. **Restaurants.** Food in town is uniformly unsatisfactory.
At ancient Corinth. *Xenia* (M), tel. 31 208. 3 rooms.
At the Canal. *Isthmia* (M), tel. 23 454. Motel. 76 rooms; very noisy.

DIMITSÁNA. *Dimitsana* (I), tel. 31 518/20. 27 rooms; restaurant. Traditional settlement.

DREPANO. *Plaka* (I), tel. 59 420/3. 120 rooms; beach.

EGIO. *Galini* (I), tel. 26 150. 31 rooms. *Telis* (I), tel. 28 200. 30 rooms; restaurant.

EPIDAUROS. *Xenia* (M), tel. 22 003. At the ruins. Most of the 24 bungalows with showers.
At Lygourio. *Avaton* (I), tel. 22 059. 10 double rooms; no restaurant. Several simple eating places. Many more souvenir shops, amongst which the *Argo* offers the widest choice.
At Palea (Old) Epidauros, 12 miles east, on the sea. *Apollon* (I), tel. 41 295. 38 rooms. *Maik* (I), tel. 41 213. 14 rooms; disco. *Maronika* (I), tel. 41 391. 18 rooms. *Paola Beach* (I), tel. 41 397. 27 rooms. *Saronis* (I), tel. 41 514. 39 rooms. Enchanting site, poor beach.

ERMIONI. *Costa Perla* (M), tel. 31 111/4. 191 rooms, bungalows; pool.
At Petrothalassa, 4 miles southwest. *Aquarius* (M), tel. 31 430/4. 415 rooms; pool. *Lena-Mary* (M), tel. 31 450/1. 120 rooms; airconditioned.
At Plepi, 5 miles east. *Kappa Club* (E), tel. 41 206. 272 rooms. *Porto Hydra* (E), tel. 41 270/4. 272 rooms, airconditioned.
Self-contained holiday complexes; half or full board available, disco, tennis, minigolf.

GARGALIANI. *Ionian View* (I), tel. 22 494. 6 double rooms command a splendid view indeed over the coast; restaurant, disco.

GÝTHIO. *Lakonis* (E), tel. 22 666. 74 rooms, pool; on private beach outside town. *Belle Hélène* (M), tel. 22 867. 98 rooms, tennis; on private beach outside town. *Laryssion* (I), tel. 22 021. 78 rooms. *Pantheon* (I), tel. 22 284. 53 rooms.

ISTHMIA. *King Saron* (E), tel. 37 201/4. 161 rooms, airconditioned; beach, pool, tennis, disco.

ÍTYLO. *Itylo* (I), tel. 51 300. 15 rooms.

KAIAFAS. Several old hotels near sulfurous springs, but only *Jenny* (I), tel. 31 234, has 8 double rooms with showers; no restaurant.

KALAMATA. *Filoxenia* (M), tel. 23 166. Two miles from town on secluded beach. 118 rooms; tennis, disco. Still farther out, at Verga, *Elite* (M), tel. 25 015. 49 rooms. On town beach, *Flisvos* (I), tel. 82 282. 41 rooms. *Haikos* (I), tel. 82 886. 30 rooms. *Valassis* (I), tel. 23 849. 37 rooms. None with restaurants.

KALÁVRYTA. *Helmos* (M), tel. 22 217. 27 rooms, most with showers.

KASTANIA. *Xenia* (M), 17 rooms, in fir forest.

KASTRO. *Kyllini Golden Beach* (E), tel. 95 105/10. 332 rooms in four blocks on excellent beach; airconditioned; pool, tennis, minigolf, disco.

KIATO. *Triton* (M), tel. 23 421. 32 rooms, airconditioned; no restaurant. *Pappas* (I), tel. 22 358. 44 rooms; no restaurant.

KOKONI. *Angela* (I), tel. 32 486. 136 rooms; pool, tennis, disco.

KOSTA. *Cap d'Or* (M), tel. 51 360/3. 107 rooms; pool, tennis, minigolf. *Lido* (M), tel. 51 393. 40 rooms.

KRANIDI. *Hermionida* (I), tel. 21 750. 27 rooms.

KYLINI. *Glarentza* (I), tel. 92 397. 30 rooms.

KYPARISSÍA. *Artemis* (I), tel. 22 145. *Ionion* (I), tel. 22 511. 33 rooms.

LAKOPETRA. 22 miles west of Patra. *Grecotel Stamac* (E), tel. 22 845. 199 rooms. Pool, tennis, beach, disco. *Ionian Beach* (M), tel. 51 300. 79 bungalows; pool, tennis, minigolf, disco.

LEHEO. *Corinthian Beach* (I), tel. 25 666. 57 rooms; tennis.

LOUTRA KYLINIS. *Xenia* (E), tel. 96 270. 80 double rooms, airconditioned; tennis, disco. *Xenia* (I), tel. 96 275. 75 double rooms; disco. This is the name of all state-owned hotels; both are near the hydrotherapy center and close to the beach.

LOUTRO ELENIS. *Politis* (I), tel. 33 249. 26 airconditioned rooms. *Seaview* (I), tel. 33 551. 22 rooms.

MELISSI. *Xylokastron Beach* (I), tel. 23 190. 80 rooms, pool, disco.

MESSINI. *Messini* (I), tel. 23 002. 21 rooms.

METHANA. *Avra* (M), tel. 92 550. 55 rooms.

METHONI. *Alex* (I), tel. 31 219. 20 rooms, airconditioned; restaurant. *Methoni Beach* (I), tel. 31 544. 12 rooms; disco, restaurant.

METOHI. 22 miles southwest of Patra. *Kalogria Beach* (M). 96 rooms in central block and bungalows; tennis, minigolf, disco.

MONEMVASSÍA. *Minoa* (I), tel. 61 209. 16 rooms. Traditional settlement. Fish taverns on waterfront.

MYCENAE. *La Petite Planète* (I), tel. 66 240. 13 rooms; garden restaurant.

MYSTRAS. *Vyzantion* (M), tel. 93 309. 22 rooms; at entrance of medieval town.

NÁFPLIO. *Xenia's Palace* (L), 48 rooms, 3 suites, and *Xenia's Palace Bungalows* (L), tel. 28 981, 54 rooms; pool; on Akronafplio, fine view. Slightly lower, *Xenia* (E), tel. 28 981/3. 58 rooms. *Amalia* (E), tel. 24 401. 175 airconditioned rooms, large pool, garden, 1 mile out of town, on the sea.
  Agamemnon (M), tel. 28 021, on waterfront, 40 rooms, small roofgarden pool. *Dioscouri* (I), tel. 28 550. 51 rooms; *Nafplia* (I), tel. 28 167. 41 rooms; *Park* (I), tel. 27 428. 70 rooms, airconditioned.
  Restaurants. *Savouras* (I), on the waterfront, is the leading seafood taverna. *Hellas* (M), on Syntagma Square, is the most popular town restaurant. *Kondogiorgis*, on the waterfront is the most elegant cafe/sweetshop.

NERANTZA. *Nerantza* (I), tel. 32 329. 30 rooms, on beach.

NIFOREIKA. *White Castle* (M), tel. 23 390. 34 airconditioned rooms, pool.

NIKOLEÏKA. 4 miles west from Egio. *Poseidon Beach* (M), tel. 81 400/2. 90 rooms, pool, tennis.

OLYMPIA. *Amalia* (E), tel. 22 190. 147 rooms; pool; well-situated and comfortable. *Antonios* (E), tel. 22 348. 65 rooms; roofgarden. *Olympic Village* (E), tel. 22 211. 51 rooms, airconditioned; disco. *Apollon* (M), tel. 22 522. 86 rooms. *Ilis* (I), tel. 22 547. 57 rooms; restaurant. *Kronion* (I), tel. 22 502. 23 rooms; restaurant. *Pelops* (I), tel. 22 543, 25 rooms; restaurant.

PALEO KALAMAKI. 4 miles southwest of Corinth. *Kalamaki Beach* (E), tel. 37 331/4. 74 rooms, airconditioned.

PATRA. *Astir* (E), Agiou Andreou 16 (tel. 276 311.) 120 rooms, airconditioned; roofgarden; pool. *Moreas* (E), Iroon Polytehniou (tel. 424 541/5). 105 rooms.
  Acropole (M), Agiou Andreou 32 (tel. 279 809.) 33 rooms. *Galaxy* (M), Agiou Nikolaou 9 (tel. 278 815). 53 rooms, airconditioned.
  Delfini (I), Iroon Polytehniou 102 (tel. 421 001.) Halfway to town beach;

71 rooms; pool; airconditioned; restaurant. *Mediterranee* (I), Agiou Niko-laou 18 (tel. 279 602.) 96 rooms, airconditioned; restaurant.

At Paralia Proastiou. 2 miles west on the sea. *Achaia Beach* (M), tel. 991 801/4. 87 rooms; halfboard; pool. *Tzaki* (M), tel. 428 396. 38 rooms.

Restaurants. *Evangelatos* (M), Agiou Nikolaou 7. The restaurants (I) on the waterfront have a fine view, but little else.

PORTOHELI. *Hinitsa Beach* (E), tel. 51 401/4. 206 rooms, airconditioned; on beach; pool, tennis, minigolf, disco. *Kosmos* (E), tel. 51 327. 151 rooms, airconditioned; on beach. *PLM Portoheli* (E), tel. 51 490/4. 218 rooms, airconditioned; on beach; pool, tennis, minigolf, disco. *Apollo Beach* (M), tel. 51 431. 151 rooms in bungalows. *Galaxy* (M), tel. 51 271/6. 171 rooms, airconditioned, roofgarden. *Giouli* (M), tel. 51 217/8. 163 rooms, airconditioned. *Ververoda Holiday Resort* (M), tel. 51 343/5. 244 rooms in central block and bungalows. *Alcyon* (I), tel. 51 479. 89 rooms, airconditioned; disco; 300 yds from beach.

Restaurant. *Papadias* (E), good seafood in the port near the church.

PÝLOS. Insufficient and rather unsatisfactory accommodations. *Galaxy* (I), tel. 22 780. 34 rooms; restaurant; 150 yds from the very small town beach. *Kastro* (I), tel. 22 264, 10 rooms, on seafront above beach.

PÝRGOS. *Letrina* (I), tel. 23 644. 68 rooms; restaurant. *Olympos* (I), tel. 23 650. 37 rooms.

RIO. *Averof Grand Hotel* (E), tel. 992 102/12. 267 rooms in central block and bungalows, airconditioned; pool, tennis, minigolf, disco. 40 yds from beach. *Rion Beach* (M), tel. 991 421. 85 rooms; disco.

SALADI. 5 miles north of Kranidi. *Saladi Beach* (M), tel. 71 391. 404 rooms in central block and bungalows, airconditioned; tennis, minigolf, disco. One of the few nudist beaches.

SKAFIDIA. 7 miles northwest of Pyrgos. *Miramare Olympia Beach* (E), tel. 94 364/9. 354 rooms in hotel, bungalows and villas on fine beach; pool, tennis, minigolf, disco.

SPARTA. *Lida* (E), tel. 23 601. 40 rooms. *Xenia* (E), tel. 26 524. Quiet in its own grounds. 33 rooms. *Dioskouri* (M), tel. 28 484. 35 rooms. *Menelaïon* (M), tel. 22 161. 48 rooms. *Apollo* (I), tel. 22 491. 44 rooms. *Maniatis* (I), tel. 22 665. 80 rooms. Airconditioned.

SYKIA. *Paradissos* (I), tel. 28 121. 26 double rooms; no restaurant; the name is rather an overstatement.

TOLO. Large number of hotels on the excellent beach; only those with restaurants are listed. *Dolfin* (M), tel. 59 192. 22 rooms. *Sofia* (M), tel. 59 567. 52 rooms.

Aris (I), tel. 59 231. 30 rooms. *Electra* (I), tel. 59 105. 18 rooms. *Epidavria* (I), tel. 59 219. 39 rooms. *Minoa* (I), tel. 59 207. 44 rooms. *Possidonion* (I), tel. 59 345. 36 rooms. *Tolo* (I), tel. 59 248. 35 rooms.

TRIPOLI. *Arcadia* (M), tel. 225 551. 45 rooms; roofgarden. *Artemis* (I), tel. 225 221. 60 rooms; no restaurant. *Galaxy* (I), tel. 225 195. 80 rooms; no restaurant.

VALIMITIKA. 4 miles east of Egio. *Eliki* (I), tel. 91 301/4. 144 rooms; on beach, pool, disco.

VATHIA. Traditional settlement.

VYTINA. In the Arcadian mountains, 3,000 ft. *Villa Valos* (M), tel. 21 210. 51 rooms; in fine setting; halfboard only. *Vytina* (I), tel. 21 262. 12 double rooms; no restaurant.

XYLOKASTRO. *Arion* (E), tel. 22 230. 64 double rooms; halfboard; on beach. *Fadira* (M), tel. 22 648. 48 rooms; no restaurant; near beach. *Rallis* (M), tel. 22 219. 74 rooms, halfboard; near beach. *Periandros* (I), tel. 22 272, 23 rooms; restaurant.

CAMPING SITES. The best equipped among some 30 organized camps are the GNTO camping grounds: *Agia Patron,* 3 miles from Patra, tel. 424 131, accommodating 600 persons; and *Kylini,* at Vartholomio 4 miles east of Loutra Kylinis, tel. 96 278, accommodating 500 persons; both near beaches.

HOLIDAY VILLAGES. See page 21.

MONASTERY HOSTELRIES. *Agia Lavra* and *Mega Spileo,* both modern with running water; near Kalavryta.

SKI CENTERS AND MOUNTAIN REFUGES. Two each on Panahaïko and Ziria, the latter the most important skiing center in the Peloponnese; one each on Helmos, Menalo, Parnonas and Taygetos.

USEFUL ADDRESSES. *GNTO,* Iroon Polytehniou, Glyfada, Patra, tel. 420 305.

NORTHWESTERN GREECE

Epirus and Aetolia-Acarnania

North-western Greece, which stretches from the northern shore of the Gulf of Corinth to the Albanian frontier west of the Píndos range, has been aroused from its centuries-old slumber by the advent of the ferry-boats from Italy. Epirus (Ipiros) is a splendid massive landscape. Epirus indeed, means continent, in contrast to the islands—Corfu, Paxi, Lefkada—strung along the littoral. The abrupt changes from the delicately shaded green of the idyllic olive and orange groves on the coast to the tremendous solidity of the bare mountains have been faithfully depicted by that versatile Victorian, Edward Lear, of limerick fame. But few travelers would nowadays put up with the discomfort, hardship and very real danger from bandits that Lear seems to have enjoyed. The scenery has kept its grandeur, but has become easily accessible by a good road network, giving access to plenty of hotels.

Mountainous provinces are often spared a surfeit of history, but in Greece the last 4,000 years have been so crammed with momentous events that Epirus received its fair share, though fair in this case refers to size rather than to pleasurable enjoyment by the inhabitants. Mountain barriers and the absence of anchorages kept the invasions of the second millennium B.C. on a manageable scale, though not preventing one of Achilles' vaguely scattered sons from founding a kingdom in a remote vale. History started in deadly earnest in the 12th century B.C. with the Dorians spreading from this bastion all over Greece, while their rearguard, the Hellenes, imposed the worship of Zeus on the native population so successfully that eventually all the various inhabitants of the mainland came to be known as Hellenes.

Republican constitutions, which became fashionable in more sophisticated communities in the 8th century B.C., never penetrated into the mountain fastness. During the classical period Epirus remained a stormy backwater of tribal warfare, highlighted by the traditional hospitality extended to the fugitive Themistocles by the king of the Molossians. That generous act must have brought them luck, as their tribe soon dominated the Epirotic confederation.

The Molossian Princess Olympias married her uncle Philip II of Macedonia in 357 B.C. How far that amiable lady was implicated in her husband's assassination has never been fully ascertained, but Alexander the Great would not permit his dangerous mother any part in the government. Her great hour came after Alexander's death in 323 B.C., when, as regent for her nephew in Epirus, and her grandson in Macedonia, she was free to intrigue to her heart's content. After her murder kings ascended and descended the shaky throne of Epirus at a bewildering speed with the system of co-kings greatly adding to the fun, until Pyrrhus reconquered the crown for a third time and entered the fray as sole ruler.

His fame, however, rests on his intervention in Italy, where he caused consternation and panic with his war-elephants. After defeating the Romans in two bloody battles in 279 B.C., he made his often quoted statement: "Another such victory and we are lost." Yet he continued to indulge indiscriminately in wars west and east, until an old woman made a lucky hit with a tile thrown from her rooftop, killing the king during an attack on Argos.

For having changed sides at the wrong moment, Epirus was crushingly punished by the Roman Consul Aemilius Paulus in 167 B.C. One hundred and fifty thousand Epirotes were sold into slavery, while the 70 principal towns were razed to the ground, before history stopped for the blissful 400 years of the Pax Romana. The battle of Actium in 31 B.C. was a naval engagement, which for all its momentous consequences caused only moderate upheaval in the peaceful province.

Epirus shared the vicissitudes of the Byzantines to the full, offering a haven to the imperial dynasty of the Angeli after they had caused the ruin of the empire by some particularly unsavory family squabbles. Little more successful in their diminished station, the Angeli despotate of Arta was incorporated in 1263, after less than 60 years, in the resuscitated empire of the Palaeologi.

Turkish Misrule

The conquest of Ioanina by the Turks under Sinan Pasha was hardly an improvement. Pashas were appointed haphazardly from among the leading Moslem families, while the country was reduced to near anarchy by inherited feuds, frequent rebellions and constant brigandage. Christianity of a sort survived. In a popular poem St. George was first bribed by a Christian maiden to hide her from a pursuing Turk, to whom the saint promptly betrayed her hiding place on receipt of a more lavish gift. But if things spiritual were in a bad way, they were at least housed in splendid bodies, dressed, according to Byron, in the most magnificent clothes in the world.

Against that colorful background there rose in the second half of the 18th century the most extraordinary figure in modern Greek history, Ali of Tepelen, who established his rule over the greater part of continental Greece and Albania, and then imposed the appointment of his sons to the governorship of the outlying provinces. But in the end Ali committed the one unforgivable sin in Turkish eyes: growing ever more avaricious with age he fell in arrears with his tribute. In 1820 a Turkish army invaded Ioanina, where Ali Pasha had to rely on Christian support, because his Moslem subjects were unwilling to fight against the Sultan. Greek help was not intended to perpetuate Ali's despotism, but to keep the common enemy, the Turks, occupied. This facilitated the outbreak of the Greek revolution in 1821, which was heavily subsidized by Ali, but failed to save him. Epirus remained a Turkish province till the first Balkan war, when Ioanina was conquered by a Greek army under Crown Prince Constantine in 1913.

Etolia and Akarnania (Aetolia and Acarnania) played only a small part in antiquity, except between 332 and 189 B.C., when the Aetolian League became a dominant power. The capital of the League was at Thermon, east of the river Aheloos, and that of Acarnania at Stratos, west of it, were the ramparts and some other remains are still visible.

Exploring Northwestern Greece

The crossing from Corfu to Igoumenítsa (18 nautical miles) is enchanting, with the lush green of the island slowly receding and the stark outlines of the mainland dramatically ahead. Try to enter the small bay in the early morning or evening, when the grey rocks flame with deep pinks and violets in an unforgettable welcome.

Igoumenítsa is the northwestern port of entry for motorists, but even without private transport there is no problem. The ubiquitous Greek buses shamble up the most improbable mountains, though heavily biased in favor of cruelly early morning hours. Peasant women and children are, moreover, very much given to being sick in public conveyances, while the radio is going full blast, indiscriminately and mercilessly for the entire program of religious service, learned discourse on handicraft and a fair share of bouzouki music.

Right at the start of the journey there is a tantalizing choice between the 62 miles northeast to Ioanina, on the first leg of the newly reconstituted Via Egnatia, once the main artery of the Roman Empire, linking Rome via Brindisi and Thessaloniki to Constantinople. (In antiquity, the eastern port on the Ionian Sea was at Dyrrhachium, in modern Albania, which sufficiently explains the shift further south.) Or the coastal highway to Preveza, taking in Parga (25 miles), the main attraction on the coast. But this means bypassing the varied sites in and around Ioanina as well as the superb Alpine scenery of the Píndos range.

So northeast it is, climbing and descending mountains along the left bank of the Kalamas river. After 15 miles there is a branch road south to Paramythiá (eight miles), once the seat of a Turkish Pasha, who resided in the imposing fortress on the slopes of Mt. Komilas.

Heroic Souli, Enchanting Parga

Paramythiá hardly justifies the detour, but the road continues south below Souli, celebrated in Greek folklore and by Byron. Fourteen miles south, after crossing the Áheron a narrow track follows the torrent—one of antiquity's favorite entrances to the Underworld—up to Souli. Soon you catch the first glimpse of the main fortress—Koungi—guarding the entrance to the almost inaccessible highland.

Throughout the period of Ottoman rule the Christian Souliots maintained their independence. They were divided into clans like the Highland Scots, and their rivalry made it at last possible for Ali Pasha to subdue them in 1803 by a gruesome mixture of bribery, treachery and force. By the terms of surrender the Souliots were free to leave with their possessions, but the solemn promise was not worth the paper it was written on. A few hundred men succeeded in reaching Parga and eventually Corfu, to be enlisted in Byron's bodyguard in 1823; but most of the Souliots took shelter in the Zalongo Monastery, which was attacked and taken by Ali's army. Only 60 women escaped to the summit of the cliffs, where they began to sing the old Souliot songs, dancing in a circle with their babies in their arms, ever closer to the edge, working themselves into a frenzy of defiance before jumping one by one down the fearful precipice. The tragic ballad of Zalongo is a common theme of the *kalamatianós*, the most popular of Greek dances, performed in a circle, the leader waving a handkerchief, swirling and bounding, while the chain of dancers shuffles around in a basic step, accompanied by a lyre, drum, clarinet and scratchy violin.

The heroic episode is commemorated by a startlingly modernistic huge monument of the dancing women on the cliff above the monastery, now accommodating a few nuns. The monastery's painted church, dedicated to St. Michael and St. Gabriel and reputedly built in the 8th century, is interesting, but pales before the splendid view embracing the open sea, the land-locked Ambracian Gulf, at whose entrance the momentous battle of Actium was fought, the island of Lefkada and the distant mountains of central Greece. Descending the four winding miles to the main road, it is then only another ten miles to Preveza.

The shortest route south from Igoumenítsa is also the loveliest, 57 miles to Preveza and the ferry to Aktio. Twenty-three miles along the coastal road ("coastal" not to be taken too literally), turn right (west) for eight miles to the most picturesque town on the west coast. The intimate square dominated by the Venetian castle high up on a rock, the smaller ruined fort on a wooded islet offshore, the dense olive groves covering the slopes down to the fine beaches, make Parga the outstanding holiday resort in the northwest.

Parga was founded in the 14th century, became Venetian in 1447 and remained a cherished possession of the Republic till the end of the Doges. After having been ceded by the British to Ali Pasha, the inhabitants, without exception, determined to leave. On Good Friday 1819 the bells were tolling, while the Pargiots disinterred the bones of their dead, burnt them and took the ashes together with the holy icons to Corfu. Ali's troops entered a town where all was solitude and silence, the only sign of former life being the smoke rising from the funeral pyres. Ali had a country house built on the promontory and settled the town with Mohammedans, who in turn were returned to Turkey in the general exchange of populations in 1924.

Ioanina, the Lair of Ali the Lion

Not that the Via Egnatia, on which we had set out before deviating to Paramythiá, lacks in scenic beauty. Stop above the village of Polýdrosso to enjoy the view over the mountains and river. A later branch road to the left (north) leads to Zitsa, a mountain hamlet a few miles off, where Byron stayed at the monastery of the Prophet Elias in 1809. He wrote enthusiastically of the situation, which he called "perhaps the finest in Greece." Zitsa, in addition to its literary associations, produces a very sweet sparkling wine.

The promontory of Ioanina juts into the melancholic lake that forms the center of a fertile valley hemmed in by ranges of imposing mountains: Mitsikeli in the north, snow-covered from December to May, links with the massif of Peristeri and Tsoumerka, Olitsika to the southwest overshadows the ruins of Dodona.

Ioanina was probably founded by the Emperor Justinian in about 540 A.D., as one of the forts in the defensive system stretching from the Ionian to the Black Sea. The impressive pentagonal citadel within 11th-century Norman walls, surrounded on three sides by the lake, dominates the town, which, in spite of the destruction during the epic siege of 1820–2 and modern progress, has retained a marked oriental character; the minarets and domes of the two mosques remain the most conspicuous feature. The mosque of Aslan Pasha, built in 1618, is now the Museum of Popular Art, housing a miscellaneous collection of weapons, icons and specimens of Epirote art. A refectory, library and baths flank the disused cemetery where Ali's body, minus the head, is buried next to his favorite wife, Umm Gulshun. The wrought-iron canopy and, inexplicably, even the marble tombstones were stolen during the German occupation in World War II. It was then that the Jewish community, which had so notably contributed to the city's prosperity, was exterminated.

Gone are the palaces of barbaric splendor, where Ali held his colorful court and received the ambassadors of the great powers. But his seraglio has been faithfully reconstructed and now accommodates cultural manifestations, next to the dilapidated Fethyé mosque on the citadel's second eminence. The fortress-palace of Ali's son, Muhtar Pasha, has likewise been partly rebuilt, rising above the main square. The small park atop is flanked on one side by a café affording a fine view, on the other by the Museum, whose exhibits range from antique finds to a well-meant collection of 19th-century paintings. Muhtar's betrayal of his father hastened the downfall of Ali who, after defeating the French forces, which had invaded his dominions from the Ionian islands, had become a factor in European politics. After becoming Vizier and Pasha of three tails, he described his methods in these simple terms: "I sent some heads to Constantinople to amuse the Sultan, and some money to his ministers, for envy never sleeps."

Yet when Ali stopped sending tribute, the Sultan was not amused and his army, led by the former Grand-Vizier Kurshit Pasha, pillaged and burnt Ioanina, then the biggest town in Greece and center of an early Hellenic revival.

The Lake and the Island

The rock of the citadel rose formerly straight from the lake, thus greatly facilitating the disposal of unwanted bodies sewn in sacks. A stately avenue of plane trees now encircles the grim walls to the landing-stage of Kyra Frossyni, named after the Greek mistress of Ali's eldest son. According to popular ballads she refused Ali's advances and was drowned together with 15 other ladies, erroneously referred to as maidens, one dark night in 1801. Possessed by a perverse desire to interfere in his children's love-life, Ali shortly afterwards raped the wife of his second son. Little wonder the sons were easily won over by the Turks, but instead of the promised high honors they were beheaded and their heads, together with that of Ali's eldest grandson, were displayed at the gates of the Constantinople Seraglio. The grandson's head led Sultan Mahmud II to make what must surely rank high among the truly perspicacious remarks in history: "I'm sorry now that I condemned him to death; I thought he was as old as his father."

To the left of the landing-stage are a number of cafés and restaurants, center of Ioanina's nightlife and scene of the traditional *volta*, the evening promenade of the younger set. Motorboats leave frequently for the village on the far side of the island, where six small Byzantine and post-Byzantine monasteries are scattered among the gardens. The most interesting are Philanthropinon (13th cent.), Diliou (11th cent.) and Agios Panteleimon. The first of these was founded by the great Byzantine family of the Philanthropinoi, whose last three members joined the monastery, and figure in the fresco inside the porch of the church dedicated to St. Nicholas the Hairless. Also depicted among conventional saints are Plato and Socrates as proof of the tolerant acceptance of the most unlikely candidates in the Orthodox hagiarchy, a charming continuation of the ancient hospitality extended to foreign divinities by the Olympians.

Agios Panteleimon was the scene of the dramatic death of Ali Pasha on January 24, 1822. It is ironic that Ali, who in all his 82 years had never kept a promise, should have trusted Kurshit's assurance of the Sultan's pardon. Ali, accompanied by his Greek wife and some faithful retainers, occupied the guest-house of the monastery, when the Turkish emissary, Mehmet Pasha, brought the *firman* ordering instant execution. Ali fired at Mehmet, wounding him in the hand, but was himself mortally wounded by a fusillade through the wood and plaster floor. Ali's head was cut off and exposed throughout his former domains. The monastery has been turned into a museum with interesting engravings of the period.

Swimming in the muddy lake is made no more attractive by the thought of Ali's countless victims lying at the bottom, than by the eels and watersnakes competing playfully with the bather. Better take a boat to Dobratova on the mainland just opposite to enjoy the eels fried at a moderately good fish restaurant.

Stalactites and Hospitality

A visit to the magnificent stalactite cave of Perama, though attacked by mold because of ecological upset, is a must. After three miles along the Métsovo road turn left to an undistinguished low hill, which covers a fantastic succession of lofty halls. Discovered in 1942 by a shepherd hiding from the Germans, a well-lit concrete path meanders now for over a thousand yards through a weird growth of stalactites and stalagmites to the further end, making all the explored parts accessible without retracing one's steps. The late King Paul and his family were entertained by the Ioanina municipality in one of the halls, an entertainment remarkable for originality rather than intrinsic enjoyment, what with the cold and constant dripping.

The road to Métsovo (36 miles) and Kalambaka (78 miles) is not only the shortest east-west connection across the Píndos range to either Athens or Thessaloniki, but also the most spectacular, winding up Mt. Mitsikeli to reveal splendid views over Ioanina and the lake. Snow-chains are required in winter for the drive through the fir forests to Métsovo (3,950 ft.), an attractive wintersports center. Métsovo held a unique place in the Turkish dominions thanks to a story of hospitality and gratitude which seems to be taken straight from the pages of the *Arabian Nights*. In the 16th century a Grand Vizier incurred the Sultan's disfavor and considering prudence to be the better part of valor he took refuge in the remote mountains of Epirus. For one year he was entertained by a Greek villager who remained ignorant of his visitor's identity. When at last restored to favor the Vizier promised his host anything he might desire. But instead of the expected request for money, the Greek begged freedom from Turkish rule for his home town. The demand was unprecedented, but the Vizier kept his word. Four *firmans* with golden seals in the Town Hall bear proof of the autonomy granted by successive sultans.

The inhabitants still wear the local costume of dark-blue homespun on feast days or touristic occasions, and speak Greek and also Vlach, a Latin dialect akin to Rumanian used by the villagers and nomad shepherds in the Píndos country. The Metropolis dates from 1511, but is in an exceptionally good state of repair, with its original roofing, baroque arches and interesting modern Italian mosaics. The Tositsa mansion, rebuilt in 18th-century style, houses a collection of Epirote arts and crafts.

The road tunnel under the 5,600 ft. Katara pass opens this Alpine landscape the year round. The branch left (north) at the Mourgani fork enters Macedonia via Grevena (38 miles) to either Kastoria (56 miles) or Kozani (33 miles); straight on (east) leads to Kalambaka (6 miles) and the Thessalian plain.

Zagoria, Wild Gorges and Painted Churches

From the road junction two miles north of Ioanina, an equally scenic 123 miles lead past the airfield north via Kónitsa to Kastoria. After 11 miles, a branch turns right (northeast) into the Zagoria district, once the feudal domain of Ali Pasha's youngest son. The road passes Kipi, the administrative center, on the seventeen miles to Negades (3,400 ft.). The deep-green waters of a nameless stream, locally known only as *parapotamos* (tributary of the Arahthos) are spanned by a number of old stone bridges, veritable architectural gems matched by the surprisingly large churches of the once prosperous 44 villages of the region. Owing to the poverty of the soil the male inhabitants have always had to emigrate. Epirus provided the skilled masons who built the great mosque in Constantinople; Epirote merchants founded Greek colonies in Italy and Russia in the 17th and 18th centuries. On their return they built fine houses and proud churches with their savings. Later emigrants went to the United States, but though many were driven back by homesickness, they had not made good to the same extent as their predecessors. The latest migration wave was directed to Germany, but the returning workers settle in towns rather than in the dying grey villages, where life continues without the modern distractions they have become used to.

The Basilica at Negades is unique, being three churches in one. The nave and each aisle lead to three separate altars, dedicated respectively to the Holy Trinity, Agios Georgios and Agios Dimitrios. The pulpit and iconostasis are richly carved and gilded, while vivid frescos by local artists cover every inch of space. Particularly remarkable is the naïvely conceived stream of hell, sweeping Judas, bishops and priests, followed at a distance by the lesser sinners, into the devil's mouth. The church, surrounded on all sides by cloisters, is a fine example of the highly original rustic architecture of Epirus, which differs radically from the usual Byzantine ecclesiastical style.

The middle branch left (north) three miles before Kipi leads via Vitsa to the village of Monodendri, with the painted church of Agios Athanasios. From the village square, where you can have a meal as rustic as the paintings, continue another half mile to the abandoned monastery of Agia Paraskevi (a female St. Friday, 1412), from whose balcony you have a stupendous view over the Vikos (Voidomatis) gorge. Better still, climb the stairs left of the church, and follow the path high up on the rocks a few hundred dizzy yards to a cave.

In spite of the varied beauty of the Zagoria, it would for the time being be rash to spend a night there. The village guesthouses are of the simplest, and when the locals wish "may you see the dawn" instead of the usual "sleep well", they know what they are talking about.

The next branch, left from the mainroad, would take you into Albania, in the unlikely case that your visa application has been granted. The wary traveler will content himself with skirting the barren mountains of that forbidden country to Kónitsa (40 miles), which nestles picturesquely at the foot of the thickly-wooded Mt. Trapezita. The Aoos gorge is entered by a new bridge, alongside one of the finest old Turkish bridges in the Balkans. The footpath on the right of the gorge continues for five miles to the monastery of Stomion. There is trout fishing in the river.

Dodona, Birthplace of the Hellenes

Thirteen miles south of Ioanina is Dodóni (Dodona), seat of an ancient oracle of the Great Goddess dating as far back as 2,000 B.C. Zeus worship was introduced in the 13th century B.C. and the new god manifested himself through the rustling of oak leaves or the sound of a metal whip blown by the wind against a brass basin.

These sounds had to be interpreted by priests, the *Selloi* or *Helloi,* whose faithful followers, the Hellenes, spread the cult of Zeus, champion of male supremacy, over the lands once ruled by the Triple Goddess.

Zeus was victorious, but the oracle had its ups and downs. Consulted in the heroic age by Heracles, Achilles, Odysseus and all the best people, it went later into a gentle decline, because of its failure to equal the masterly ambiguity of Delphi. Enduring for a time as the poor man's Delphi, Dodona became again fashionable under the Macedonian dynasty, which favored an oracle near the seat of government.

The temple was destroyed by the Aetolians in 221 B.C., rebuilt, sacked together with all Epirus by the rapacious Aemilius Paulus, restored once more to be converted into a church in the 4th century A.D. Bishops of Dodona disputed at the great ecumenical councils, and it is interesting to speculate how far the political acumen and psychological insight gained by their *Helloi* predecessors proved useful. The Goths, more thorough than previous despoilers, succeeded in erasing the very memory of Dodona's location for over a thousand years. Byron, the eager sightseer, complained angrily that all traces of the sanctuary had been obliterated.

It was only in 1876 that the Greek amateur archeologist Karpanos discovered the ruins below 30 feet of rubble and earth. Foundations of temples and the priests' houses, broken grey columns of severe Doric, and a large theater, recently restored for the performances of ancient tragedies, are all that remain. Dodona ranks high among the minor festivals that have sprouted prolifically all over Greece, but it is astonishing how hard the stone benches seem after two hours of culture. So bring cushions to Dodona, to listen in comfort to the heart-rending woes of ancient heroes, unless you prefer the tranquillity on off-nights, so much closer to the spirit of the sacred valley.

Nikopolis, City of Victory

After returning the nine miles to the junction with the highway south, you drive through a narrowing plain, parched in summer, but green with corn in spring. Abundant winter rains make Epirus the wettest province, as the mountain barriers prevent the rain clouds that drift up from the Ionian Sea from penetrating further inland.

At the inn of Emin Agha, near the highest point of the Kanetta gorge (2,000 ft.) Crown Prince Constantine received in 1913 the surrender of the Turkish forces defending Ioanina. A bust of doubtful taste commemorates that event. The descent is alongside the Louros river, lined with plane trees and wild laurel. The Roman aqueduct once carried the clear water from the springs of Agios Georgios to Nikópoli (Nikopolis), while the barrage one mile downstream now supplies Epirus with electricity. The most extensive orange groves in Greece begin at Filipiáda, and the fragrant perfume of the blossoms pervades the entire plain in spring. Forty-one miles from Ioanina the road divides: left (southeast) to Arta (6 miles), right (southwest) to Preveza (25 miles) and the vast ruins of Nikopolis just outside.

Founded by Octavianus Augustus in 30 B.C., on a grand scale, Nikopolis immortalized the new emperor's resounding victory over Mark Anthony's and Cleopatra's superior forces in the battle of Actium the previous year. There was a fatal flaw in Anthony's strength, as the 60 biggest ships of his fleet were under the command of Cleopatra. Suddenly, inexplicably, in the thick of battle, with all the odds in their favor, Cleopatra's ships broke line and set course towards the Peloponnese. Plutarch dramatically describes what ensued: "No sooner did Anthony see her ship sailing away, than, forgetting everything and deserting those who were fighting and dying in his cause, he got into a five-oared galley and followed after her who had already ruined him and was destined to complete his ruin." Anthony's 120,000 infantry and 12,000 cavalry encamped near Apollo's temple at Actium (Aktion) across the narrow entrance to the gulf, hailed Octavian as master of the world without a blow being struck on land.

Nikopolis was built on the site of Octavian's camp, populated from the surrounding districts, exempted from taxes and adorned with splendid palaces and temples. Ubiquitous St. Paul did not fail to visit the most Roman town in Greece, to lay the seed of Christianity. In the 5th century Nikopolis became the seat of a bishop, and a 100 years later Justinian was still adding churches and strengthening the walls.

What was left after the devastating Bulgarian raids of the 9th century was destroyed by an earthquake. Parts of the town sank into the Ambracian Gulf (Amvrakikós), where walls and columns are still visible in the clear water. Further out are the wrecks of Roman war galleys which an American-Greek venture is planning to raise. Above ground remain the impressive though broken line of the ramparts, two theaters, the larger with the inevitable performances of ancient drama in summer, an aqueduct, the stadium, temples of Ares and Poseidon. The ruins of the four early Byzantine churches are no less interesting, especially the lovely mosaic in the basilica of St. Dumetius (about 530 A.D.), representing the universe.

Preveza, five miles south, at the tip of the long promontory between the Ionian Sea and the Ambracian Gulf, is a town of 13,000 inhabitants. Some minor Venetian fortifications bear witness to the century-long connection with the Ionian Islands, only broken by Ali Pasha's conquest. There are several good beaches on the Ionian coast, but Preveza is only just being opened up to tourism.

Byzantine Arta

Arta has maintained a rare prosperity ever since its foundation as a Corinthian colony in the 7th century B.C. under the name of Ambracia. It became twice the capital of Epirus, first under Pyrrhus in 294 B.C. and again at the time of the Despotate of the Angeli in the 13th century. Even after the Turkish conquest the astute town-fathers obtained the singular privilege of excluding all Moslems, except the Turkish governor, from the city.

Foundations of classical and Hellenistic buildings cover a large area below the ancient acropolis; an equally ruined theater, a temple of Apollo and the huge blocks of ancient walls are scattered about. But some well-preserved monuments bear witness to Arta's medieval glory. First and foremost the church of the *Panagia Parigoritissa* (Our Lady of Consolation), built by the Despot Michael II and his consort Anna. It stands on a spacious square above the market, the late Byzantine style of the brick and stone construction strangely modified by Italian influence, owing to the Angeli dynasty's close connection with the Norman and Angevin courts of Naples and Kefalinia. The mosaics in the cupola are interesting, but most remarkable are the projective pendentives above the pillars, a unique architectural device, supported by horizontal columns traversing the wall. The refectory nearby has been restored as a small archeological museum.

The churches of Agios Vassilios, with exterior decorations, and Agia Theodora, built by the consort of Michael II, belong to the same period. The convent of Kato Panagia is two miles south of the town, while the monastery of Vlachernae, containing the tomb of Michael II, stands on a hill to the north-east. All have been expertly restored and are as easily accessible as the Byzantine fortress. You drive straight through the double gate in the crenellated ramparts, built with the stones of the ancient acropolis, to the pleasant surprise of a comfortable hotel commanding a splendid view over the orange groves sloping down to the river, whose course can be traced through the fertile valley to the distant Tsoumerka mountains.

The beautiful bridge over the Arahthos, which was built in the

18th century at the expense of wealthy Thiakoyannis Ghatophagos (The Cat-eater), is celebrated in many old ballads. Completion of the bridge was long held up, because the river destroyed each night the day's work. At last a bird revealed to the master-builder that the foundations had to be reinforced with the body of his wife to withstand the onrush of the stream. More enamored with his work than his wife, the builder consented, but though the bridge was finished in a miraculously short time he repented and committed suicide.

The next 27 miles south lead first through orange and lemon plantations and then along the flanks of Mt. Makrinóros to Amfilohía, founded by Ali Pasha on the east end of the vast Ambracian Gulf.

Aetolia-Acarnania

A scenically lovely road hugs the southern shore of the land-locked gulf for 25 miles to Vonitsa. From the road junction just beyond that pleasant fishing village below an imposing Venetian castle, the nine miles northwest lead to the airport of Aktio, close to the site of the temple of Apollo Aktios, and the ferry to Preveza; 12 miles southwest take you past the romantic Santa Maura castle and good beaches to the island of Lefkada, accessible over a long causeway, a highly recommended excursion; the 84 miles south more or less follow the coast via Mytikas to the attractive bay of Astakos—though this means lobster, the local diet knows nothing of such delicacies—and then through occasional oak groves to Etolikó, thus providing the shortest link between Igoumenitsa and the Peloponnese or Delphi.

South of Amfilohia, the highway passes two lakes and crosses the Ahéloos near the very ruined ruins of Stratos, ancient capital of Acarnania, to the extensive tobacco plantations round Agrínio (30 miles). One mile south of this prosperous town, bypassed at no great loss, is the branch left (north) to Karpeníssi (70 miles) via the large artificial lake of Kremastá, formed by damming up the Ahéloos (see page 254). Another branch east after a further mile climbs 18 miles through the luxuriant olive and cypress groves on the northern shore of Lake Trihonída, past the pretty monastery of Mirtiá, to Thermó, the sanctuary of the Aetolian League. The temple of Apollo dates from the 6th century B.C., but there are also remains of a temple belonging to the geometric period, three stoas, the longest being no less than 185 yards, and extensive walls. The curious painted heads in the museum are probably of the Mycenaean period. The wish to preserve self and car precludes an attempt on the atrocious 30 miles north over the Panetolikó to the

Proussos Monastery, which is at present only accessible from Karpeníssi (see page 254).

If you skirt the south shore of Trihonída to Makrinou—but don't be too distracted by the delightful contrasting colors of the green shores, blue lake and snow-capped mountains; there are some hidden gullies within the villages, that become torrents after heavy rain—it is possible to continue straight on (southeast) to Nafpaktos (21 miles), crossing a mountain range with lovely views before descending the valley of the Evinos river.

The highway south from Agrínio passes between the lakes Lissimahia and Trihonída, then cuts five miles off the scenically more rewarding narrower parallel road to the right (west) through the Klissóura Gorge, whose towering sides are the nesting place of eagles, hawks and kites. Emerging at a wide lagoon you see the houses of Etolikó mirrored in the surrounding shallow water. It all looks very picturesque from the mainland, but the island is somewhat disenchanting on closer acquaintance. Eight miles west, across the Aheloos, extensive walls enclose the ruins of the antique Aetolian port Oeniadae.

Messolongi on the edge of the lagoon is famous for the heroic siege during the War of Independence (May 1825–April 1826) and for its romantic association with Lord Byron, who died there of fever, shortly after having been appointed commander-in-chief of the Greek forces.

The town was closely besieged by a Turco-Egyptian army. After hunger had reduced the inhabitants to the direst extremities, the defenders, escorting their women and children, attempted to break through the enemy lines on the night of April 22, 1826, but most of them perished in the attempt. This sortie, known as the exodus, is commemorated every year by a solemn celebration. At the memorial cemetery, the *Tabia* (Bastion), stand the monuments of the Philhellenes of all nations who fell there during the siege fighting for the liberty of Greece. The fall of the town made a tremendous impression throughout Europe and more than any other event helped to arouse sympathy for the Greek cause.

If your visit coincides with the sunset, drive out to Tourlída, three miles along the narrow strip extending into the lagoon. The islets scattered at its entrance were defended by the forts of Vassiladi and Kleissoura, which played an important part during the siege.

The remaining 25 miles to the Antirio-Rio ferry wind along the northern shore of the gulf of Patra, after crossing the Evinos. Two miles before reaching the sea, the road forks right (south) to the ferry and the Peloponnese, straight on to Náfpaktos (6 miles) and Delphi (a further 68 miles).

PRACTICAL INFORMATION FOR
NORTHWESTERN GREECE

WHEN TO COME. Thanks to the protecting mountains the climate is delightful in spring and autumn, while the heat is rarely oppressive in summer. Winters are cold in the interior and very wet on the coast. The outstanding cultural events are the *Epirotica,* musical, theatrical and folkloric performances; in Ioanina in August; ancient drama at Nikopolis in July, and at Dodona in August.

HOW TO GET ABOUT. Twice daily flights between Athens and Ioanina (50 min.); thrice weekly via Agrinio (1 hr.); four times weekly to Aktio (1 hr. 20 min.) for Lefkada, and Preveza.

The ferry-boat Brindisi-Corfu-Patra calls at Igoumenitsa, but there is also a local ferry service between Corfu and Igoumenitsa, ten times daily in summer. The 62 miles from Igoumenitsa to Ioanina are the beginning of the modern version of the antique Via Egnatia, under reconstruction to Thessaloniki; Ioanina is the hub of the system, 123 miles northeast to Kastoria in west Macedonia; 40 miles south to Arta, another 28 miles to Amfilohia, thence bypassing Agrinio and Messolongi to Antirio, ferry (half-hourly) to Rio, where it links with the toll motorway along the northern shore of the Peloponnese to Corinth and then to Athens. The daily bus takes about eight hours for the 260 miles.

But there are three shorter west-east crossings to the Athens-Thessaloniki motorway: the *first* from Ioanina along the lake and through the magnificent scenery of the Pindos range via Metsovo and Kalambaka (Meteora) to Larissa (128 miles); the *second* from Agrinio across the Kremasta lake by the Tatarna bridge and through the foothills of the Panetoliko via Karpenissi to Lamina (121 miles); the *third* branches left (east) at the road-fork before Antirio to Nafpaktos (6 miles) and then via Delphi to Thebes (130 miles). Daily hydrofoil service Nafpaktos-Patra.

Coastal steamers on the Patra-Preveza-Corfu run call at Parga. Parga is reached by branching eight miles left (west) off the coastal highway which connects Igoumenitsa with Preveza, avoiding the mountains of the interior (57 miles); a half-hourly ferry takes cars in ten minutes to Aktio. Twelve miles southwest is the Lefkada ferry across the narrow channel separating the two causeways, which can also be reached by skirting the Ambracian Gulf from Amfilohia (34 miles); nine miles east of Aktio is Vonitsa, whence the shortest road south connects via Mytikas and Astakos at Etoliko (65 miles) with the main artery.

HOTELS AND RESTAURANTS. The hotel restaurants are on the whole the safest, though the *tavernas* certainly have more local color, sometimes too much. The single restaurant at the Ioanina lakeside opens only in summer. The lake fish, carp, pike, eel, are palatable enough, especially the baked eel (*helí sto harti*). The cloyingly sweet sparkling wine from neighboring Zitsa is sacrilegiously referred to as Greek champagne. Ioanina has some good oriental pastry, besides the usual *baklava, kadaïf* and *galaktoboureko* try *ravani* and *bougatsa* (made with cheese). Of regional dishes there are few. In Messolongi ask for fish roe appetizer *avgo taraho* (expensive); in Preveza for shrimps (*garides*); shrimps with rice (*garides pilaffi*) are among the better fare in coastal region, but pies are the real Epirote specialty.

AGRÍNIO. *Galaxy* (M), tel. 23 551/3. 36 rooms. *Soumelis* (M), tel. 23 473. Motel on bypass one mile out; 20 rooms; restaurant. *Alice* (I), tel. 23 056. 34 rooms. *Leto* (I), tel. 23 043. 36 rooms, most with showers.

AHELOOS. *Filoxenia* (M), tel. 71 201. Motel at the ruins of Stratos, near the Aheloos bridge 8 miles north of Agrinio: 3 double rooms.

AMFILOHIA. *Amvrakia* (I), tel. 22 213. 39 rooms; restaurant. *Mistral* (I), tel. 22 287. 40 rooms; restaurant.

ARTA. *Xenia* (M), tel. 27 413. Lovely location within the Byzantine fortress, book well in advance in summer. 22 rooms; tennis. *Kronos* (I), tel. 22 211/3. 55 rooms; restaurant, disco.

ASTAKOS. *Astakos Beach* (M), tel. 41 096. 30 rooms, 4 suites. On beach.

IGOUMENITSA. *Xenia* (M), tel. 22 282. Motel on the sea. 36 double rooms. *Astoria* (I), tel. 22 704. 13 rooms. *Jolly* (I), tel. 23 970. 27 rooms. *Oscar* (I), tel. 23 338. 34 rooms. Airconditioned.

IOANINA. *Xenia* (M), Vassileos Georgiou II 33. Far from lake; 60 rooms. *Alexios* (I), Poukevil 14 (tel. 24 003). 92 rooms. *Dioni* (I), Tsirigoti 10 (tel. 27 864). 44 rooms. *Egnatia* (I), Dagli 2 (tel. 25 667). 52 rooms. *Olympic* (I), Melanidi 2 (tel. 25 888). 44 rooms. *Vyzantion* (I), Leoforos Dodonis (tel. 23 898). 104 rooms; the only (I) hotel with a restaurant.
Restaurant. *Ta Litharitsia,* cafe-restaurant and disco in the park.

KASTROSSYKIA. *Preveza Beach* (M), tel. 51 483. 264 rooms in central block and bungalows. 10 miles north of Preveza. Airconditioned; pool, tennis, minigolf, disco.

MESSOLONGI. *Theoxenia* (M), tel. 28 098. On the sea, 80 rooms, roofgarden. *Liberty* (I), tel. 28 050. 60 rooms.

METSOVO. *Diasselo* (M), tel. 41 719. 20 rooms, 2 suites. *Victoria* (M), tel. 41 771. 30 rooms; disco. *Bitounis* (I), tel. 41 545. 24 rooms. *Galaxy* (I), tel. 41 202. Only half of the 10 double rooms with showers. Restaurant on tree-shaded terrace. *Kassaros* (I), tel. 41 662. 24 rooms.

MYTIKAS. *Simos* (I), tel. 51 380. 27 rooms; restaurant.

PARGA. *Lichnos Beach* (M), tel. 31 257. 84 rooms in central block and bungalows. *Parga Beach* (M), tel. 31 293. 80 bungalows; minigolf. These two are at opposite ends of the village. Of several (I) hotels, only the *Bacoli*, tel. 31 200, has all of the 34 rooms with showers, and a restaurant.

PLATARIA. 4 miles south of Igoumenitsa. *Plataria Beach* (M). 22 rooms.

PREVEZA. *Zikas* (M), tel. 27 505. 54 rooms. *Dioni* (I), tel. 27 381. 30 rooms; restaurant. *Minos* (I), tel. 28 424. 19 rooms, no restaurant.
Restaurants. Two very simple restaurants on the waterfront.

VONITSA. *Bel Mare* (I), tel. 22 394. 33 rooms.

 SHOPPING. Ioanina used to be famous for its metalworkers and embroiderers. Metalwork (small silver boxes with enameled designs, brooches, buckles, ashtrays etc.) are still made in traditional designs, though the quality of the silver has somewhat deteriorated. These as well as some fine needlework, rugs and bags of good color and design, in the traditional Metsovo style, can be bought in numerous tourist shops.

EXCURSIONS. Those with a special interest in archeology are recommended to visit—in addition to Dodona—the following sites:

Amotopos, 6 miles northeast of Filipiada, ancient walls dating from the 4th-3rd century B.C.

Doliani, near Riziani, to the right of the Ioanina—Igoumenitsa highway, with the ruins of a walled town of the 3rd–2nd century B.C.

Kassopi, near Kamarina, north of Nikopoli (about an hour by bus from Preveza) where there are the ruins of a 4th-century B.C. town.

Kastri-Mesopotamos. This is the site of the ancient Ephyre with the remains of the Oracle of the Dead, dating from Homeric times. It can be reached by the Preveza—Paramythia road. The excavated portion begins some 2½ miles to the east of Kanalaki.

USEFUL ADDRESSES *GNTO,* Napoleon Zerva 2, Ioanina, tel. 25 086; also in the port of Igoumenitsa.

THE IONIAN ISLANDS

In the Realm of Odysseus

There are seven islands, which accounts for the Greek name Heptanesa. Six—Kérkyra (Corfu) of which the neighboring islet of Paxí is a part, Lefkáda, Itháki (Ithaca), Kefalonía (Cephallonia) and Zákynthos (Zante)—are strung in a chain off the western shores of Greece. The seventh, Kýthira (see earlier) lies far to the south, close to the eastern promontory of the Peloponnese, and has more often than not followed a destiny apart, ever since Aphrodite chose it for her first sensational appearance.

Ruins and tombs on Lefkáda and Kefalonía prove the existence of a flourishing Mycenaean civilization at the time of the Trojan war, in which Odysseus, King of Ithaca played such a decisive part. Leucadius, Penelope's brother, gave his name to one of the isles, while on Corfu, the land of the Phaeacians, was enacted the charming idyll between Princess Nausicaa and the shipwrecked Odysseus. These Homeric associations formed a common bond, which however was broken in classical times. Though the northern islands were colonized from Corinth in the 8th and 7th century B.C., Corfu soon revolted and its conflict with the mother city led to the Peloponnesian War, when the colony appealed for help to Athens, while Corinth, allied to the other islands, turned to Sparta. After subjection to the tyrants of Syracuse, the kings of Epirus and of Macedonia, the islands passed in the 2nd century B.C., under Roman rule.

With the break up of the Byzantine empire each island again resumed a separate and stormy existence. Resisting Germanic and Saracen invasions with varying degrees of success, the old ties with Sicily were at last re-established in the 11th century, and for 300 years Norman and Angevin kings ruled either directly or through their vassals, of whom the counts of Cephallonia and Zante were the most powerful. Corfu was the first to place itself under Venetian protection in the 14th century, and in spite of two momentous Turkish sieges has the distinction of being the only part of modern Greece never to have experienced Ottoman rule. The other islands suffered severely from the Turks, before being slowly gathered under the protective wings of the mighty maritime republic. The astute diplomats of San Marco won the loyal support of the leading Greek families by a liberal scattering of high-sounding titles, which, to the islanders' great regret, are not recognized by the Greek constitution. The life of the island aristocracy centered on their elegant country houses, and the general prosperity led to a flowering of arts and letters in happy contrast with the prevailing material and spiritual misery on the mainland. Italian became the official language till 1851, when a British governor reintroduced Greek, which had decayed into a peasant dialect.

The fall of Venice in 1797 started an unparalleled game of musical chairs among the great powers. Under the treaty of Campo Formio the French occupied all Venetian territories, but Russo-Turkish forces established in 1800 the Republic of the Seven Isles under the sultan's sovereignty. In 1802 the Russians took over, to be in their turn dispossessed by the French in 1807. Britain joined the game in 1810, but the French garrison in Corfu held out against the English blockade until 1814, when the treaty of Paris re-established the Ionian Republic under British protection.

The senate and legislative assembly had little real authority under the personal rule of the Lord High Commissioners, who were great individualists, to put it mildly. The first Commissioner, Sir Thomas Maitland, was notorious for his rudeness, especially to bearers of letters on introduction. He was known to have exposed an unmentionable part of his anatomy to unwanted visitors, yet his eccentricity was no greater than that of his successor. Sir Frederick Adam married an ambitious Corfiote, whose moustache, according to contemporary comments, would not have shamed a dashing hussar. This peculiarity did not prevent the misguided second Commissioner from lavishing the revenue of the islands on the bearded lady.

Successive commissioners built roads, hospitals, asylums and prisons, reformed education, law and agriculture, but these benefices could not stem the rising tide of nationalism. Ruthless suppression failed as also Gladstone's attempt at reconciliation by a liberal constitution. Britain acknowledged the trend by using the Ionian islands to secure the election of Prince William George of Holstein-Glücksburg, son of the King of Denmark, to the Greek throne, and after his accession as George I, the islands were ceded to Greece in 1864.

Earthquakes had been a fairly common calamity, especially in Zákynthos, but never as widespread and devastating as the series of shocks which in summer 1953 leveled the towns and villages on Itháki, Kefalonía and Zákynthos. By 1959 the reconstruction was completed, a remarkable feat in a poor country, largely due to the active help of the army and generous support from foreign welfare organizations. But the fine old houses of Venetian Zante are gone, replaced by modern buildings, perhaps pleasanter to live in, but infinitely less pleasing to the eye.

Exploring the Ionian Islands

The ferry-boat from Brindisi as well as most ships coming from Italy or down the Dalmatian coast call at Corfu, thus giving the best possible introduction to Greece. The unrivaled beauty of the island is enhanced by the inhabitants' famed courteousness, the happy result of centuries of unbroken civilization. Corfiotes have been accused of being overcivilized—as if that were possible—of not conforming to the accepted pattern of the dashing, reckless Greek. Moreover, to some fanatical purists the island is too lush and luxuriant, lacking in the classical barrenness of Attica and the Cyclades. A much more valid objection is the touristic overdevelopment which has degraded numerous beauty spots.

Corfu

Boats coming from Italy and Yugoslavia pass through the narrow channel separating the northern bulge of the island from Albania, so the traveler from abroad is presented with the entire east coast on his way to Athens. But he should break the journey for a while, to enjoy the tranquil dignity of the tall 18th-century buildings lining the arcaded streets, little changed since Venetian times, though the Italian bombing of 1941 destroyed the opera house and other public buildings.

The road from the harbor ascends past the mansion where John Capodistrias, Greece's first President, was born in 1776, now a school for interpreters. The cathedral (Metropolis), a little higher up, dates from 1577 but of greater interest is the church of St. Spyridon (1589), the island's patron saint, which lies just off the main square and is easily recognizable by its red dome. Corfu's sensuous beauty seems to preclude sanctity, though a patron had to be found in saintlier parts. The embalmed body of Agios Spiridon, Bishop of Cyprus in the fourth century, was smuggled out of Constantinople in a sack of straw after the Turkish conquest and after an adventurous journey, placed in a silver casket in the chapel to the right of the altar. Most efficacious in saving the town from the plague in 1630 and the Turks in 1716, his prestige was further enhanced when a bomb hit the church, but failed to explode in World War II during an air raid that destroyed a third of the town. No wonder his name is proudly borne by a good half of the male islanders.

British rule has left some unexpected marks, especially on the large central, the Esplanade, square where cricket is still played. The game has inevitably undergone certain local modifications, together with some English words and drinks, as for instance *tsintsibira,* no other than ginger beer. On the north side of the square rises the elegant colonnade of the former Royal Palace, built after the plans of Sir George Whitmore between 1816 and 1823. The attractive residence of the High Commissioners and seat of the Ionian Senate, known as the Palace of St. Michael and St. George, as it was also the headquarters of the newly-founded order, became a favorite residence of George I. The staterooms are open to the public and beside the stern portraits of the High Commissioners there is the remarkable Sino-Japanese collection donated by a former Greek ambassador to those countries.

The British High Commissioners, a self-assured lot, scattered monuments all over the Esplanade, the most original being an Ionian rotunda to the memory of Sir Thomas Maitland, near the bandstand where the municipal orchestra performs on Sundays. Capodistrias' statue faces the empty shell of Lord Guilford's Ionian Academy on the upper Esplanade, bombed out but scheduled for reconstruction. According to contemporaries Lord Guilford was "a queer fish, but very pleasant; he goes about dressed up like Plato, with a gold band round his mad pate and flowing drapery of purple hue. The pretty dress of the students consists of a tunic and cloak, with buskins of red leather reaching to mid-leg. The professors bind fillets round their heads. Medicine wears the tunic citron and the cloak orange; Law light green and violet; Philosophy green and blue." In spite, or perhaps because, of the fancy dress, this nucleus of a university started Greece's literary revival round the poets Solomos and Mavilis.

The west side of the Esplanade was the exclusive reserve of the nobility till revolutionary France swept away feudal privileges and substituted a local adaptation of the Rue de Rivoli. The arcades below the tall houses, the Liston, are taken up by souvenir shops and cafés, overflowing into the square after sunset.

The old fortress on the east is cut off by a deep canal. This artificial island was a suburb of the ancient town, but the center of the Byzantine settlement. The Venetians, recognizing its strategic importance, transformed it into a fortress, which decisively contributed to the successful resistance against the Turkish attacks in 1716. The hero of the siege, Count Schulenburg, is honored by a statue near the bridge. English barracks were built in the fortress area and the former Anglican Chapel of St. George, in the Doric style, has been converted to Orthodoxy. The massive walls of the new fortress, on a hill dominating the harbor, are a good example of the solid military Venetian architecture. Today it houses the town's archives. From the top there is a fine view over the town and the surrounding villages half hidden in cypress and olive groves, while the distant mountains of Epirus and Albania seem to merge with the island's highest peak, Mount Pantocrator.

On the south the square narrows to the shady Dimokratías Boulevard. A favorite evening stroll is along the bay past the 7th-century B.C. Cenotaph of Menecrates to the ruins of the Artemis temple, whose colossal Gorgon pediments are (together with the lioness of Menecrates) the pride of the museum behind the Corfu Palace Hotel. Above the Anemomilos suburb rise the cupolas of the 12th-century church of Agios Iason and Agios Sosipater.

The Haunt of Royalty

Paleopolis, the antique capital, occupied most of the promontory where several sanctuaries have been excavated. Within the precincts of the large archaic temple stood two minute shrines, one dedicated to Hermes, the other to Aphroditos, patron of transvestites, judging from the clay statuettes depicting Aphrodite with moustache and beard, a curious anticipation of things to come in the shape of Lady Adam.

A Russian general was the first to rediscover the serenity of the wooded promontory, and instead of a gun emplacement he built himself a pavilion. It would be going too far to say that this aesthetic indulgence led to the loss of the island, but soon afterwards the second Lord High Commissioner outshone his Russian predecessor by building the villa of Mon Repos, surrounded by a beautiful park, for his bearded spouse. "Sir Frederick's Folly" became the summer residence of the Greek royal family; the Duke of Edinburgh was born there. The beach of Mon Repos is well provided with cabins and a café under huge plane trees; it is open to the public and within easy reach of the town, but the bathing is marred by the seaweed in the shallow water.

The road continues through gardens and parks to Kanoni, one of the world's great beauty spots, made deservedly famous by countless pictures. The name derives from a French cannon that once stood there, no doubt utterly incongruous in that sublimely peaceful landscape. The open sea is separated by a long, narrow causeway from the lagoon of Halikiopóulou, with the intensely green slopes of Mount Agia Deka as a backdrop. A shorter breakwater leads to the white convent of Vlahérna on a tiny islet. Beyond, tall cypresses guard the chapel on Pontikonisi, the Mouse Island, a rock rising dramatically from the clear water, which mythology has identified with the Phaeacian ship turned to stone by enraged Poseidon for bringing Odysseus home to Ithaca. The sunset over the lagoon is one of those experiences that will not be forgotten in a lifetime.

The long causeway's main function is as an aqueduct, built by Sir Frederick, though pedestrians and even cyclists may pass. The road south skirts the lagoon, past the international airport. One branch of the road continues to the open sea, to be rejoined by the other branch shortly before the pretty village of Benítses. That other branch first climbs to the village of Gastouri nestling among the trees, and then turns to the Achilleion, the palace of the Empress Elizabeth of Austria, at an altitude of 476 feet, 12 miles from Corfu.

This remarkable monument to bad taste is redeemed by the lovely garden stretching to the sea. Halfway down, in an open pavilion, stands the statue of the empress, her beauty marred by the impossibility of reproducing modern clothes in marble. The street façade of the palace is fairly inoffensive, but the interior is a preposterous hotch-potch of a pseudo-Byzantine chapel, a pseudo-Pompeian room and a pseudo-Renaissance dining hall, culminating in an hilariously vulgar fresco of "Achilles in his Chariot." It is astonishing that a woman as fastidious as the empress so entirely succumbed to the appalling taste of her period. Yet she was independent enough to choose for her retreat an island that until then had been unfashionably remote.

Worse is to come on the terrace which commands a superb view over Kanoni and the town. In what was seriously intended as an Ionic peristyle stand a bewildering number of statues (from the

Muses down to somebody's Aunt Fanny), in various degrees of undress, but uniformly depressing or funny, according to the visitor's mood. Almost artistic is the marble "Achilles Wounded," Elizabeth's favorite hero, in whose honor the palace was named.

To prove that he could do everything bigger and better, the German emperor inscribed his colossal Achilles with the modest dedication: "to the greatest Greek from the greatest German." Always the Supreme War Lord, the Kaiser had a riding saddle fixed up as a chair for the writing desk; the imposing throne of the lavatory, complete with electric bell, witness that Wilhelm II insisted on his illustrious status even in his most intimate moments. He bought the Achilleion after the assassination of the Austrian empress, and resided there regularly till the outbreak of the First World War. Before being turned into a casino the palace was completely renovated in 1962, but the historic monstrosities have been well preserved.

Paleokastritsa

Lacking the comic touch, but scenically equally splendid is the longer excursion to Paleokastritsa. The road, constructed by the Eleventh Regiment of Foot to a convalescent camp, but according to gossip, to Lady Adam's favorite picnic spot, crosses the island between orange and olive groves to the rugged bays and promontories of the west coast. On a rock towering over the crystal clear water of the creek stands the monastery facing the open Ionian Sea. The steep mountain behind the monastery rock is crowned by the grim ruins of Angelokastro, built in the 13th century by Michael I Angelos, Despot of Epirus, during his brief rule over Corfu. To enjoy the magnificent view over the wild coast drive up to the restaurant on the Bella Vista terrace, a favorite vantage point of Wilhelm II. The twin bays below are the traditional site of the Phaeacian capital ruled by Alcinous, when Odysseus was washed ashore and found by Nausicaa, playing ball with her maidens, at the mouth of the Ermónes river further south.

Another monastery on the west coast that should be visited for the lovely site is the hermitage of the Myrtiotissa, an hour's walk from the village of Pelekas, lying below Mount Agios Georgios. Then there is the drive north to Kassiópi along the east coast, past the Castello, an early 20th-century Florentine-Renaissance counterpart of the Achilleion where King George II liked to spend the few summers he was allowed in his country; the splendid bay of Dassia, Ypsós, Pyrgí and Nissaki, to return over mighty Mount Pantokrator. But then any road on this blessed island reveals some new beauties.

Lefkáda and Itháki

The annual Festival of Art and Literature attracts, by its varied folkloric manifestations, large crowds in August and has put Lefkás deservedly on the tourist map. But hotel accommodation is totally insufficient, though complemented by what the French edition of this volume so charmingly and ambiguously terms *on couche chez l'habitant*. Here, as on all Ionian islands with the exception of Kefalinía, the capital has given its name to the whole island. Lefkáda is easily reached; either by boat from Athens calling at the lesser ports of northwestern Greece; or in about two hours by motorboat from Preveza, over the site of the naval battle of Actium, which Cleopatra's cowardice or treachery lost for Mark Anthony; or by road from Amfilohia (38 miles) along the shores of the Ambracian gulf, and then by ferry boat across the canal that separates Lefkáda from the mainland.

This canal through the marshy isthmus was originally dug by the Corinthians in 640 B.C., but silted up again. Augustus ordered a new excavation and also linked the town to the land, as he was interested in the island which lay so close to the scene of his greatest victory. The canal was sufficiently important to be kept open by successive conquerors, and in the 13th century the Franks built the Santa Maura Fortress to guard the entrance. An aqueduct of 260 arches brought water to the castle, which was later occupied by the Venetians and Turks.

A ten-mile-long strip of sand, on which windmills and trees seem to rise straight out of the water, separates the open sea from the lagoon on which the town stands, connected by a long causeway to the port. Lefkáda suffered severely in the earthquakes of 1867 and 1958, though it escaped the still greater devastation of 1953. The damaged Venetian churches are undistinguished, but the 13 miles to the bay of Vlího, hugging the coast, are a sheer joy. Some Mycenaean ruins at Nidri led the German archeologist Dörpfeld to elaborate an ingenious theory that there was the site of ancient Ithaca. But without going into complicated archeological arguments the traveler will be able to appreciate the scenic beauty of the drive. After Vlího the road climbs into the mountainous but fertile interior, to rejoin the sea at the fishing village of Vassiliki in the south, halfway (27 miles) on the island circuit. The island of Skorpios, a few miles off, belongs to Onassis' daughter. Both he and his son are buried there. The return journey, on a pretty road high up in the cliffs of the west coast, presents another facet of this lovely island, the laboriously terraced mountain slopes and the beaches on the Ionian Sea.

To include the four northern islands in one tour, it is possible to proceed from Vassiliki on Lefkáda to the port of Koliéri in the northern bay of Itháki. The journey takes about four hours, for the first part in the shelter of the Lefkatos, the White Cape, once crowned by a temple of Apollo, near the modern lighthouse. From the cliff 236 feet high the Lefkadian leap was performed as a divine judgment for certain crimes, but curiously enough also as a drastic cure for love-sickness. It was indeed a case of kill or cure as the poetess Sappho experienced to her detriment. Disappointed lovers of the Roman period were less reckless and equipped themselves with feathers to break the fall, while boats were waiting to haul them out of the water. Apollo's priests performed the dive as a routine observance.

A steep scenic road crosses the island over the narrow waist below Mount Aetos. From the highest point of the road, without climbing the 1,246 feet to the summit, one enjoys a magnificent view: to the west Kefalonía, separated only by a strip of water, and to the east the entrance to the gulf of Patra, guarded by high mountain sentinels.

The capital is locally called Vathý (Deep), as it lies at the head of a deep inlet, branching off from the big eastern bay. Vathý as well as Ithaca, the Precipitous, are indeed singularly apposite and in perfect agreement with Homer's description in the Odyssey. Though the smallest of the four islands over which Odysseus ruled, it was, owing to its strategical position and ports at every point of the compass, the obvious center of a maritime kingdom.

Kefalonía and Zákynthos

Kefalonía is the largest of the Ionian islands, the central mountain chain rising to 5,313 feet. Though the plains are fertile and there are even forests of a local variety of fir, it is only at the lovely fishing villages of Assos and Fiskárdo, in the north that Kefalonía rivals the enchantment of Corfu and Zákynthos. From Sami opposite Itháki, near the extensive but dull ruins of ancient Samaea, it is 16 miles to Argostoli, the modern capital in a fjordlike bay in the south. The drive takes in the main sights: in the central plain the monastery of Agios Gerasimos, Kefalonía's patron saint, who failed to protect his sanctuary in the terrible disaster of 1953; the 83 Mycenaean tombs at Mazarakata, partly of the beehive variety, partly hewn into the rocks, which have yielded numerous Bronze Age vases and implements; and about four miles before Argostoli the village of Kastro, on the ruins of San Giorgio, the Venetian capital, destroyed by an earthquake in 1636 and finally abandoned in favor of Argostoli in 1757. The empty shells of churches and houses straggle up to the solid ramparts of the castle, unscathed by repeated upheavals. Just behind the drawbridge are the ruined British barracks.

Argostoli, originally the port of San Giorgio, lies inside the branch of the long Linadi Bay. Razed to the ground in 1953, it has been rebuilt on occasionally startling modernistic lines, following utilitarian principles mitigated by wide, tree-lined avenues. The *Katovathres,* deep clefts in the coastal cliffs in subterranean communication with the sea, are a local attraction. The Melissani seacave can be explored by boat, while one of the green-colored chambers of the Drongorati caves has been transformed into a subterranean, stalactite-roofed concert hall, renowned for its acoustics. The fine sandy beach of Platys Gialos is two miles out of town. The second town, Lixouri, across the bay, is fringed by good beaches.

Last, but certainly not least, comes Zákynthos, long known as *Zante, fiore di Levante.* Till 1953 the flower of the Levant rivaled Corfu in natural beauty as well as in the attractiveness of the arcaded town and of the country houses scattered over the plain. The architectural gems are all gone and the new box-like arcades, so indispensable in the torrential winter rains, are but a sad substitute for their rounded, elegant 18th-century predecessors. But at least the local patron saint, Agios Dionysios, proved here more efficacious, as only his church and the National Bank building survived the last great earthquake. This curious juxtaposition has been attributed by the faithless to good, solid masonry, a belief reinforced by the inevitable Venetian fortress, which on the hill dominating the town proved itself impervious to the successive violent upheavals afflicting the island during the last 150 years. But even here there is the proverbial silver lining in the richness and fertility of the volcanic soil, and the view from the castle over the wide, intensively cultivated plain between the two seas only presents the luxuriant vegetation of the flowering island.

Zante hospitably welcomed the artists who fled Crete after the Turkish conquest in the 17th century. The museum thus contains an outstanding collection of paintings belonging to the Ionian School, especially the superb *Christ as Highpriest,* by Nikolas Kallergis. The closest beach is at Argássi (three miles); the longest stretch of fine sand is to be found at Laganás (six miles south); while Pórto Róma (seven miles) is an idyllic bay below a rocky promontory. The two mineral springs at Keri, the southernmost point, where pitch bubbles up at the rate of three barrels a day to be used for the caulking of boats, were described by Herodotus in the 5th century B.C.

PRACTICAL INFORMATION FOR THE IONIAN ISLANDS

WHEN TO COME. Decidedly not in winter. The torrential rains from November to March make the islands an earthly paradise in spring and summer, but are most depressing in their persistency while they last. Unfortunately the feasts of Agios Spiridon, patron of Corfu, and of Agios Dionysios of Zákynthos, with their display of ecclesiastical pomp and ceremony, fall respectively on December 12 and 17, but lesser processions in honor of the former saint take place on Palm Sunday, Easter Saturday and August 11. The International Ionian Regatta is held in June. During the numerous local fairs you can see national costumes and watch popular dances. Performances by theater groups and folkloric dances in Corfu, Itháki, Lefkáda and Zákynthos during August and early September hardly deserve to be classified as festivals, but the Sound and Light at the Old Fortress, Corfu, May through September, is well worth watching.

HOW TO GET ABOUT. Corfu's international airport is connected with several European capitals, as well as Brindisi, and four times daily with Athens; in summer also with Thessaloniki via Ioanina; Kefalonía and Zákynthos are linked daily with Athens; Zákynthos also by charter flights with some European capitals.

Frequent steamer services from Venice, Trieste, Rijeka and Brindisi to Corfu, operated by Greek, Italian and Yugoslav lines.

Daily car ferries from Ancona, Bari and Brindisi to Corfu continue to Patra from April to October; less frequent in winter.

Local ferry boats link Corfu twelve times a day to Igoumenitsa in Epirus, once daily to Pasí and Itháki; Lefkáda to Preveza; Itháki and Kefalonía (Sami) to Patra; Zákynthos to Kylini on the Peloponnese.

Daily hydrofoil service, weather permitting, from Argostoli and Zákynthos to Patra.

Frequent bus services to all points of interest by the extensive road network on the islands. Daily coach service from Athens, Kifissou 100. For deluxe Pullman service, enquire at travel agencies.

HOTELS AND RESTAURANTS. Hotels are crowded from May to September with package tours. Most hotels, except at Lefkáda, face the sea; all with restaurants, unless otherwise stated; many offer halfboard or fullboard only. On the islands, food at the usual water-front taverns is uninteresting, in spite of the long connection with Italy. Some wine, on the other hand, is pleasant. *Theotoki,* produced by Corfu's leading family is difficult to obtain. Kefalonía produces the excellent *Robola* and Lefkáda produces a very drinkable rough red wine, *Santa Maura,* that goes well with the local sausages. The Corfu Barbecue and Wine Festival offers wine, folk dancing and cabaret combined with a folkloric museum and handicrafts in the making in the *Village* five miles north of town. A major tourist attraction.

Corfu
All distances are from Corfu town

AGIOS GORDIS. 9 miles southwest. *Agios Gordios* (E), tel. 36 723. 209 rooms; pool, tennis, disco; above the beach. *Chrysses Folies* (I), tel. 30 407. Nothing to do with follies, but the Golden Nests, which is almost equally off the mark. 20 double rooms, 300 yds. from beach.

ALYKES. 2 miles north. *Kerkyra Golf* (E)—rather confusing because the golf course is near the west coast—tel. 31 785/7. On beach; 240 rooms, not airconditioned; pool, roofgarden, tennis, disco. *Salina* (I), tel. 36 782. 16 rooms.

ANEMOMYLOS. Suburb opposite Mon Repos beach. *Arion* (M), tel. 37 950. 105 rooms; disco, minigolf, pool, roofgarden. *Marina* (M), tel. 32 783. 102 rooms, airconditioned; pool, roofgarden.

BENÍTSES. 7 miles south. *Odyssey Apartments* (E), tel. 92 227. 56 furnished apartments. *San Stefano* (E), 92 292. 250 rooms; pool, tennis, 800 yds from beach. *Potamaki* (M), tel. 30 889. 149 rooms; beach, pool, roofgarden, disco. *Corfu Maris* (I), tel. 38 684. 25 rooms; no restaurant.

CORFU TOWN. *Corfu Palace* (L), tel. 39 485/7. 106 rooms; pool, tennis. Guests are taken to bathe at Miramare Bungalows at Moraitika. *Cavalieri* (E), tel. 39 336. In a converted 18th-century mansion on the upper Esplanade. 48 rooms, not airconditioned. *Astron* (M), tel. 39 505. 33 rooms; tennis. *King Alkinoos* (M), tel. 39 000. 61 rooms; roofgarden. *Olympic* (M), tel. 30 532. 50 rooms, tennis. *Arcadion* (I), tel. 22 670. 55 rooms. *Atlantis* (I), tel. 35 560. 58 rooms, airconditioned; on seafront, *Ionion* (I), tel. 39 915. 81 rooms; in port.

Restaurants. *Averof* (E), Alipiou 4 (tel. 31 468), with a shaded courtyard near the old harbor, good choice of local dishes, *sofrito* (veal with garlic and vinegar sauce). *Bella Napoli* (E), Skaramanga 11, tel. 33 338. Ionian dishes in an Italian setting. There are Expensive fish restaurants in the Mandouki suburb. *Aegli* (M), Kapodistriou 23 (tel. 31 949) is in the Liston, among the numerous cafe-sweetshops, crowded from morning till late at night. *Bouzoukia* in *Corfu by Night* (E), tel. 38 123, and *Kastro* (E), tel. 32 154; both Potamou. Among the discos on the port road, *Bora Bora* (M) and *Koukouvaya* (M).

DAFNILA. 8 miles north, promontory with olive groves. *Eva Palace* (L), tel. 91 286/7. 174 rooms; pool, tennis, disco. *Robinson Club Hotel* (E), tel. 35 732. 260 rooms, not airconditioned; pool, tennis, disco; close beach.

DASSIA. 7 miles north. *Castello* (E), tel. 93 201. Though not all the 72 rooms have baths—especially in the two small annexes—this is one of the very few hotels in Greece with an atmosphere, as befits a former royal summer retreat; not airconditioned but large, high rooms, kept cool by the surrounding park; lovely dining terrace; tennis; shuttle service to the beach; with *Diktya* Restaurant-Nightclub (E).
  Chandris Corfu (L), tel. 93 351. 301 rooms in central block, bungalows and villas; *Chandris Dassia* (E), tel. 33 871/5. 251 rooms; beach, pool, tennis, disco. Slightly cheaper but still Expensive: *Elaea Beach,* tel. 93 490. 198 rooms, halfboard. *Paloma Bianca* (M), tel. 93 317. 34 rooms, airconditioned; pool, tennis. *Dassia,* (I), tel. 93 224. 54 rooms; beach.

ERMONES. 9 miles west. *Ermones Beach* (E), tel. 94 241/2. 272 bungalows, not airconditioned; pool, tennis.

GAENA. 6 miles south. *Achilleus* (M), tel. 92 425/6. 74 rooms.

GASTOURI. 3 miles southwest. *Achillion* (I), tel. 30 531. 15 rooms. *El Greco* (I), tel. 31 893. 14 rooms. The *Casino* has a good restaurant.

GLYFÁDA. 10 miles west. *Grand Hotel* (E), tel. 94 201/2. 242 rooms; excellent beach; pool, tennis, disco. *Glyfáda Beach* (M), tel. 94 257. 35 rooms.

GOUVIA. 5 miles north. *Corcyra Beach* (E), tel. 30 770/2. 252 rooms in central block and bungalows, not airconditioned; pool, tennis, disco. *Park* (M), tel. 91 310. 125 rooms. *Pheakion* (I), tel. 91 264. 36 rooms.

KANONI. 2 miles south. *Corfu Hilton* (L), tel. 36 540. 274 rooms in hotel and bungalows above beach; pool tennis, nightclub. *Ariti* (E), tel. 38 885. 171 rooms. *Corfu Divani Palace* (E), tel. 38 996/8. 165 rooms; disco. Both have pool but are over 1 mile from beach. *Royal* (M), tel. 37 512. 114 rooms; pool, disco; about 200 yds from beach. *Salvos* (I), tel. 31 693/4. 92 rooms; pool, disco; 200 yds from beach.

KAVOS. 29 miles south. *Cavos* (I), tel. 22 107. 21 rooms.
  Restaurant. *O Naftis* (M), excellent fish cooked by the owner's American wife. Also 10 apartments.

KOMENO. 6 miles north. *Astir Palace Corfu* (L), tel. 91 481/6. 308 rooms in central block and bungalows; pool, tennis, nightclub. *Radovas* (E), tel. 91 218. 115 airconditioned rooms and bungalows; pool.

KONTOKALI. 4 miles north. *Kontokali Palace* (L), tel. 38 736/9. 238 rooms; beach, pool, tennis, nightclub. *Pyrós* (I), 26 rooms.

MESSONGI. 14 miles south. *Messongi Beach* (M), tel. 38 684/6. 796 rooms; beach, pool, tennis, minigolf, disco. *Melissa Beach* (I), tel. 92 429. 32 rooms. *Rossis* (I), tel. 92 352. 30 rooms, airconditioned; beach.

MORAITIKA. 13 miles south. *Miramare Beach* (L), tel. 30 226/8. 149 bungalows; tennis, minigolf. *Delfinia* (E), tel. 30 318. 83 rooms; beach, pool. *Margarita* (I), tel. 92 368. 26 rooms.

NISSAKI. 14 miles north. *Nissaki Beach* (E), tel. 91 232. 239 rooms, halfboard; pool, tennis, minigolf, disco.

PALEOKASTRITSA. 14 miles northwest. *Akrotiri Beach* (E), tel. 41 275/6. 126 rooms, not airconditioned; pool. *Oceanis* (M), tel. 41 229. 71 rooms; pool. *Paleokastritsa* (M), tel. 41 207. 150 rooms; 200 yds from beach; disco, pool. *Apollon* (I), tel. 41 211. 23 rooms. *Odysseus* (I), tel. 41 209. 36 rooms.
Restaurants. Renowned for lobster (astakós).

PERAMA. 5 miles south. *Alexandros* (E), tel. 36 855/7. 75 rooms; pool. *Aeolos Beach* (M), tel. 33 132/4. 231 bungalows; pool, minigolf; on beach. *Akti* (M), tel. 39 445. 55 rooms; pool; on beach. *Aegli* (I), tel. 39 812. 37 rooms; on beach; roofgarden. *Oassis* (I), tel. 38 190. 66 rooms; pool, disco; roofgarden; on beach. *Pontikonissi* (I), tel. 36 871. 49 rooms, restaurant.
Restaurant. *Yannis* (M), for seafood.

PYRGÍ. 9 miles north. *Emerald* (I), tel. 93 209. 58 rooms, airconditioned; beach, roofgarden disco; outstanding for the price.

RODA. 22 miles north. *Roda Beach* (M), tel. 31 225. 360 rooms, airconditioned; beach, pool, tennis, minigolf, disco. *Silver Beach* (I), tel. 31 408. 33 rooms; beach 300 yds.

SGOMBOU. 7 miles northwest, halfway to Paleokastritsa. *Lucciola Inn* (M), tel. 91 419. 10 rooms in a genuine Corfiote setting with country inn atmosphere; excellent fixed menu; book well in advance.

SIDARI. 21 miles north. Among the three (I)s, *Mimosa*, tel. 31 363, 35 rooms, is the largest and closest to the beach.

SINARADES. 8 miles southwest. *Gyaliskari Palace* (E), tel. 31 400. 208 rooms, 4 suites; pool, tennis, disco.

TSAKI. 8 miles south. *Regency* (E), tel. 92 305/8. 185 rooms, airconditioned; beach, pool, disco.

YPSÓS. 8 miles north. *Anatoli* (M), tel. 93 414. 36 furnished apartments. *Ypsos Beach* (M), tel. 93 232. 60 rooms; pool. *Mega* (I), tel. 93 208. 32 rooms; beach; good value.

Itháki

Mentor (M), tel. 32 433. Most of the 36 rooms with bath; on seafront.

Kefalonía
All distances are from Argostoli

AGIA PELAGIA. 6 miles south. *Irinna* (M), tel. 41 285/7. 169 rooms, halfboard; beach, pool, tennis.

ARGOSTOLI. *Aenos* (I), tel. 28 013. 40 rooms. *Cephalonia Star* (I), tel. 23 180. 36 rooms.
Restaurants. *Aenos* (I), *Kephalos* (I), *Limenaki* (I) and *Lorentsatos* (I), all on water front and indistinguishably undistinguished.

FISKARDO. Traditional settlement. Converted mid-19th-century houses (M), accommodating 6 to 18 guests.

LASSI. 1 mile south. *Mediterranée* (E), tel. 28 760/4. 227 airconditioned rooms; beach, pool, disco. *Lassi* (I), tel. 23 126. 20 rooms, near beach.

LIXOURI. *Summery* (I), tel. 91 771. 56 rooms, near beach on town's outskirts.

PLATYS GIALOS. 2 miles south. *White Rocks* (E), tel. 28 332/5. 102 airconditioned rooms in central block and bungalows; beach, disco.

POROS. 25 miles north. *Hercules* (I). 6 rooms; beach.

Lefkáda

Lefkas (M), tel. 23 916. 93 rooms; easy walking distance from fine beach. *Nirikos* (M), tel. 24 132. 36 rooms; even closer to beach.

Paxi

Paxos Beach (I), tel. 31 211. 27 simple bungalows close to beach; disco.

Zákynthos
All distances are from Zákynthos town

ALYKES. 10 miles northwest. *Montreal* (I), tel. 83 341. 31 rooms; beach.

ARGASSI. 3 miles southeast. *Captain* (M), tel. 22 779. 37 rooms, pool. *Chryssi Akti* (M), tel. 28 022. 61 rooms; tennis, on beach. *Levante* (M), tel. 23 608. 63 rooms. *Mimosa Beach* (M), tel. 22 588. 32 bungalows; on beach.

LAGANAS. 4 miles southwest. *Esperia* (M), tel. 24 505. 35 rooms. *Galaxy* (M), tel. 72 271. 80 rooms; roofgarden; on beach. *Zante Beach* (M), tel. 72 230. 252 rooms in central block and bungalows; tennis, disco; on beach. *Alkyonis* (I), tel. 72 267. 19 rooms. *Ionis* (I), tel. 72 241. 50 rooms; the only one with a restaurant among some 15 (I)s near the beach.

PLANOS. 3 miles north. *Mediterranean* (E), tel. 24 550. 80 airconditioned rooms, beach, pool. *Orea Heleni* (I), tel. 28 788. 22 rooms; tennis. *Tsilivi* (I), tel. 23 109. 55 rooms; beach.

ZÁKYNTHOS TOWN. *Reparo* (E), tel. 23 578. 15 rooms, airconditioned. *Strada Marina* (M), tel. 22 761. 56 rooms; roofgarden. *Xenia* (M), tel. 22 232. 39 double rooms. *Bitzaro* (I), tel. 23 644. 42 rooms; no restaurant. *Diana* (I), tel. 28 547. 36 rooms. *Phoenix* (I), tel. 22 719. 38 rooms. ½ mile inland, *Lina* (M), tel. 28 531. 44 rooms, pool, tennis, disco. 1 mile, *Varres* (M), tel. 28 352. 34 rooms.

HOLIDAY VILLAGES. Of the *Club Méditerranée's* three (see p. 22), the *Valtour Marbella*, tel. 39 755, 296 rooms, at Agios Ionnis; and the *Ilios*, tel. 22 144, 240 rooms, at Nissaki. Both are (L) hotels, with rooms occasionally available for outsiders. Bamboo huts in the *Ypsos* (I).

CAMPING SITES. Some 15 in Corfu, Kefalonía and Lefkáda.

 SPORTS. All nautical sports at the hotel beaches, which in Corfu are better on the north and west coasts. *Bathing* is most enjoyable from the miles of lonely sand dunes that separate Límni Korissíon, Corfu's only lake, 16 miles southwest, from the sea. Fine beaches at Platys Gialos on Kefalonía, between lagoon and sea at Lefkáda, Laganas on Zákynthos. Tennis in most of the (L) and (E) hotels.

Corfu possesses an 18-hole golf course on an 175-acre sporting center at Livádi Rópa (Ropa's Meadow), 11 miles from town on the way to Ermones. Unique in Greece, visitors can play cricket at the Byron Cricket Club on the Esplanade.

CASINO. Baccarat, chemin de fer, roulette all year round in the Achilleion Palace on Corfu.

USEFUL ADDRESSES. *British Vice Consulate,* Mavili 2; *GNTO* in Government House, tel. 30 520; *Post Office* in same building.

CENTRAL GREECE AND THESSALY

Home of Gods and Romans

Central Greece is officially called Stereá Ellás (mainland Greece), but locally known as the Roumeli, because the inhabitants proudly insist on their Roman heritage, if not descent. The Roumeli then is the land of Rome, bounded by Epirus, Thessaly and the Parnassós, rich in natural beauty, made easily accessible by an adequate road network.

Further north, at the confines of ancient Greece, but in the center of the modern state, lies the province of Thessaly, once a vast inland sea, later divided into two fresh-water lakes, which ultimately forced an opening through the gorge of Tempe. The surrounding mountains, the Pindos, Orthris, Pílio, Ossa and, above all, the great Olympos range, now tower over a fertile plain.

This desirable land was the goal of a greater number of invaders than usual even in Greece, ever since the Pelasgians started the fashion in about 2000 B.C. In 1200 the Thessalians, a Doric tribe, made their appearance and divided the country into three principalities, which in classical times formed a military league of particularly quarrelsome members.

In the 3rd century A.D., the invasions were resumed as of old. Goths, Huns, Bulgars, Serbs and Franks pillaged and burnt, sometimes incorporating Thessaly in their short-lived kingdoms. Ruled by the Turks from 1389 to 1881, it returned at last to Greek sovereignty in that year, thanks to Gladstone and Gambetta.

Exploring the Roumeli

The Athens-Thessaloniki highway sweeps from the Boeotian plain back to the coast and continues along the narrow sea, hemmed in by the island of Euboea. The branch right leads to the beach of Theológos, and another, left, inland to Atalánti, near which German archeologists are unearthing an important sanctuary of Artemis. After the pleasant spa of Kammena Vourla and the two huge dishes of the Earth Satellite Tracking Station, the road turns to historic Thermopylae, 18 miles southeast of Lamia. Hot Gates was indeed a fitting name, as the steaming sulphur springs of Thermopyles Spa, which now empty through an alluvial coastal strip into the sea, in antiquity further limited the narrow pass between the water and the towering rocks, where 300 Spartans under Leonidas offered a heroic resistance to the immense army of Xerxes in 480 B.C. Asked to surrender, because the Persian arrows would black out the sun, Leonidas gave his famous reply: "All the better, then we can fight in the shade." But the gallant defenders were overwhelmed when a Persian detachment, led over a mountain path by a local traitor, attacked them in the back. A simple inscription commemorates their supreme sacrifice: "Stranger, tell the Lacedaemonians that we lie here, obedient to their command."

It is 133 miles on the toll motorway from Athens to Lamia, but this prosperous provincial town, dominated by a Frankish castle, can also be reached by the old road from Livadia, over the scenic Pournaraki pass. Karpeníssi is 51 miles from Lamia. Separate branch roads lead to the spas of Ýpati, up-to-date, Platýstomo and Smókovo, without modern accommodation.

After the branch left (southwest) to Ýpati, the main road enters the valley of the Sperhiós leading to Makrakómi. At Agios Georgios a road turns right (north) to Smókovo and Karditsa (61 miles), the most difficult but loveliest approach to the Thessalian plain. Over thickly wooded mountains you reach Rentína (2,800 ft.), where it suffices to visit the interesting church, though two hills are crowned with the remains of an acropolis, while antique walls are scattered on remote slopes. At Smókovo (38 miles) the road widens and continues in improved state to Karditsa.

Past Agios Georgios, the main road ascends through fir forests to the Ráhi ridge (3,500 ft.) and then descends the southern slopes of Mt. Tímfristos, whence an adventurous branch left (south) leads via Domnísta to Náfpaktos. Karpeníssi, a small town in the heart of the Roumeli, is an excellent center for excursions by car and on foot. The site is pleasant under plane trees shading the fast-flowing Aspropotamos, the food less so, at Kefalóvrysi three miles south. On the little island is a monument to Marko Botsaris, one of the Souliot leaders in the War of Independence, who died there valiantly fighting a superior Turkish force. The valley narrows at the Mikró Horió (Little Village, eight miles), rebuilt after destruction by a gigantic landslide in 1963. The Megalo Horió (Big Village) is across the river.

The next very rough 15 miles mostly follow the Aspropotamos through spectacular mountain scenery to the Proussos Monastery in a formidable gorge below Mt. Panetolikó. Though possessing a miraculous picture of the Virgin attributed to St. Luke, Proussos is not only visited by pilgrims but also by those who really want to get away from it all.

The 70 miles from Karpeníssi to Agrínio are kept open in winter by snow ploughs (snow chains required). Several forest roads penetrate deep into the mountain fastness to isolated hamlets. The Tatárna bridge, little short of half a mile long, spans the Kremestá lake, formed by the damming up of the Afrifótis, Ahéloos and Tavropós rivers.

A branch leads to the large dam and hydro-electric plant at the narrowest point of the impressive Ahéloos gorge. The last part of the journey is along the northern flanks of Mt. Panetolikó to the fertile plain of Agrínio and the highway to Epirus.

Thessalian Battlefields

The inland road from Lamia to Larissa (70 miles) winds over the Fóurka pass, where the Greek army under Crown Prince Constantine made a last stand against the superior Turkish forces in 1897. The first village in the Thessalian plain below is Fársala, famed for its sticky sweet *chalvas* (nougat).

The Romans were partial to Greece as a battlefield, as Pharsala was shortly followed by the equally decisive battles of Philippi and Actium. In 48 B.C., Pompey led his great army against the smaller forces of Julius Caesar and suffered a crushing defeat. But Pompey also lost his nerve and, abandoning his troops to their fate, fled to Tempe. Never stopping in his flight, he took ship to Egypt, where he was treacherously murdered, leaving Caesar master of Rome and the world.

In spite of these fascinating historical associations, it is pleasanter to enter Thessaly by the toll road which, after bypassing Lamia, more or less follows the coast via Stylída to Mikrothíves, where it turns inland to Larissa (81 miles). To visit Pílio, branch right (east) at Mikrothíves to Néa Anhíalos on the site of Byzantine Thebes and ancient Pyrasos, not so much for the remains of four basilicas and a small museum, but for the drive along the Pagasitic gulf, with its superb views over the Pílio massif to Volos. Another way of enjoying the magnificent scenery is by boat from Halkida to Volos, a 10-hour trip, with stops on both sides of the narrow channel separating the mainland from the steep cliffs of Euboea, opening at last into the majestic sweep of the Pagassitikós. This vast, circular gulf seems entirely landlocked, its entrance masked by the foothills of the Pílio range, whose gentle slopes are covered with vineyards and olive groves almost to the summit.

The Pílio (Pelion) Country

Pagasses (Pagasae), the port of ancient Iolkos, stood on a promontory opposite Volos. It was from here that Jason set out in the *Argo,* the first sizeable ship ever built by man, to make good a vague claim to the Golden Fleece. With the help of his formidable companions, the carefully chosen Argonauts, including such celebrities as Heracles, Theseus, Orpheus, the sons of the North Wind, and Asklepìos as ship's doctor, he brought back not only the Golden Fleece from Colchis, but also the Witch-Princess Medea. She had stopped her father's pursuit by chopping up her brother and throwing the morsels overboard, forcing the fond parent to strike sail to collect the sad remains. Medea continued her happy family life by killing Jason's uncle, the former king of Iolkos, in a spurious rejuvenation operation. Exiled to Corinth, she murdered her two children before her husband's eyes and escaped to Athens in her dragon-car.

Pagasae was conquered by Demetrius Poliorcetes, who finally ended his adventurous career in the town that was renamed Demetrias in his honor. Except for some sculptures, mostly funerary, in the museum, only a few walls remain of the favorite residence of successive Macedonian kings, who ruled Greece from behind the massive fortifications.

And little more remained of Volos after the two devastating earthquakes of Easter 1955. It was rebuilt with commendable speed, but stark utility prevailed and has spread over the large industrial zone. The port is choked with the ferry traffic to Syria, making the lovely surroundings all the more enticing. A 5000 B.C. settlement has recently been unearthed, but a greater thrill awaits fans of the Neolithic at Dimini, 2½ miles west, where six concentric rings of fortifications surrounded the chieftain's dwelling, while surprisingly artistic pottery sheds a favorable light on life in the 4th millennium B.C. And to top it all, another 2½ miles west, mud-brick houses were built round the chief's larger residence in the Sesklo citadel, Europe's oldest fortified settlement.

In the suburb of Ano Volos, straggling up the lower slopes of the 5,252 foot high Pílio, a few 18th-century towerhouses still rise picturesquely above the orchards. Once they were considered the only possible habitation in a region rich enough to be pillaged by Turks, pirates and bandits alike. Here was the site of Iolkos, whose throne Jason claimed, after descending from the wise centaur Cheiron's cave near the summit. But Cheiron, the tutor of every self-respecting legendary hero, was an exception. The centaurs, those strange beings, half man and half horse, who haunted the dense forests of Pelion, were notorious for their lasciviousness and drunkenness.

The extraordinary frescos of the painter Theóphilos (1867–1934), one of the really original primitives, are displayed in a museum at Anakássia, harmoniously furnished in the style of the period. More of his work is in the Museum of Varia at Mytilini.

On a cypress-clad hill overlooking Volos and the calm waters of the gulf, stands the Episkopí, a charming small Byzantine church. This is the traditional site of the wedding banquet of Peleus, one of the Argonauts, and the sea-nymph Thetis. The Olympians honored the feast with their presence, but Eris, the uninvited goddess of discord, flung a golden apple among them, inscribed "For the fairest." Hera, Athena and Aphrodite all claimed it, and their bitter recriminations must have stood in tragic contrast to the serenely peaceful setting. At last Prince Paris of Troy was chosen as judge, and awarded the apple to Aphrodite, thus incurring the undying hatred of the other two goddesses. The fate of Troy was sealed.

Local Color

The slopes of Mount Pílio are dotted with 24 attractive villages, gay with rushing mountain streams among beech, chestnut and olive groves. Portaria, high above Volos, is a popular summer resort, whose excellent *kokkineli* (red wine) has to be consumed on the spot, as it does not stand up well to transport. Neither visitors nor locals complain of this.

Separated by a deep ravine is Makrinítsa, less sophisticated, but richer in *couleur locale*. The two frescoed 17th-century churches of an abandoned monastery contain the portraits of the most unheard-of saints. Several 18th-century mansions have been converted into hotels as parts of the *Traditional Settlements* program. The village square would not be amiss in fairyland; a large, paved terrace, overhanging the town and gulf below, keeps its intimacy by a backdrop of huge plane trees, which shade a small Byzantine church and an exquisite fountain. On the numerous feast days there is dancing till late at night, and in their natural surroundings the national dances have none of the stiff artificiality they assume in town. Local custom prescribes that every *zembeikiko* dancer should perform for his friend, squatting at the edge of the dance floor and keeping time by clapping his hands. Each dancer executes the intricate steps separately, rewarding the partner with an occasional high kick over his head.

The Pílio is crossed on a good road below the summit. Zagorá, the largest village, still retains an air of quiet 18th-century dignity, enhanced by the luxuriant vegetation, and the Church of the Savior, built in 1100, is well worth a visit. The other approach to the Pílio along the northern shores of the gulf is equally pleasing. Agriá is famous for its excellent bottled lemonade. The road continues through the lush orchards on the Lehónia promontory and dense olive groves, turning inland at the 19th mile and over the low ridge of the Pílio to Tsangaráda, 35 miles from Volos, in the middle of a chestnut forest. From Móuresi, two miles further on, a steep branch road descends to the idyllic beach of Agios Ioánnis facing the open sea, while the Pílio roundtrip is continued to Zagorá and Horeftó.

It is 37 miles from Volos to Larissa, mainly on the Lamia toll road parallel to the Kinoskefalé hills (dogs' heads), which divide the plain. Velestino, in the midst of modern market gardens, is the ancient Pherae, where Apollo served King Admetus for a year to atone for his murderous attempt on the Cyclopes. Not only did he help his master to win the hand of Alcestis by yoking a lion and a boar to a chariot, but Apollo even prevailed on the Fates to let Alcestis die in place of her husband. This noble sacrifice was eagerly accepted by the far-from-gallant Admetus, but not by the gods, who sent Heracles to wrestle with Death. Victorious in this supreme contest, the hero returned triumphantly with the faithful wife.

By returning to the road juntion at Mikrothíves and then turning west, battlefield addicts may still visit Fársala on the way to Karditsa, a prosperous market town, the abode of numerous storks. Before rushing off on the treeshaded straight 18 miles to Trikala do not miss the excursion to the artificial Plastiras Lake (27 miles), past the hydroelectric plant a few miles west, to which huge water pipes descend from the mountain ridge. The monastery of Korona (13 miles), burnt by the Germans in 1943, has been rebuilt with a comfortable guesthouse overlooking the vast Thessalian plain to Mt. Olympos. A little higher, but still in sight of that plain, you partake of a sudden dramatic transformation scene into an idyllic alpine valley. Fields and fir forests slope gently to the shores of the blue lake, while the jagged summits of the Pindos range, snow-clad most of the year, tower in the background. You can drive for several miles along the lake to the dam at the far end.

In Trikala, on the banks of the Lítheos river, the Lethe of the ancients, the search is on for a presumed temple of Asklepìos following the excavation of an Hellenistic stoa and some Roman baths. A clocktower on a wooded eminence rises above the insignificant ruins of Justinian's fortress, later the palace of the 14th-century Serbian Emperors. There is also a pretty but neglected mosque on the Karditsa road built by Sinan Pasha in 1550.

The Meteora

The next 12 miles approach the mighty Pindos range on the left (west), while on the right strange rock formations rise ever higher from the plain. Below a dramatic sheer cliff nestles Kalambaka, whose 14th-century Metropolis is decorated with frescos, providing a suitable introduction to one of the wonders of the later Middle Ages.

A circular road winds four miles through an unearthly forest of gigantic pillars rising to 1,820 feet above sea level. These rock-needles were believed to be meteors hurled by an angry god, though in fact they were split and twisted into their fantastic shape by the erosive power of the sea.

These inaccessible pinnacles offered a safe refuge to pious hermits in the turbulent 14th century, when the Serbian emperors of Trikala were competing with Byzantium for the fertile valley, retreating before the incursions of soldiers and brigands to their impregnable rocks. Within a few years the monk Athanasius founded the Monastery of the Transfiguration on the Great Meteoron and imposed the austere rules of the Holy Mountain, rigorously excluding women. Other hermitages followed the example and expanded into monasteries, but the Meteoron retained a dominant position, counting among Athanasius' disciples members of the rival imperial houses of Constantinople and Serbia. A scion of the latter, the Hermit-King Joasaph, richly endowed the monastery; but it was the advent of John Cantacuzene, expelled by his joint emperor from the Byzantine throne, that gave the Meteoron imperial prestige. The abbots refused to recognize the overriding authority of the Superior of the Ascetics any longer, but instead sought to secure their own domination. The ensuing bitter struggle was sharpened by the contest for arable soil, and the violation of all the founder's precepts led inevitably to a rapid decline. Only 6 of the 24 imposing monasteries that once rose proudly on the black rocks remain today while snow and wind have swept away all vestiges of the others from the towering summits they crowned.

The expropriation of Church land for the settlement of refugees in the 1920s sealed the fate of the already decaying monasteries, which have become too poor to serve the traditional liqueur or coffee to the crowds of visitors. Loss of refreshment, however, is more than compensated for by less perilous access, through awesome, but perfectly safe, staircases.

Pinnacled Monasteries

The days of jointed ladders, pulled up in an emergency, are no more, and the nets are now strictly limited to hauling up supplies. Occasional romantics, who misguidedly hanker after the good old days when the traveler was pulled up uncomfortably squeezed into an outsize stringbag, are quickly cured of their rash desire by one look at the rusty and rotting windlass; especially if accompanied by the gruesome story that the rope was never changed until it broke.

The architecture of the monasteries is conditioned by the restricted space available, with buildings rising from different levels. Some are whitewashed, while others display the pretty Byzantine pattern of stone and brick, the multiple domes of the many churches dominating the wooden galleries and balconies, that hang precariously over frightening abysses.

Agios Stephanos is connected to the main cliff by a drawbridge. This ancient hermitage was transformed into a monastery by the munificence of the Emperor Andronicus III Palaeologus and still preserves some of its former treasures. There are fine wood carvings in the main church, a few old icons, but the votive offerings have been pillaged or sold, and the priceless manuscripts eaten by worms. From the windows one enjoys a sublime view over the vast plain to the sea, just discerned on the horizon. North and west rise the formidable barriers of Olympus and Pindos, still snow-covered when the almond and peach trees below are in bloom, shading the green corn and the flaming red poppy fields. But the last monk has departed, and 20 nuns are kept busy preventing 30 orphans from falling into the awesome abyss.

A nunnery in the retreat of the Ascetics—what would Athanasius have said to that? Though even the severe Master might have considered the venerable age of the surviving handful of monks a certain guarantee for their impeccable behavior, with intervening precipices dampening any remaining sinful ardor. Agia Roussani was the first to be converted to a convent, while recently restored Agios Nikolaos, on the lowest rock, is still untenanted.

Agia Triada, on a particularly forbidding pinnacle, is reached by a flight of steps cut into the rock face. The reward for the steep climb lies more in the position of the monastery, perched perilously atop, than in any artistic merit of the Church of the Holy Trinity.

But it is different at fortress-like Agios Varlaam, founded as late as the 16th century. The frescos in the Chapel of All Saints have been skillfully restored and retain some of their original freshness, and some manuscripts remain in the library.

The Great Meteoron is only a stone's throw away, yet only reached after a breathtaking climb. The path faces the tallest rock-needle, bearing the ruins of the deserted Monastery of the Manuscripts, which was renowned for its illuminated missals. Looking at the perpendicular rock, one easily credits the story about the original ascent being achieved by way of a rope fastened to an eagle's leg, whose nest lay on top of the peak. Just below are the traces of a large painting representing the Virgin and Child. Yet even the perils of painting in such an unpropitious place pale before the awe-inspiring prison cells, shallow caves situated at a dizzy height, where the trespassers against the monastic discipline had to crouch on a narrow ledge, exposed to the rigors of the climate for long periods.

At the top of galleries hollowed out of the rock, the massive gate of the Great Meteoron opens on a large, irregular courtyard. The cloister, the refectory, the churches and chapels are a moving monument to an extinct way of life, whose infinite pain and labor required a religious fervor incomprehensible to later generations.

The Meteoron poignantly epitomizes the glory and decline of Eastern monasticism. The former abode of emperors and kings is now unable to recruit novices even among the poor peasantry. The lovely Church of the Transfiguration bears all the signs of continued neglect, and the fine frescos have suffered by time and dampness. The day seems near when this relic of a great past will be completely abandoned. The medieval splendor can never be recaptured, but the empty shell at least will be preserved as a national monument.

The Olympos Country

The road westwards crosses the Pindos range at the Katára pass, in the magnificent alpine approach to Epirus, while the branch right (north) after five miles provides via Grevena the shortest approach to western Macedonia. Following the Pinios downstream, it is 52 miles from Kalambaka to Larissa, in the heart of the fertile plain. This position assured Larissa of a predominant place in Thessalian history. Reputedly founded by Acrisius, the luckless grandfather of Perseus, it fell later to the progeny of Heracles, at whose brilliant court Pindar and Hippocrates shone. Christianity was appropriately introduced by St. Achilles, the namesake of the great Homeric hero, who ruled somewhere in the vicinity. Under the Turks Larissa gained new importance, but lost all remains of the past to provide building material for the extensive fortifications. The most agreeable feature of the modern town is the Nymphs' Wood, beyond the Pinios bridge, a park with open air restaurants and cafés.

Tírnavos is ten miles along the old road to Macedonia. Only in this large village has the old fertility symbol survived and been sanctioned by Orthodoxy. On Shrove Monday *ouzo* is served in outsize phallic vessels painted in gaudy colors.

The whole countryside rising slowly towards the Olympos is a living museum of folklore. The conservative mountaineers have retained their traditions and customs intact over the centuries. The Church adopted most, with slight modifications, and the funeral rites and dirges, the beating of the ground with the forehead, the rhythmic calling of the departed.

The upper reaches of the Olympos range were the favorite hideout of the *klephtes,* terror of the Turks. These young Greeks, finding life under foreign rule intolerable, fled into the mountain fastnesses of the country, raiding Turkish posts and caravans. They were the nucleus of the 1821 revolutionary forces.

Elassóna, 37 miles from Larissa, lies in the foothills of Olympos, the highest in mountainous Greece. A paved road crosses the lower range from five miles north of Elassóna to Katerini (38 miles), reaching the highest point at the forlorn village of Agios Dimitrios. On no account attempt the crossing by turning right at Kallithea, the first road fork, to Kariá, surrounded by chestnut and fir forests, to join the toll road 38 miles north of Larissa. Better is the branch to the Alpine Club Refuge B (6,500 ft.), within a three-hour easy climb to Skólio, an exciting ski-ascent in winter and the second highest of the peaks standing in a semi-circle round the wild, desolate Mavrolongos valley. The highest summit, Mýtikas (Pántheon), 9,574 ft., was only scaled in 1913. In antiquity no mere mortal dared to climb the abode of the gods. The rebellious Titans were duly punished for their sacrilegious attempt to reach the Throne of Zeus, the third of the great peaks.

The toll-highway to Thessaloniki shortens the distance from Larissa by 50 miles to 115 miles, besides being scenically more interesting than the old inland route via Kozani. The highway follows the railway to Gortyne, once ruled by Ixion, a kind of Greek Cain.

Vale of Tempe

The six-mile-long vale of Tempe is entered at Baba, whose name and mosque recall the Turkish occupation. This gateway to ancient Greece has been fortified since time immemorial, yet the elaborate fortifications were turned by successive invaders, by Xerxes in 480 B.C., Alexander the Great, and most spectacularly by the Roman general Q. Marcius Philippus in 169 B.C. Hauling his war elephants over the mountains, he outflanked the strong fortress of Gamos, and the last Macedonian king, Perseus, withdrew in panic to final defeat.

Only once was successful resistance offered in this seemingly impregnable defensive position. The Emperor Alexius annihilated the Norman army during the first Crusade, thus postponing for over a 100 years the dismemberment of Greece into feudal principalities. This was left to the shameful Fourth Crusade, when the Franks poured through the abandoned valley.

The varied history is fittingly illustrated by the ruins of fortresses belonging to all ages, culminating in the romantic medieval Castle of the Beauty, Kástro tís Oréas, on top of a precipitous rock. The orderly Romans even left an inscription, now barely legible, recording the fortification of Tempe by Caesar's legate Cassius.

For 3,000 years poets have extolled the beauties of Tempe, which provided the idyllic background to a host of myths centering on Apollo, from the time he was still in his mother's womb. Yet there is many a gorge in Greece, the Vouraïkos and Langada in the Peloponnese, Vikos and Aoos in Epirus, which surpasses Tempe in scenic grandeur. The beauty of the peaceful vale lies mainly in the delightfully refreshing contrast with the burning plain of Thessaly. A profusion of trees on both banks of the icy-cold Pinios provides welcome shade.

Through the trees arching over the river at the Fountain of the Nymphs one catches a glimpse of the sea, bounded by the Halkidiki peninsula. Here the mountain walls of the lower Olympos and Ossa are most formidable, bearing witness to the tremendous convulsion, when the waters of the inland sea forced an outlet, an event that gave rise to the legend of Deucalion's flood.

The narrow valley opens out and the highway turns north, along the coast to Thessaloniki. The road to the right (south-east) leads to the pretty little port of Stomio, where the lovely long beach has become an international camping ground, and for good reasons: it ideally combines the attractions of sea and mountain, by being the natural center for excursions up the thickly wooded slopes of Ossa.

The return to Larissa can be made by following the coast south to Agiókambos and then turning inland via Skíti and Agía; a branch right (northeast) rises to Anatolí, from which the ascent of the 6,490 ft. Ossa is best undertaken. The easy climb is well rewarded by the superb view over the Aegean to the distant shores of Asia Minor.

PRACTICAL INFORMATION FOR CENTRAL
GREECE AND THESSALY

WHEN TO COME. The Olympos and Pílio regions are pleasantly cool even in summer, but the Thessalian plain bakes in the vast oven formed by the surrounding high mountains. June is harvest time, and the stubble fields are here no more attractive than anywhere else. Maximum enjoyment will be obtained in spring, especially at the famed Meteora monasteries, when the mountains are still snowcovered and blend harmoniously with the green fields, the red poppies and the white and pink fruit trees. The winter is cold, with snow and rain; February is the worst month.

HOW TO GET ABOUT. There are several flights weekly from Athens to Larissa. The railway traverses the province from south to north: Lamia, Larissa, Tempe; with a branch from Larissa to Volos, a ferry port and popular stopping point for cruise ships. The tollroad keeps closer to the coast, thus avoiding the mountains of the old interior road via Farsala. After bypassing Lamia and Almyros, the motorway turns at Mikrothives inland to Larissa, hub of the road network. The branch to the right (east) skirts the Pagastic Gulf to Volos, then continues southeast to Tríkeri at the Gulf's entrance, with a branch to Platánia, opposite Skiathos. The circular road of the Pilio (68 miles) leaves the coast 17 miles southeast of Volos, turning north to Tsangarada, returning via Zagorá over the summit at Hania and down through Portaria. There are two lateral connections with the west coast: Lamia-Karpenissi-Agrinio (121 miles) and Larissa-Kalambaka-Ioanina (128 miles), both very mountainous but wellgraded. The quickest approach to Meteora (Kalambaka) from Athens is along the inland road north from Lamia, turning left (northwest) 11 miles after the Domokos Pass on a treeshaded branch to Karditsa and Trikala (38 miles). The quickest way to western Macedonia is from the road junction 3 miles northwest of Kalambaka via Grevena to Kastoria (95 miles). Of the two roads crossing the Olympos range north of Elassóna, the southerly via

Karia has deteriorated into impassability, the northerly via Agios Dimitrios to Katerini is entirely paved.

HOTELS AND RESTAURANTS

AGIOKAMBOS. *Golden Beach* (I), tel. 22 222. 17 rooms.

AGIOS KONSTANTINOS. *Motel Levendi* (E), tel. 31 756. 28 double rooms; beach. *Astir* (I), tel. 31 625. 31 rooms; no restaurant; 50 yds from beach.

ARKITSA. *Kalypso* (M), tel. 91 392. 178 bungalows, most with showers, airconditioned; pool, tennis, minigolf, disco. *Helena* (I), tel. 91 270. 16 rooms; no restaurant.

ATALANTI. *Anessis* (I), tel. 22 147. 15 rooms; no restaurant.

GLÝFA. *Akroyali* (I), tel. 51 312. 19 rooms.

KALAMBAKA. *Motel Divani* (E), tel. 23 330. 165 rooms; airconditioned, pool. *Xenia* (M), tel. 22 327. 22 double rooms; airconditioned. *Atlantis* (I), tel. 22 476. 26 rooms. *Galaxias* (I), tel. 23 333. 24 rooms. *Rex* (I), tel. 22 372. 32 rooms.

KAMMENA VOURLA. Among the large number of hotels along the seashore of this popular spa, only the *Galini* (E), tel. 22 247/8, 131 rooms, airconditioned, pool, tennis, disco, and the *Radion* (M), tel. 22 308/10, most of the 62 rooms with bath, no restaurant, possess their own thermal installations. *Possidon* (M), tel. 22 721/5, 93 rooms; *Sissy*, tel. 22 190/1, 102 rooms; both pool, tennis, minigolf, disco, are the only M's with restaurant, directly on the beach. *Delfini* (I), tel. 22 321. 22 rooms; the only one among some 40 (I)s with showers to all rooms, restaurant, beach across the road.

KARAVOMYLOS. *Stylis Beach* (I), tel. 41 201/5. 154 rooms, airconditioned; pool, tennis, disco; good value.

KARDITSA. *Astron* (I), tel. 23 551. Most of the 47 rooms with showers; no restaurant.

KARPENISSI. *Lecadin* (M), tel. 22 131/5. Above the town, commanding a fine view; 104 rooms. *Anessis* (I), tel. 22 840. 25 rooms.

LAMÍA. *Delta* (I), tel. 21 600. 39 rooms; the only with restaurant. *Elena* (I), tel. 25 025. 51 rooms. *Samaras* (I), tel. 28 971. 64 rooms, airconditioned; all central.

LARISSA. *Divani Palace* (E), tel. 252 791/4. 77 rooms. *Astoria* (M), tel. 252 941. 84 rooms; airconditioned, pool. *Metropole* (M), tel. 229 911/5. 95 rooms, airconditioned; roofgarden, pool. *Motel Xenia* (M), tel. 227 002. 30 double rooms, airconditioned; 2 miles out on motorway. *Ambassadeurs* (I), tel. 254 825. 89 rooms, airconditioned; restaurant. *El Greco* (I), tel. 252 411. 90 rooms, airconditioned; restaurant.

NÉA ANHÍALOS. *Protessilaos* (I), tel. 76 310. 25 rooms; no restaurant.

PÍLIO. Afyssos, 16 miles from Volos. *Alexandros* (I), tel. 33 246. 9 double rooms. *Katia* (I), tel. 33 297. 12 double rooms.

Agios Ioannis, 38 miles. *Aloe* (M), tel. 31 241, 44 rooms. *Maro* (M), tel. 31 477. 47 rooms. *Kentrikon* (I), tel. 31 232. 20 rooms. *Zephyros* (I), tel. 31 335. 12 double rooms; restaurant. All on beach.

Agria. 4 miles. *Barbara* (I), tel. 92 367. 9 rooms; no restaurant.

Horeftó. 29 miles. *Katerina* (I), tel. 22 772. 9 double rooms; no restaurant.

Kala Nera. 8 miles. *Alcyon* (I), tel. 22 364. 11 double rooms. *Izela* (I), tel. 22 379. 31 double rooms. *Roumeli* (I), tel. 22 217. 14 double rooms, most with showers; the only restaurant.

Makrynitsa. 10 miles. *Archontikon Mousli* (M), tel. 99 228. 8 rooms; converted old mansion. *Archontikon Sissilianon* (M), tel. 99 556. 7 double rooms; old converted mansion. *Archontikon Xiradakis* (M), tel. 39 250. 7 double rooms; old converted mansion; no restaurant.
Restaurants. At the two Inexpensive restaurants on the village square, the splendid setting has to compensate for the very inadequate food, but the local red wine is drinkable.

Portaria. 8 miles. *Xenia* (M), tel. 99 158/9. 76 double rooms; openair dining terrace; disco. *Alkistis* (I), tel. 99 290/2. 47 rooms. *Pelias* (I), tel. 99 175. 28 rooms; no restaurant.

Tsangarada. 31 miles. *Xenia* (M), tel. 49 205. 46 rooms. *San Stefano* (I), tel. 49 213. 37 rooms; restaurant; in chestnut forest 4 miles above a lovely beach.

THEOLOGOS. *Economo's Silver Bay* (M), tel. 51 491. 196 rooms in central block and bungalows; airconditioned, pool, tennis, minigolf, disco. On beach. *Nafsika* (I), tel. 51 004. 8 double rooms; restaurant.

THERMOPYLES. *Aegli* (I), tel. 93 304. None of the 45 rooms with showers; restaurant. A hydrotherapy center including Moderate hotels is under construction at these hot sulphur springs, mentioned by Herodotus, for the treatment of rheumatism.

TRIKALA. *Achillion* (M), tel. 28 192. Most of the 73 rooms with baths. *Divani* (M), tel. 27 286. Half of the 66 rooms with baths. *Dina* (I), tel 27 267. 51 rooms. *Rex* (I), tel. 28 375. 58 rooms, some with showers; no restaurant.

VOLOS. *Alexandros* (M), tel. 31 221/4. 78 rooms. *Electra* (M), tel. 32 671/3. 38 rooms. *Park* (M), tel. 36 511/5. 119 rooms. *Xenia* (M), tel. 24 825/7. 48 rooms; the only one on the rather polluted beach. *Admitos* (I), tel. 21 117. 31 rooms. *Galaxy* (I), tel. 20 750. 54 rooms. *Sandi* (I), tel. 33 341. 39 rooms; no restaurant.

Alykes Beach. 4 miles south. *Filoxenia* (I), tel. 38 336. 17 double rooms; no restaurant.

YPATI. *Xenia* (M), tel. 59 509. 81 rooms. *Alfa* (I), tel. 59 507. 27 rooms. *Astron* (I), tel. 59 595. 27 rooms.

CAMPING SITES. The best equipped among some 10 organized camps is the GNTO camping ground at *Kammena Vourla*, tel. 22 053, accommodating 1,500 persons.

MOUNTAIN REFUGES. Two on Pílio; one on Iti, Ossa and Timfristos.

TRADITIONAL SETTLEMENTS. In 3 Pílio villages.

USEFUL ADDRESSES. *GNTO,* Koumoundourou 18, Larissa, tel. 250 919; and Riga Fereou Square, Volos, tel. 23 500.

MACEDONIA AND THRACE

The Drama of Contrast

Macedonia and Thrace, cut off by the vast mountain ranges of the Olympos and Pindos, give the illusion of having more in common with the adjoining Balkans than with peninsular Greece. Only a part of what once was known by the name of these two provinces has been included in the modern Greek nation. The region has always been particularly desirable to its northern neighbors, as it is geographically the culmination of the fertile river valleys of Serbia and Bulgaria, and this has ensured an unsettled history. This is best documented in Thessaloniki, where stratum upon fascinating stratum from every era of the city's turbulent past can easily be traced.

The vegetation differs from the rest of the country, and the climate, too, is continental, with bitterly cold winters spiced by the local demon, *vardari,* the icy north wind. The Axios (Vardar) river, flowing into the Thermaïkós Gulf west of Thessaloniki, divides Macedonia into two distinct regions—the western forest-clad mountains and the fertile eastern plains stretching inland from the sea, near which trees and buildings are mirrored in glassy lagoons. In both regions are large lakes and rivers that actually flow all the year round. Thrace, separated by the Nestos river and the Rodópi mountains, is an extension of the eastern plains, with vast fields of maize, cotton and, above all, tobacco. The excellent beaches of the mountainous three-pronged peninsula of Halkidikí are attracting a rapidly increasing number of tourists.

The landscape of this northern region is varied and beautiful enough to warrant a prolonged visit, all the more as there is also a wealth of Hellenistic and Byzantine remains.

Historic Background

Though invasions from the north started in the fourth millennium B.C., it was only in the Mycenaean period that contacts were established with the rest of Greece, where the Macedonians and Thracians, to their chagrin, continued to be considered foreigners and barbarians, even after the glorious exploits of the Great Alexander.

In the 8th century B.C. Greek colonization began on a large scale, resulting in constant strife with the Macedonian kings, whose endeavor at unification finally succeeded in the 5th century with the foundation of a popular infantry based on free yeomanry as a check on the cavalry of the feudal nobles. During the Persian wars the north bore the brunt of the Asiatic invasions. The revenge came in the 4th century B.C., after Greece had been subjected first by Philip II of Macedon, then by his son Alexander the Great, who brilliantly carried out his father's plans and conquered the Persian empire with his invincible Macedonian phalanx.

After Alexander's death in 323 B.C. there followed 50 hectic years of undignified scramble for the succession, ephemeral empires and kingdoms fighting over the Macedonian homeland till Antigonos Gonatas firmly established his dynasty in 276 B.C. Antigonid Macedonia served as a useful shield against the outer barbarians, but after the final defeat in 168 B.C. of Perseus, the last king, Macedonia became a Roman and later a Byzantine province. Centuries of vicissitudes followed, invasions by Slavs, Arabs and Turks, who remained in possession until the Balkan War of 1912.

Liberation proved only a temporary solution, as Greeks, Serbs and Romanians now quarreled with their former ally Bulgaria over the spoils. The resulting second Balkan War was no more successful in appeasing conflicting aspirations than the First World War. The same regions were fought over in the Second World War and the Bulgarian occupation distinguished itself by exceptional cruelty, retarding all progress. But the efforts of recent years in such diverse fields as land reclamation, irrigation, hydro-electric plants and the industrial zone as well as the International Trade Fair have transformed the region.

Exploring Macedonia

The Larissa-Thessaloniki toll road (94 miles) runs parallel to the railway on entering Macedonia across the Piniós bridge at the northeastern end of the vale of Témpe. It is a lovely drive along the shore of the Thermïkos Gulf to Platamónas (8 miles) sprawling down the foothills of Olympos to the sea, below the romantic ruins of a 14th-century castle.

The first branch road left (west) is practicable only to the mountain village of Kariá in the lower Olympos. The second begins with 3 paved miles to Litóhoro, whence a forest road continues for 11 miles to the parking place at Prioniá in the National Park. An easy ascent leads in 2½ hours to the Alpine Refuge A and about the same time is required to reach the highest peak, Mytikas (9,574 ft.). The third branch, a wide avenue of 3 miles leads to Dio, the sanctuary of Zeus embellished by King Archelaos at the end of the 5th century B.C. with a temple, theater and stadium, and surrounded by a wall with defensive towers. The Romans added a temple of Artemis-Isis, two large baths and, in A.D. 375, a Christian basilica with well-preserved mosaics. The museum holds the usual antique miscellanea, and the theater shares with the castle of Platamónas the performances of the Olympos Festival in July–August, but Dio's attraction lies in the splendid site at the foot of the Olympos range, convincingly chosen as the abode of the gods. The fourth branch from Kateríni, bypassed at no great loss, crosses the Olympos chain fairly comfortably to Elassona.

The toll road follows the coast north, above a string of small beach resorts; Skotiná, Leptokariá, the beaches at Litóhoro and Katerini, Korinós, Makrygialós and Methóni. At Pydna the Macedonian kingdom finally succumbed to the Roman Consul Aemilius Paulus in 168 B.C.; tombs from that period have lately been discovered nearby. The toll road then avoids the marshy shore of the fertile coastal plain, crossing successively the Aliákmon, Loudias, Axios and Galikos before entering Thessaloniki. Between the last two rivers a motorway branches north to Evzoni (29 miles) on the Yugoslav border.

Turning left (west) at the Methoni junction to Veria, you may link up with the inland road from Larissa and start on a round trip of western Macedonia without ever retracing your steps. Shortly before the Aliákmon, the longest river course in Greece, rise the impressive ruins of the 3rd-century B.C. palace of King Antigonus Gonatas (he of the Big Knee).

The plain stretching to the village of Vergína is freckled with tumuli of the Early Iron Age (1000–700 B.C.). The largest tumulus, 325 feet in circumference and 37 feet high, has yielded to a team of villagers, directed by Professor Andronikos from Thessaloniki University, a large number of 4th-century B.C. grave monuments, most thoroughly looted, but the first complete ancient Greek painting ever found, the Rape of Persephone by Hades was perfectly preserved in a marble tomb. Even deeper, 17 feet below ground level, a much larger tomb, in the form of a Doric temple with two chambers, was excavated and has been hailed as one of the outstanding finds of this century, as all antique European tombs of this caliber had been previously plundered. The painted frieze is a brilliant composition of a lion hunt. A marble sarcophagus enclosed a casket of solid gold weighing 24.2 pounds, whose lid, bearing the exploding star, symbol of Macedonian kings, opened on bones and teeth topped by a delicate diadem of oak leaves and acorns. Silver vessels and goblets, armor and helmet, a unique gold, bronze and ivory shield, another diadem and scepter, but above all five marble heads, which Professor Andronikos claimed to be those of Philip II and his family, supported the belief that this was the tomb of the great Macedonian king and the bones in a smaller gold casket those of his seventh wife, Cleopatra (Macedonian royalty being given to polygamy). This shifts Macedonia's antique capital, Aigai, from Edessa to Vergina, a claim strengthened by the continuing discovery of ever more royal grave monuments, dated by vases to 375–350 B.C., perhaps including those of Philip's two brothers.

Final proof came in 1982, when Professor Andronikos unearthed the remains of a theater near the even scantier vestiges of a palace. Philip was murdered in the theater of Agai. In 336 B.C. the wedding of Cleopatra, daughter of Philip II and Olympias, with the latter's brother Alexander, King of Epirus, was celebrated with great magnificence to impress Greece with Philip's might before he started on his Persian campaign.

The Delphic oracle had been all that could be expected: "Crowned to the altar comes the Bull, the Sacrificer stands," an obvious reference to the Persian king being poleaxed by Philip. Or had the Delphic intelligence service some inkling of the assassination that was to follow? Had Persian gold bribed the oracle as well as hired the murderer, or was Olympias revenging herself for Philip's neglect? Philip was walking in solemn procession behind the images of the Twelve Gods (as though thirteenth the crowd whispered) when Pausanias, a former guardsman, dashed forward and stabbed him. Pausanias had almost reached the gate where two horses were picketed, when he stumbled, fell and was transfixed by a spear, before he could be tortured into confessing. Philip's son Alexander was immediately acclaimed as king by the army, thus ending one of the great murder mysteries of history with a resounding triumph for Delphic prophecies.

At Véria, 13 miles beyond the Aliákmon, Saint Paul was well received by the Jewish community, after his hasty exit from Thessaloniki, and was allowed to preach where a ruined mosque now stands. Houses have been built into the ramparts in an intriguing way, often using the old blocks. Several small Byzantine churches tucked away in courtyards were so built to escape the notice of the Turks: Agios Nikolaos, with a fresco of the Sleeping Virgin; Agios Christos, with many 14th-century frescos; Agia Photini, with a carved wooden door, capitals and more frescos; Agios Georgios, again for woodwork and frescos; and Prophet Elias, which has a bishop's throne and a beautiful icon.

If pressed for time you might make the abridged circuit, north to Naoussa (13 miles), Edessa (25 miles further on), returning via Pella to Thessaloniki. If you have time visit Naoussa, a prosperous little town on the slopes of Mount Vérmio. From the public gardens you enjoy a splendid view over the vast orchards below.

For lovely mountain scenery, drive up Mount Vérmio to Kato Vérmio (13 miles, 4,600 ft.) or Seli, the two main skiing resorts. Back in the plain, three miles along the Edessa road, it is possible to indulge further in any newly-acquired passion for Macedonian tombs. Near the village of Lefkádia, in the orchards to the right (east), the 3rd-century B.C. tomb of a Macedonian general was accidentally unearthed by peasants in 1954. The hideous modern concrete structure is unfortunately necessary to preserve the paintings—the general himself, Hermes Conductor of Souls, two of the judges in Hades—on the half Doric, half Ionic façade of the small temple. Nearby a larger tomb fronted by three Ionic columns was discovered 20 years later. Across the road, not signposted and closed to the public, is the tomb of the Lyson and Kallikles families.

The 38 miles from Veria to Kozani, on the wider circuit, wind along the southern flank of Mount Vérmio, below the new monastery of Panagia Soumela, where the miraculous icon of the Virgin found refuge after the destruction of the great mother-house in Asia Minor in 1923. Between Kastaniá and the pass of Hantóva you have a wonderful view over valleys and mountains.

Kozani has no intrinsic merit, but is the hub of western Macedonia: it lies roughly halfway between Larissa, reached over Greece's longest bridge, almost a mile, across the artificial lake

Poliphiton created by damming up the Aliákmon for the country's largest hydroelectric plant, and Thessaloniki on the inland road (173 miles); the road north leads to the big thermo-electric plant of Ptolemaída and then forks at Vevi left (west) to Florina (50 miles) and right to Edessa (68 miles); the branch to the right, 14 miles west of Kozani, leads to Siatista, with some well-preserved 18th-century houses, two of which can be visited, the painted church of Agia Pareskevi (1611), modern Agios Dimitrios and a Paleontological Museum full of skeletons. After a further two miles the road forks left (south) across the Aliákmon to Grevena and over a lonely highland affording fine views of the Pindos range to the Mourgani junction (72 miles from Kozani) near Kalambaka on the Ioanina-Trikala road; right (northwest) following the upper course of the Aliákmon for 41 miles to Kastoria.

Kastoria, the Town in the Lake

Kastoria's particular charm is largely due to its site on a promontory joined to the mainland by a narrow isthmus. It thus has two fronts on the lake, which is appropriately called Orestias, after the town's reputed founder, Orestes, son of Agamemnon. The Byzantine governors of this imperial frontier outpost left monuments to their piety in the multiplicity of miniature churches. Not all 72 are, however, medieval, as several were built as private chapels to the 17th- and 18th-century houses of the rich merchants. These patrician abodes, called *archontica*, their upper painted stories projecting over the windowless lower floors, are sadly decayed, except one on Kapetan Lazarou St. converted into a folkloric museum.

The tiny churches are: the 11th-century Panagia Koubelidiki, named after its singular cylindrical dome, in the court of the high school; a little further down Mitropoleos street is the 12th-century Agios Nikolaos, a tiny single-naved basilica with impressionist frescos; the 14th-century Taxiarches (Archangels) has interesting frescos, as also Agios Athanasios (1385), still nearer the large modern Metropolis; the 11th-century Agios Stephanos, a triple-naved basilica, is in the eastern quarter, not far from Agii, and is probably the oldest. But these architectural gems are lost among large apartment blocks which have spread beyond the promontory, for Kastoria's 400-year-old industry has once again brought prosperity to the town—the skilful piecing together of scraps of fur left over from cutting. It is a surprise to see fur on the roll, like any woven textile. The rather heavy finished product is sold cheaper than orthodox fur coats.

A one-way anti-clock-wise road, shaded by large plane trees, circles the promontory. Halfway, at the extreme point (one mile), stands the monastery of the Panagia Mavriotissa with two old churches. That of Agios Ioanis has well-preserved frescos; particularly interesting is the *Stilling of the Waters*, featuring the typical Kastorian fishing boats, flat-bottomed and blunt at both ends. To immerse yourself in local color you might punt to that lovely spot, which is an ideal camping site. Bathing, however, is prohibited in the badly polluted water.

Kastoria lies at 2,500 ft., but for the return journey you have to climb higher still, up Mount Vérno. Over the southern flank to the junction with the Kozani-Edessa road (38 miles) past the village of Klissóura (3,900 ft.), whose church of Agios Dimitrios possesses an admirably carved 15th-century *iconostasis*; over the northern flank, even higher, on a worse but scenically more rewarding road across the Pisoderi pass, allowing for a short side-trip to the bird sanctuary in the solitude of the Little and Big Prespa Lakes, the latter bordered by Greece, Yugoslavia and Albania, to Florina (44 miles) near the Yugoslav frontier post of Niki (12 miles).

Three Ancient Capitals

Close to Florina, archaic statues were unearthed in 1978 in what is believed to have been the first Macedonian capital, before the kings moved to Aigai, in about 800 B.C. Though it revived in the Middle Ages, nothing of interest remains.

The 42 miles to Edessa climb after the Vevi junction to an altitude of 3,150 ft. Mount Kaïmaktsalan (8,260 ft.), another favorite in innumerable Balkan skirmishes, on the left (north) forms the border with Yugoslavia; on the right is Lake Vergorítida, with the pretty village of Arnissa on a promontory. At Ágras is a hydroelectric station powered by the 82-foot falls of the Voda river with important fish hatcheries down stream.

Edessa, till recently identified with antique Aigai, lies on a northwestern ledge of Mount Vérmio. It is a pleasant town crossed by several rivulets uniting into spectacular waterfalls hiding a small stalactite cave. The view over the sea of fruit trees in the valley below even surpasses that at Naoussa, in spite of the hydroelectric installations.

After descending into the orchards you reach the branch road to Naoussa and Veria at the village of Skydra (nine miles). Continuing straight on (east) an ancient reservoir on the left, the so-called "Bath of Alexander" heralds the extensive ruins of Pella.

Towards the end of the 5th century B.C., King Archelaos transferred the capital from Aigai to Pella, to which he attracted the greatest artists of his time, as for instance Euripides. In the year of the 106th Olympic Games, subsequently computed by Christian historians as 356 B.C., Queen Olympias gave birth in the royal palace to Alexander, deservedly called the Great. Pella, protected by vast swamps and the island fortress of Phakos, remained the seat of the Macedonian kings till Perseus' defeat in 168 B.C.

Intermittent excavations since 1958 have thus far brought to light several public buildings, whose peristyles surround open courtyards. Excellently preserved pebble mosaics depict the story of Helen of Troy, Dionysus riding a prancing panther, Alexander being saved by Krateros at a lion hunt, each surrounded by a border design. Remarkable are the huge roof tiles, some of marble, others of clay, bearing the names of people or of the city. The huge agora, surrounded by late 3rd-century B.C. stoas, was uncovered in 1982, but not yet the palace, for whose decoration Archelaos commissioned the painter Zeuxis, to be severely criticized by his nobles for this un-Macedonian extravagance. Tools in bone, iron and bronze have been found, besides clay vessels and figurines, also many coins ranging from the reign of Philip to Roman times. The museum's chief glories are a superb vase decorated with the battle of the Amazons, and a bronze statuette of Poseidon.

Just beyond Géfyra (bridge) on the Axios river is the junction with the motorway north to Evzoni (29 miles) on the Yugoslav border; continuing east, across yet another river, the Galikós, you reach Thessaloniki (55 miles from Edessa).

The Halkidiki, Macedonia's Playground

All the beaches southeast of Thessaloniki have been appropriated by huge hotel and bungalow complexes. The mountainous, thickly-wooded Halkidikí Peninsula is bounded north by the two elongated lakes of Koronia and Volvi, west by the Thermaïkós Gulf, east by the Strymonikós, while in the south three prongs jut far into the Aegean. It offers infinite scenic (and on Mount Athos, architectural) variety, easily accessible by an adequate road network. To avoid having to retrace your steps for any great distance, start with the westernmost prong, the Kassandra, named after the Great Alexander's general and not after Priam's sinister daughter. That prophetess of doom would indeed have been quite out of place in the idyllic setting.

At Mikra, just after Thessaloniki's international airport, the road branches right (west) to the beaches of Perea and Agía Triáda, southwest to the coast beyond Epanoní, and due south (left) to rejoin the sea at Néa Kalikratía before turning inland. Finds dating back 500,000 years justify the five mile sidetrip north to the cave of Petrálona, before continuing southeast to Nea Moudania (38 miles). Beyond the canal cut across the narrow isthmus, but on the Gulf of Kassandras, are the insignificant ruins of Potidea, whose revolt against Athens was one of the causes of the Peloponnesian War. Destroyed by Philip II, refounded by Kassander as Kassandría, it was finally razed by the Huns. As the promontory widens, the enchanting view over both coasts is limited to the eastern, studded with fishing villages. The coastal road passes through Néa Fokéa, Kalithéa and Kryopigí to Palioúri. After a last glance at the seemingly land-locked Gulf of Kassandra and the Sithonia prong topped by the unmistakable triangular summit of Mount Athos, the road climbs into the hills and pine woods, with a branch extending to the headland. Again you view both gulfs before reaching the west coast at Ágia Paraskeví. Along the sea to Kalandra, where you turn inland to complete the circuit two miles after Kassandría, the dull main village.

After this appetizer proceed to the even lovelier middle prong, Sithonia. Recrossing the isthmus turn right (northeast) to Ólynthos (four miles), in 392 B.C. the capital of an important confederation. All that is left is a huge mound crowned by scattered foundations and broken sections of the ramparts. At the Gerakiní road fork (five miles) continue right (south) along a series of fine beaches below thickly wooded hills.

The next 36 miles skirt the tranquil pine forests past Metamórfossi and Néos Marmarás to Pórto Carrás where almond and olive trees as well as vineyards producing Greece's best wine, surround a luxurious tourist complex; two miles of murals, open-air and indoor theaters, exhibition hall and handicraft center emphasize the cultural slant of this high-income-bracket resort. After the yacht harbor of Koufos near the tip of the promontory the round trip along the east coast via Sarti and Ormos Panagias is completed.

From Gerakini it is nine miles to Polýgyros (1,755 ft.), the attractive capital of the Halkidiki. The next seven miles climb through densely-wooded mountains to the pass (2,996 ft.), whence there is another one of those fine views over the Kassandra Gulf and promontory. The inland road is joined at the 36th mile from Thessaloniki, but the Halkidiki has still much to offer, so turn right (east) to Arnéa and the forest beyond.

Among the unremarkable ruins of Stágira stands the remarkably ugly statue of its greatest son, the philosopher Aristotle, tutor of Alexander the Great. Ierissos (72 miles from Thessaloniki) has an excellent beach, a mediocre medieval castle and some ancient walls; Nea Roda has only the first. Crossing from the east to west coast along Xerxes' canal, long since filled in, the road hugs the shore to Ouranóupoli (eight miles). This is the last village on the Athos promontory at which women and children are allowed, and that only since 1923, when refugees from Asia Minor were settled on the confines of the monks' republic. The fortified tower at the end of the splendid beach was built by the Emperor Andronicus II, and served later as a look-out against the pirates, who infested the four surrounding islands. Ouranóupoli is an ideal spot to leave your womenfolk while visiting the Holy Mountain, and to recover from the rigors of that journey.

A quick and scenic alternative for the return journey is provided by continuing north from Stratóni through pinewoods to Olympiáda, then for 21 miles along the shore to Stavros, a deservedly popular summer resort, whence it is two miles to the Kavala highway.

This is the usual tourist route from Thessaloniki east to Komotini in Thrace, mainly along the sea, but there is an inland alternative via Seres and Drama, among fertile plains and mountains with a lesser road in between. Along this rather dull middle road is Langadás (13 miles northeast of Thessaloniki) where on the feast of St. Constantine and his British-born mother St. Helena—May 21—the firewalkers (anastenárides) brandish the saints' ikons above their heads and dance barefoot on glowing charcoal embers, and are none the worse for it. A similar event, reminiscent of ancient Dionysiac rituals including the sacrifice of a calf in whose ears lighted candles have previously been stuck, attracts large crowds to the village of Agia Eleni near Seres.

Just before the Strymónas bridge, it is possible to join the shortest west-east road from Thessaloniki along lake Koronia and then lake Volvi, beside which is the spa of Apolonia. A picturesque fortress heralds the Rendína gorge, at whose other end is the branch to Stavros.

The next 15 miles follow the sea to the bridge over the Strymónas, flowing down from Bulgaria. The huge stone lion was found in the river bed, probably washed down from the ruins of Amfípoli, less than a mile from the crossroad. Ancient Amphipolis was founded by Pericles on a spur of Mount Pangéo on the river's left bank; it was the object of constant dissent among the Thracians, Athenians, Persians and Macedonians before the advent of the Romans, owing to the rich mineral deposits in the area. Imposing ramparts strengthened by round towers, one of antiquity's most formidable fortifications, surrounded the acropolis where—between the remains of early-Christian basilicas—new finds are constantly coming to light. The more important, especially jewelry, are sent to the Kavala museum, the remains are exposed in the village museum over the hill. The 1,200 tree trunks buried in the sands of the river supported a wooden bridge, used for a thousand years after its construction in about 425 B.C., as witnessed by the remains of Byzantine towers. There is a wide view from the acropolis over the coastline across to Mount Athos and the Halkidiki.

Continuing straight on (north) from Amfípoli you reach either

Dráma or Séres if you are in hurry to return, while the first branch to the right (northeast) climbs to Rodólivos, starting point for climbing or skiing on Mount Pángeo. The monastery of Ikossifiníssis, supposedly founded in 518, possesses rare old manuscripts, though the frescos in the church of the Zoodóhos Pigí are modern.

Thou Shalt See Me At Philippi

So says Caesar's ghost in Shakespeare's tragedy, and as this is eastern Macedonia's outstanding archeological site, to Filípi (Philippi) it shall be.

Eleftheróupoli can be reached from Rodólivos along the road circling Mount Pangeo. The usual approach, however, is by the highway east from the Amfípoli junction through the southern foothills of the mountain. Three miles before Kavala you meet the road from Drama; if it happens to be summer afternoon this is the time to visit Philippi, six miles along that road, as the heat haze will have lifted and the plain looks its best, when you drive along the tree-lined avenue.

Anxious to protect his newly acquired gold mines on Mount Pangeo, Philip II settled numerous Macedonians in 358 B.C. in the Thasian colony of Krinídes to which he graciously gave his name. Here it was that Brutus had his fatal rendezvous with Caesar's ghost, when he and Cassius were defeated by Mark Anthony and Octavian in 42 B.C., the second of the three momentous encounters that decided the fate of Rome on Greek soil. Brutus and Cassius committed suicide, but the victors enriched and embellished Philippi, which continued to prosper in the following centuries, thanks to its privileged position on the Via Egnatia, the empire's main artery. Standing at the edge of the plain, under the Thimodes Mountains, the town was a natural stopping place for cross-empire travelers. Here Saint Paul preached his first sermon in Europe, extempore, to the women washing their clothes in the river, and baptised Lydia, the cloth merchant. After spending some time in prison, Saint Paul departed for Thessaloniki by way of Amphipolis and Apollonia, only to make a hasty retreat to Veria, and yet another to Athens. In spite of this erratic course he made a great impression and laid the seeds of Christianity in Macedonia.

The extensive remains of the town lie mostly below the road on the left, entered through the restored propylaeum. The large *agora* contains the ruins of many Roman buildings; beyond stand the remains of a huge 5th-century basilica, two imposing pillars supporting an arch, which catch the eye from afar. Their large blocks and sculptures had been used in some previous edifice, while in the 6th century another basilica with a dome was superimposed on the earlier one. Further on were the Roman baths. Among the various scattered ruins on the rocky ledges on the right, above the road, is the so-called prison where Saint Paul and Saint Silas were thrown, with their feet "made fast in the stocks." The small cave hardly seems adequate for housing several prisoners.

In the rocks are niches of ancient shrines, with inscriptions and carved reliefs of deities. The climb up to the acropolis (which affords an excellent view) leads past the Egyptian shrine; the crumbling ramparts above are partly Macedonian and partly Byzantine, but the three towers, which stand out so well from a distance, are later additions. The grey stone theater backing on to the rocks dates from the time of Philip II, but it was actually converted into a gladiatoral arena (like the one on Thasos), supplementary tiers supported by arches as well as an underground entry for the wild beasts were then added. Returned to its original use, ancient tragedies are now again performed in summer.

Excavations have recently brought to light the foundations of the oldest known octagonal church, built by Constantine the Great and rebuilt by Justinian, the Propylaea on the Via Egnatia, a large bath establishment and mosaics.

By Rivers and Lagoons

Returning from Philippi, stop at the height above Kavala to enjoy the great panorama of the town and of Thasos, the island which once held it in thrall; on a clear morning you might even be able to see the distant Dardanelles. Kavala, forming an amphitheater on the lower slopes of Mount Symvolon, is, with over 50,000 inhabitants, the fifth largest town of Greece, a big fish market and the center and port of the tobacco trade. The middle of the town is given over to warehouses. The coastal road via Loutrá Elefthéron, Néa Péramos, Néa Iraklitsa and Kalamitsa leading straight into the busy waterfront, is scenically lovelier.

Known as Neapolis by the Romans, Christopolis by the Franks, Kavala's present name—meaning on horseback—indicates its importance as a relay station for changing horses. It was here that Brutus stationed his fleet during the battle at Philippi; and here too, that Saint Paul landed, having sailed from Samothrace. The Roman aqueduct curving across the center of the town is still its distinguishing feature, while the decaying Byzantine fortifications are less interesting than the climb through the somewhat Oriental eastern quarter of old Turkish houses and Mohammed Ali's badly neglected religious foundations. Mohammed Ali was the son of a rich tobacco merchant, and after a chequered career almost as colorful as that of his contemporary, Ali Pasha of Ioanina, became the founder of the Egyptian royal dynasty, whose last reigning member was the late King Farouk. The house where Mohammed Ali was born in 1769 stands on a promontory, behind his equestrian statue. Now a museum, it gives a good idea of Moslem family arrangements, with carved cupboards for storing the rugs and cushions, which would be brought out for sleeping, and wooden latticed screens, whence the women could look out of the harem quarter without being seen. The doors to the women's apartments are strongly bolted, and there is even a lift by which the food was sent to the exclusively male gatherings. On the opposite side of the waterfront crescent is the archeological museum with most of the Amphipolis and Avdira finds.

It is 111 miles from Kavala to Alexandróupoli. After 16 miles is the branch right (south) to Hrissóupoli airport and the port of Keramoti (13 miles), the ferry terminal for Thasos (four nautical miles). The highway follows for a short distance the romantic Nestos valley and then crosses the river into Thrace. This is still tobacco country, but the villages become markedly Oriental, as Thrace is the one province where the Moslem population was not exchanged after World War I. In the villages the older women still wear full Turkish trousers, and slim minarets of mosques dominate the skyline, especially at Xanthi. This small town clings to the hilly sides of the Eskeje Remma valley, and is the market for the Pomaks, descendants of Bulgarians who embraced Islam about 500 years ago. It is pleasant to sit on an evening in one of the numerous cafés or restaurants on the large central square. Visits to the convent of the Panagia and the monastery of the Taxiarches, now a school, are justified by the magnificent view they command from their vantage points.

The coastal road to Komotini (35 miles) bypasses Xanthi by turning again towards the sea. The first branch to the right (southwest) leads to Avdira (10 miles), near the walls and tombs of ancient Abdera where Democritus propounded the Atom Theory in the 5th century B.C. Lágos lies on a narrow strip of sand between the sea and Lake Vistonis. It is an attractive landscape in its own melancholy way, rich in all sorts of water birds and extensive fisheries. The road runs on a dyke, along which bridges, trees and the church of Agios Nikolaos are perfectly mirrored in the still water of the lagoon. One of the best beaches of the north is only five miles to the right at Fanári. The incongruous signpost "Byzantine Temple" points to nothing more sensational than a small medieval church. Prehistoric tombs and the pavement of the Roman Via Egnatia are likewise indicated.

Komotini resembles Xanthi, but in a less attractive setting.

Continuing southeast, the last branch west (right) shortly before reaching the sea leads to the excavations of Messimvría (Mesembria), a Hellenistic town dependent on the Kingdom of Samothrace. Ramparts climb two miles from the sea up to the acropolis and back to the sea, enclosing a sanctuary of Demeter; rich finds are coming to light in the vast cemetery. Back on the mainroad, the Cyclopean sea cave of Mákri claims a rather doubtful place in the *Odyssey*. The road follows the coast via Néa Hilí to Alexandroupoli (40 miles), which makes up for its surprising lack of historical remnants—considering it was founded by Alexander the Great and the first of some 20 towns to bear his name—by finds from the neighborhood in the Archeological Museum.

Close to the Turkish border, the road turns again inland, along the west bank of the Evros river, which divides Greece from Turkey, but has its source near the Bulgarian capital, Sofia. The wide fertile river valley is apt to be flooded in winter and springtime, especially the delta opposite the island of Samothrace. Important flood-prevention works are under execution on both banks, while the long bridge between Kipi (27 miles) and Ypsala is the main border crossing to Istanbul.

Further up the valley is Soufli, renowned for its silks. In the Byzantine castle above Didymótiho the Emperor Ioannis Paleologus was born in 1349, and later the Sultan Bayazit. At Pýthio the railway, which has previously run roughly parallel to the road, divides; the direct line to Istanbul crosses the Evros, while the line to Adrianople continues on the right bank to Orestiáda. The road bridge and frontier station is still further north, at Kastaniés (85 miles from Alexandróupoli) within sight of Adrianople (Edirne).

As there is no alternative route back as far as Komotini, few travelers, except those proceeding to Turkey, venture up the Evros valley, in spite of its undoubted picturesqueness. From Komotini, however, it is possible to take the shorter inland road to Xanthi (31 miles), through the plain divided by a wall that extends at Amaxades from the foothills to Lake Vistonis, and has from time immemorial failed to keep out invaders from the east.

It is possible to drive north up the Eskeje Remma valley where the Pomak shepherds graze their flocks, but there is no crossing over the formidable Rodópi mountains into Bulgaria. The road west via Stavróupoli to Drama to scenic, especially along the Nestos valley to Paranésti.

The Golden Plain

This was the name given by the Turks to the plain of Drama, not only for its great fertility, but also for the diffused golden light in the late summer afternoons. For the sake of that light Philippi was included in the outgoing journey, as that is the time the motorist from Thessaloniki is likely to arrive, after a swim at Satvros and with the prospect of comfortable accommodation close at hand in Kavala.

Nobody will begrudge retracing the nine miles to Philippi, which, like the remaining 12½ miles to Drama, are shaded by huge poplars. Trees—poplar, elm, lime and plane—line many of the Macedonian roads, and often form a roof, to the driver's delight. Drama was the scene of an Athenian defeat by the Macedonians in the 5th century B.C.; nothing remains of that period and neither some insignificant Roman ruins nor the Byzantine chapel near the walls warrant more than a cursory glance; you might, however, take a meal on the island at the Agia Varvara springs within the town.

Séres deserves much closer attention. About half way along the unexciting 44 miles from Drama is the junction with the road from Amfipoli (18 miles). Séres has seen much fighting since its foundation in pre-Hellenistic times. Xerxes stabled the sacred mares of the Sun Chariot in the rich plain, watered by the Strimon; while after bearing the brunt of repeated attacks by the Bulgars on their way to Thessaloniki, Séres was temporarily relieved when the Emperor Basil II, the Bulgar-slayer, defeated Tsar Samuel in the Strimon gorge. Ten thousand of the latter's troops were blinded by the emperor's orders, leaving only every hundredth man with one eye to lead his comrades home. The Turks stayed from 1368 to 1913, but liberty did not come gently to this old stronghold, for in the same year it was burnt down by the "liberating" Bulgars. During the last war it was to suffer yet again under Bulgarian occupation.

Little is left of the old Christian and Turkish quarters, which have been replaced by a busy, prosperous modern town. Ancient Agios Theodoros, near the new Metropolis, has been restored as a museum, containing some Roman sculptures. The triple-naved basilica possesses several unusual features, such as the raised *Synthronum* behind the aspe. In the large mosaic of the Last Supper, Our Lord is shown twice, offering the bread and wine to those on the left and right respectively. The small sunken side-chapel was used as a secret school under the Turks.

Brightly colored hand-woven rugs are on display in the mosque on the central square, but the two other mosques are left to decay as symbols of the hated Turkish domination. Yet, the mosque on the river, standing forlorn among the weeping willows, is one of the finest and most romantic buildings in Macedonia.

An easy climb from the town, or a short drive on the further side, along the nameless tributary of the Strymonas, past a swimming pool, cafés and taverns, brings you to the acropolis, crowned by the ruins of the 13th-century castle. Within the walls is the

Byzantine church of Agios Nikolaos, which also has a crypt that was used secretly, entered between two rocks. From the height you have a wonderful view in all directions; the outlines of the town are softened and beyond the valley, in which the most varied architectural styles of churches can be discerned, are range after range of mountains. It is through that tempting landscape that you might either proceed to Bulgaria (frontier station 28½ miles) via Sidirókastro, a picturesque township below a medieval castle; or visit the spa of Nigrita (14½ miles)—whose bottled water is drunk for digestive disorders—crossing the Strymonas, on a tree-lined avenue; or return to Thessaloniki (59 miles) across the plain and over a mountain rising to 2,130 ft., whence you enjoy some spectacular views over Lakes Koronia and Volvi and the country beyond as far as the sea. Seven and a half miles before Thessaloniki is the junction with the road on which you set out for Kavala.

PRACTICAL INFORMATION FOR MACEDONIA AND THRACE

WHEN TO COME. Late spring or early summer is the best time for traveling about, since snow and ice frequently block the roads in winter. The summer is hot and dusty in the eastern plains, though not in the western mountains, and obviously best for the lovely beaches in the Halkidiki, at Porto Lagos, Fanari and near Alexandroupoli.

Carnival is ebulliently celebrated in Naoussa, the Dionysian tradition being particularly strong in the Halkidiki villages and at Kozani during the traditional three weeks before Orthodox Lent, rising to its gayest for the last two days. Kastoria's Carnival is held at the unusual season of Epiphany, while Litóhoro extends the festivities for a week.

In midwinter, a Hunting Week is organized in the Evros delta and the Hellenic Alpine Club holds six races on Mount Vermio.

Among the most popular Saints' days is that of Saints Constantine and Heleni, on May 21. Crowds visit Langadas and Agia Eleni (Séres), to watch the *Anastenarides*, or Firewalkers. So great a draw is this ancient custom whose origins are pagan, that it is very difficult to get near enough to view the spectacle. On May 14, Komotini presents Thracian folkloric customs.

Your visual senses are catered for by a flower festival in early June at Edessa; your palate by a strawberry festival at Florina in July, and a wine festival extending into August at Alexandróupoli; your intellect by the performance of ancient drama at Philippi and the Olympús festival in the castle of Platamónas and the ancient theater of Dio from July to August; and your spiritual needs suitably high up in the Kastania Pass between Kozani and Veria, where the miraculous icon of the monastery of the

Panagia (Our Lady) *Soumelas* attracts large crowds of pilgrims for the Feast of the Assumption on August 15. There is an international windsurfing competition in the Halkidiki at the end of September.

HOW TO GET ABOUT. Thessaloniki, lying roughly halfway on the reconstituted *Via Egnatia* between the port of Igoumenitsa in Epirus and the Turkish border, is the obvious center of excursions, if not in actual mileage at least in time, as progress in the western mountains is necessarily so much slower than in the eastern plains. The journey north from Athens takes about eight hours by train, ten by bus. Thessaloniki can be reached by plane directly from several European capitals, from Athens by eight flights daily (50 min), from Alexandróupoli and Ioanina three times weekly.

Three flights daily between Athens and Alexandróupoli (55 min), two daily to Kavala's international airport at Hrissoupoli (1 h 25 min), three flights weekly to Kastoria (2 h 5 min) and Kozani (1 h 30 min).

If you are entering Greece from the north, the international trains cross the Yugoslav border at Evzoni and go on to Thessaloniki. This route is also followed by the road from Belgrade and Skopje, while the road from Bitola crosses the border near Niki. From Turkey, the railway crosses the border at Pýthio, while the two main frontier posts on the road are Kipi at the Evros bridge and north at Kastanies, opposite Adrianople (Edirne).

Daily buses connect not only all towns, but also the outlying villages. The beaches on the Halkidiki peninsula are well served from Thessaloniki, whence there are also trains to Florina and to Alexandróupoli and intermediary stations. It is advisable, when traveling by provincial buses in this region, to buy the ticket the evening before. If not, go half an hour before departure time. On the long distance trains it is essential to get your ticket beforehand (this also bears your seat number). Kavala can also be reached by sea in a 12-hour trip from Thessaloniki, and Dafni, the port of Athos, in about eight hours. The frequency of these journeys is dependent upon the weather and the season.

HOTELS. The best accommodations are offered by the beach hotels and bungalows of the resort in the Halkidiki; most insist on halfboard, and it is safest to keep to the hotel restaurants.

Specialties here include *lagos* (hare) in walnut sauce or stewed in wine; quail, woodcock and wild duck in season; *salata piperies*, a salad of fried red peppers mostly found in Florina; the excellent and inexpensive *brik*, red caviar, which comes from the river Evros; *manouri* in western Macedonia and *telemes* in Thrace are good cheeses. Naoussa produces Greece's most popular red wine, while the Domaine Carras in the Halkidiki produces the country's best wines of any color.

AGIA TRIADA. *Sun Beach* (M), tel. 51 221/4. 120 rooms, airconditioned;

pool, disco. *Galaxy* (I), tel. 22 291/3. 80 rooms; beach, roofgarden, disco.

ALEXANDRÓUPOLI. *Motel Astir* (E), tel. 26 448. 53 rooms, pool; on beach. *Motel Egnatia* (M), tel. 28 661. 96 rooms; on beach. Both near town. *Alex* (I), tel. 26 302. 28 rooms. *Alkyon* (I), tel. 27 465. 30 rooms.

ASPROVALTA. *Strymonikon* (I), tel. 31 209. 13 rooms; no restaurant.

DIDYMOTIHO. *Plotini* (M), tel. 23 400. 67 rooms; disco. *Anessis* (I), tel. 22 050. 13 rooms.

DISPILIO. 2 miles south of Kastoria. *Tsamis* (M), tel. 43 330/5. 81 rooms; beach on the lake.

DRAMA. *Xenia* (M), tel. 23 195. 48 rooms, airconditioned; disco. *Apollo* (I), tel. 25 551. 40 rooms; no restaurant.

EDESSA. *Katarraktes* (M), tel. 22 300. 44 rooms; at the waterfall, fine view. *Xenia* (M), tel. 22 995. 20 rooms. *Alfa* (I), tel. 22 221. 30 rooms.

EVZONI. *Evzoni* (M), tel. 51 209. 25 rooms.

FLORINA. *King Alexander* (M), tel. 23 501. 38 rooms, on the outskirts; food above average. *Lyngos* (M), tel. 28 322. 40 rooms. *Tottis* (M), tel. 22 645. 32 rooms. *Antigone* (I), tel. 23 180. 80 rooms.

GEFYRA. *Gefyra* (I), tel. 51 287. Motel; 12 rooms.

HALKIDIKI. Afytos. *Afytis* (M), tel. 91 273. 27 rooms.

Agia Paraskevi. *Aphrodite* (M), tel. 71 228. 24 rooms.

Gerakini. *Gerakina Beach* (M), tel. 22 474. Hotel and bungalows; 503 rooms; pool, tennis, minigolf, disco.

Haniotis. *Dionyssos Apartments* (M), tel. 51 402. 32 suites. *Soussouras* (M), tel. 51 251. 17 bungalows on beach; tennis. *Pella* (M), tel. 51 679. 179 rooms. *Ermis* (I), tel. 51 245. 28 rooms. *Strand* (I), tel. 51 261. 45 rooms, disco.

Ierissos. *Mount Athos* (M), tel. 22 225. 42 rooms; beach, tennis.

Kalandra. *Mendi* (E), tel. 41 323/7. 172 rooms, not airconditioned but on cool promontory. Beach, pool, tennis, minigolf, disco.

Kalithea. *Athos Palace* (E), tel. 22 100/10. 599 rooms and bungalows; on beach; pool, tennis, minigolf, disco. *Pallini Beach* (E), tel. 22 480/10. 495 rooms in central block and bungalows; on beach; pool, minigolf, tennis, disco. *Ammon Zeus* (M), tel. 22 356. 112 rooms, airconditioned; beach, disco. *Belvedere* (I), tel. 22 910. 34 rooms; no restaurant; near beach.

Kryopigi. *Kassandra Palace* (E), tel. 51 471/5. 192 rooms; pool, tennis, disco. *Alexander Beach* (M), tel. 22 433. 129 rooms; tennis.

Metamorfossi. *House Danai* (M), tel. 22 310. 15 suites. *Golden Beach* (I), tel. 22 063. 41 rooms.

Nea Moudania. *Kouvraki* (I), tel. 21 292. 21 rooms; no restaurant; near beach.

Ormylia. *Sermili* (M), tel. 51 308/11. 123 rooms; beach.

Ouranoupoli. *Eagle's Palace* (E), tel. 71 230. 162 rooms in central block and bungalows; on beach; pool, tennis, disco. *Xenia Motel* (M), tel. 71 202. 42 rooms; beach tennis. *Xenios Zeus* (I), tel. 71 274. 20 rooms; no restaurant; near beach.

Paliouri. *Xenia* (M), 72 bungalows on beach.

Porto Carras. Greece's largest and most luxurious holiday complex, managed by Grand Metropolitan Hotels of London. 200 Villas with service; *Meliton Beach* (L), 445 rooms; *Sithonia Beach* (L), 468 rooms; tel. 71 381. *Village Inn* (M), tel. 71 381. 85 rooms, airconditioned, the only beach hotel to remain open November through March. 26 restaurants, 3 nightclubs, casino, convention center, theater; pools, tennis, golf, riding.

Sani. *Robinson Club* (E), tel. 31 221/3. 218 bungalows on beach; pool, tennis, minigolf; wooded grounds; camping site.

KALAMITSA. *Lucy* (M), tel. 83 2600/5. 217 rooms, airconditioned; beach, pool, disco.

KASTORIA. *Xenia du Lac* (M), tel. 22 565. Fine view over the lake but only a few of the 26 rooms with baths. *Kastoria* (I), tel. 29 453, 15 rooms; *Keletron* (I), tel. 22 676, 21 rooms; no restaurant. Food is below the already low provincial standard. If touring by car better stay at *Dispilio*.

KATERINI. *Alkyon* (M), tel. 61 613. 34 rooms; beach.
Among the 20 (I) hotels on or near the beach are: *Aktaeon*, tel. 61 424. 36 rooms. *Dion*, tel. 61 506. 15 rooms; no restaurant. *Muse's Beach*, tel. 61 212. 60 rooms.
Olympion (I), tel. 29 892. 56 rooms; in town.

KAVALA. *Tosca Beach* (E), tel. 224 866. 100 bungalows nearly on beach; pool. *Egnatia* (M), 7th Merarhias 136, tel. 832 636. 38 rooms; roofgarden. *Galaxy* (M), Venizelou 51, tel. 224 521. 149 rooms. *Oceanis* (M), Leoforos Erythrou Stavrou 32, tel. 221 980. 168 rooms, airconditioned; roof garden, pool, disco. *Esperia* (I), tel. 229 621. 105 rooms, airconditioned; 500 yds from beach. *Nefeli* (I), tel. 227 441. 94 rooms; 500 yds from beach.

KILKIS. *Evridiki* (I), tel. 22 304. 44 rooms; no restaurant.

KOMOTINI. *Orpheus* (M), tel. 26 701/5. 79 rooms, airconditioned; roofgarden, disco. *Xenia* (I), tel. 22 139. 26 rooms.

KORINOS. *Europa* (I), tel. 41 382. 17 double rooms; 300 yds from beach; tennis.

KOZANI. *Xenia* (M), tel. 30 484. 30 double rooms. *Aliakmon* (I), tel. 36 015, 85 rooms. *Helena* (I), tel. 26 056. 39 rooms; no restaurant.

LANGADAS. *Lido* (I), tel. 22 653. 18 rooms.

LEPTOKARIA. *Olympian Bay* (M), tel. 31 311/5. 228 rooms in central block and bungalows; beach; minigolf. Among some 15 (I)s, near the beach, *Galaxy,* tel. 31 224. 26 rooms. *Matos,* tel. 31 266. 29 rooms.

LITÓHORO. *Aphroditi* (M), tel. 81 415. 24 rooms. *Myrto* (I), tel. 81 398. 31 rooms; no restaurant. 3 miles west, on the beach at Plaka *Leto* (M), tel. 22 122. 93 rooms, pool, tennis, disco. *Olympios Zeus* (M), tel. 22 115. Bungalows and camping, 100 rooms; tennis.

MAKRYGIALOS. *Achillion* (I), tel. 41 210. 28 rooms. *Panorama* (I), tel. 41 269. 52 rooms.

METHONI. *Arion* (I), tel. 41 214. 39 rooms. *Ayannis* (I), tel. 41 216. 28 rooms.

NEA HILI. *Aphroditi* (I), tel. 26 165. 20 rooms. *Dionyssos* (I), tel. 26 845. 33 double rooms. Both with restaurants.

NEA IRAKLITSA. *Vournelis* (I), tel. 71 353. 12 rooms.

NEA PERAMOS. *Plage* (I), tel. 71 401. 42 rooms; on beach.

NEAPOLI. *Galini* (I), tel. 22 329. 35 rooms; no restaurant.

NEI EPIVATE (near Thessaloniki airport). *Europa House* (I), tel. 22 455. 28 rooms, airconditioned. 100 yds from beach.

OLYMPIADA. *Germany* (I), tel. 51 255. 19 rooms.

OREOKASTRO. *Haris* (I), tel. 696 174. 29 rooms.

ORESTIADA. *Selini* (I), tel. 22 636. 41 rooms. No restaurant.

PEREA. *Aegli* (I), tel. 22 243. 24 rooms. *Lena* (I), tel. 22 755. 42 rooms.

PERIVOLI (in the Pindos range). *Perdika* (I), tel. 22 102. 24 rooms. No restaurant.

PLATAMÓNAS. *Platamon Beach* (M), tel. 41 212. 170 rooms, pool, tennis, minigolf. *Alkyonis* (I), tel. 41 416. 33 rooms. *Dias* (I), tel. 41 267. 24 rooms. All are on the sea. Higher up on the toll road, *Maxim* (M), tel. 41 305. 73 rooms. *Artemis* (I), tel. 41 406. 16 rooms.

PTOLEMAÍDA. *Kostis* (I), tel. 26 661. 27 rooms; no restaurant.

SÉRES. *Xenia* (M), tel. 22 931. 55 rooms, on river. *Galaxy* (I), tel. 23 289. 49 rooms; no restaurant.

SIATISTA. *Arhontikon* (I), tel. 21 298. 26 rooms, disco.

SKOTINA. *Lefkes* (I), tel. 41 408. 9 rooms.

SKYDRA. *Adonis* (I), tel. 89 231. 20 rooms; no restaurant.

SOUFLI. *Orpheus* (I), tel. 22 305. 18 rooms; no restaurant.

STAVROS. *Aristotelis* (I), tel. 61 474. 15 rooms. *Athos* (I), tel. 61 353. 24 double rooms; no restaurant. Several very simple taverns near the sea.

VERIA. *Aristidis* (I), tel. 26 355. 50 rooms. *Polytimi* (I), tel. 23 007. 32 rooms; *Veroï* (I), tel. 22 866. 48 rooms.

XANTHI. *Nestos* (M), tel. 27 531. 74 rooms; airconditioned. *Democritus* (I), tel. 25 111. 40 rooms; no restaurant.

CAMPING SITES. The best equipped among some 39 organized camps, mostly on the coast, are the GNTO camping grounds at: *Akti Thermaikou*, Agia Triada, tel. 51 360; *Akti Asprovalta*, tel. 31 249; *Akti Kryopigi*, tel. 22 321; *Alexandroupoli*, tel. 28 735; *Batis*, Kavala, tel. 227 151; *Epanomi*, tel. 41 378; *Fanári*, tel. 31 270; *Kalandra*, tel. 41 345; *Olympos*, Skotina, tel. 41 487; *Paliouri*, tel. 92 206.

MOUNTAIN REFUGES. Four on Olympos as well as on Vérmio, half at read terminals; three on Falakro; two on Pangeo; one on Pieria, Vitsi and Vrondou. Most open for skiing in winter. Information from *Hellenic Alpine Club*, Karolou Dil 15, Thessaloniki.

YOUTH HOSTELS. At Agia Triada and Litohoro.

THESSALONIKI

The Byzantine City

Thessaloniki is not very old as towns go in Greece; the 2,300th anniversary is celebrated in 1985. Kassandros, one of Alexander the Great's generals, strengthened his precarious hold on the Macedonian throne by marrying the last surviving member of the ancient royal family, Alexander's step-sister, Thessaloniki. In her honor, he named the town built in the form of an amphitheater at the head of the Thermaïkos Gulf below the Hortiates Mountains, one of the few good harbors on this northern coast.

The origin of its founder was a definite handicap under the succeeding rival Antigonid dynasty, but after the Roman conquest in 168 B.C., it became the capital of the Macedonian province. The building of the *Via Egnatia,* the Empire's main east-west artery linking Rome and Byzantium, further enhanced the prosperity already assured by the trade route up the Axios valley into the Balkans.

The historic nucleus of narrow winding lanes, where the picturesque, if flimsy, wooden houses with overhanging balconies are increasingly giving way to utilitarian concrete structures, has been engulfed by similar huge blocks of flats, partly saved from the dreary uniformity of their likes all over the world by neo-Byzantine features in many public buildings, the lavish use of pastel colors, but above all, by the lovely situation.

The population has undergone no less radical changes, first by the exchange of the Turkish minority against Greeks from Asia Minor in 1923, then by the extermination of almost all the 50,000 Sephardic Jews during the German occupation in World War II, so that there are at present only some 1,400 among the almost one million inhabitants of Greece's second town; a homogenity unique in the city's proud but stormy history.

Owing to the visits of Saint Paul, it became an early center of Christianity. The Emperor Galerius, who made it an imperial capital after his victory nearby over the Goths, was responsible for the martyrdom in A.D. 306 of Saint Dimitrios, the patron and protector of the city. As the result of a bloodthirsty demonstration during his absence, a later emperor, Theodosius the Great, inflicted upon the town a punishment as stark and horrible as anything in its history. The citizens appear to have been great racing enthusiasts, and so furious were they at the imprisonment of a favorite charioteer for making improper advances to one of the Gothic commander's attendants, that they lynched the general, Botheric, and several of his men. It is held by some that this was really an excuse for demonstrating the resentment of the people against the Gothic officers and troops. Theodosius carried out his brutal revenge with great cunning. The townsfolk were invited to the Hippodrome to attend the Games in his honor. When they were all enclosed, the Gothic troops massacred them by the thousand.

After the loss of Egypt and Syria in the seventh century, Thessaloniki became the second city of the Byzantine Empire, not only an important commercial but also a spiritual center, sending forth the brothers Cyril and Methodius in the ninth century as the Apostles of the Slavs. A prosperity rare for the age and the region attracted a highly undesirable number of greedy contenders from near and far. Bulgars and Serbs were successfully repulsed, but in 904 a Saracen force managed to enter and plunder the town, making off with thousands of slaves. In 1185 the city was sacked by the Normans, and in 1204 it was made into a feudal kingdom under Marquis Bonifacio of Montferrat, as a consolation prize for having missed the Latin imperial crown of Constantinople. In 1246 it was re-united with the Byzantine Empire, later to be sold to Venice. In 1430 it was to suffer the worst siege of its history led by Murad II, after which it remained under Turkish domination for nearly 500 years.

During all the centuries of Byzantine rule, the building and decorating of numerous churches was pursued vigorously. In its heyday, a wealth of mosaics was produced, succeeded in poorer days by frescos. A period of renewed prosperity accompanied the arrival of 20,000 Jews, exiled from Spain in 1492, whose nucleus of cultured and energetic leaders made vast improvements to the city and its trade. But only a few who survived World War II still speak among themselves in medieval Spanish. Many of the Oriental buildings, including practically all the minarets, were destroyed by the Greeks when they recaptured the city in 1912. Then a great deal more was gutted in 1917 by the worst of the many fires the city has known.

Yet Thessaloniki offers something from almost every period of its two thousand and more years of history. The Hellenistic walls were extended by the Romans, who left their own remarkable monuments. Among the many early Christian edifices are the galaxy of Byzantine churches whose beauty of exterior design, or of interior decoration in mosaic or fresco, is the main interest of many visitors, and after which the Macedonian School of Byzantine Art is named. A Venetian tower and some sadly dilapidated Turkish mosques and baths remain from subsequent occupations, having survived siege and sack, fire and fighting. The citadel still crowns the hill above.

Exploring Thessaloniki

The Thessaloniki bypass connects Western with Eastern Macedonia, but arrival in the city is fairly simple, not only by the less glamorous successors of the spy-thriller favorite, the Orient Express. The railway station is conveniently situated in Monastiriou which, after crossing Vardari Square, becomes the Via Egnatia, now as for the last 2,000 years the town's main thoroughfare, lined by a wide choice of hotels. The 14 miles from the junction of the toll motorway from the Yugoslav border to Athens with the road network to western Macedonia likewise lead into Monastiriou, while the motorist from Seres or Kavala arrives by Langada on Vardari Square. The town terminal of Olympic Airways is situated at a corner of Vassileos (King) Konstantinou along the sea. Nearby, in Triti Septemvriou, the foundations of Thessaloniki's oldest Christian church were discovered in 1981.

This is not only the most favored spot for the *volta,* the traditional evening stroll, but also the most useful all-purpose waterfront; if you have, Heaven forbid, lost your passport or have to call at your consulate for less dramatic affairs; or are seized by the irrepressible desire to see some of the neo-Byzantine government

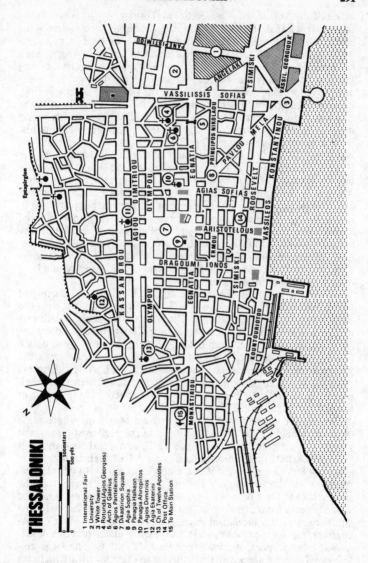

THESSALONIKI

50 meters
500 yds

1 International Fair
2 University
3 White Tower
4 Rotunda (Agios Georgios)
5 Arch of Galerius
6 Agios Panteleimon
7 Dikastirion Square
8 Agia Sophia
9 Panagia Halkeon
10 Panagia Ahiropitos
11 Agios Dimitrios
12 Agia Ekaterini
13 Ch. of Twelve Apostles
14 Post Office
15 To Main Station

offices from the inside, the National Tourist Organization, Post Office, Town Hall, all just around various corners; or simply want to enjoy the splendid view over the Thermaïkos Gulf from a sidewalk café after indulging in seafood in the adjoining restaurants; or are taking a motorboat to one of the beaches or attractive fishing villages on the opposite shores; Vassileos Konstantinou is the answer to the tourist's prayers, including the first dose of sightseeing.

At the eastern end rises the massive circular White Tower, the city's emblem, constructed by Venetian craftsmen probably working for Turkish masters and not for their own Serene Republic during an ephemeral occupation. This bastion, where land and sea walls met till the latter's destruction in 1866, is also known as the Bloody Tower, owing to the massacre of the Janissaries (elite troops, recruited from among forcibly converted Christian boys, who made and unmade sultans for centuries till Sultan Mahmoud freed himself in 1826 from their somewhat oppressive protection). It is a strange irony of history that the same town where imperial authority over the army was reestablished also witnessed the army uprising which led to the deposition of Turkey's last absolute ruler in 1909, while one of the conspiring officers, Kemal Atatürk, brought sultanate and caliphate to an end almost exactly one hundred years after the massacre.

Across the square is Macedonia's cultural center, the Society of Macedonian Studies with the Art Gallery, the State Theater, the military center and the Officers' Club. In the adjacent public gardens is a marble statue of Crown Prince Konstantine, who led the liberating army on Saint Dimitrios Day (1912) into the town, only a few hours ahead of the Bulgarians. A stone marks the spot nearby, where King George I was assassinated in 1913 while taking his morning stroll, unaccompanied as usual. The murderer was neither Bulgar nor Turk, as might have been expected in the middle of the Balkan Wars, but a Greek lunatic.

Beyond the gardens is the Archeological Museum, where pride of place is held by the treasures found in the Hellenistic tombs at Derveni in 1961 and Vergina since 1977. Among the magnificent jewelry, caskets and armor is an almost 3-foot high bronze vase, whose splendid embossment seems to belong to 17th-century baroque rather than to the 4th century B.C. Exhibits range from the Geometric Age via the archaic to the classic, with many gold and silver objects from 5th-century B.C. tombs in ancient Sindos, now submerged in the industrial zone that pollutes air and sea. Sarcophagi, glass vases and mosaic floors were unearthed in Thessaloniki, other important finds come from Ólynthos. The large collection of Roman sculpture from the 1st to the 5th century includes a rare likeness of the 14-year-old Emperor Alexander Sebirus.

Across the road the pagoda-like Telecommunication Tower,

even more incongruously far-eastern at night, dominates the extensive grounds of the International Fair, whose over 3,000 exhibitors from 20 countries attract a million visitors every September. Though started only in 1926, the fair is in fact a revival of the *Dimitria*, a popular annual occurrence attended by many foreign merchants, held at least as early as the 12th century in memory of Saint Dimitrios. The cultural part of the *Dimitria*, under its old name, now comprises religious and artistic events in the Byzantine tradition, leading up to the celebration of Saint Dimitrios Day, October 26, followed on the 28th by a big military parade before the president of the republic on Greece's second National Day, commemorating the historic "No" to the Italian ultimatum in 1940.

In Vassilissis (Queen) Olgas, running southeast, parallel to the gardens on the seafront of the elegant residential district, large blocks of flats overshadow the sham-baroque of the Villa Alatini, in 1909 the home of the leading Jewish family and the town's most elegant building, where the deposed Sultan Abdul Hamid II was imprisoned by the Young Turks till he had divulged the whereabouts of his vast private fortune to the revolutionary officers. The Folkloric and Ethnological Museum is housed in the one-time Governor's Residence at No. 68.

The road leading inland from the White Tower, Vassilissis Sofias, leads to the university, named after Macedonia's greatest mind, the philosopher Aristotle. The large, well-equipped university town extends over what was till the Second World War the Jewish cemetery, beyond the intersection with Egnatia in which, to the left, rises the Triumphal Arch of Galerius. Built in A.D. 303, the worn bas-reliefs depict the Emperor's victories over the Persians. The arch spanning the remaining pillars is an unmistakably modern restoration in brick. Not far off the pink wooden house where Kemal Atatürk, the creator of modern Turkey, was born, looks rather forlorn among the uniformly uninspiring modern buildings.

Byzantine Monuments

Thessaloniki is constantly being likened to a museum of Byzantine Art, and as the most interesting churches are fairly well grouped together, it may be found convenient to arrange one's visit in the same way as a museum, chronologically. From the Arch it is a mere hundred yards up to the earliest church, Agios Georgios. This large Roman Rotunda, once connected by a gallery to Galerius' long-vanished palace, was intended to serve as the Emperor's mausoleum. His Christian successor Constantine the Great denied such magnificence to the body of the pagan persecutor, and used it as the palace church, the first of its kind in Europe. Theodosius the Great dedicated it to St. George and adorned it with the most splendid fifth-century church mosaics in existence; a striking ring of saints around the dome, set against a unique illustration of contemporary Roman architecture on the glittering golden background that was to become typical of such mosaics. In 1591 the Turks made it into a mosque, adding a minaret which is one of the only two remaining in Thessaloniki. There is also a Dervish's tomb of the early 19th century, besides the 15th-century ones on a lower level. Briefly restored as a Christian church in 1912, the Rotunda is now a museum but at present closed because of the damage suffered in the 1979 earthquake. To the left is Agios Panteleimon, another church of the 12th century.

To reach the next church, return to the Egnatia. On the junction at your right with Agias Sofias is the church of the Panagía Ahiropíitos, which means Our Lady Made Without Hands. This triple-naved basilica was built in the fifth century and was probably originally the church of Agia Paraskevi (Friday), the principal church of the city. It was the first to be turned into a mosque by the Turks as a triumphant gesture and was named Eski Djouma (also meaning Friday). The arches are decorated with patterns in mosaic.

Agias Sofias ascends past the Museum of the Macedonian Struggle, dedicated to the fight before the Balkan Wars, to Agiou Dimitriou. On the left is apparently modern Agios Dimitrios, the city's largest church, originally built in the 5th century, as a paleo-Christian basilica, with five naves. It was partially destroyed by a fire during the celebrations of Agios Dimitrios in 538 and rebuilt, only to be burnt and again rebuilt in the 7th century. The present building was erected after a fire in 1917. Some of the 8th-century mosaics are still to be seen near the choir, one depicting Agios Dimitrios as protector of children and another showing him with Leontius (who built the church) and a bishop. Two more show Our Lady and Agios Sergios. Then there is an interesting painting on the south wall. Also there are some of the original pillars of colored marble with carved capitals. The side-chapel of Agios Euthemios was built about 1303 in the time of the Emperor Andronicus II, by Michael, his Master of Horse. In the crypt, which is on the site of the martyrdom of Agios Dimitrios by Galerius, is the so-called Baptistry, near the saint's legendary tomb. From here flowed the sweet-smelling and miraculous healing oil which attracted pilgrims and gave Agios Dimitrios the name *Myróvlitos* (Flowing with Myrrh). The relics of the saint were returned piecemeal from San Lorenzo in Italy in the oecumenical spirit prevailing between the Catholic and Orthodox Churches.

Going back down Agias Sofias it is easy to pick out the Basilica of Agia Sofia (Holy Wisdom) by its large green dome, similar to its namesake in Constantinople. This spacious building (dating from the 8th century) heralds a change in architecture; the basilica, besides being crowned with a dome, shows the first signs of what was to develop into the Greek Cross plan. Converted into a mosque, the mosaics were restored by the Turkish government at the beginning of the century, and in 1912 it became a church again. In spite of bomb damage and redecoration, the 8th and 11th century mosaics are very impressive. Besides the Madonna and Child in the apse, the great work is the Ascension in the cupola, showing Our Lord seated on a rainbow, surrounded by a ring of angels and apostles alternating decoratively with olive trees. Walk along Ermou and turn right up Aristotelous into vast central Dikastiríou Square, in whose upper part the Roman Agora is being excavated. Below stands a picturesque but dilapidated Turkish bath and in the other corner the only surviving medieval Guild church, the graceful *Panagia Halkeon* (Our Lady of the Coppersmiths). This church, built in 1042, is typical of the Byzantine Greek cross. Note the frescos of the Apocalypse and Last Supper; also the tomb of Christoforus, the founder.

The next two churches, also in the Greek Cross shape, date from the 13th and early 14th centuries and are close together. At Metaxa Square, turn right for the church of Dodeka Apostoli (the Twelve Apostles), with its ornamental brickwork and its high dome surrounded by four smaller ones. There are interesting frescos inside. Agia Ekaterini, right up Sahini, is very similar in shape and of a slightly earlier date. Unless you have someone to guide you to Profitis Ilias Church (which is quite close), it is easier to go down to Kassandrou, continue left till above Agios Dimitrios Cathedral, then go left up Profitis Ilias. This 14th-century church, also domed, has the trefoil or triple-shell feature often seen on Mount Athos. The buttresses were added when it became a mosque.

It is interesting to walk around the remains of the city walls. Only the northern one is still intact and it gives opportunities for wonderful views. It is best reached by Venizelou, which continues as Dragoumi Street. On the way up Venizelou, you may notice the old Turkish baths with their cluster of domes, on the corner of what is now the Bezestini Market, while at the junction with Via Egnatia is an old mosque. A few of the old gates and towers (a short distance apart) are still standing, such as the 4th-century Eski-Delik Gate and the 14th-century Manuel Paleologos Tower. Near the junction with the Citadel Wall is a rock on which perches the monastery of Vlatadon. This is traditionally the place where Saint Paul addressed the Thessalonians. Its small 14th-century church is cruciform, dwarfed by the Neo-Byzantine Institute of Patriarchical Studies. Below its terrace the whole town spreads down to the sea, beyond which are the lofty peaks of Olympos and Ossa.

Still higher up rise the ramparts of the *Eptapyrgion* (Castle of the Seven Towers), now being restored as a national monument. The city walls descend past a big tower to the university city, but it is not possible to go down that way. Below Vlatadon, 14th-century Ossios Dadid incorporates a 6th-century apse with a Christ mosaic.

PRACTICAL INFORMATION FOR THESSALONIKI

WHEN TO COME. Spring and early autumn are the best seasons, but the International Fair, lasting two weeks in September, attracts such large crowds that accommodations are difficult, especially as an International Film Festival, followed by a Greek Film Festival, are held at the same time. October is given over to the *Dimitria*, a Festival of Music and Drama with a Byzantine slant. A Fur Fair takes place in March. Summer can be stifling, while late autumnal rains do not enhance the appearance of a city designed for sunshine, and in winter icy winds sweep down the Axios valley from the Balkans.

HOW TO GET ABOUT. Information on how to reach Thessaloniki is under *Practical Information for Macedonia and Thrace*. In Thessaloniki itself, there are plenty of buses in town; these also go up to the city walls. Taxis are blue and white.

The main sites are all within easy walking distance. A popular excursion is to Panorama, some six miles away, on the slopes of Mt. Hortiatis.

The east coast of the gulf is studded with small resorts and fishing villages with facilities for bathing and for meals. Many can be reached by boat from the White Tower as well as by bus. The beach of the Aretsóu suburb is closed because of pollution, so to have a swim it is necessary to cross the head of the gulf to Perea, Nea Epivate or Agia Triada, about 16 miles by road or seven by sea. Nea Mihaniona is 18 miles by road and 13 by sea.

HOTELS. Thessaloniki is well-equipped with hotels in all prices ranges, but it is essential to book ahead during the annual International Fair in September. All the hotels in our listings are airconditioned and have restaurants, unless otherwise stated.

Deluxe

Makedonia Palace, Leoforos Megalou Alexandrou (tel. 837 520/9). 287 rooms, 15 suites. In quiet residential district with fine view over the bay, plus roofgarden, restaurants and garage.

Expensive

Capitol, Monastiriou 8 (tel. 516 221/9). 194 rooms, 7 suites. Near the railway station; garage.

Electra Palace, Platia Aristotelous 5 (tel. 232 221/9). 131 rooms, 6 suites. Comfortable and central.

Nepheli, at Panorama, 6 miles away (tel. 942 002). 70 rooms. No airconditioning; disco.

Moderate

Astor, Tsimiski 20 (tel. 527 121). 88 rooms. No airconditioning; garage and roofgarden.

Capsis, Monastiriou 28 (tel. 521 421/9). 428 rooms. Roofgarden pool, nightclub, garage; near railway station.

Egnatia, Leontos Sofou 11 (tel. 536 321/9). 142 rooms. Public rooms only are airconditioned.

El Greco, Egnatia 23 (tel. 520/9). 90 rooms.

Metropolitan, Vassilissis Olgas 65 (tel. 824 221/8). 118 rooms. No air-conditioning.

Queen Olga, Vassilissis Olgas 44 (tel. 824 621/9). 148 rooms.

Philippion, at Asvestohori, 2 miles out in the hills (tel. 203 320/4). 92 rooms. Public rooms only are airconditioned; pool, tennis, minigolf, night-club.

Rotonda, Monastiriou 97 (tel. 517 121/3). 79 rooms. Public rooms only are airconditioned.

Victoria, Langada 13 (tel. 522 421/5). 68 rooms. Public rooms only are airconditioned.

Inexpensive

A.B.C., Angelaki 41 (tel. 265 421/5). 112 rooms. Not airconditioned, no restaurant.

Amalia, Ermou 33 (tel. 268 321/5). 66 rooms. No restaurant.

Esperia, Olympou 58 (tel. 269 321/5). 70 rooms.

Olympia, Olympou 65 (tel. 235 421/5). 111 rooms.

Park, Ionos Dragoumi 81 (tel. 524 121/4). 56 rooms. No restaurant.

Pella, Ionos Dragoumi 61 (tel. 524 221). 79 rooms. No restaurant.

Telioni, Agiou Dimitriou 16 (tel. 527 825). 63 rooms. Not airconditioned.

Vergina, Monastiriou 19 (tel. 527 400/8). 133 rooms.

Ymca Hostel, Platia Han (tel. 225 277).

Ywca Hostel, Agias Sofias (tel. 276 144).

 RESTAURANTS. On the whole, these are better than in Athens, though the hotel dining rooms tend to be uniformly uninteresting. The *Roof Garden* in the Makedonia Palace is improved by the splendid view. The *Capsis Piper Roof Garden*, in the Capsis Hotel, is helped by a lively orchestra. The bar-restaurant high up in the *Telecommunication Tower* is not improved by the fact that it revolves, though its view provides some compensation. The *Grill House* in the Electra Palace Hotel serves excellent meat dishes. All these restaurants are Expensive.

Among the Moderate restaurants are: *Krikelas*, Gramou Vitsi 32 (tel. 414 690) and *Soutzoukakia*, Venizelou 8 (tel. 277 694), both of which are outstanding taverns. *Stratis*, Vassileos Konstantinou 19 (tel. 276 353), is one of the few restaurants among the numerous cafe/pastry shops that line the waterfront; this is *the* place for the local specialty *mídia tiganitá* (fried mussels), best washed down with white Macedonian *Korona* wine. *Tottis* is the most popular spot on the seafront, but they also have another popular branch on Platia Aristotelous opposite the Salon Olympion. Creamy cakes, sticky pastries and ices are complemented by snacks at the *Castello* and *Corfu* on Vassileos Konstantinou.

At Aretsou, *Chez André*, Plastira 5 (tel. 413 715) varies French with Greek dishes, while *Remvi*, Nea Krini (tel. 941 129) specializes in sea food.

The only Inexpensive tavern that might be singled out is the *Kefallinia*, Botsi 5 (phone reservations not accepted), for rough but tasty food and wine. Otherwise, look for *donér kebáb* turning on a spit outside any Psistaría.

DISCOS. *Lavalbone Disco-Nightclub*, Platia Aristotelous 10 (tel. 228 670) is the most elegant and central, but you might also try *Arigate*, Sofouli 100 (tel. 411 874). At Panorama are *Kounies* and *Nepheli*. All are Moderate in price.

 SHOPPING. The main shopping street is Tsimiski, and you should be able to find everything and anything you need here, and in the surrounding streets. There are a number of good department stores as well as antique shops, leather shops (leather is perhaps one of the very best things to be had in Greece, and the leather goods available can make excellent souvenirs), clothes shops, pharmacists and shoe shops (these are also very good value in Greece).

Other, lesser shopping streets include Agias Sofias, Egnatias, Ermou and Venizelou.

 USEFUL ADDRESSES. *American Consulate,* Vassileos Konstantinou 59. The *British Consulate*, in the same avenue at no. 15. The *National Tourist Organizaiton* office is at Aristotelous Sq., 8, tel. 271-888. *American Express,* Vassileos Erakliou 21; *Wagons-Lits/Cook*, Venizelou 1; *Olympic Airways*, Komninon 2; *Tourist Police*, Agias Sofias 11; *Automobile and Touring Club of Greece*, Vassileos Konstantinou; *Telegraph office*, Heraklion 56; *Post office*, Megalou Alexandrou 28; *Bank of Greece*, Megalou Alexandrou 12. For car hire, try: *Byron*, D. Gounari 5; *Hellas cars*, Venizelou 8.

HOLY MOUNT ATHOS

A Visit to the Monks' Republic

Byzantine hierarchic and hieratic tradition has continued in splendid immutability on the 131 square mile peninsula below the Holy Mountain of Athos. For 1,000 years generation after generation of monks have dedicated at least one third of every 24 hours to the exacting service of the Eastern Church, which does not prevent them from retaining an absorbing interest in earthly matters.

Perhaps the greatest resemblance to paradise lies in the difficulty of entering the monks' republic. Access is only through Dafní, the mountain's port, by an occasional boat from Thessaloniki; or, more usually, first by road across the mountainous Halkidiki peninsula, 89 miles to Ierissos, a pleasant fishing village on an excellent beach. Then fifteen more miles across the gently undulating narrow neck of the Athos promontory, near the canal Xerxes cut in 480 B.C. to avoid the disaster his predecessor's fleet suffered off the stormy cape, and you reach Ouranoupoli. In fair weather a motorboat leaves every morning for Dafní.

Since 1977 non-orthodox laymen are only allowed overnight on Mount Athos when they can prove religious or scientific reasons. Their stay is limited to four days. Foreign visitors require a letter of introduction from their respective consulates to the Greek Ministry of Foreign Affairs in Athens, or the Ministry of Northern Greece in Thessaloniki, which then issue another letter to the Port Authorities of Ierissos and Ouranoupoli, responsible for administering not more than ten permits per day. It should be noted that all regulations regarding visits to Mount Athos are very strictly observed.

The tourists who land from a cruise ship—forbidden to approach within 500 yards if women are on board—merely for a few hours at one or two monasteries may avoid a lot of fuss and bother, which, however, is richly rewarded by the unique experience of a land where time has stood still.

Athos is organized on the lines of a theocratic republic, ruled by the Holy Community in Karies, consisting of one representative from each of the 20 monasteries since 1920 under the benevolent supervision of a Greek governor. Though the number of monks has more than doubled from an all-time low in the 1970s to almost 1,500, with a concomitant lowering of the average age to a mere 40 years, it is still a dramatic decline from the 15th century, when the mountain rang with the prayers of a 1,000 monks in each of 40 monasteries, not to count the host of hermits. Clever diplomacy succeeded in maintaining a large degree of autonomy and prosperity under Turkish rule, one of the sultans, Selim I, even paying a state visit. The present lack of novices is a more serious problem than the infidels ever were.

After Ouranoupoli the pine-clad cliffs rise steeply from the sea. The first *skiti*, a community of semi-independent monks, is an agglomeration of surprisingly large houses, founded in the period of Russian preponderance in the 19th century. The czarist government cultivated this foothold in the Mediterranean, claiming that the Holy Mountain belonged to the whole of Orthodox Christianity. The revolution of 1917 put an end to the influx of Russian monks, until suddenly in 1958 the Patriarch of Moscow expressed a desire to replenish the dwindling contingent of his compatriots. The Greek government has long kept a wary eye on this unexpected religious zeal and only recently again admitted novices from Eastern Europe, as under the constitution every monk becomes a Greek citizen.

Further along the coast vast buildings of every conceivable architecture are separated by the dense forest coming down to the sea: impressive Dochiariou, Xenophontas with 16th-century frescos, and the Russian Agios Panteleimon, where only a few old men remain of the former fifteen hundred.

Nine Centuries without Women

For the thousand-year celebrations in 1963 a road was constructed from Dafní to Kariés, and an incongruous bus shambles through the thickets of pink and white oleanders, while the bare triangular peak of Athos towers above the tall trees. The guest-wing of Xiropotamou, on a hill overlooking the sea, has fallen to one of those periodical fires that are inseparable from wood stoves and candles; the valuable library suffered no loss. Placid bulls graze on lush meadows, but of course no cows, in deference to the edict of the Emperor Constantine IX in 1060, forbidding access: "To any woman, any female, to any eunuch, to any smooth visage." The part excluding females is still strictly enforced, though it is no longer necessary to grow a beard. In 1976, the government showed an admirable sense of tradition, if little understanding for the eccentricities of modern life, by upholding this discriminatory regulation.

Stately buildings dot a well-watered valley, which slopes, lush and green, down to the sea. At Karies, man has helped nature to perfect a Greek Shangri-la.

The 10th-century church of the Protation is decorated with exquisite frescos by Panselinos, the leading representative of the Macedonian school of painting. The palace of the Holy Community faces the Athonian Academy, where the peasant monks receive a high-school education. The governor's pleasant residence is on the way to Agios Andreas, which, like all Russian foundations on Athos, relies more on size than artistic merit; damaged in a recent fire, it is now deserted. The few shops and the stuffy inn are run by monks, but it is preferable to stay at the Koutloumousiou Monastery, in the midst of lovely gardens. The building, badly damaged by fire in 1980, is the usual large rectangle, with wooden balconies along the upper floors. In the courtyard the domed cruciform church faces the refectory.

There are several monasteries on the west coast, south of Dafní, of which Simonos Petras, perched high on a cliff, spectacularly evokes Tibet. It has long been swathed in scaffolding, as there is no money to restore the crumbling walls. Perhaps the thrill of very real physical danger contributed to making it a center of Athos' spiritual revival. On rounding the cape where the Persian fleet was wrecked, the wooded slopes give way to barren rocks rising steeply to the 6,670-foot high summit, crowned by a chapel. In caves precariously connected with the world by ropes and ladders dwell hermits in all the primitive fervor of the early Christians. Yet, as a concession to Greek sociability, they usually live in pairs.

The community of monks at Kapsokalivia earn their livelihood by making rosaries, woodcarving and a variety of handicrafts, unfortunately less artistic than the pretty village itself.

The Oldest Monastery—Lavra

Lavra, the oldest, richest and most powerful monastery, is not far off. Founded in the year 963 by St. Athanasius with the help of the Emperor Nikephorus Phocas, Lavra alone has never suffered from fire and retains its original aspect of a large, fortified hilltop village, the perfect unity of the Byzantine architecture not marred by later additions.

This vision of Byzantium becomes all the more real on the numerous feast days, when the abbot receives important visitors riding up on mules, with the immutable pomp and ceremony his predecessors must have shown to the imperial dignitaries of old. White-bearded monks and boy novices prostrate themselves during the all-night service in the 1,000 year old church, under the eyes of the abbot seated in hieratic immobility on a gilded throne. The liturgy ends with a solemn procession at dawn, moving to the refectory, where clergy and pilgrims eat in silence at marble tables, under the menacing frescos of the Last Judgment, while a monk reads from the lives of the martyrs.

Iviron, higher up the eastern coast, is another of those improbable immense constructions surrounded by virgin forest. Here the monastic peace is for once unbroken, as the persistent beating of an oak-board, the call to prayers, does not penetrate the thick walls of the deep-blue guest room.

Vatopedi Monastery

That champion of progress comes suddenly and dramatically into sight, behind a promontory crowned by the ruins of the original Athonian Academy, later transferred by an exiled patriarch to Karies. The gaunt ruin among olive trees, the tranquil bay with white houses submerged by creepers and hibiscus, compose the perfect romantic landscape down to the last detail of the mill's giant waterwheel. The stupendous rectangle of Vatopedi stands on a slight eminence, the styles ranging from Byzantine to Renaissance, connected by incongruous wooden balconies. Besides the refectory and a fountain there are no less than three churches in the vast courtyard, dominated by a massive medieval tower. Yet somehow this incredible mixture achieves a serene harmony.

According to legend the Boy-Emperor Arcadius was traveling to Constantinople in A.D. 395, when a huge wave swept him overboard. He was mourned as lost, until hermits found him sleeping under a mulberry tree. In gratitude Arcadius later founded a monastery where he had been washed ashore, and named it Vatopedi, the Greek for mulberry and child. A pretty tale, but though several monasteries cherish their Roman origin, history does not bear them out.

The grim walls of Esphigmenou rising straight from the sea enclose some charmingly naive rustic wall paintings. A road, marvelous to relate—bearing the mark of a tractor donated by the Yugoslav faithful—leads inland to Chiliandariou, founded in 1197 and richly endowed by successive Serbian princes. The church, an exceptionally good example of the Athonian triple style, displays its delicate pattern of colored bricks without the dark-red coating which protects and disfigures many architectural gems nearer the sea.

In spite of a multitude of ugly wires, the more congenial oil-lamps and candles still light the long vigils, as another gift, an electrical installation, only rarely works. Or perhaps they considered it tactless to use this gift for the illumination of the late King Peter's numerous pictures.

Tucked away behind the library are the most beautiful icons on Athos: a moving 13th-century Madonna and four large panels depicting the archangels, which testify to the beginning of the Renaissance in the studios of the 14th-century Constantinople. A portable mosaic of a rosy-cheeked Virgin is interesting rather than beautiful, and there is also a three-handed Virgin, nobody quite knows why.

One wing of Bulgarian Zographou, in the center of the promontory, was burnt down in 1976. The remaining monasteries are no less richly endowed by nature and pious princes. But it is hardly possible to visit them all during one stay, without suffering from a surfeit of monastic art and especially of monastic food and beds. They may better be left for another dream-like return in time, while the relative comfort of Ierissos is only five hours by boat from Esphigmenou.

INTRODUCING THE AEGEAN
ISLANDS

Heart of the Greek World

by
ROBERT LIDDELL

Robert Liddell is an authority on the eastern Mediterranean and author of these chapters on the Aegean Islands. He has written travel books about the eastern Mediterranean, including Aegean Greece, Byzantium and Istanbul, The Thracian Ships, *etc.*

The Aegean is the heart of the Greek world which, since the dawn of history, had looked for guidance to the sanctuary of Apollo, on the sacred island of Delos. Round this small island circle the Cyclades, and to this fact they owe their name. These link up with other islands, forming stepping-stones to East and West. In ancient times (and even today, in this mountainous country) it is the land that separates, and the sea that unites. These islands were stations en route between the city-states of mainland Greece, such as Athens, Corinth and Sparta and the no less important Greek states in Asia, Miletus and Ephesus.

Though most visitors now come for the sun and sea, few fail to respond to the beauty of the place-names, and the age-old romantic associations of the archipelago. Even if these islands had no story, they would have the appeal of their great and varied beauty, their exquisite outlines and the superb colors of rock and sea.

King Aegeus must have had wings, not reported by mythology, to fling himself from the Acropolis into the sea which has borne his name ever since Theseus' thoughtlessness drove his parent to suicide. Since these pre-historic times, the 1,425 Aegean islands, of which only 130 are inhabited, have known many rulers. After Roman domination they formed part of the Byzantine empire. Later they were occupied by Frankish and Italian crusaders and eventually by the Turks who were sometimes less hard on them than the Christian Venetians, who also held temporarily some of the islands. History and geography have created a widely different architecture. Medieval Rhodes is Gothic, the work of crusading knights; Venetian influence can be felt in Naxos and Thira. Hios, Lesbos and Samos have adopted Turkish features but the most widespread is the cubistic cycladean style—which extends to the Sporades and the Dodecanese—with its characteristic houses and churches, all whitewashed. Nearly all the present port-capitals, often on antique sites, bear the name of the island, while the medieval inland capitals, now mostly insignificant villages or even totally abandoned, are with few exceptions called Hóra (the Place). One of the few welcome touches of modernity is the spreading use of solar energy in the remoter islands.

What to See, Where to Go

Rhodes attracts by far the largest number of visitors, both as a result of the variety of its historical monuments as well as for the relatively high standard of its accommodations. The next favorite is Mykonos, the best island from which to visit Delos, followed by Kos, Límnos, Skíathos and Thira. The Argo-Saronic Islands are becoming increasingly overcrowded, especially at weekends.

The main attractions on the islands are classical antiquities, medieval monuments and some charming towns, scenery and beaches.

PRACTICAL INFORMATION FOR THE AEGEAN

 WHEN TO COME. Crete and Rhodes strive for winter tourism, but on the whole, May to October is the season for the islands, though a fine April or a mellow November can be pleasant for a visit. Most of the island hotels open at Easter (whenever that happens to fall), though outdoor restaurants or taverns are hardly going until June even if there is an early heat-wave. Greek families generally take their holidays between July 15 and early September, and the islands are therefore emptier and pleasanter before and after those dates, and there is more room on the boats. The Cyclades should especially be avoided round August 15 (Assumption of the Virgin) when nearly all boats are diverted to take pilgrims to Tinos or Paros. August is also the season of the *meltémi* (the prevailing north westerly summer wind), and the sea is very rough. You should also try to avoid making a return journey to Piraeus during the last week of August and the first week of September—the rush season.

 HOW TO GET ABOUT. Starting point for island trips is nearly always Athens (by air) or Piraeus and some Attic ports (by sea). Communication within each group of islands is relatively easy, but though the Cyclades, the Eastern Islands and Crete are connected by some of the older boats, it is often more convenient to return to Piraeus. Local *caiques* should be sternly refused except by the hardiest sailors. Greek island boats are a law unto themselves. The schedules warn that timings are subject to alterations without notice, which, in the case of inter-island hopping boats, is the understatement of the century, so check with a local travel agent, especially for remoter islands. Double bookings still occur. By far the most comfortable, but also fairly expensive, way to explore the Aegean is on one of the numerous cruise ships, some of which are up to the highest standards. The same cannot be said for the island boats in general—more remarkable for their age than their speed or comfort.

To encourage visits to the remoter islands, third class passage is free from Rhodes to the lesser Dodecanese, as well as between some of the Cyclades, during April and May, September and October.

There are regular air services to all the bigger islands, thence helicopters to most of the smaller, at least in summer. Thus this unique island world has become easily accessible, which makes it unlikely that it will remain unique much longer.

The three standard excursions for a brief glimpse are: a flight to Rhodes, most popular of the Aegean islands (seeing on the way a great deal of the archipelago from the air).

Or fly to Mykonos, visit Delos and be back in Athens within 27 hours.

Even a visitor who only has time for a day trip can take the hydrofoil from the Zea Marina, Piraeus, for Aegina (35 minutes), take a taxi or bus to the temple, bathe at Agia Marina, and be back in Athens that night. Another hydrofoil leaves in the morning for Poros (1 hr. 5 min.) and Ýdra (1 hr. 40 min.), returning to Athens in the evening. There are, moreover, organized daily excursions to the offshore islands.

Cars and motorcycles can be hired on all the bigger islands. On the smaller there is often only one road from the port to the Hora.

 HOTELS AND RESTAURANTS. Despite the great number of hotels and bungalows which have opened in recent years, it is necessary to book well in advance for July and August. Deluxe and Expensive hotels are airconditioned unless otherwise stated. Almost all the beach hotels close from November through March, but in the towns, especially on Crete, Halkis and Rhodes, some remain open all year. Villas are for rent in the larger resorts, but being expensive and modern does not necessarily mean that plumbing, electricity and other amenities work. They should all be tried *before* renting; similarly in the numerous furnished flats (see p. 21). The private rooms available are unpretentious, clean, inexpensive, but often very noisy. Again, check first, especially the number and age of the family's children.

Unless otherwise stated, all the hotels in our lists have restaurants, but they are uniformly uninspiring and sadly neglect seafood. If that's what you're after, walk along the seafront taverns guided by your eyes (and nose). Fish will be brought out for your inspection and you can go into the kitchens and look into the pots with no obligation. With luck and judgment, you shouldn't fare badly as a rule. But generally there are no restaurants that deserve special praise, though a few have been singled out for the convenience of readers.

THE OFFSHORE ISLANDS

Euboea and the Argo-Saronic

The five islands, situated in the Saronic Gulf (Saronikós), and off the shores of the Argolid—known as the Argo-Saronic—are more easily visited than any others. There are several boats daily, the sea is rarely rough, and the close proximity of land makes this a particularly interesting and beautiful voyage.

Salamis and Aegina

The largest and most populated of the offshore islands is probably the best-known among those who have never visited Greece, the least among those who have. A very justifiable paradox, because in the narrow straits dividing it from Attica raged in 480 B.C. the famous naval battle in which the Greeks decisively defeated the numerically vastly superior Persian fleet. After watching the massacre of his troops on the islet of Psittalia from a marble throne on Mount Egaleo, King Xerxes hastily embarked and Europe was saved.

As for the scarcity of visitors, Salamína (Salamis) quite frankly does not live up to so glorious a name. The pretty white church of the monastery of the Faneroménis (Apparition of the Virgin), on the north shore facing the landlocked gulf of Eleusis, is noteworthy for a 17th-century fresco of the Last Judgment; the domestic architecture of the capital and the smaller villages is pleasing, but the beaches are poor and overcrowded.

Egina (Aegina), which can be reached in half an hour, displays the most varied scenery. Its beautiful outline, with the pure peak of Mount Oros (1,745 ft.) provides the fitting centerpiece for the Saronic Gulf as seen from Athens.

Zeus abducted the nymph Aegina to the island, where their son Aeacus became king, before assuming a judgeship in the underworld. To provide him with subjects, Zeus changed the island's ants (*myrmex*) into the Myrmidons, a name still borne by the followers of his grandson, Achilles. The capital, named after the island, but locally known like every island capital as *Hora* ("the place") has returned to the ancient site, continuously occupied from about 2500 B.C. to A.D. 1,000, as witnessed by rich ceramic finds now in the museum. From the middle of the second millennium B.C. onward, Aegina sent its ships far afield and the discovery of silver mines in Spain enabled it to mint the first coins in Europe in 700 B.C., the famous Turtle Drachme eagerly coveted by collectors.

The 5th-century B.C. Doric temple of Apollo and the 2nd-century B.C. theater and stadium were built by the kings of Pergamon to whom the island had been sold for 30 talents. They were used as convenient quarries by too many conquerors to present any great interest today except to the ardent archeologist. Opposite the temple, the English shipping agent George Brown built a house in the 19th century over a Mycenaean tomb to extract the superb Minoan jewelry, probably hidden there by an antique grave robber. This Aegina Treasure was sold to the British Museum for £4,000 in 1892. Even Capodistrias' first Greek government used the temple for the construction of an orphanage, now a prison for capital offenders, and the first high school, now the museum. In a typical Greek return to square one, the first coins of modern Greece were minted in Aegina during its brief glory as capital in 1828. The port, partly neo-classical, partly cycladic, is protected by two long spits, one bearing the dazzling-white church of Agios Nikolaos, crowned by a pastel-blue cupola. On the sidewalks, below the multicolored houses, stand rows of porous clay jars of the type that has served since time immemorial as an efficient water cooler; of somewhat more contemporary usefulness are the sponges and delicious pistachio nuts for which the island is rightly famous. The view south-ward extends to the serrated ridge of the volcanic isthmus of Methana, which is flanked by two satellite islands, Moni and Angistri; in the distance are the mountains of the Peloponnese.

The road traversing the island passes the Omorfi Eklisia (Beautiful Church), built in 1289 but not as beautiful as all that, on the way to Paleohóra, the medieval capital, which was only abandoned in 1826, when the danger from corsairs had at last disappeared. The houses were removed stone by stone to the antique site of the capital, so that now only 27 crumbling Byzantine chapels cling to the bare cliff. But below, a huge modern church rises above the white convent, the goal of many a pilgrim, because it contains the embalmed body of Agios Nektarios, though it is far from clear who canonized the latest Greek saint, who died in 1920. There is no recognized procedure for beatification in the Orthodox Church, as such occasions have become so exceedingly rare.

Another eight miles lead to the great Doric temple of the goddess Aphaia (perhaps a local goddess, perhaps the name under which the Aeginetans worshipped Artemis), dominating the east coast from a beautiful mountain site, surrounded with pine woods. The temple, built with the spoils of victory at Salamis, is in a remarkably good state of preservation. No other Greek temple in the islands is so well preserved, and, on the mainland, its only rivals are the Theseion in Athens, and the temple of Bassae in the Peloponnese. Its fine sculptures were bought by Prince Louis of Bavaria, father of Greece's first king, Otto, in 1813 and are now in Munich.

The road descends to Agia Marina, where a popular summer resort has developed on the excellent bathing beach, which can also be reached by boat from Piraeus or the *Hora*.

From Aegina, the boat coasts the Methana peninsula, and puts in, near the isthmus, at a spa locally called Vromolimni ("stinking lake," from the sulphur springs) but officially known as Methana, which, beside its curative properties for rheumatism, is also a convenient center for excursions along the Peloponnesian east shore. The boat then enters a beautiful landlocked bay.

Poros

Poros consists of a largish limestone island, thickly wooded, and a small, bare volcanic projection on which the town is built. The pink, white or yellow houses climb up the rock, and face another village—Galatás—on the mainland opposite, across a narrow strait. It has seemed to some people like a small scale Bosphorus, hence its name. It is of very great charm, particularly if the houses are shining in the afternoon sun. The view of the Peloponnesian mainland is most beautiful; the green plain of Trizína is backed by rugged mountains, of which a noble range is generally called—on account of its form—the Kimoméni or Sleeping Woman.

Poros is naturally very full of Athenians, especially at weekends in the summer. The bathing is not more than moderately good—best at the beach of the Neório, among pinewoods (reached by caique) or below the 18th-century Monastery of the Virgin, which may be reached either by sea, or by the one road on the island.

Delightful excursions may be made; on Poros, to the site of the temple of Poseidon (few remains, but exquisite view), where Demosthenes, last champion of Greek-independence, poisoned himself in 322 B.C. to avoid capture by the Macedonians, and on the mainland to the *Lemonodasos* (lemon grove), full of fragrance in the spring, or the beautifully situated ruins of ancient Trizína, a steep 30-minute climb above the village eight miles from Galatás.

There is a naval school in Poros, and this, the good communications, and the proximity of Athens give the place a bustle and gaiety rarely met with in the islands.

From Poros the boat passes through the strait, follows the long mountain, Adera, and rounds the point where it ends in the sea as Cape Skylli, the southern end of the Saronic Gulf.

Ýdra and Spétses

The first of these two is a long, bare, high rocky island. Little of the town can be made out until one is actually entering its narrow harbor. It is then seen to be something unique in Greece, being a homogeneous town, full of tall handsome houses, all built in the years round 1800.

Not long before that date, a number of mountaineers from Epirus moved here, to escape from Turkish oppression. The barrenness of the island forced them to turn to the sea for a living; they became adventurous merchants, and many of them made a large fortune by running the British blockade during the Napoleonic wars. They built these stately houses, one of which has been converted into a historical museum. Each was a self-contained world, and ready to resist a siege with bakery, store-rooms, and great cisterns for water (most essential on this waterless island). There are also beautiful smaller houses, generally white, but sometimes with brightly colored doorways or other features.

When the revolution against the Turks broke out, Ýdra mustered an important fleet, led by two brilliant naval men, Tombazis and Miaoulis. Because of the island's maritime superiority and substantial riches it helped considerably to win the war of independence, but it lost the peace by its subsequent bankruptcy. Today its principal industry is tourism, though there are no roads or "modern" developments.

Ýdra is a natural center for artists and there is a sizeable foreign colony of writers and painters. If they don't outstay their welcome—as occasionally happens—they can find accommodation in the Tombazis mansion, acquired by the Athens School of Fine Arts.

Though crowded in season, Ýdra is not altogether a suitable summer resort; most of the town is only approachable up ankle-breaking flights of steps, and, in the heat of summer, the place feels shut in. One has to go a long way for a good bathing beach, and excursions are very limited—the steep ascent to the monasteries near the summit of the mountain ridge (1,285 ft.) can be made on a mule, and is to be recommended, on account of the beautiful view of the little town, which exudes great dignity.

After Ýdra the journey is again most attractive. The boat enters the bay of Ermioni, adorned by curiously shaped rocks and islands, and backed by the high twin peaks of Mount Didyma.

Spétses is a low, wooded, undulating island, lying off the shores of the Peloponnese, and at no distance. It's a lively spot, favored alike by international residents and Athenian families bringing their children for the summer holidays. It is more bracing than the other Argo-Saronic islands, and generally cooled by the breezes. Motorboats cross frequently to the beach of Kosta, on the mainland; it is a longer trip to Agii Anárgyri, a fine beach on the other side of the island. Though the shores are not of great interest, there are fine distant views to the south of the great mountains on the other side of the gulf of Náfplio.

The town of Spétses is white, clean and pretty, but lacks Ýdra's distinction in architecture or in situation. There are, however, a great number of small churches and chapels of a quality much superior to that often found in the islands. Excursions may well be made to the convent (with a charming view of the small satellite island, Spetsopoula, the property of the Niarchos family and once stocked by the famous shipping magnate with game for his hunting parties), or to the fine wood of Brellos. Unlike Ýdra, where there is no wheeled traffic, Spétses has a great number of horsedrawn cabs. The *plateia* is pleasant to sit in in the evening, and the view towards the islands of Dokos and Ýdra, and their attendant rocks is very fine. Spétses, though the least exciting of the Argo-Saronic islands, is in many ways the best for a prolonged stay.

It might also be a center for excursions; the other islands may easily be visited by boat, and those who have left their car at Kosta or Porto Heli—connected by road to Corinth via Epidaurus as well as to Náfplio—can make interesting explorations on the mainland.

Euboea

Évia (Euboea) is, strictly speaking, an island, for the channel of the Evrípos completely separates it from the Boeotian mainland; nevertheless it seems like an extension of northern Greece, to which it is so very near, and has no insular qualities. The principal town, Halkída (Chalkis), is bisected by the Evripos, here contracted to a river, and spanned by a toll draw-bridge, so that ships may pass through. This is an agreeable, airy place. One may swim from a mainland beach opposite, or on the Artaki promontory, five miles north on the island.

A tourist pavilion has been installed in the Venetian castle on the hill; the Byzantine church of Agia Paraskevi was transformed by the Frankish lords of Euboea into a Gothic cathedral. But the main curiosity remains the Evripos itself, that strange, inexplicable current of eight miles per hour, changing its direction six or seven times a day; there is a legend that the philosopher Aristotle threw himself into it, in despair of ever understanding its cause.

The spa of Edipsós, whose sulphur springs have brought relief to sufferers from rheumatism since Roman times, can be reached by steamer from Halkis, frequent ferry boats from Arkitsa on the mainland opposite, or over 93 miles of road north from Halkída, through superb mountain and forest scenery with views over both coasts of the island. The branch to Límni continues along the west coast to Edipsos. Near Liháda, on the northwestern promontory, stands the self-contained resort complex of Gregolimano, more conveniently reached by its own launch from Agios Konstantinos on the mainland.

The coastal road south passes Lefkánti, where a large 9th-century B.C. site, recently unearthed, vies with a similar excavation at Kommos in Crete for Greek seniority. Eretria (14 miles) was destroyed by the Persians before they sailed to their defeat at Marathon in 490 B.C., but the strategic position was quickly reoccupied—as witnessed by the ruins of the temples of Apollo and Dionysos, of a large theater, fortifications on the acropolis as well as the finds now in the Archeological Museum. The small beaches hardly justify the conglomeration of holiday complexes.

The road continues through Amarynthos to Alivéri, where a thermo-electric plant supplies Athens with electricity. Turning inland and up the island's mountainous spine, the road divides after seven miles. One branch continues south, offering spectacular views—at one point over both shores—before touching on the up-and-coming beaches of Néa Stýra, Marmári and Kárystos, which can also be reached by ferries from the Attic east coast.

The other branch leads to Kými on the east coast, looking towards Skyros. Kými is finely situated on a plateau, beneath which an olive-covered amphitheater opens out. The daily bus from Athens takes only four hours via the Oropo-Eretria car ferry, and from Kými's small port Skyros can be reached within two hours.

PRACTICAL INFORMATION FOR THE
OFFSHORE ISLANDS

 HOW TO GET THERE. Halkída, on Evia, is connected to Athens by road and rail. There are ferries from Arkitsa, which is on the Athens-Lamia motorway, to Edipsos and from Glýfa, which is off the Lamia-Larissa motorway, to Agiokampos in the north, as well as from Oropos to Eretria, from Agia Marina (northwest of Marathonas) to Néa Stýra, from Rafina to Marmári and to Kárystos in the south of Evia.

Salamis, the closest of the Argo-Saronic islands, can be reached by hourly ferry from the main harbor of Piraeus as well as by frequent car ferries from Perama, a Piraeus suburb, and Néa Peramos on the Athens-Corinth motorway. There are ten ferries daily from Piraeus to Aegina, some of which continue on to Porós.

There are at least four boats every day calling at Aegina, Porós, Ermioni and Porto Heli from the Zea Marina in Piraeus. Porós can also be reached by car ferry from Galatás, which is connected by road to Epidauros, while there is also a car ferry to Spétses from Kosta.

HOTELS AND RESTAURANTS

Egina

AGIA MARINA. *Apollo* (M), tel. 32 271/4. 107 rooms. Beach, pool, tennis. *Argo* (M), tel. 32 471/3. 60 rooms. Airconditioned, halfboard, tennis. Among some 20 Inexpensive hotels on or near the beach are: *Galini,* tel. 32 203, 35 rooms, *Kyriakakis,* tel. 32 222, 30 rooms, *Marina,* tel. 32 301, 29 rooms and *Pantelaros,* tel. 32 431, 55 rooms.

ANGISTRI ISLAND. Among some 10 very simple Inexpensive hotels are: *Kekryfalia,* tel. 23 895, 8 double rooms and *Mylos,* tel. 23 892, 10 rooms.

EGINA TOWN. *Danaë* (M), tel. 22 424. 52 rooms. Pool. *Nafsika Bungalows* (M), tel. 22 333. On a not particularly attractive beach just outside town. *Areti* (I), tel. 22 806, 21 rooms. No restaurant. *Avra* (I), tel. 22 303. 33 rooms. Airconditioned. *Klonos* (I), tel. 22 640. 46 rooms.

PERDIKA. *Aegina Maris* (M), tel. 25 130/2. 164 rooms in central block and bungalows, airconditioned. *Moondy Bay* (M), tel. 25 146/7. 72 bungalows, pool. Both on beach, with tennis, minigolf, disco.

SOUVALA. *Efi* (I), tel. 52 214. 32 rooms.

Evia

AGIOS MINAS. *Saint Minas Beach* (E), tel. 98 411. 80 rooms. Tennis, disco. *Drossia Beach* (I), tel. 98 248. 28 rooms.

AMARYNTHOS. *Blue Beach* (M), tel. 22 467. 210 rooms. Airconditioned, pool, tennis, minigolf. *Stefania* (M), tel. 72 485. 80 rooms. Both on beach and with disco. *Flisvos* (I), tel. 72 385. 26 rooms.

EDIPSOS. *Aegli* (M)`, tel. 22 215. 80 rooms, and *Avra* (M), tel. 22 226, 71 rooms, modernized, half the rooms have private baths, thermal facilities. *Kapolos* (M), tel. 23 331. 51 rooms. *Galaxias* (M), tel. 22 184. 36 rooms. Pool, near beach. *Heraklion* (M), tel. 22 247. 37 rooms. *Taenaron* (M), tel. 23 250. 28 rooms. Among the over 30 (I) hotels the most modern are: *Anessis,* tel. 22 248, 55 rooms, *Capri,* tel. 22 496, 45 rooms, *Irene,* tel. 22 981, 30 rooms; and *Mitho,* tel. 22 780, 36 rooms.

ERETRIA. Large concentration of hotel and bungalow complexes. *Eretria Beach* (M), tel. 62 411. 234 rooms. Airconditioned. *Golden Beach* (M), tel. 61 012. 100 rooms. Airconditioned. *Holidays in Evia* (M), tel. 62 611. 334 rooms. *Malakonta Beach* (M), tel. 62 510. 155 rooms. All are on rather small beaches, pool, tennis, disco. *Delfis,* (I), tel. 62 380, 88 rooms.

GREGOLIMANO. *Gregolimano* (E), tel. 33 282. The Club Méditerranée's hotel, bungalow and villa complex.

HALKÍDA. *Lucy* (M), tel. 23 831/5. Not all 92 rooms have baths. Airconditioned, disco. *Hilda* (M), tel. 28 111/9. 122 rooms. Airconditioned. *John's* (M), tel. 24 996. 57 rooms. *Paliria* (M), tel. 28 001/7. 118 rooms. Airconditioned. *Hara* (I), tel. 25 541. 47 rooms. No restaurant.
Among the excellent Moderate seafood taverns on the seafront, no singling out is justified.

KÁRYSTOS. *Apollon Resort* (M), tel. 22 045/9. 79 rooms. Beach. *Karystos Beach* (M), tel. 23 141/4. 85 rooms. Airconditioned, pool, tennis, disco. *Amalia* (I), tel. 23 311/4. 158 rooms. *Galaxy* (I), tel. 22 600/3. 72 rooms. Airconditioned. *Karystion* (I), tel. 22 391. 39 rooms.

KÝMI. *Beis* (I), tel. 22 604. 30 rooms. Beach.

LEFKÁNTI. *Lefkanti* (I), tel. 52 853. 39 rooms.

LIMNI. *Limni* (I), tel. 31 316. 47 rooms. Beach.

MARMÁRI. *Marmari Bay* (I), tel. 31 301. 114 rooms. Pool, disco. *Michel-Marie* (I), tel. 31 347. 30 rooms.

NÉA ARTAKI. *Bel Air* (M), tel. 42 263. 44 rooms. Beach, pool. *Angela* (I), tel. 42 330. 60 rooms.

NÉA STÝRA. *Aegilion* (I), tel. 41 204. 27 rooms. *Aphroditi Beach* (I), tel. 41 226. 80 bungalows. *Delfini* (I), tel. 41 210. 44 rooms.

PEFKI. *Galaxias* (I), tel. 41 325. 25 rooms. No restaurant. *Galini* (I), tel. 41 208. 30 rooms.
There are a number of Inexpensive seafood taverns on seafront.

POLITIKA. *Euboean Beach* (I), tel. 31 121. 48 rooms.

STENI. *Steni Motel* (I), tel. 51 221. 36 rooms.

Poros

Poros (M), tel. 22 216. 91 rooms. Beyond the village; beach, disco. *Saron* (M), tel. 22 279. 24 rooms. On noisy waterfront; no restaurant. On pine-fringed beaches nearby are: *Neon Aegli* (M), tel. 22 372, 72 rooms; *Pavlou* (M), tel. 22 734, 36 rooms, no restaurant; *Sirene* (M), tel. 22 741, 120 rooms, pool, disco; *Angyra* (I), tel. 22 432. 53 rooms. On beach.

Among the Inexpensive waterfront taverns, remarkable only for the splendid view, are several sweetshops and discos.

3 miles north on the mainland, across the narrow channel, *Stella Maris Holiday Center* (M), tel. 22 562. 93 rooms in central block with bungalows on beach, plus pool, tennis, minigolf, disco.

Spétses

Kasteli (E), tel. 72 311/3. 72 rooms in central block and bungalows on beach outside village. *Spétses* (E), tel. 72 602/4. 77 rooms. Airconditioned; small beach *Roumanis* (M), tel. 72 244. 35 rooms. No restaurant. *Ilios* (I), tel. 72 488. 27 rooms. *Star* (I), tel. 72 214. 37 rooms. Both airconditioned and near beach.

The best restaurant is the *Trehandiri* (E), in the old port.

Ýdra

Unsatisfactory and insufficient accommodations only. *Hydroussa* (M), tel. 52 217. Half of the 36 double rooms with baths. Among some 10 Inexpensive hotels, only the *Delfini*, tel. 52 082, has showers to all 11 rooms, but no restaurant; on seafront. Private lodging also available.

Better try the *Miramare* (M), tel. 52 300, on Mandraki beach 1 mile from town. 28 rooms. Or better still, the large holiday complexes at Plepi and Petrothalassa on the mainland opposite. (See H213.)

Among the numerous waterfront restaurants are: *La Grenouille* (E), rather pretentious, and *Xerí Eliá* (M), for those content with simpler fare.

THE CENTRAL ISLANDS

The Cyclades

Bearing out many of the ancient legends, the islands of the Aegean are the tops of drowned mountains rising from a submerged plateau which lies southeast from Attica. Of recent years they have begun to attract a swarming tide of visitors, with the result that several of those which were once idyllic hideaways are now in the forefront of the package tour market. The sheer simplicity of life which was so attractive to earlier visitors has given way on many of the islands to prefabricated holidays in large international complexes, the sense of remoteness and individuality gone for ever. Many of the islands, however, by their isolation and lack of such facilities as fresh water have managed to resist the changing times. These can usually be approached only by local boat and need a very flexible timetable if they are to be enjoyed.

Naturally, lying as they do full in the path of routes crisscrossing this end of the Mediterranean, the islands have been under constant influence from a vast variety of peoples. During the Bronze Age they were part of the great civilization which created Cnossos and Mycenae—as can be seen in the frescos from Thira which are on view in the National Archeological Museum in Athens. The Minoans were followed by the Ionians who were followed by the Persians who gave way to the Athenians, when the great Delian League came under the Athenian empire. The Macedonians, the Ptolomies, the Romans and the Goths all came and went. As a microcosm of the fate of this part of the world, the islands passed from the hands of the Venetians to those of the Turks, were plundered by the English, were partly occupied by the Russians and then, in this century, were the focus of violent conflict in the two world wars.

Delos

The Kyklades (Cyclades) are so called because the inner ring of this archipelago circles round the holy island of Delos. But the most important island in antiquity is now sadly deserted, though still of fascinating interest in its serene isolation.

Dilos (Delos) is the birthplace of the twins Apollo and Artemis, whose mother, Leto, was relentlessly pursued by the serpent Python, by the order of Hera, the jealous wife of Zeus by whom she was pregnant. She could find nowhere to rest until Poseidon, moved with compassion, anchored the floating island of Delos with a diamond column, just in time for Artemis to be born; in truly divine, if somewhat precocious fashion, she helped her brother Apollo into the world the following day.

From at least the 8th century, Delos was a holy place for the Ionian Greeks; when Athens rose to power, and had aspirations to Ionian Leadership, she began to have eyes on Delos. In 540 B.C., the tyrant Pisistratus of Athens purified the island, removing all human remains buried there; another such purification was made by the Athenians in 425, and two years later they deported all living Delians to Asia Minor—the sacred island was held to be defiled if birth or death took place there.

Delos, the sacred isle, receives Mykonos' two- and four-legged flocks. Sheep stay the year round, tourists for the day, as accommodation is negligible. The safest anchorage within the circle of central islands was a natural halt for vessels sailing between the Greek mainland and the shores of Asia, the geographical as well as the religious center of the Aegean.

After the defeat of the Persians in the 5th century B.C., the confederacy of Delos was founded for future mutual defense of the Greek states against Persia, and its funds were kept here, until in

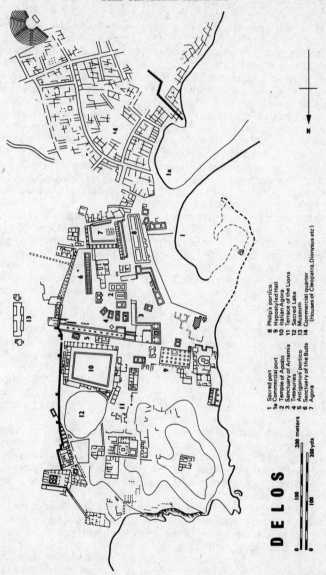

N

1 Sacred port
1a Commercial port
2 Temple of Apollo
3 Sanctuary of Artemis
4 Treasuries
5 Antigonus portico
6 Sanctuary of the Bulls
7 Agora

8 Philip's portico
9 Hypostyled Hall
10 Italian Agora
11 Terrace of the Lions
12 Sacred Lake
13 Museum
14 Commercial quarter
(Houses of Cleopatra, Dionysus etc)

D E L O S

0   100   200 meters
0   100   200 yds

454 they were transferred to the acropolis of Athens for safe keeping. In Hellenistic times an international merchant community settled on Delos, which flourished even more under the Romans, as witnessed not only by the impressive public buildings but also the sumptuous private villas of that period. It is hardly imaginable that this small islet, three miles long and only one mile wide, supported in 88 B.C. a population of some 20,000, who were massacred to the last person by order of King Mithridates of Pontus, the ally of Athens; Roman attempts at revival ended in failure due to a raid by pirates twenty years later. Religion proved an insufficient substitute for commerce, and by the second century B.C. tourism was the mainstay for the upkeep of the magnificent monuments. But in the Middle Ages, neighboring islanders, and even worse, the Venetians, helped themselves to what remained of marble and stone. A museum houses some remarkable archeological finds but the best are now at the National Museum in Athens.

The columns of the sanctuary are mostly broken off at a low level, as are those of Apollo's archaic temple as well as of two classical Athenian shrines and, impartially, of miscellaneous Greek, Egyptian and Syrian divinities. Likewise of Antigonus Gonatas' 410-foot-long portico and the slightly smaller of Philip V of Macedon, facing the portico of Attalus II of Pergamon. For the Hellenistic kings vied with each other in the construction of splendid monuments. But an earlier protective power, Naxos, left the most impressive memorial, the Terrace of the Lions, where five archaic beasts (7th century), lean, vigilant, with tapering waists, still crouch on their hindlegs. The Venetians appreciated these heraldic guardians, one of which has for centuries been standing sentinel before the arsenal in Venice.

Otherwise, the Hellenistic and Roman commercial city has most to offer in the way of remains. Roman bankers as well as Egyptian and Phoenician merchants settled in the elegant residential quarter round the theater. The walls of several villas rise 10 feet, bright with painted stucco on the restored colonnaded courts. The House of Cleopatra is named after the imposing statue of an Athenian matron, but the others after the delicate floor mosaics. Outstanding are the House of the Trident, of the Dolphin, of Dionysos, where the handsome god is riding a tiger, changing over to a panther in the House of the Masks.

The easy ascent of Mount Kýnthos (368 ft.) up a flight of steps is recommended, particularly at sunset, for the wonderful view of the encircling Cyclades—to Syros, which inherited Delos' trade, Naxos and Paros dominating the distant south, Tinos, the new holy island, to the north, while nearby Mykonos has obtained the heritage of tourism. The nearer view, to be enjoyed on the way up the street, is also of remarkable beauty.

Mykonos

Mykonos was of little importance in ancient times and until the 1950s, mainly visited for its proximity to Delos. But the sun-drenched bare hills rising from a deep blue sea and dotted with dazzling white chapels, windmills and dovecotes converging on the attractive port, whose cubic houses are whitewashed twice a year, while the innumerable little churches introduce delicate pastel shades with their cupolas, were bound to make it a great tourist resort, corresponding so exactly to what an Aegean island should look like. It is apt to be very crowded in August which is, for another reason also, the worst summer month to visit it—the *meltémi* blows very strongly and can make sea travel rather unpleasant.

The characteristic cubist, white architecture can be seen better only in such remote islands as Sifnos and Folegandros. There is a good deal of variety in the size and shapes of houses, but color is not admitted except on doors or shutters, or on the pink or blue domes of the little churches. The architectural gem is the Paraportiani, four chapels on different levels forming one church on the site of the old fortress. The Athens School of Fine Arts enjoys a superb view from the town's highest point. Visitors are attracted by the round, white, thatched windmills with canvas sails, and it is agreeable to wander at random, even to get lost, in the narrow winding lanes. Particularly to be mentioned is Enetica (Venice), a row of old houses, lashed by the sea. It is a pleasant drive to Áno-Méra, the one other village, to visit the pretty monastery, on a day when one wants a change from the sea.

The beaches of Ágios Stéfanos, Kalafáti, Megáli Ámos, Órnos and Platys Gialós are also accessible by road, but an enterprising walker may find lonely coves suitable for swimming.

Sýros and Tínos

Sýros is the capital of the Cyclades, with its great port Ermoupoli dominating sea transport in Greece until 1870; afterwards Piraeus rose, and Sýros declined till the opening of shipyards and docks exactly 100 years later brought about a modest revival. The shipyards and associated industries of Ermoupoli, and so the presence of industrial workers, give the town a different feeling from the peasant and fishing based communities of most other islands. A replica of Milan's opera house, where, alas, no opera has been performed since 1914, large private houses, and handsome public buildings round the big, rectangular, inland plateia where there is no traffic, testify to the former wealth of the island. In the countryside are many villas built by rich Greeks from Egypt.

The harbor, full of Aegean craft of every kind, is always lively, and the square is amusing on a Sunday evening, when the band plays, and it is full of people strolling about. The hills behind the lower town—Ano-Sýros, covered with white houses, and predominantly Catholic, on account of the long Venetian dominance in the island; and the Orthodox hill, Vrontádo—look well from the sea. It is interesting to spend an hour or two in Ermoupoli, but if you stay on the island, go to the charming bays of Galýssas, Fínikas, Possidonia or Vári where there are good beaches.

Tínos has assumed Delos' position as the Aegean's religious center. The pleasant capital contains some very pretty traces of Venetian architecture. Its great glory is the enormous church of the Blessed Virgin, the Evangelistria, a modern church of no distinction, though its courtyard, with fine trees, is not unattractive. It was built as a shrine for an icon discovered at the time of the Greek war of independence, to which miraculous powers are attributed. It is crowded with pilgrims on August 15, the feast of the Virgin's Assumption. After the church service, the miraculous icon is borne aloft by sailors over the prostrate bodies of the sick and maimed. Thousands of ex votos witness frequent miracles. The second Marian feast, the Annunciation, is celebrated on March 25, but the faithful pray before the diamond- and pearl-encrusted *Megalohári* (Great and Gracious Lady) the year round. In the white marble stoas round the vast courtyard are a Byzantine Museum, a Picture Gallery and a Sculpture Museum. The Archeological Museum is in the wider street leading up from the port; the narrower is lined with shops selling religious articles, souvenirs and wicker baskets, a local handicraft. The Orthodox Kehrovóuni Convent above the town was a favorite retreat of Princess Andrew of Greece, mother of the Duke of Edinburgh; the nuns sell embroideries.

Tínos is mountainous, unlike low-lying Sýros, and it is worth going into the interior for the sake of the wonderful view, and for the prettiness of the white Cycladic architecture. Towered dovecots are a special Cycladean feature. Like Sýros, this island also has a large Catholic population.

Andros and Paros

Andros may be approached in two ways; the island capital on the east side is reached by a boat which passes between the narrow strait dividing Andros from Tinos—it is said that people can converse across it. A pleasanter journey is from the Attic port of Rafina to Gávrio on Andros' east coast. Further south is Batsí in a pretty bay.

A deep and wide valley crosses from west to east, descending to the capital—which is admirably situated on a long spit of rock. As in Euboea, the scenery is almost more continental than insular. The mountains are high, bare, and squarish; in their folds are several charming oases of greenness, and tall, white houses.

The capital looks fine from the sea, or from above on the hills; inside, it is a little disappointing—one is almost surrounded by the sea, but it is only to be seen down long and narrow lanes. The mountain spa of Sariza, with its iron spring, is beautifully situated. The best bathing is at Korthi, in southern Andros—cut off from the capital by high mountains—but here the landscape is much less impressive.

Other lines of boats connect Piraeus to the southern Cyclades. Paros and its white capital, Paros or Paríkia, on the west coast, are particularly attractive, the high central mountains are bare, but there are several areas of greenness, objects for delightful excursions.

The great glory of Paros town is the church of Ekatontapyliani (Our Lady of the Hundred Gates)—it has not, of course, a hundred gates, but if all the openings, arches, windows, etc., are counted, they may well come to a hundred or more. This is a rambling building, for it includes a great church of the Virgin, a small church of Agios Nikolaos, and a baptistery; they may date from the reign of Justinian (6th century).

The interior is at first puzzling. In the seventeenth century the nave vault was replaced by another, resting on baroque piers and arches; at first one seems to have entered a large baroque church. It is then seen that an ancient triforium gallery with square-headed openings runs round three sides of the church (everywhere except at the east end). This should be ascended, and is the most beautiful feature of the church. It is a fascinating building, with cross-vistas, and many nooks and corners; apart from Nea Moni in Hios, it is much the most important church in the Aegean. Only traces of the once-marvelous frescos remain, but the stonework itself, in bold patterns of white, red and green, is impressive; also note the "patriarchal" seats round the apse, behind the high altar, and the early cruciform font, with steps down to the water.

Paros was, in ancient times, most celebrated for its white marble—much used at Delos. The quarries are worth the short trip by car.

A more popular excursion is that to the caves of Anti-Paros, a large satellite island connected by regular boats. At the village of Anti-Paros, mules may be hired. The ride to the entrance of the caves is most beautiful; in fine weather there is a marvelous view of the southern islands. The caves may now be visited with ease; a staircase has been constructed, and electric light is laid on. But the stalactites must have looked their weird best in the torchlight during the celebration of Christmas mass in 1673, organized by the French ambassador.

Paros is an island that invites a lengthy stay. It accommodates the Aegean School of Fine Arts. There is fairly good bathing at Agia Anna and in the bay, opposite the capital (reached by boat), though the finest beaches are around the lovely bay of Naoussa on the northeastern shore. The extensive walls of antique Asty have long supplied the building material for the picturesque Cycladic fishing village of Naoussa. But recent excavations on the Acropolis hill have brought to light a Mycenaean palace complex, whose finely dressed huge blocks are blackened by the fire by which the Dorian invaders put an end to the Bronze Age civilization throughout Greece round 1200 B.C. For men only, a short bus ride from Paríkia, the monastery of Longovarda, where some of the monks paint icons, rises from the shore. An hour and a half by donkey, for the hardy only, to the southwest of Paríkia is the Garden of the Butterflies, where, on a smaller scale but in a quieter and more attractive place, the same moths can be seen as in the famous Valley of the Butterflies at Rhodes.

The wine of Paros, dark and sweet, will only please a few.

Naxos, Halki and Ios

The sea is often rough between Paros and mountainous Naxos, the largest of the cyclades. The boat puts in at Naxos, the capital, largely the creation of the Venetian dukes of the archipelago, who made it their seat. The palace of the dukes forms the upper part of the town, clearly seen from the sea above the picturesque lower quarter, in which Venetian features blend with the characteristic architecture of the Cyclades; exhibits in the museum are, however, mainly Byzantine. Here, also, is a strong Catholic minority.

On a small islet to one side of Naxos, rises the tall marble gateway of a temple of Dionysos. It is here that he found Ariadne, when Theseus had deserted her on Naxos, after she had guided him by a thread out of the Cretan Labyrinth.

The island of Naxos is large enough to have a supply of water sufficient to support a prosperous agriculture, and so has less need to rely on tourism. The narrow, winding lanes below the flowering balconies of the old mansions in the white town contrast intriguingly with the surrounding green valleys. In the distance are high craggy mountains, and all around the island charming, traditional villages. In the marble quarries of Flerio lies the gigantic unfinished statue of a youth; further south, Upper Sagri is dominated by the Byzantine monastery of Kaloritsa, Lower Sagri by a Venetian castle. In the northwest, at Avlonitsa, Byzantine churches still display some fine frescos not far from the grim castle of Apalyros.

The central village of Halki preserves its pure Cycladic aspect within medieval fortifications. There are still more worthwhile excursions, to the Frankish castle of Filoti, the Hellenistic fortress of Rimera and the charming village of Apiranthos.

At Ios another halt is made in a large and beautiful bay cutting deeply into the olive-clad hills. The island capital can be seen, an attractive white town, on the hill above. In recent years Ios has been overrun by the knapsack set, which has made the hospitable islanders unfriendly and distrustful. If you want to get any impression of Cycladic atmosphere you have to decamp to the interior of the island. A tumulus on the other side of the island is called "Homer's grave"; and he has but this one, though seven cities claim the honor of his birth.

Thira (Santorini)

Thira is undoubtedly the most extraordinary island in the Aegean. A volcano rose here from the sea in prehistoric times, deposited its lava on the flanks of a high rock already there, and an island was born. The hottest argument in archeology centers at present on what remains several thousands of years and natural phenomena later. Egyptian papyri, describing Atlantis, the Happy Isle, submerged by the sea in an unparalleled catastrophe, were quoted by many ancient writers, among them Solon and Plato. The latter insisted that he was neither presenting a moral fable nor a man's eternal desire for a lost paradise, but recounting a true story. His descriptions singularly fit the last bloom of Bronze-Age Thera, from the town built of red, white and black stone—the strange coloring of the island's cliffs—where ritual bull dances played a major part in the cult, to the tragic end when Atlantis sank in a day and a night.

Only the date did not tally: Solon claimed Atlantis disappeared 9,000 years before his time. The late Professor Marinatos from the Athens Academy ingeniously explained that Solon had simply added one nought too many. Though one of the seven Wise Men of Antiquity, Solon was after all no mathematician, and 900 years corresponds miraculously to the fateful date of about 1450 B.C. when the volcano exploded, the middle of the island sank, the surrounding circle split and the sea poured in, only to be spewed out in an unprecedented tidal wave which swept across the Aegean and engulfed Crete, some 70 miles away. Devastating earthquakes caused by the upheaval completed the ruin of the Minoan empire.

That calamity has been followed by further, if less violent, eruptions; in 236 B.C. the islet of Thirassia was splintered off the northern rim of the circular gulf, 37 miles in circumference, surrounded by fragments of the broken crater; throughout the centuries islets have risen and sunk; and Néa and Paleá Kaméni (the Burnt Islands), which appeared between 1573 and 1925 in the middle of the gulf, are still active.

In 1967 the theory that the legend was based on reality was put to the test. A tunnel dug through the 160 feet of pumice at Akrotiri, the southernmost promontory, almost immediately revealed a Bronze-Age town of some 30,000 inhabitants. Buildings standing two and three stories high, with traces of balconies on the 50-foot street fronts, had been preserved by the ash that enveloped them before the final explosion. They were decorated with delightful frescos of men, plants, birds, antelopes and apes, the last never before depicted in Minoan paintings; those in the governor's palace seem to illustrate the story of the Argonauts. They surpass in artistic delicacy all other famed Mediterranean frescos, those of Crete as well as the later Roman variations at Pompeii, and after having been painstakingly reassembled are on temporary loan to the Athens Archeological Museum till arrangements are made to exhibit them on Thira. No human skeletons have come to light, so obviously the islanders had been warned by some volcanic activity before the final disaster.

The small museum in the capital contains mainly finds from ancient Thira, but the much more exciting Minoan discoveries await the construction of a museum at Akrotiri. It is necessary to make sure on the island if the excavation site is open to visitors.

The island has reverted to its ancient name of Thira, after the 9th-century B.C. Dorian colonizer Thiras, though it is also known as Santorini, a name derived from its patroness, St. Irene of Thessaloniki. Sailing into the gulf, one sees gaunt and sheer cliffs rising all round; they seem to shut you in, for one islet or another blocks the view of the outlets. The colors, black, pink, brown, white or pale green, are never beautiful; and the dead texture of the volcanic rock is a great contrast to the living, warm limestone of most Greek islands. In one place the bare peak of Profítis Ilías rises to 1,856 feet; otherwise nothing shows above the cliff-top but a string of white villages—like teeth on the lower jaw of some monster.

Six cable cars relieve all but the most incurably romantic from the perilous ascent from the tiny port to the island capital is made up a zigzag cliff path on expiatory mules piously believed to contain souls of the dead who are thus doing their purgatory.

From below, on the sea, Thira looks much as it was before the great earthquake of 1956; a line of whiteness above the cliffs. Most of the houses have been restored, though not always to the harmonious mixture of Cycladic architecture and Venetian elegance, which so greatly enhanced the amazing natural scenery of the island. The village has spread to the safer, gentler outer slopes, away from the dramatic cliff-top of the volcanic crater.

Every excursion reveals new facets of the unique scenery; by boat to the Burnt Islands to visit the active craters; a strange and infernal landscape, set against the backdrop of the multicolored 1,000-foot cliff; along the cliff-top northeast to Ia, reborn as a traditional settlement; southwest to the ancient city of Thira, in the south of the island; best by taxi to a point near the monastery on Profítis Ilías (from whose terraces there are fine views); thence over the mountain flank, covered with pumice stone or loose earth, to a 1,200-foot altitude.

The remains of a large city were thoroughly excavated and studied at the turn of the century by Hiller von Gärtringen. There are relics of a very ancient Dorian city, one of the pioneers of early Greek colonization, and the mother-city of Cyrene in North Africa. At the sanctuary of Apollo, graffiti dating back to the 8th century B.C. record the names of some of the boys who danced naked at the god's festival.

Later, the Ptolemies of Egypt kept a garrison here, to maintain their rule over the Aegean. They too have left their traces. The Romans, when they in turn came, restored a charming Ptolemaic portico, and built a very pretty little theater of their own. There is a wide view of encircling islands from the plateau where the ancient city was built. On the site of the antique port far below stands the village of Kamari, and further south the sweep of fine black sand at Perissa contrasts with the translucent sea. The dazzling white church of Ágios Stavós (Holy Cross) owes its strange circular shape with flying buttresses partly to the exigencies of frequent earthquakes.

Thira produces potent sweetish wine; the rich volcanic soil is friendly to viniculture, and to the growth of small sweet tomatoes.

Amorgos, Sýkinos and Folegandros

Amorgos, a remote island, with an archipelago of small islands lying between it and Naxos, is scenically no less attractive than Thira. The island, narrow and high, rises abruptly to considerable altitudes. Its great eastern cliffs, in particular, are very grand; they have been called the natural defense wall of Europe—for the Dodecanese beyond is really Greece in Asia. In the splendid orange limestone cliffs of Amorgos nestles the small white monastery of the Virgin, the Panagía Hozoviótissa, probably meaning "life-saving" from shipwreck in these perilous seas. From Katapóla, the port on the west coast, it is 4 miles inland to the capital, a typical white Cycladic town built at 1,000 ft above sea level around a 13th-century castle. The only road then curves southwest through some fine mountain scenery past the magnificently situated monastery, to terminate at Arkessíni, site of one of the three ancient towns now being excavated.

The small islands which lie between Ios and the western Cyclades, Sýkinos and Folegandros, are seldom visited. And yet the ascent from the tiny harbors to the capitals is rewarding on both islands, especially on Folegandros, where a mosaic path climbs beside the only road from Karavostássis to the Hora, a white Cycladic town built between the walls of an old fort, and on the edge of a beetling precipice. The cliffs of Folegandros (in which is the Golden grotto, very difficult of access, and not worth the trouble and hazard) are, with those of Amorgos, the finest cliff scenery in the Cyclades.

Milos, Sifnos, Serifos, Kýthnos and Kea

The western Cyclades are less visited than others; cruises sometimes stop at Milos, either because it is, geographically, convenient as a halting-place on the way to Crete, or because everyone will have heard of the island where the famous Aphrodite was found in the nineteenth century—forcibly carried away on a French ship, and now known as the "Venus de Milo" in the Louvre. This is the southernmost of these islands, in form like a ring round a huge bay. There is a tall mountain, and the shape of the island is lovely, with views of small islets as one approaches. But Milos is, like Thira, volcanic, its strangely white soil fringed by purple-blossomed trees on the shores.

From Adamas, the main port, it is three miles to Milos, capital since 1100 B.C. and today nestling below the inevitable medieval fortress. The catacombs, where early Christians sought refuge are closed because of the danger of cave-ins. The second port, Apolonía, is more frequented by tourists because of its proximity to Filakopi, where excavations are bringing to light three Minoan and Mycenaean towns, the oldest dating back to 2500 B.C.

Milos gained unwanted fame by the cruel treatment it received at the hands of the Athenians during the Peloponnesian war, so poignantly related by Thucydides, whose "Melian Dialogues" is perhaps the most moving account in all literature of an aggression by a greater power.

Sifnos is more pleasing to the eye, and also to the limbs by providing better accommodation: in the west at Kamares, the principal port with a fine beach; and at another Apolonía, the capital, which extends over the amphitheater of three hills overlooking the east coast. It is a smiling island, its bare hills terraced on their lower slopes for cultivation or for olive trees. It produces the best olive oil in the Cyclades, and in consequence Siphniac cooking is better than the average in this region. Another product of Sifnos is pottery; it is made at several places on the island, always by the sea, so that it may be shipped with ease.

It is on this island that the Cycladic cubic type of architecture, seen with small variations in so many islands, is found in its greatest perfection. Here a projecting ledge, over every door or window, adds to the interest of the exteriors (a feature also to be seen on Folegandros, where the houses are also very beautiful).

Most of the inhabitants live in a line of almost connecting white villages on the crest of a hill, but the finest architecture is to be seen in the old island capital, Kastro, down by the eastern shore, looking towards Paros; here one street passes over the roofs of one storied buildings below, and it is joined by bridges to the upper stories of the opposite houses.

Ancient Sifnos enjoyed a brief period of great prosperity when gold was found there; the remains of the Siphnian treasury which was erected at Delphi are impressive. The Siphnians were supposed to give Apollo at Delphi a golden egg annually: once they tried to fob him off with a gilded stone, and in anger he sunk their gold mines. Indeed, in antiquity they had a name for sharp practice. Today they are singularly gentle and pleasant people, with the reserve that characterizes those islanders whose life is lived remote from their principal port.

The next island, northward, is Serifos, where the boat enters the deep gulf of Livádi. The capital is a labyrinth of steep lanes climbing a pyramidal hill topped by a formidable Venetian fortress. A rare kind of pink, indigenous to Serifos, grows out of the walls in abundance. This is where the infant Perseus came to land in a chest, with his mother Danäe who later married the island's king, Polydectes; and it is here that, when he came to manhood, he petrified the ruthless king with the head of the Gorgon Medusa. A cave is shown as that of the Cyclops, whom Odysseus blinded, but the geography of the Odyssey is much in dispute, and other islands claim to be the scene of this event.

Kýthnos also has a fine bay, and is renowned for warm springs; it is one of the barer islands, but has a great appeal for those who like the treeless scenery of the Cyclades.

Kýthnos is little visited, but Kea (locally known as Zia), a mere 40 nautical miles from Piraeus, is increasingly appreciated for its splendid beaches, antique ruins, Venetian castle and the superb view over a wide sweep of the Aegean from the monastery of the Panagía Kastriní.

The capital, which curves like the letter S round a high hill, is particularly attractive, being distinguished by a great number of arches that cross its one long street. Some way beyond, in the hillside, is a huge antique lion, carved out of the rock, which has apparently fallen from its original position to the site that it now occupies under some olive trees.

PRACTICAL INFORMATION FOR THE CENTRAL ISLANDS

HOW TO GET THERE. In summer, daily flights from Athens to Milos, Mykonos, Paros and Thira. Also from Iraklio to Mykonos and Thira. Helicopters from Paros and Thira to several of the lesser islands. At least one boat daily (not Sunday) from Piraeus to Mykonos, Naxos (car ferry *Naxos*), Paros, Syros, Thira and Tinos, on different itineraries, but usually comprising Syros; there are boats three times weekly to Milos, Serifos and Sifnos. There are less frequent boats to Amorgos, Folegandros and Sýkinos.

From the Attic port of Rafina, there are daily car ferries to Andros (Gavrio), Ios, Syros and Tinos, and there is also a car ferry from Lavrio to Kea and Kýthnos. Daily motorboats, usually part of an organized tour, run from Mykonos to Delos (weather permitting) which, like Thira, is included in most tours.

HOTELS AND RESTAURANTS. Beach hotels are closed from November through March. As far as food is concerned, the Cyclades do not differ greatly from the mainland. If you happen to call in at Amorgos, try the *fava*, a purée of beans and oil; it's quite tasty. The only cheese of some distinction is *kopanista*, pride of Mykonos.

The best Turkish Delight in Greece comes from Syros and the same can be said of Sifnos for honey-pies (*melopita*) and cakes (*melomakarona*). The volcanic soil of these islands is favorable to the cultivation of grapes and their wines are justly famous: Paros and Naxos produce a dry red, Santorini the dark *Nihtéri* and the white *Atlantis*. Kea has chosen a promising French name: *Bouquet*. You can round off a meal with a lemon liqueur, *Kítra*.

Amorgos

EGIALI. *Mike,* (I), tel. 71 247. The island's only hotel, some of the 10 rooms with shower; on beach.

Andros

ANDROS TOWN. *Paradissos* (M), tel. 22 187. 41 rooms. *Xenia* (M), tel. 22 270. 26 rooms. On a cliff above the beach.

BATSÍ. *Chryssi Akti* (I), tel. 41 236. 61 rooms. *Skouna* (I), tel. 41 315. 18 rooms. On beach.

GAVRIO. *Aphrodite* (I), tel. 71 209. Most of the 23 rooms with showers.

KORTHI. *Korthion* (I), tel. 61 218. 15 rooms. Beach.

Ios

IOS TOWN. *Armadoros* (I), tel. 91 201. 27 rooms. *Corali* (I), tel. 91 272. 14 double rooms. *Flisvos* (I), tel. 91 315. 13 rooms. No restaurant. *Sea Breeze* (I), tel. 91 258. 14 rooms.

MANGANARI. *Manganari* (M), tel. 91 215. 31 bungalows. Disco.

Kea

KORISSIA. *I Tzia Mas* (I), tel. 31 305. 24 double rooms. *Karthea* (I), tel. 31 222. 35 rooms. Both on the beach.

KOUNDOUROS. *Kea Beach* (M), tel. 22 144. 80 rooms in central block and bungalows. Plus disco.

Kýthnos

LOUTRA. *Xenia Anagenissis* (I), tel. 31 217. 46 rooms. Thermal facilities; near the beach.

MERIHAS. *Possidonion* (I), tel. 31 244. 83 rooms.

Milos

ADAMAS. *Milos* (M), tel. 41 837. 27 rooms; on own beach beyond the port. *Venus Village* (M), tel. 41 770. 91 rooms in central block and bungalows; with beach pool and disco. *Chronis* (I), tel. 41 625. 16 rooms. *Delfini* (I), tel. 41 741. 25 rooms. No restaurant.

Mykonos

AGIOS STEFANOS. *Alkistis* (M), tel. 22 332. 102 rooms in bungalows. On beach. *Artemis* (I), tel. 22 345. 23 rooms. No restaurant. *Panorama* (I), tel. 22 337. 27 rooms. Tennis, minigolf and disco: good service, but lack of hot water.

ANO MERA. *Ano Mera* (E), tel. 71 215. 67 rooms.

KALAFATI. *Aphroditi Bungalows* (M), tel. 71 367. 95 rooms.

MEGALI AMMOS. *Mykonos Beach* (I), tel. 22 572. 27 bungalows.

MYKONOS TOWN. *Despotika* (M), tel. 22 009. 21 rooms. Airconditioned. *Konhyli* (M), tel. 22 107. 29 rooms. *Petassos* (M), tel. 22 608. 16 rooms. *Rohari* (M), tel. 23 107. 45 rooms. None with restaurant. *Korali* (I), tel. 22 929. 28 rooms. *Magas* (I), tel. 22 577. 19 rooms. *Manto* (I), tel. 22 330. 15 rooms. None with restaurant.

ORNOS. *Ornos Beach* (M), tel. 22 243. 27 rooms. *Paralos Beach* (I), tel. 22 600. 40 rooms.

TOURLOS. *Rhenia* (M), tel. 22 300. 37 rooms in bungalows. *Irene Beach* (I), tel. 22 306. 14 rooms. Neither has restaurant.

VRYSSI. *Konhyli* (M), tel. 22 107. 29 rooms. *Korali* (I), tel. 22 929. 28 rooms.

Restaurants. Prices are above the country's average, but not the quality. *El Greco* at Tria Pigadia, and *Katerini* are Expensive. *Georgos* and *Marko Polo* are Moderate. Discos: try *Nine Muses* and *Remezzo*, both Expensive.

Beaches. Very crowded near town. Better to go a certain distance, by bus to *Psarou*, by boat to *Ilia, Paradise* and *Super Paradise*. The last two are nudist preserves, respectively hetero and gay. Least crowded is *Kalafati,* across the island by bus.

Naxos

Aegeon (I), tel. 22 852. 21 rooms. *Barbouni* (I), tel. 22 535. 14 rooms. *Iliovassilema* (I), tel. 22 107. 21 rooms. *Koronis* (I), tel. 22 626. 32 rooms.

The only one with restaurant. *Naxos Beach* (I), tel. 22 928. 25 double rooms. *Sergis* (I), tel. 22 355. 28 rooms.

Several undistinguished and indistinguishable Inexpensive taverns on the waterfront.

Paros

DRYOS. *Annezina* (I), tel. 41 364. 13 double rooms. *Julia* (I), tel. 41 249. 12 rooms. No restaurant.

MARPISSA. *Leto* (I), tel. 41 283. 14 double rooms. *Pisso Livadi* (I), tel. 41 309. 12 double rooms. No restaurant.

NAOUSSA. *Hippocambus* (M), tel. 51 223. 49 rooms in bungalows. *Ambelas* (I), tel. 51 324. 16 double rooms. *Kalypso* (I), tel. 51 488. 24 rooms. *Mary* (I), tel. 51 249. 34 rooms. *Minoa* (I), tel. 51 309. 26 rooms. All are on or near the island's best beaches.

PAROS TOWN. *Polos* (I), tel. 22 173. 21 rooms. *Xenia* (M), tel. 21 394. 23 rooms. Halfboard; beach. *Alkyon* (I), tel. 21 506. 24 rooms. *Argo* (I), tel. 21 367. 44 rooms. *Argonaftis* (I), tel. 21 440. 14 rooms. *Asterias* (I), tel. 21 797. 26 rooms. *Dilion* (I), tel. 21 479. 14 rooms. *Nikolas* (I), tel. 22 259. 43 rooms. None of the (I)s have restaurants.

There are many (I) seafront taverns, but it's worth wandering round the back streets, where you'll find more variety and, on the whole, better quality.

PUNTA. *Holiday Sun* (M), tel. 22 731. 53 airconditioned rooms, pool, tennis.

Serifos

LIVADI. *Maïstrali* (I), tel. 51 381. 20 double rooms. No restaurant. *Serifos Beach* (I), tel. 51 209. 33 rooms. Near beach.

Sifnos

APOLONIA. *Sofia* (I), tel. 31 238. 11 rooms.
Restaurant. *Cyprus* (I), Cypriot specialities.

KAMARES. *Kamari* (I), tel. 31 641. 18 rooms.

PLATYS GIALOS. *Platys Yalos* (M), tel. 31 224. Most of the 22 rooms with bath. Beach.

Syros

ERMOUPOLI. *Nissaki* (I), tel. 28 200. 42 rooms. No restaurant, near beach.

FINIKAS. *Olympia* (I), tel. 42 212. 40 rooms. Airconditioned; beach.

GALYSSAS. *Françoise* (I), tel. 42 000. 24 rooms, beach.

POSSIDONIA. *Eleana* (I), tel. 42 601. 27 rooms. *Poseidonion* (I), tel. 42 300. 42 rooms.

VARY. *Alexandra* (I), 42 540. 30 rooms. *Domenica* (I), tel. 61 216. 22 rooms. *Romantica* (I), tel. 61 211. 30 rooms. All on beach.

Thira

AKROTIRI. *Akrotiri* (I), tel. 31 295. 17 rooms.

EMBORIO. *Arhaea Elefsina* (I), tel. 22 643. 15 rooms. No restaurant.

IA. *Traditional Settlement* (M), 45 rooms in modernized old houses. Original rather than comfortable accommodations.

KAMARI. *Kamari* (I), tel. 31 243. 55 rooms. Beach, pool, tennis, disco. *Zorbas* (I), tel. 31 433. 40 rooms.

MESSARIA. *Artemidoros* (I), tel. 22 502. 16 rooms. *Loïzos* (I), tel. 22 359. 12 rooms. No restaurant.

THIRA TOWN. *Atlantis* (E), tel. 22 232. 25 rooms. *Kallisti Thira* (M), tel. 22 317. 33 rooms. *Panorama* (I), tel. 22 481. 20 rooms. The only restaurant in this category; disco. *Santorini* (I), tel. 22 593. 24 rooms. *Theoxenia* (I), tel. 22 740. 11 rooms. Reserve well in advance during the festival in the first week of August.

Tinos

Tinos Beach (E), tel. 22 626. 180 rooms in central block and bungalows. 1½ miles from town, pool, tennis, minigolf, disco. *Aeolos Bay* (M), tel. 23 339. 69 rooms. *Alonia* (M), tel. 23 541. 34 rooms. *Asteria* (I), tel. 22 132. 48 rooms. No restaurant. *Delfinia* (I), tel. 22 289. 38 rooms. On seafront. *Meltemi* (I), tel. 22 881. 43 rooms. No restaurant. *Oceanis* (I), tel. 22 452. 47 rooms. On seafront.

THE EASTERN ISLANDS

The Dodecanese, Sámos, Híos and Lesbos

The Dodecanese are islands scattered off the southwest coast of Asia Minor; though called the "twelve islands" they come to more, on most of the varied enumerations. Travelers seldom visit others than Pátmos, Kos and Rhodes, though some of the lesser-known islands well repay exploration. This group of islands was taken from Turkey by Italy in 1912; the islanders believed that it was a step towards their immediate liberation, but the Italians established themselves there, and the Dodecanese achieved union with Greece only in 1948. Kos and Rhodes still have Turkish minorities, who enjoy full cultural and religious liberty, and live in friendship and harmony with the islanders—they even join in each other's feasts. The Italian occupation, at first benevolent, became in the later years of Fascism vain and tyrannical—a few buildings, beautiful gardens and good roads remain, otherwise it might never have been.

Exploring the Dodekánissa (Dodecanese)

Pátmos, the northernmost island, is a place of pilgrimage, because it was here that St. John the Divine wrote the Apocalypse, and because of the famous monastery founded here in the 11th century. It was declared sacred by the Greek Parliament in 1980. The southern part of the island is particularly famed for its charming white "cubist" architecture.

From the port, Skála, on a deep bay, one ascends a hill on the south. Towards the top is the church of the Apocalypse, which enshrines the cave where St. John received the Revelations; the voice of God spoke through a threefold crack in the rock, and St. John (to whom alone it was audible) dictated to his disciple Prochorus. A slope in the rock wall is shown as the desk where Prochorus wrote, and silver haloes are set on the stone that was the apostle's pillow, and the grip by which he raised himself from his knees. Tradition says that St. John was sent here in A.D. 95 by the emperor Domitian for preaching Christ in Ephesus, but returned to Ephesus on Domitian's death the next year.

The pleasant small capital is dominated by the great monastery. This was not founded until late in the 11th century, when St. Christodoulos, a hermit, begged the Emperor Alexis I to make the foundation. For centuries the island had been deserted, and a prey to pirates.

The island was granted to the monastery, and, if the monks had their rights (which might not be convenient to them) Pátmos should really be today, like Athos, an independent monastic republic under Greek protection. The church contains a noble 11th-century icon of St. John the Divine, the gift of Alexis, and the silver shrine of St. Christodoulos; there is also a fine carved screen of early 19th-century work. The treasury of the monastery is very rich, and has never been plundered. There are fine Byzantine jewels and embroidery, and an 11th-century mosaic icon of Agios Nikolaos.

The well-arranged and spacious library is famous: its greatest treasure is the *Codex Porphyrius* of the Gospels, 33 leaves containing most of St. Mark's gospel. This beautiful book was written in silver, on purple-stained vellum, in the 5th century; other leaves from the same manuscript are preserved in Leningrad, the Vatican, the British Museum and Vienna. Famous manuscripts from Pátmos (including an important text of Plato) were bought by the traveler Edward Daniel Clarke in 1808.

The terraced roofs and the bell towers are the most attractive feature of the monastery—which commands a superb view over the whole island with its many creeks. The visitor should also see the refectory, with its long stone tables.

There are many coves, mostly with pebble beaches; the best bathing is at lovely Gríkos.

Léros and Kalymnos

Léros is, like Pátmos, an island of many creeks and promontories, but it is very much less attractive. Practically all property on this island belongs to women, due to an age-old tradition of bequeathing estates to daughters. More pleasant than Láki, the port, are the capital, Plátanos, built in tiers below a fortress, as well as the fishing villages of Alínta and Agía Marína.

The crossing to Kalymnos, the main port and capital of that mountainous island, is one of very great beauty. Prehistoric remains have been discovered in a cave, and Horió, the old inland capital, features the usual fortress (this time Byzantine), but it is for the splendid varied scenery that Kalymnos deserves a visit. Yet the port is impressive from the sea, with its blue, white or yellow houses piled on the reddish rock. The Kalymnians particularly delighted in painting their houses alternately blue and white—the Greek colors—to annoy their Italian keepers during their occupation. In the summer most of the active male population is absent, sponge-fishing; of the remaining inhabitants, many leave the capital for the lovely beaches of Linária, Myrtíes and Pánormos.

Kos

Kos is much better prepared for summer visitors when the town is aglow with flowering oleanders and hibiscus. After the devastating earthquake of 1933, a low, white modern town was built to withstand earthquake shock. The catastrophe at least afforded opportunities for further excavations of the Greek and Roman antiquities.

Kos preserves traces of all the different civilizations that it has known: remains of Hellenistic and Byzantine sanctuaries, the castle of the Knights of Rhodes, and Turkish mosques and fountains. The pretty 18th-century mosque of the "Loggia" contains marble from a Byzantine basilica, which had in its turn been constructed out of the remains of an Hellenistic arcade.

By this mosque is an ancient plane tree, called after Hippocrates, the "father of medicine," who was born on the island. There is no reason for this ascription; a plane tree does not live above five hundred years; nor is it likely that this is a remote descendant of a plane tree under which Hippocrates could have sat in the fifth century B.C. In his day the Koan capital was at the far, western end of the island—it was called Astypalaia, and Thucydides recounts its destruction by an earthquake.

The site of modern Kos was inhabited from 366 B.C., and it was in the century following that the island had its greatest period. It was in the Ptolemaic sphere, after the death of Alexander the Great, and it is here that Berenice, wife of Ptolemy I, gave birth to Ptolemy II Philadelphus—who earned that title by resuming the immemorial tradition of Pharaonic arrogance and marrying his sister Arsinöe II. At the beginning of the third century B.C., a famous school of pastoral poetry flourished here. The greatest exponent of this type of poetry, Theocritus, probably came from Sicily, but certainly remained for some time in Kos, and immortalized some Koan scenes.

From the town's shingle beach, lined by restaurants and cafés under shady trees, there is an exquisite view across to Bodrum on the Turkish mainland (Halicarnassus, the birthplace of Herodotus). Outstanding among the widely scattered Hellenistic and Roman remains are the noble statue of Hippocrates in the museum, and the exquisite floor mosaic of fish, a very fine and delicate work, in the Casa Romana, an antique villa. At the partly restored Hellenistic Asklipiio (2½ miles), a sanctuary and a medical school, terraced in the hillside, the Hippocratia, a minor musical festival, is held in August. Nearby, the renowned South African surgeon, Christian Barnard, opened in 1984 the Olympic Health Center, based on Hippocrates' teaching that prevention is better than cure.

The town of Kos is at the east end of a northern coastal plain, on the south of which is a great mountain range, whose principal peak is called Dikeos, or Christ the Just. On the northern slopes of this range are many charming villages, from which the inhabitants descend to cultivate the plain below. After the westward end of the mountain range, there is a long tail to the island: a wild volcanic country where once the ancient city stood.

The Lesser Isles

The southern sea journey from Kos is most beautiful, passing several smaller islands. Níssyros is sometimes visited for its thermal establishment. It is a strange, square-shaped island, rising on all sides towards a central ring of hills which surround the large volcanic depression of Laki, in which there are two extinct craters, Alexandros and Polyvotis. All the outer slopes are planted with almond trees, an exquisitely beautiful sight in February. The ancient acropolis of Níssyros, a short walk from the modern town of Mandráki, has magnificent "Pelasgian" walls of black trachyte.

Sými is a beautiful island, almost encircled by the mountains of the Turkish mainland. Unlike volcanic Níssyros, it is an island of warm-colored earth and rock. Its mountains are as impressive as those of Kalymnos and Karpathos, and entitle it to rank with them as the finest in the Dodecanese. The vast and ugly monastery of Panormitis, in Greco-Russian baroque, is beautifully situated in a bay on the remoter side of the island, and is a place of pilgrimage for enormous crowds on feasts of its patron saint.

Tílos is deeply indented by several bays. In the far end of one lie the attractive arcaded houses of Livadiá, encircled by the ruins of four Genoese castles. Megalo Hirío, the capital, is four miles inland, below yet another fortress, amidst vineyards and fig trees, which extend to the monastery of Ágios Panteléimon.

Hálki, connected by caique three times a week to Kámiros on Rhodes, though the smallest in this group, displays the whole lot: Pelasgian walls, vestiges of no less than three temples of Apollo, two Byzantine monasteries, a castle and some fine beaches.

Ródos (Rhodes)

The great island of Rhodes, with its fine walled town, is Greece's biggest and most cosmopolitan resort, with some 22,000 beds in hotels of all categories accommodating almost a million visitors annually. Congresses extend the foreign influx, and there is some winter tourism, despite the abundant rainfall which favors the luxuriant vegetation.

The first town-planner in Europe, the Milesian architect Hippodamos, designed, in 408 B.C. the checker-work layout of Rhodes, named like the island after the nymph Rhodos, beloved by the sungod Helios, patron of the island. Succeeding Athens as the main commercial power in the Aegean, Rhodes introduced maritime law, while its wealth made possible the development of a new School of Sculpture tending towards the colossal, in the manner of Alexander the Great's court artist, Lysippos, who executed the famous bronze Quadriga of the sun. Rhodian sculptors created the superb Laocoon excavated by Michelangelo in Rome, the victory of Samothrace, now in the Louvre, and the original of the Farnese Bull in the Naples Museum. Allied to Rome, Rhodes suffered the common fate of these allies by being finally annexed. The decline in political and commercial eminence in the 1st century B.C. meant the end of expensive sculpture, but a new School soon flourished, that of Rhetoric, rivalling that of Athens.

In 43, the Apostle Paul brought Christianity; while, in 654, the Saracens started depredations which still left enough in 1191 for Richard Coeur de Lion to wonder at the mighty works of art. Rhodes made news when in 1306, the chief admiral of the Byzantine empire sold it to the military Order of Saint John of Jerusalem, which was then established in Cyprus, after the loss of the Holy Land. The Emperor Andronicus II objected to such a powerful vassal and it took four years of hard fighting before some knights were able to enter the town mixed with a flock of sheep on a dark misty night and to open the gates to their comrades. The Order was composed of Knights, Brothers (hospitalers) and Clerks; it was organized into eight national sub-divisions or "Languages": Provence, Auvergne, France, Italy, England, Germany, Castile and Aragon. It was ruled by a Grand Master, who was elected for life by the General Chapter. Nineteen Grand Masters ruled in Rhodes, fourteen of French origin, which proves the preponderance of French knights.

Rhodes was made so firm a stronghold, that in 1480, the Grand Master Pierre d'Aubusson was able to resist the attacks of 70,000 Turks led by Mohammed II, the conqueror of Constantinople. In 1522, Villiers de l'Isle Adam was obliged to surrender to Suleiman the Magnificent's 200,000 men, but only after a six months' siege that captured the imagination of all western Europe. Thereafter the Order retired to Malta, where an equally heroic Grand Master, La Valetta, victoriously beat back the Sultan's final onslaught.

The modern port is a part of the Knights' fortifications, topped by an iron deer, Rhodes' emblem, on the harbor pillars. Walls encircle the old town and the three-mile circuit of the battlements affords a fine view over the Byzantine, Latin and Turkish architecture framed by luxuriant parks across the moat.

Apart from the Castellania (the Knights' market-building) the best of Gothic Rhodes may be seen by walking up the famous street of the Knights, which follows a steep, straight ancient road that once led from the acropolis of Rhodes to the port. On one corner is the Knights' hospital, now the museum, which contains a handsome court with cloisters. The exhibits in the beautifully-proportioned refectory and spacious pillared infirmary range from the Mycenaean period to the Middle Ages, highlighted by two lovely Hellenistic statues of Aphrodite. On either side of the street are the restored inns of the different "Languages"; the fine battlemented French inn, with large square windows, and the cardinal's hat and arms of the Grand Master Pierre d'Aubusson should be noted, also the heavy round Aragonese door to the Spanish inn. A small church projects out of line, with a battered Madonna in a niche. The street is spanned by an arch, below the Provençal inn, and then comes the modern archway of the Grand Master's palace. Helion de Villeneuve (1319–1346) copied the papal palace of Avignon for this grandiose residence, which survived the sieges but was wrecked in an accidental explosion in 1856. The last, somewhat megalomaniac, Italian governor finished the reconstruction in 1940. It is commonly maligned, but though ostentatious, with much of the interior a monument of bad taste, it is a fairly convincing Gothic replica—especially in the flattering illumination of the Sound and Light performance from April through October. The interior should be visited, for it contains many mosaic pavements, which the Italians removed here from Kos.

The Knights' town survives as within the walls of the Turkish town, narrow streets spanned by anti-seismic arches, further propped against shock by flying buttresses forming a charming labyrinth of round squares, where huge plane trees shade the fountains. Slim minarets rise over the cupolas of mosques and Byzantine churches, tiled eaves and overhanging wooden balconies. The fine dome of the Mosque of Regib Pasha tops a double portico and it is worth entering the Hammam of Suleiman to see the plasterwork in the great room.

The modern town centers on the small port of Mandraki, used by caiques, windmills and yachts. Three windmills stand on the breakwater which terminates at the Agios Nikolaos lighthouse. Here was the ancient harbor, whose entry was bestridden by the largest of all Rhodian sculptures, the Colossus of Rhodes, one of the Seven Wonders of the World. Chares of Lindos' 100-foot bronze statue of Helios was overthrown by the devastating earthquake of 227 B.C., having guarded the port for a mere 65 years. Despite generous donations by Hellenistic rulers, the technical difficulties of raising the statue could not be overcome. Broken up by the Saracens, the fragments were shipped to Syria, where 980 camels were loaded with the ponderous debris for the final purchaser at Edessa. This chief water-front of the town is marked by pseudo-Venetian and massive pseudo-Roman buildings, the octagonal Italian market-building, which is pleasant enough, the Bishop's palace and the church of Evangelismou giving on to the same courtyard with a fountain, the rather lamentable Post Office, Theater and Municipality and the Venetian Gothic Prefecture, beside which the Mosque of Murad Reïs looks all the more graceful.

Except for the Hydrobiological Institute with its well-stocked aquarium, the northern promontory is almost entirely taken up by modern hotels, from the sea to Mount Smith, from which Sir Sydney Smith, commander of the English fleet, kept an eye on the French during Napoleon's Egyptian campaign. Scattered over the eastern slopes are the remains of the 2nd-century B.C. acropolis, with the temples of Zeus and Athena, the partially restored temple of Apollo, gymnasium and stadium, and the small theater.

A waterlily pond reflects a ruined aqueduct and Ptolemaic tomb in the beautiful park of Rodini, site of the annual Wine Festival from July through September, one mile along the east coast. It is pleasant to dine by the sea in the tavernas of the small port of Kóuva, just outside the city walls, after a day on the superb sands, or stroll through the town of the Knights, or in the charming gardens.

Three Ancient Cities

The Dorian invaders of the 11th century B.C. founded on Rhodes the cities of Ialisos, Kamiros and Lindos, which were leagued with Kos, and with the Asiatic cities of Halicarnassus and Knidos, in a religious and political confederacy, called the Dorian Hexapolis. Such local leagues are found in other parts of Greece, and preceded larger systems of Hellenic unity. In 408 B.C. the three Rhodian cities founded Rhodes itself as their administrative and religious center.

Of the three ancient cities, not very much is to be seen of Ialisos, five miles inland. On the hill stands the now derelict Franciscan monastery of Filerimo, and there are extensive views. More interesting than the antique foundations, the remains of an early Christian basilica and the 4th century B.C. Doric fountain on the hillside is the little chapel of St. George with its Gothic wall-painting. Seventeen miles along the west coast, the extensive ruins of Kamiros, on the slopes of a hill that is crowned with a handsome colonnade, give a much better picture of a 3rd century B.C. town.

But the gem of the three is undoubtedly Lindos, a lovely 35-mile drive along the east coast. The entire town has been officially designated an archeological site, thus ensuring its intact preservation. A small masterpiece of cubism, its architecture includes Byzantine and Arabic influences and all of it is ancient and impressive.

Its acropolis is on the top of a high headland, whose flank falls abruptly to the sea; from sea and land it is a grand sight, even finer than the site of the temple of Sounion, with which it may in some ways be compared. It is a very ancient foundation, attributed to Danaos and his fifty daughters, who came here from Egypt on their flight from Aegyptos and his fifty sons. There is a beautiful colonnade, and, on a high platform, the temple of Athena Lindia; no acropolis, except that of Athens, has so much to show. There is also a Byzantine church (in ruins), a castle of the Knights, and Turkish fortification. Lindos thus contains a history of its island in epitome.

In a small gulf at one side of the cliff foot, St. Paul is believed to have landed, no doubt greatly vexed by the great veneration accorded to Athena Lindia, whose mantle Alexander the Great wore in battle and to whom he dedicated the shields taken at Issos. In the charming white town, the Church of Our Lady of Lindos was built by the Knights of Rhodes. It has a tunnel-like frescoed nave, with a black and white pebbled floor. Some of the pretty seventeenth century houses have pebbled courtyards. In several of them collections of early "Rhodian" pottery may be seen. The legend that a Grand Master of the Order captured some Persian potters, and made them work for him, has no foundation. No fragments of this ware have ever been found on the island, and not until recent times has "Rhodian" pottery been manufactured in Rhodes. It has, however, now developed into a local industry, known especially for its ornamental tiles.

On the road from Rhodes to Lindos one may visit Kallithea, where the medicinal springs of the seaside spa, specializing in the cure of digestive and kidney disorders are closed at present. Further along the coast are two villages in the white style of the Cyclades; Afándou, in the hills above the golf course, and Archangelos, below a medieval castle.

Valley of the Butterflies

Beside the attraction of antique and medieval sites, as well as fine beaches, there is the heavily-wooded and pleasantly-cool mountain retreat of Profitis Ilias (Prophet Elias), 31 miles from the capital.

At only half that distance lies the famous Valley of the Butterflies, a long wooded gorge, crossed by many rustic bridges. The golden moths have not taken to the innumerable visitors, so an EEC grant is employed to preserve them from ecological catastrophe. In summer swarms settle thickly on the leaves, and inside hollow *amber orientalis* trees. In repose, their protective coloring makes them look like dark leaves, with yellow veins. If stirred, they fill the air with a thick shower of reddish gold. The wood and waterside walks of the Seven Springs (Eptá Pigés) among plane and pine trees up in the mountainside, are cool even in the height of summer.

The Outlying Isles

Kárpathos, lying with its attractive companion Kássos halfway between Rhodes and Crete, deserves a place on the tourist map. Southern or "European" Kárpathos, though pleasant enough, is nothing extraordinary. The wild northern part is almost unique in two things: it preserves its forests, and local costume is still worn by the women as ordinary working dress.

In many islands women treasure the beautiful traditional clothes of their grandmothers. They will show them to interested visitors, and may sometimes wear them at Easter, at weddings, or on other festive occasions. But they are best dresses, and have nothing to do with everyday life. The women of northern Kárpathos wear long boots, into which they tuck their white Turkish breeches; their white skirts are looped up, when they work in the fields. Over all is worn a graceful cloak of night blue, and a black handkerchief patterned with colored flowers covers the head. The women here take a large part in the heavier work; "we will find a woman to carry your things," is a typical remark. This grand, if grim region, so little influenced by the outer world, preserves a life of its own, and must be one of the last happy hunting-grounds for folklorists.

Far to the east, barely a mile from the Turkish coast, Kastelórizo, though the smallest of the 12, is perversely also known as Megísti, the Biggest, which it is of its own group of tiny islets. The houses of the present 270 inhabitants cluster below the reddish Venetian fortress from which the island's name derives. The oblong harbor is so perfectly sheltered that it once provided a safe landing-ground for hydroplanes from Paris; it forms a vast pool where the bathers glimpse ancient amphora through the crystal clear water, hardly ruffled by some fishing smacks; though only a handful, they provide an abundance of seafood, comprising delicious sea snails and crabs. All the other food is brought by the twice-weekly boat from Rhodes.

At the western periphery of the archipelago, Astypalea is the nearest to the Cyclades, and is clearly seen from Thira and Amorgos; with the latter it is connected twice a week, as well as with Kos and Rhodes, towards which its main harbor is turned.

Remoteness, however, is not the only charm of this island. Its great bay, Maltezána, with its rocks and satellite islets is of great beauty; and the capital (which from below looks strangely like that of Pátmos, with a large castle in the place of the monastery of St. John) is a particularly attractive white village, chiefly distinguished by an enormous number of wooden balconies in criss-cross trelliswork. There is a line of nine windmills to one side, in varying stages of disrepair. Halfway to the Cyclades, the island has a marked Cycladic character.

Sámos

Sámos, Hios and Lesbos, these great islands, so near the coast of Asia Minor (of which they are geographically a part) should, with the Dodecanese, be called "Greece in Asia." They are all that is left to Greece of the glorious Greek civilization which flourished on the Asiatic coast at a very early period, long before the rise of Athens as an important state and city. Few parts of the Aegean have greater variety and beauty of landscape.

Sámos, the southernmost, is not connected with the other two by regular communications. Boats from Piraeus and Mykonos first call at Agios Kírykos, the port of Ikaria, a large rocky island with Europe's most radioactive springs. Sámos' highest mountain Kérkis (4,720 ft.) is seen from miles away. It is near the western tip of the island, and seems to float above the sea, like a mountain in a Japanese print. On a nearer approach its great bald head is seen, rising out of surrounding forest. Early travelers saw a mysterious light shining out of this mountain; superstitions and scientific conjectures were made about its origin, but it has never been explained.

During the century that followed the fall of Constantinople (1453), Sámos was completely depopulated, except for a few people who hid on this mountain, and perhaps continued the line of aboriginal Samians till the next century, when the Turkish admiral, Kilidj Ali Pasha, fell in love with the island (where he had gone hunting) and obtained permission from the sultan to repopulate it with Greeks from other parts and grant them autonomy. From 1834 onwards Sámos was a Christian principality under Turkish dominion until its union with Greece in 1912.

Sámos is an island in which the mountains are disposed in a singularly fortunate way; after Kérkis there is a pass, and then the chain of Ámbelos (3,740 ft.) forms the backbone. Ámbelos sends out a number of spurs towards the sea in all directions, and they enclose many well-shaped small coastal plains. Every good view in Sámos, and there are so many, includes one or other of these mountains, and sometimes the grand peak of Mycale in Asia Minor, separated by a narrow strait. The island is almost everywhere well-wooded, and extremely fertile, growing some of the best grapes in Greece.

In 1854 the Christian prince moved to Vathý (Deep) on a long, narrow gulf on the north coast. Pythagora Square is the center of modern Samos; the princely Council Chamber is now the Town Hall, flanked by no less than three Museums, Archeological, Byzantine and Paleontological. The partly wooden houses in the attractive upper town, still called Vathý, rise on terraces in the red-tiled Turkish style; a great contrast to the cubist, white houses of the woodless Cyclades. There are pretty excursions to be made particularly above the town, to the monastery of Zoödochos Pigi, with its wonderful view towards Asia, or a longer excursion (by bus or taxi) to the village of Vourliótis, on the northern slopes of Ámbelos. This village is in itself attractive (its plateia would make an exquisite stagesetting) and it is a short walk to the monastery of Vrondianí, below a medieval castle. Sámos' beach of Gagóu is one mile out of town, and despite the tourist pavilion, nothing much to write home about.

Much better bathing can be enjoyed below the formidable walls of Sámos' ancient capital, now the attractive port of Pythagório (10 miles), named after the famous 6th-century B.C. philosopher and mathematician, Pythagoras. Framed by two good beaches, it commands an exquisite view of Mycale and Asia Minor, but occupies only an insignificant part of the vast rectangle enclosed by well-preserved ramparts stretching six miles up and across the Astypalean hill. These fortifications were constructed by the political prisoners of the Tyrant Polycrates, whose corsairs were, from 535 to 527 B.C., the terror of these seas, plundering friend and foe alike "for he argued," Herodotus tells us, "that a friend was better pleased if you gave him back what you had taken from him, than if you spared him at the first''; Herodotus, who had a warm partiality for this island, was especially interested in "the mighty works of the Samians" in which Polycrates showed his power. One of these was a harbor mole (part of which can be seen under the water), another was a tunnel to bring water through a hill (an astonishing feat of engineering by Eupalinos, and still accessible for a considerable length below a deep stalactite cave), the third was the temple of Hera, patroness of Sámos, which was ranked among the Seven Wonders of the World. One column of Europe's biggest 6th-century B.C. temple is still standing four miles west of Pythagório, in the coastal marsh past the airport. The statue of the largest antique *Kouros,* a 15-foot-high colossus, dating from 570–560 B.C., unearthed in continuing excavations, is the pride of the Sámos museum. Higher up is Hóra, a pleasant village that was the capital from 1560 to 1854.

A road more or less encircles the island, and the round trip is a highly desirable excursion, because of the great variety and beauty of the scenery. The old houses of Karlóvassi, the second town and port, extend to the 10th-century monastery of the Panagía tóu Potamóu (Our Lady of the River).

Some boats go on from Sámos to the Dodecanese; this is a most interesting journey, for you pass through the Boghaz (strait) of Sámos, which is only about one and a half miles broad, and enjoy beautiful views of Mycale and of the plain of the Maeander.

Híos (Chios)—Birthplace of Homer?

The scenery ranges from barren rocks without any sign of vegetation to four small fertile plains. The capital is devoid of any particular interest, despite a ruined mosque, the tiny prison where Bishop Platanos and 75 leading citizens were held before being hanged in 1822 as part of the massacre of 30,000 islanders by the Turks, as depicted in Delacroix's famous painting and described in Victor Hugo's poem. Another mosque on the main square is surrounded by cafes and pastry shops. Nor can much enthusiasm be raised by the mainstays of most islands, a museum of antiquities and a medieval castle—Genoese this time.

Híos is one of the seven traditional birthplaces of Homer, and the author of an Homeric hymn describes himself as "the blind old man of rocky Chios". Modern scholars, who tend to believe that he was a single individual, and not a company, are disposed to think it possible that he did indeed live and work here. The village of Kardámyla in the northeast is his traditional birthplace, and he is said to have lived and worked at Volissos on the west; there is no evidence to support either of these traditions. The *Pétra Omírou* (The Rock of Homer), four miles north of the town, was a rupestral shrine of the Asian goddess Cybele, represented with two lions, though it was once believed that the great bard had sat on a knob on the flattened top, and that rhapsodes sat round the edge, listening to him. The taverns under the plane trees are pleasant on a summer evening, and the stony beach is much frequented. Another four miles on, at Vrontados, is the seat of the International Society of Homeric Studies.

The town beach is inadequate, but possesses tremendous snob value for Híos society, as it extends to the house of one of the richest of the fabulous Greek shipping magnates. If bathing is the object, better take a bus four miles south to Karfás.

One curious result of Híos' connection with shipping is the almost complete absence of its sons between the ages of 18 and 35, which gives the town an aspect more expected on neighboring Lesbos.

No round trip is feasible, as all roads, rough in the remoter parts, radiate from the capital. There is, however, one excursion of outstanding interest, to Nea Moni, high up on the mountain, where in the first half of the 11th century three holy hermits found a miraculous icon of the Virgin; they were commanded in a vision to go to Lesbos and seek Constantine Monomachos, then living there in exile, and to get him to promise to build a church for the icon if ever he became emperor. When the eccentric empress Zoë, by a third marriage, raised him to the throne as Constantine IX in 1042, the hermits went to Constantinople, and exacted the fulfillment of the promise. He sent them back to Híos with masons and artists. On his death, the work was temporarily held up for lack of funds, but these were eventually supplied by Zoë's sister, the empress Theodora.

At one time this was a vast monastery, inhabited by 600 monks; for lack of novices a few nuns have now taken over. Turkish vandalism, earthquakes and neglect have done great harm to the church, but there is a most interesting cycle of mosaics depicting the life of Christ.

Of other monastic buildings, the refectory, on the south of the church is an uninteresting 17th-century building, but should be visited on account of the fine stone table, which runs the length of the room. There are niches in it for knives and forks and napkins, and there are remains of ornaments in *opus Alexandrinum* on the top. Northwest of the church, you may look through a door down into a vaulted cistern; this 11th-century structure is reminiscent of the subterranean cistern of Constantinople.

The town lies in a green plain, Kampos, where high mud-brick walls hide the country houses of the older Chian families—and Híos, under the Genoese Trading Company that was its ruler until 1566 was almost unique among Greek islands in fostering the growth of a local aristocracy. A Dutch traveler of the 18th century gives a description of these dwellings that is still true today: "These houses are walled round, and from the outer gate is a walk of trellis-work covered with vines, and supported with stone pillars from an adjacent quarry. At the end of this walk is a garden of about an acre of land, planted with orange and other trees."

In the southwest lie the mastic villages, prosperous from the gum exuded from the terebinth lentisk, a round bushy tree with dark green leaves. It is gathered, in the form of crystals, in the autumn and late summer. In its natural state, it is a scented chewing gum of extreme adhesiveness. It is made into a liqueur, into chewing gum, and into a white sticky jam, served in Greek cafés as a "sweet of the spoon"—a spoonful in a glass of water, and it is called *ypovrýhio* (submarine). In Turkish times mastic was a strict monopoly of the sultans; it was much valued in Constantinople, where the ladies of the Serail liked to chew it, to lessen the boredom of their lives, and to sweeten their breath.

Of the mastic villages, Pýrgi is most frequently visited. It is built within medieval walls, and near the middle is a ruined *pyrghos,* (tower), once the keep. The town is a labyrinth of narrow lanes, overshaded by vines or other creepers, and often spanned by arches, as a protection against earthquake shock. The women of Pýrgi are unique in the island in wearing a native costume; the big kerchief on the head—fringed at the side—is colored for a married woman, black for one recently widowed, and white for a widow of long standing. They are of a strange, unmediterranean type, and are probably descendants of Saracen marauders. It is worth continuing to Mésta, a perfect example of the island's fortified villages, restored as a traditional settlement.

Lesbos—Where Sappho Lived and Loved

In the eighth century B.C. the Tyrant Pittacus united the towns of Lésvos (Lesbos) and made his capital Mytilíni the center of the

Aeolian Greeks and of a famous school of poetry. When "Burning Sappho" practiced what she preached in about 600 B.C., Mytilíni was perhaps the most advanced and civilized city in the ancient world; it was prosperous, possessed a considerable sea-power, and a remarkable intellectual life. Aesop, the great storyteller, was native of Lesbos. Another great lyric poet, Alcaeus, was Sappho's exact contemporary. It is she, however, who has captured the imagination of posterity; the first and the greatest of woman poets. Her erotic poems addressed to girls, in which the physical effects of love on the human frame are described as no other writer has described them, earned her the reputation which has clung to her ever since, and were the reason for the burning of those poems by the church in Constantinople in 1073; fortunately many fragments survive. The biographical tradition about her is apocryphal, and there is no reason to credit the tale that she died as a result of a leap from a cliff at Lefkada in the Ionian islands, on account of her unsuccessful love for a young boatman called Phaon. Legendary inhabitants of Mytilíni (at a much later date) were Daphnis and Chloë, the hero and heroine of the charming pastoral romance by Longinus.

Modern Mytilíni is an agreeable island capital, though most of it is architecturally regrettable. There is a wide water-front, there are good views of Asia Minor, and the Genoese castle is well preserved; it deserves a visit for the sake of the views over the island and the sea, even if only a ruined mosque and baths remain of the large Turkish town that was once built within its vast perimeter. The ancient theater, a relic of antiquity above the town, near the chapel of Agía Kyriakí is hardly worth a visit, except for the very beautiful view (afternoon best). The museum has a rich collection of *Tanagra* figures, and of ancient lamps, beside some good mosaic pavement, found at Eressós, and two very beautiful seventh-century capitals of the rare Aeolic style. The Theophilos Museum is at Variá.

On the water-front, the specialties of Lesbos may be enjoyed, olives, ouzo from Plomári, and the excellent fresh sardines from the gulf of Kalloní. Bathing in town is poor, but some of the hotels have swimming pools. Eight miles north is a beach at Thérmi, a small thermal establishment for rheumatic conditions.

Eastern Lesbos—very much the best part of the island—is a country of high mountains and olive groves. Excursions are greatly to be recommended, particularly round the lovely, olive-surrounded gulf of Géra, which is like an inland lake. This is some of the most idyllic scenery in Greece. It is well to drive thence to the small town of Agiássos, situated under the bald frowning peak of the Lesbian Olympus. The site is attractive, and gives charm to the town though, like everywhere in Lesbos, it has no architectural appeal. Skópelos is another lovely, pastel-colored village, buried in fig-trees and poplars.

The drive continues further up to the admirably situated sanatorium, through a fine chestnut forest, and down to the coast at Plomári. There are superb views over the Lesbian Olympus, over the gulf of Géra, and over the hills behind that to the sea, and Asia. Plomári, with its ouzo factories, is unattractive, but not far away is the lovely, though pebbly, beach of Ágios Isidóros.

Mithýmna

The 36 miles to the north coast skirt the gulfs of Gera and Kalloni in succession, before crossing the tip of the island to the pleasant fishing village of Pétra,whose splendid beach is dominated by the church of the Panagía Glykophilóusa (Sweet-kissing Virgin) perched on a rock. A number of paintings by Theophilus on show in a private house here provide an unexpected artistic touch, strengthened at nearby Mithýmna which has been chosen by the International Academy of Engraving for annual summer courses.

Mithýmna stands on the site of ancient Methymna, second most important city after Mytilíni, and its constant rival. Arion, the musician who was shipwrecked and saved on a dolphin's back, was a citizen of Methymna, and it is here that the current bore the head of the singer Orpheus, after it had been torn off by the Maenads (the bacchantes whose advances he disdained), and thrown into the river Evros in Thrace.

Mithýmna is the island's most attractive town, built on a high headland, under a fine Genoese castle—this was saved from a Turkish assault in the fifteenth century by the "Lady of Lesbos" Onetta d'Oria, wife of the ruling Genoese prince, who astonished the townsfolk by appearing in full armor, and leading them to victory. The bay below is lined by a pebbly beach, and the view of the Trojan mountains across the sea is admirable. The return trip is best made along the northeast coast via Mystégna and Thermi to Mytilíni, the variety of scenery compensating for some rough patches.

Eressós, in the southwest, is by some accounts the birthplace of Sappho (the ancient city put her head upon its coins). The village lies in a valley, under fine rocks; in the summer its entire population goes down to other quarters by the sea. The hill that overlooks a beautiful sandy beach, was the acropolis of the ancient city, and nearby are the outlines of two sixth-century basilicas.

The much recommended excursion to the petrified forest seems rather over-rated. A rough climb over the hillside is rewarded at the end by no more than a number of fossilized tree trunks.

PRACTICAL INFORMATION FOR THE
EASTERN ISLANDS

HOW TO GET THERE. Rhodes' international airport is linked by direct flights with several foreign countries, with Athens by five flights daily and with Iraklio (Crete), Karpathos, Kassos, Kos, Myhonos, Thessaloniki and Thira. There are two flights daily between Athens and Kos and three flights daily between Athens and Mytilíni, which is also connected to Thessaloniki. There are two flights everyday from Athens to Híos and Sámos and daily ferries from Piraeus to Híos and Lesbos and between Ikaria and Sámos, Kalymnos, Kos and Rhodes; less frequent ferries to the smaller Dodecanese islands but Patmos is included in most cruises. Daily ferries from Híos to Cesme, from Mytilíni to Dikeli; daily from Sámos to Kusadasi, in Turkey.

HOTELS AND RESTAURANTS. Rhodes has plentiful modern accommodations in all categories. A number of hotels are open all year round. Except in the luxury hotels, the food is remarkably indifferent, with no trace of any Italian influence, which would certainly be welcome.

Híos is famous for its fruit preserves (*glyko*) and its aperitifs (*mastika* and *ouzo*). Though Byron praised the Samian *Moscháto* in his *Isles of Greece,* it is almost too sweet to drink even as a dessert wine. The light white Rhodian wines, especially *Lindos,* go well with fish.

Astypalea

Aegeon (I), tel. 61 236. 20 rooms. No restaurant. *Astynea* (I), tel. 61 209. 20 rooms.

Híos

HÍOS TOWN. *Chandris Chios* (M), tel. 25 761/8. 156 rooms. Airconditioned, halfboard, pool, 100 yds from beach, disco. *Diana* (I), tel. 25 993. 51 rooms. *Kyma* (I), tel. 25 551. 59 rooms. No restaurant.

KARDÁMYLA. *Kardámyla* (M), tel. 22 378. 32 rooms. Airconditioned, beach, tennis, disco.

MESTA. *Traditional Settlement* (M). 33 rooms in modernized old houses in a very original setting.

Ikaria

AGIOS KIRYKOS. *Toula* (M), tel. 22 298. 151 rooms and bungalows. Beach, thermal facilities, pool, tennis, disco; 1 mile from town.

THERMA. *Apollon* (I), tel. 22 477. Some of the 39 rooms with showers.

Kalymnos

KALYMNOS TOWN. *Olympic* (I), tel. 28 801. 42 rooms. No restaurant.

MASSOURI. *Armeos Beach* (M), tel. 47 488. 34 rooms. Pool. *Ioanna* (I), tel. 47 208. 14 rooms.

MYRTIES. *Delfini* (I), tel. 28 914. 18 rooms. Beach.

PANORMOS. *Drossos* (I), tel. 47 301. 51 rooms. Minigolf.

Karpathos

Porfyris (I), tel. 22 294. 22 rooms. *Romantica* (I), tel. 22 460. 20 rooms.

Kastelórizo

Xenon Dimou Megistis (I), tel. 29 072. 17 rooms. No restaurant.

Kos

KARDAMENA. *Carda Beach* (M), tel. 51 332. Bungalows. 67 rooms. Tennis, disco. *Valinakis* (I), tel. 51 358. 73 rooms. No restaurant.

KEFALOS. *Carlos Village* (E), tel. 23 020. 266 rooms. All facilities; on beach. *Hellas* (I), tel. 23 017. 17 rooms.

KOS TOWN. *Caravia Beach* (E), tel. 41 291. 297 rooms in central blocks and bungalows. *Continental Palace* (E), tel. 22 737. 180 rooms. *Dimitra Beach* (E), tel. 28 581. 134 rooms. Not airconditioned. All on beaches near town with pool, tennis, disco.
Agios Konstantinos (M), tel. 23 301. 91 rooms. *Alexandra* (M), tel. 28 301. 79 rooms. *Atlanta Beach* (M), tel. 28 889. 44 rooms. *Kos* (M), tel. 22 480. 137 rooms. Beach. *Theodorou Beach* (M), tel. 22 280. 54 rooms. *Theoxenia* (M), tel. 22 310. 42 rooms.
Anastasia (I), tel. 28 598. 43 rooms. *Captain's* (I), tel. 22 961. 28 rooms. *Elli* (I), tel. 28 401. 78 rooms. *Elma* (I), tel. 22 920. 35 rooms. *Maritina* (I), tel. 23 241. 68 rooms. *Oscar* (I), tel. 28 090. 193 rooms. The only (I) with restaurant. *Zephyros* (I), tel. 22 245. 52 rooms.

LAMBI. *Atlantis* (E), tel. 28 731. 297 rooms in central block and bungalows. Pool, tennis. *Atlantis 2* (M), tel. 23 755. 85 rooms. *Irene* (I), tel. 28 186. 55 rooms. *Laura* (I), tel. 28 981. 23 rooms.

Leros

ALINTA. *Maleas Beach* (I), tel. 23 306. 48 rooms.

LAKI. *Leros* (I), tel. 22 940. Half of the 19 rooms with showers.

Lesbos

KRATIGOS. *Katia* (M), tel. 21 736. 38 bungalows. Thermal facilities, pool, tennis.

MITHYMNA. *Delfinia* (M), tel. 71 315. On pebble beach. Most of the 50 rooms with baths. Pool. *Molyvos* (M), tel. 71 386. 30 rooms. On beach.

MYSTEGNA. *Petalidi* (I), tel. 71 471. 19 rooms.

MYTILÍNI. *Blue Sea* (M), tel. 23 994. 56 rooms. Disco. *Xenia* (M), tel. 22 713. 74 double rooms. Pool, minigolf. *Sappho* (I), tel. 28 415. Most of the 31 rooms with showers. No restaurant.

PETRA. *Petra* (I), tel. 41 257. 18 rooms. No restaurant.

PLOMARI. *Oceanis* (I), tel. 32 469. 42 rooms.

THERMI. *Votsala* (M), tel. 71 231. 47 double rooms. Beach, tennis, minigolf.

Patmos

GRÍKOS. *Xenia* (M), tel. 31 219. 35 rooms. Beach.

SKALA. *Astoria* (I), tel. 31 205. 14 rooms. *Chris* (I), tel. 31 001. 26 rooms. *Kastro* (I), tel. 31 554. 15 rooms. No restaurant.
The Moderate seafood taverns on the waterfront occasionally serve excellent crayfish.

Rhodes

AFANDOU. *Xenia* (M), tel. 51 121/9. 26 double rooms. Pool, beach and 18-hole golf course.

FALIRAKI. *Apollo Beach* (E), tel. 85 251. 293 rooms. *Blue Sea,* tel. 29 271. 296 rooms. *Colossos Beach,* tel. 85 295. 516 rooms. *Esperides* (E), tel. 85 267/9. 550 rooms. Public rooms only airconditioned. *Faliraki Beach* (E), tel. 85 301/3. 298 rooms. *Rodos Beach* (E), tel. 85 471/4. 280 rooms on central block and bungalows. All are on or near beach, with pool, tennis, minigolf and disco. *Edelweiss* (I), tel. 85 442. 51 rooms. No restaurant. *Lido* (I), tel. 85 226. 20 rooms.

IXIA. Leofóros Ialyssóu, the avenue along the west coast, is lined throughout its 7 miles from Ixía to Kremastí with huge hotels. *Miramare Beach* (L), tel. 24 251/4. 179 rooms and bungalows. Not airconditioned, but one of the few directly on the beach. *Olympic Palace* (L), tel. 28 755. 333

rooms. *Rodos Palace* (L), tel. 25 222/9. 610 rooms in an 18-story block and airconditioned chalets. All with pool, tennis, minigolf, nightclub.

Avra Beach (E), tel. 25 284. 186 rooms in central block and bungalows. *Blue Bay* (E), tel. 92 352. 237 rooms. *Dionyssos* (E), tel. 23 021/5. Slightly off the coastal road and thus quieter. 273 rooms. *Electra Palace* (E), tel. 92 521/5. 216 rooms. *Elina* (E), tel. 92 466. 150 rooms. *Elisabeth* (E), tel. 92 491. 92 furnished apartments. *Golden Beach* (E), tel. 92 411/5. 225 bungalows directly on the beach; only public rooms airconditioned. *Ialyssos Bay* (E), tel. 91 841. 151 rooms. *Metropolitan Capsis* (E), tel. 25 015/25. 649 rooms, 44 suites. The largest of them all. *Oceanis* (E), tel. 24 881/6. 229 rooms. Only public rooms airconditioned. *Rodos Bay* (E), tel. 23 661/5. 330 rooms and bungalows. All with pool, tennis, minigolf, disco.

Leto (I), tel. 23 511. 97 rooms. *Solemar* (I), tel. 22 941. 102 rooms. Both pool. *Velloïs* (I), tel. 24 615. 51 rooms.

KALLITHEA. *Sunwing* (E), tel. 28 600. 389 rooms, 48 suites. Pool, tennis and nightclub.

LINDOS. *Lindos Bay* (E), tel. 31 212. 192 rooms. Beach, pool, tennis and disco.

NEOHORI. *Athina* (M), tel. 22 631. 142 rooms, pool, beach.

RENI KOSKINOU. *Eden Roc* (E), tel. 23 851/3. 381 rooms in central block and bungalows. *Paradise* (E), tel. 29 220. 495 rooms. Both with pool, tennis, minigolf and nightclub.

RHODES TOWN. All hotels are in the new quarter on the north promontory. *Grand Hotel Astir Palace* (L), tel. 26 284/99. 377 rooms. Pool, disappointing beach, tennis, nightclub; houses the casino at present.

Belvedere (E), tel. 24 471/4. 212 rooms. Not airconditioned, beach across the road, pool, tennis. *Blue Sky* (E), tel. 24 091/3. 182 rooms. Pool, disco. *Chevaliers Palace* (E), tel. 22 781/4. 223 rooms. Pool, minigolf, disco. *Ibiscus* (E), tel. 24 421/3. 205 rooms. Not airconditioned. *Mediterranean* (E), tel. 24 661/5. 154 rooms. Only public rooms airconditioned, beach across the road. *Park* (E), tel. 24 611/2. 84 rooms. Not airconditioned, pool, disco. *Siravast* (E), tel. 23 551/7 29 2154. 92 rooms. Not airconditioned.

Aglaia (M), tel. 22 061. 110 rooms. Pool. *Alexia* (M), tel. 24 061. 135 rooms. *Amphitryon* (M), tel. 26 880. 99 rooms. *Cactus* (M), tel. 26 100. 177 rooms. Beach across the road. *Esperia* (M), tel. 23 941. 191 rooms. *Konstantinos* (M), tel. 22 971. 133 rooms. *Manoussos* (M), tel. 22 741. 120 rooms. Roofgarden pool. *Plaza* (M), tel. 22 501. 128 rooms. Pool. *Spartalis* (M), tel. 24 371. 79 rooms.

Rhodes Town is the only resort with a wide choice of Inexpensive hotels, of which only the largest are listed.

Africa (I), tel. 24 979. 75 rooms. *Ambassadeur* (I), tel. 24 679. 42 rooms.

Arion (I), tel. 20 006. 47 rooms. *Caracas* (I), tel. 22 371. 52 rooms. Airconditioned. *Carina* (I), tel. 22 381. 59 rooms. *Continental* (I), tel. 28 433. 113
rooms. *El Greco* (I), tel. 24 071. 75 rooms. *Flora* (I), tel. 24 538. 98 rooms.
Helena (I), tel. 24 755. 86 rooms. *Irene* (I), tel. 24 761. 54 rooms. *Lydia* (I),
tel. 22 871. 60 rooms. *Majestic* (I), tel. 22 031. 79 rooms. *Marie* (I), tel. 22
751. 79 rooms. Beach across the road. *Minos* (I), tel. 24 041. 72 rooms.
Parthenon (I), tel. 22 351. 79 rooms. *Phaedra* (I), tel. 24 207. 62 rooms.
Semiramis (I), tel. 20 741. 120 rooms. The only one with a restaurant in this
category.

Restaurants. *Captain's House* (E), Zervou 5 (tel. 21 275). In a converted mansion; dinner only, Greek and international cuisine. *Casa Caste-
lana* (E), Aristotelous 33 (tel. 28 803). In a 15th-century Inn of the Knights;
everything from snacks to full-course meals. *Kon Tiki* (E), Limin Mandra-
kiou (tel. 22 477). On a boat in the old port; seafood specialties, dinner
only. *Neorion* (M), Platia Neoriou (tel. 24 644). Cafe-restaurant.

The string of Inexpensive establishments with open-air terraces along
the Mandraki port are sadly lacking in everything but a fine situation. The
hotel food lacks even that.

The best handicrafts shops and some jewelers are in Sokratous in the
old town; branches in Deluxe and Expensive hotels are more expensive.

THOLOS. *Doretta Beach* (E), tel. 41 441. 295 rooms, pool, tennis, disco.

Sámos

KALAMI. *Anthemis* (E), tel. 28 050. 24 suites. *Pythagoras* (I), tel. 28 422.
16 rooms. No restaurant.

KARLOVASSI. *Aegeon* (M), tel. 33 466. 57 rooms. *Merope* (I), tel. 32
650, 80 rooms.

KOKARI. *Afroditi* (I), tel. 28 530. 42 rooms. *Kokkari Beach* (I), tel. 28
538. 45 rooms. Restaurant. For excellent food and friendly atmosphere, try
Stathis (I), a real find on the harbor. Open May to mid-October.

MARATHOKAMBOS. *Kerkis Bay* (I), tel. 31 574. 25 rooms. *Klimataria*
(I), tel. 31 412. 12 rooms. *Votsalakia* (I), tel. 31 444. 17 rooms. No restaurant.

PYTHAGÓRIO. *Doryssa Bay* (E), 700 yds. from town, tel. 61 360. 176
rooms. Beach, pool, tennis, minigolf. *Phito* (M), tel. 61 314. 75 bungalows
on beach. *Glicoriza Beach* (I), tel. 61 321. 62 rooms. *Ilios* (I), tel. 61 365. 33
rooms. *Polyxeni* (I), tel. 61 359. 23 rooms. No restaurant.

SÁMOS TOWN. *Aeolis* (E), tel. 28 904. 51 airconditioned rooms. In
upper town. *Eleana* (M), tel. 28 665. 15 rooms. *Xenia* (M), tel. 27 463. 31
rooms. Central and airconditioned. *Samos* (I), tel. 28 377. 83 rooms.

THE NORTHERN ISLANDS

Sporades, Limnos, Thassos and Samothrace

Although some of them have old histories, in general, the delightful islands of the Sporades are unmentioned by history and fable, and rely on their great natural beauty to attract visitors. From each one of them, there are tempting views of other islands and their tiny satellites, and it is a constant pleasure to sail between them, in good weather. They are a delight for yachtsmen, while from the air, this thick sprinkling of islets gives an amazing beauty to the sea, when flying to or from Kavala.

Exploring the Sporades

The Sporades, the Scattered Isles, are the handful of colored pebbles the gods were left with after creating the world and, as an afterthought, they flung them over the northwestern Aegean. Skýros, the southernmost and largest, consists of two very different regions; the southern part is bare and Cycladic, while the north is forested.

From Linária the port on the east coast, to Skýros town above the west coast, the road passes through a Cycladic country of brown, terraced hills and fig trees. Skýros is chiefly distinguished by the dramatically abrupt rock which supports the castle. It is a particularly attractive white village, in the cubist style of the Cyclades. The hospitable people will gladly show visitor their houses, and one or two interiors should be seen; the carved woodwork, when it takes the form of a balustrade to the upper room in a house is often old and attractive. The contemporary arts and crafts are, on the other hand, sometimes a little depressing. The pottery is prettily painted, but tends to be awkwardly shaped.

According to mythology, Achilles was hidden on Skýros by his mother Thetis, dressed as a girl, to keep him out of the Trojan war; it had been prophesied that his participation in it was essential to the success of the Greeks, but that he himself would be killed. By throwing jewelry and a sword among the playing children, Odysseus found the youngster he was looking for. In recent history, it is still remembered that the English poet Rupert Brooke died of septicaemia, in the First World War, off the south coast and Churchill, then First Lord of the Admiralty, stopped the war for a day so he could be buried in a beautiful olive grove at Tris Bóukes (an excursion by land or water from Linária). He is rather flatteringly commemorated by a statue of Immortal Poetry, by the Greek sculptor Tombros, erected outside Skýros town, looking at the beautiful sandy beach below.

The other Sporades are generally approached from Volos, after a journey through the lovely Pagasitic gulf, and round the peninsula of Magnesia, on which an invading Persian fleet once came to grief.

Skíathos

The first is Skíathos (shadow of Athos), a low-hilled, thickly wooded island, with a quiet idyllic beauty. It has an impressive harbor, protected and adorned by a great many little islets. This island has no ancient history; its most interesting son was Alexandros Papadiamandis (1855–1911), whose short stories are based on island life and tradition.

The town dates from 1830; it is prettily built on two hills, overlooking the great harbor and smaller lagoon, where caiques were built. When the Turks occupied the island in the 16th century, the inhabitants retired to an almost impregnable rock in the north, a village called Kastro, whose crumbling remains are dominated by the church of Christ.

Skíathos is popular with tourists, particularly the English, who have built a number of pleasant houses along the indented shore. Outstanding among the tranquil bays is the wonderful beach of Koukounariés (the stonepines) one of the best in the Aegean. A magnificent grove of these trees fringes a long sweep of sand; behind there is a charming inland lagoon, backed by maize fields and olive groves.

Equally enjoyable is a visit to the next island, Skópelos. This is also a green island, but its name means "rock", and rocky it is; when approached from Skíathos, its high uneven ridge makes it appear a different world.

The first port, Glóssa, is on the western side of the island; here the vegetation is very luxurious, and through the groves of olives and of fruit trees there are exquisite views of Skíathos, of the many scattered islets that lie in between, and of distant Euboea.

The exceptionally attractive island capital rises from a semi-circular bay, which faces north and thus provides little shelter. The houses, roofed in a beautiful soft grey slate, are built in a modified form of the style prevalent on the Pilio peninsula, but a very rich use of color is made on the walls, which are washed over in white or blue or red or ocher; the ridges and eaves of the roofs are picked out in white, which emphasizes their charming variety of shape.

Several small monasteries or convents, hiding among olive trees or shining out on the hillside round the gulf are pleasant objects for a short walk. The silver-green olives shade a soil more vividly colored than any other in the Aegean, sometimes of a fine reddish purple.

The specialty of Skópelos is plums, and in the season (August) you may watch them being home-dried in slow ovens, and sample them at various stages of the process. A final polish is put on with finger and thumb.

Alonissos, though no less fertile, is only sparsely populated. The idyllic peace and solitude of its many sandy beaches make it ideal for underwater fishing among the ruins of sunken cities and to the caves of surrounding islets.

The Islands of the Thracian Sea—Límnos

These three islands, though briefly united in the late Middle Ages under the Genoese Gateluzzi princes, whose main seat was in Lesbos, present all the astounding natural and cultural variety of the Aegean.

Límnos, the largest, with the best beaches, is rich in story. Here

Hephaestos alighted, when thrown by his father, Zeus, out of heaven—he injured himself in the fall, and was represented as lame for ever afterwards. He became the patron god of this island, and when his wife, Aphrodite, committed adultery with Ares, the Limnian women neglected her worship. In revenge, she afflicted them with halitosis, and their husbands neglected *them*—in consequence of this every man on the island was massacred. Fortunately the "Argo" came this way, on the quest for the Golden Fleece; the Argonauts stayed two years in Límnos, and fathered a new generation—only Heracles remained obstinately on board the whole time, and refused to disembark. Límnos is also the scene of the legend of Philoctetes, the Greek Robinson Crusoe, who was marooned here by the Greeks on their way to Troy, left alone with an invincible bow, and an incurable wound whose stench made his proximity unendurable. Years later he was brought before the beleaguered city and killed in combat King Priam's son, Paris.

In pre-history, Límnos had a Tyrrheno-Pelasgian population, of which interesting traces remain; in history it was, in the 5th century, almost a colony of Athens. Later it went through many changes of ownership. The big, almost land-locked bay of Moúdros in the south was an allied base in the Gallipoli campaign in the First World War.

The island capital, Myrína, is a small town on the west side. There is a Genoese castle on a great rock, in whose face are also cut the outlines and streets of a pre-historic Pelasgian city. The Archeological Museum in the residence of the Turkish Pasha is noteworthy for its prehistoric exhibits.

Easy accessibility by air and the comfortable bungalows on the magnificent beach make this an agreeable place for a lengthy stay in the summer, for the climate is particularly dry and cool. In the evening, Mount Athos stands up against the sunset, a superb outline, and one of the most striking views in the Aegean. Its shadow is said to touch Límnos twice a year.

Excursions, on this low-hilled, unwooded island, are easy along paved roads. The ruins of antique Hephaestia are in the shallow Bounia bay in the north. Those seriously interested in pre-history should visit Palióhni, on the east coast, where Italian archeologists have uncovered four layers of settlements, the oldest dating from around 3500 B.C. A large Bronze Age city of about 2300 B.C. was connected with Troy, which is only some 60 miles away.

Samothrace

Samothráki (Samothrace) possesses a very distinctive beauty and interest; its high central massif, rising to the great peak of

Fengári (the mountain of the moon) makes it a landmark from far away. It is perhaps the finest of all Greek islands as seen from the sea.

The Sanctuary of the Great Gods, a panhellenic shrine, was the island's chief claim to fame in antiquity. This has been admirably excavated by New York University, under Dr. Karl Lehmann, and a museum has been built to house finds, and reconstructions. There is also a hostel for archeologists and for visitors: a small but pleasant bungalow.

The Great Gods of Samothrace, the Kabiri, were Thracian deities whom the Greeks, when they colonized the island, adapted to their own mythology. The Kabiri were gods of the underworld in a cult that centered on the least attractive aspect of the Great Goddess, as Hekate, goddess of the night and witchcraft, joined by Hades and Persephone. There was a public festival of the Great Gods every summer, and in addition there were mysteries into which candidates could be initiated at any time of the year; there were two stages of initiation, and those who sought the higher degree are believed to have been obliged to confess their major sins—a unique feature in ancient Greek worship. The historian Herodotus was an initiate, also Philip of Macedon, who is said to have met in Samothrace the Epirot princess who became his wife, and mother of the great Alexander.

Valley of the Sanctuary

The sanctuary lies in a peaceful valley, between dry streams, and under the rugged peak of St. George—the lower flanks of the mountain are grey-green with olives and above, the remarkable wall of the ancient city of Samothrace can be seen running up the slope till it reaches an outcrop of rock, under the peak. Paleópolis can be reached in some ten minutes from the hostel; from the jetty below, cruise passengers can visit the ruins with ease, if weather allows them to disembark—(this is not always the case; the Thracian sea can be very stormy).

In the sanctuary the temples and other buildings are carefully labeled by notices. The buildings were of two sorts, those belonging to the public festival of the Great Gods, and those which were used for the mysteries. The former include the base of the rotunda of Arsinöe: this was a room for the reception of representatives of various Greek states who attended the festival. It was erected by that remarkable queen of Macedon, who later married her brother, Ptolemy II, Philadelphus, and ruled Egypt with him as Arsinöe II, until her death in 270 B.C. It is the largest round building known in

Greek architecture; a reconstruction showing its elegant pilastered gallery is to be seen in the museum. Of the buildings pertaining to the mysteries, the Hieron, the holy of holies, most strikes the eye, as five Doric columns have been re-erected, composing the site into a more comprehensible and photogenic picture.

At the fountain, above the general level of the temples, Champoiseau, the French Consul in Adrianople, found the Winged Victory of Samothrace in 1863 and sent it to the Louvre. The statue is believed to be the work of a Rhodian sculptor, dedicated to Antigonus II of Macedon after the naval battle of Kos in 258 B.C., in which he and his allies defeated Ptolemy II.

Samothrace is a cool and refreshing place to stay in the summer; unfortunately the bathing, on the stony beach of Paléopolis, is not good. Those who are energetic will climb Fengari, if the weather is clear enough to promise a view. Poseidon sat on that peak to watch the Trojan war, and a mortal climber can see the Trojan Ida mountains and Athos, if the day is clear. Less enterprising walkers may follow the walls of the ancient city of Samothrace, and they will also wish to visit the towers of a Genoese fortress, on a small high rocky acropolis, overlooking the Thracian sea. On a clear day the mountains behind Alexandroupoli are seen, and you can catch a glimpse of Athos.

The Hora, a strikingly situated village, with a Genoese fort on a fine sugar-loaf rock, is under an hour's walk from Paléopolis. The best excursion to be made in Samothrace is the circumnavigation of the island, or at least a trip along the wild rocky southern shore as far as the cascade that falls into the sea from high up on a cliff face. In the course of this excursion you will enjoy a swim on the beautiful and deserted beach of Ammos. Only very calm weather is good enough for this whole day's outing.

Thassos

Greece's first off-shore oil and gas field, providing ten percent of consumption, has not interfered with the beauty and variety of Thassos or diminished the appeal of its fascinating antiquities and beautiful bathing beaches.

The capital is a pleasant village, built on the site of the ancient city, whose agora and other buildings lie among the houses. The circular memorial to the Parian colonizer Telesikles was restored in 200 B.C., when the agora was framed by marble porticos; the propylaea faced the Hellenistic altar and temple of Zeus Agoraios (Of the Market); two choragic monuments were added to the temple of Dionysos; and Heracles' 5th-century B.C. Ionic temple was enlarged with a ritual hall. But the most important vestige of the past is the grand enclosure of walls rising behind the village, up to a ridge of rock that at one point provided a natural fortification. Performances of ancient drama are once more given in summer in the Hellenistic theater, which the Romans converted into a gladiatorial arena in the 2nd century B.C. Much of the ancient *bas relief* sculpture has been allowed to remain *in situ*. Particularly noteworthy is the large statue of Silenus near the restored walls of the modern village.

Thassos was a prosperous ancient state, owning gold mines both in the island, and on the mainland. Thasian marble (to be seen both here, and in the Sanctuary of the Great Gods in Samothrace) was an important article of export, and Thasian wine was in high repute all over the eastern Mediterranean; jars in which it was exported have been found as far afield as Egypt and the shores of the Black Sea. Viniculture has dramatically deteriorated, and the present product is better avoided.

The museum contains a few things beautiful in themselves though the best finds from Thassos are in the Louvre.

Makrýammos (the long sand) is the finest bathing beach; it may be reached by a pleasant walk of half an hour, by bus, or (best) by motor boat—one sails under the ancient walls and acropolis of Thassos. As Makrýammos has become the preserve of the Xenia guests, Glyfáda, a pleasantly shady place on the west coast, is now more frequented. Beach follows beach along that coast, Rahóni being specially indicated for camping, but none are as idyllic as those below Panagia and Potamia in the north-east. The road climbs through a forest to these two villages, the first of which, with white houses in the style of architecture of the Pilio, one or two built across a running brook, is particularly worth a visit.

Thassos tends to fill up in the summer months because it is the weekend resort for eastern Macedonia. The circumnavigation of the island is as rewarding as a round trip by car, mostly along the shore. The road hugs the west coast to Limenaria (23 miles) and the infinite variety of scenery makes it worthwhile to bring over a car by ferryboat. Limenaria can also be reached by direct boat from Kavala. In spite of some mining activity, Limenaria has an attractive setting, with good bathing (both on the spot, and at the sandy beach of Pefkari, three miles south), and in the evening there is a noble view of the whole peninsula of Athos, ending in the Holy Mountain. The longer return trip (34 miles) along the east coast, passes near the marble quarries of Alyki where two ancient temples, two early Christian basilicas and numerous tombs have been unearthed, then turns north to Potamia and Panagia.

PRACTICAL INFORMATION FOR THE
NORTHERN ISLANDS

HOW TO GET THERE. There are daily flights from Athens and Thessaloniki to Limnos. In summer, there are two flights a day from Athens to Skíathos, and three a week from Thessaloniki. Daily from Athens to Alonissos. There are four ferries every day from Kavala to Thasos town, and at least one every day to Limenaria. Also at least nine ferries daily from Keramoti.

There are three boats every week from Samothrace to Alexandroupoli, as well as one every week that calls at Límnos on its way to Piraeus.

From Athens, you can get to the Sporades by taking the bus to the Euboean port of Kymi and then taking the daily boat to Linaria (Skyros) or the twice daily boat to Alonissos and Skópelos.

There is also a daily ferry from Agios Konstantinos (95 miles north of Athens) to Skíathos and Skópelos. Also from Agios Konstantinos, there is a twice weekly ferry to Límnos and a once weekly ferry to Samothrace. There is also a boat from Volos to Skíathos and Skópelos, and a daily hovercraft in the summer.

HOTELS AND RESTAURANTS. Book well in advance, unless you are happy to make do with a clean but very simple room in a private house. A pleasant diet can be based on the excellent green figs (*sýka*) of Skýros, a cheese called *graviéra* and seafood.

Alonissos

Galaxy (I), tel. 65 251. 37 rooms. *Marpounta* (I), tel. 65 219. 104 rooms in bungalows on beach.

Límnos

MYRINA. *Myrina Beach* (L), tel. 22 681/4. 125 bungalows. Pool, tennis, minigolf. *Kastro Beach* (M), tel. 22 772. 72 rooms. *Lemnos* (I), tel. 22 153. Most of the 29 rooms with showers. No restaurant.

There are several Inexpensive seafood taverns on the waterfront.

Samothrace

Niki Beach (I), tel. 41 561. 38 rooms.

Skíathos

AHLADIES. *Esperides* (E), tel. 42 245/6. 162 rooms. Pool, tennis, disco. *Belvedere* (I), tel. 42 475. 50 bungalows.

KOUKOUNARIES. *Skiathos Palace* (L), tel. 42 242/3. 201 rooms. Pool, tennis, nightclub. *Xenia* (M), tel. 42 041. 32 double rooms.

SKÍATHOS TOWN. *Alkyon* (M), tel. 42 981/5. 80 rooms. Airconditioned; disco. *Koukounaries* (I), tel. 42 048. 17 rooms. No restaurant,

TZANERIA. *Nostos* (E), tel. 42 420. 104 rooms. Not airconditioned; pool, tennis, disco.

Skópelos

GLOSSA. *Avra* (I), tel. 33 550. 28 rooms. Beach.

SKOPELOS TOWN. *Amalia* (M), tel. 22 688. 50 rooms. 500 yds from beach. *Aeolos* (I), tel. 22 233. 41 rooms. Beach; no restaurant. *Denise* (I), tel. 22 678. 22 rooms.

STAFYLOU. *Rigas* (I), tel. 22 618. 35 rooms. No restaurant.

Skýros

Xenia (M), tel. 91 209. 22 rooms. On one of the finest of the island beaches; one mile from the town.

Thassos

KINYRA. *Gerda* (I), tel. 31 278. 12 double rooms. No restaurant.

LIMENARIA. *Sgouridis* (I), tel. 51 241. 14 rooms. *Thalassies* (I), tel. 51 163. 17 rooms. No restaurant.

MAKRÝAMMOS. *Makryammos* (E), tel. 22 101. 206 bungalows on lovely beach. Pool, tennis, disco.

PANAGIA. *Golden Sand* (I), tel. 61 471. 11 rooms.

SKALA POTAMIAS. *Anagnostou* (I), tel. 61 277. 13 rooms. *Atlantis* (I), tel. 22 158. 8 rooms. *Kamelia* (I), tel. 61 463. 15 rooms. No restaurant.

SKALA RAHONIOU. *Argyro* (I), tel. 81 263. 29 rooms.

THASSOS TOWN. *Timoleon* (M), tel. 22 177. 30 rooms. No restaurant; near the inadequate beach. *Angelika* (I), tel. 22 387. 26 rooms. On beach. *Laïos* (I), tel. 22 309. 27 rooms. *Possidon* (I), tel. 22 381. 16 rooms. No restaurant.

CRETE

Europe's Oldest Civilization

by

PETER SHELDON

About 1600 B.C., while the rest of Europe was still in the grip of primitive barbarity, one of the most brilliant and amazing civilizations the world was ever to know approached its final climax. The sophisticated elegance of King Minos' court on the island of Crete (Kríti) was an appropriate manifestation of imperial power patiently built up over centuries.

Legendary Minos, son of Zeus, in the shape of a bull, and Europa, won fame for his incorruptible justice, which earned him, after his death, a place on the high court in the underworld. His name seems to have been adopted as a sacred title by his successors, ruling as priest-kings of a strange religion, over which bulls held a frightening, though ill-defined sway. If the original Minos led his Neolithic people between 4000 and 3000 B.C. from Syria to Crete, if he founded the prominent dynasty of Knossós in about 2000 B.C., or if he only united the island politically in about 1600 B.C., remains a matter for conjecture; though the latter theory is now most widely accepted. The Minoans were dark, almost certainly Asiatic; but their culture, though Egyptian-inspired, evolved in a uniquely original direction and produced a truly great civilization in the 600 years of the middle and late Minoan periods.

The strong central government gloried in the construction of the splendid palaces of Knossós and Phaestos, from which Minos ruled a maritime empire including the Cyclades, the Peloponnese and parts of Sicily. These conquests were made by the first organized royal navy in history, as distinct from earlier, individual trading ventures. The government of the islands was entrusted to royal princes, while heavy tributes were exacted from the Mycenaean principalities on the mainland. These extremely onerous tributes might have been the cause for a disastrous invasion of Crete by the subject peoples. But it might well have been a tidal wave and earthquakes caused by the explosion of the Thira volcano in 1450 B.C., even more devastating than the calamity which brought down the first palaces in about 1700 B.C., that led to the downfall of Knossós.

The last Minos was plagued with a nymphomaniac wife, Pasiphae, who, in the best family tradition, had fallen desperately in love with a gorgeous white bull. Daedalus, an Athenian craftsman of wondrous skill, undertook to satisfy the queen's desire. He built a hollow wooden cow, upholstered with a cow's hide, and concealing Pasiphae in the lifelike dummy brought about the union which she craved. The fruit of this union was the Minotaur whose bull's head on a human body confirmed the sad truth that the sins of parents are visited on the children.

To avoid scandal Daedalus constructed a labyrinth, where Pasiphae's disgrace was concealed, entertained—one wonders how—by a yearly tribute of seven youths and seven maidens from Athens. Prince Theseus insisted on being included among the victims and helped by Minos' daughter, Ariadne, returned safe from the labyrinth after slaying the unlovable cross-breed.

Ariadne, who seems to have taken all the initiative in the courtship in accordance with the hereditary strain, prevailed on Theseus to take her along. However, by the time the couple reached Naxos, Theseus was eager to effect a second escape from his one-time savior, only to succumb finally to Ariadne's sister Phaedra. Ariadne had the best of both worlds, as abandoned by her hero she found favor with a god, Dionysos.

Daedalus had become involved in the Theseus affair, as it was he who had thought of the silken thread by which the hero made good his escape from the labyrinth. Imprisoned with his son Icarus in the now empty maze, Daedalus' ingenuity proved equal to the occasion. He made two pairs of wings, attached them with wax to the shoulders and rose with his son skywards. In spite of his father's warning, Icarus could not resist the temptation of soaring higher and higher, till the sun melted the wax. He fell and was drowned near the island which is called in his memory Icaria. Daedalus succeeded in reaching the haven of King Cocalus' court in Sicily, where Minos, arriving in hot pursuit, was done to death by the king's daughters. The Cretan fleet was destroyed by the Sicilians, and the whole legend of Theseus culminating in Minos' inglorious end lends credit to the invasion theory.

The golden Minoan days were followed by the not entirely inglorious twilight of Mycenaean rule. King Idomeneus led a Cretan contingent against Troy, but by 1200 B.C. the island was again divided into primitive city-states, constantly at war. With the arrival of the Dorians in the following century, the long night of the Iron Age descended and even the subsequent flowering of classical culture on the Greek mainland found only a weak reflection on Crete. In 66 B.C. it was occupied by the Romans, as it had become a pirates' nest. But the piratic tradition was revived by the Arabs in the 9th and 10th century, when the swift Moslem galleys dominated the eastern Mediterranean up to the Byzantine reconquest in 961. As a consequence of the Fourth Crusade the Venetians installed themselves for almost 500 years, until the island fell to the last onslaught of the Turkish hordes. For 200 years one insurrection followed another, suppressed with increasing ferocity by the sultans, who were at last forced to grant home-rule under a Greek prince. But not till 1913 was Crete definitely incorporated into Greece and the exchange of population in 1923 removed the Moslem minority from the island. The undaunted resistance of Greek, British and Anzac forces against the German airborne invasion in World War II was worthy of the long heroic Cretan history.

Exploring Crete

Though some northcoast resorts like Ágios Nikólaos and Mália have been overdeveloped, the interior and the southcoast have remained largely untouched. All the 3,327 square miles of Greece's largest island are scenically rewarding, yet despite the attractions of sea and mountains, the mystery surrounding Europe's first civilization and empire draws an equal number of visitors to Crete. And Iráklio, with a population of 90,000 the biggest town and commercial center, is the obvious choice for an exploration of the fabulous Minoan palaces.

Yet the first impressions belong to a more recent past, measured in centuries and not millennia. The 13th-century church of San Marco, used for exhibitions, and the restored Renaissance Loggia overlook the baroque Lion Fountain on Iráklio's central Venizelou Square. The Metropolis of Agios Minas is garishly 19th-century, but *Agia Katerina* contains six large icons by Damaskinos, the Cretan School's outstanding representative and teacher of El Greco. Impressive ramparts (where Greece's best-known modern writer, Nikos Kazantzakis, is buried under a wooden cross bearing a quotation from his *Zorba the Greek*) and the Koulé fortress guarding the Venetian port and facing the barren island of Día, now a hunting area, bear testimony to the 24-year siege before the Venetians under Morosini finally surrendered to the Turkish Vizier Achmed Kiuprili in 1669. But the waterfront is unusually forbidding, with hardly any taverns or cafés. The Historical Museum contains a variety of Roman and Byzantine finds.

When the foundations of the Cretan University's medical school were laid alongside the Knossos road, the British Archeological School unearthed a wealth of interesting objects from an antique cemetery used from 1400 B.C. to A.D. 500. A jumble of human bones with fine knife marks like butcher's cuts seems to indicate that the Minoans were not averse to occasional cannibalism, though subsequent finds at Aharnes and Knossos allow the more charitable interpretation of human sacrifices.

Minoan Splendor

The Archeological Museum stands in a class of its own, guarding practically all the Minoan treasures brought to light by the various excavations. The civilization of 2,000 years is superbly illustrated by an unique collection of pottery and jewelry, including the famous seal-stones with Linear B script, which first attracted Sir Arthur Evans to Knossós. The discovery by another Englishman, Michael Ventris, that Linear B is Greek, and the decipherment of hundreds of clay tablets found in the Minoan palaces as well as on Mycenaean sites on the mainland, alas exclusively store inventories, might indicate that the Minos who united Crete in about 1600 B.C. was an Achaean who usurped the throne. The hieroglyphic inscription winding spiralwise on both sides of the famous terracotta Phaestos disc seems likewise Achaean Greek, a prayer to the gods for help (deciphering was further confused in 1980, when Linear A was claimed to be an unknown Indo-Germanic language). The frescos most catch the eye: delightfully sophisticated representations of broad-shouldered, slim-waisted youths; ritual processions; scenes from the bull ring, far more dangerous than any toreador would dare, as the youth or girl took the bull by the horn when he lowered his head to toss, and somersaulted over his back;

and groups of bare-breasted court ladies, whose puffed sleeves and flounced skirts led a French archeologist to exclaim in surprise "des Parisiennes"—a name still applied to the fresco.

This introduction to a brilliant culture is climaxed by a visit to the palace of Knossós, three miles inland. Only the intuition of Schliemann would have suspected that the huge mound hemmed in by low hills covered one of the most amazing archeological sites. Troy and Mycenae, Tiryns and Knossós, what a record of sensational finds, yet Turkish obstruction prevented Schliemann from exploring his last discovery. Cretan independence made it possible for Evans to start excavations in 1900 and find a forgotten civilization.

The original palace built about 2000 B.C. was destroyed some 300 years later and replaced by a more magnificent group of buildings, now partly reconstructed. Evans has been attacked for these reconstructions, paid for out of his own pocket to the tune of £250,000 in the days when pounds came as golden sovereigns and were worth a great deal more than they are today. But besides giving the layman an approximate idea of Minoan architecture, which relied largely on color effects, the much abused reinforced concrete restoration was essential to preserve the wonderfully theatrical great staircase and the throne room, where the oldest throne in Europe still stands unguarded.

Ruins in Crete tend to be particularly ruinous, not only because of their venerable age, but also because of the poorness of the building materials. The gaudily painted, downward-tapering wooden columns and beams supporting the fragile gypsum and stucco facades had been charred in the devastating fire of 1450 B.C. and only falling rubble sustained the delicate fabric. The rubble had to be replaced in the course of excavation, and reinforced concrete was used.

How much is owed to Sir Arthur Evans becomes apparent in the incomparably more splendid setting of Festós (Phaestos). Near the southern shores a conglomeration of buildings rose on a solitary hill dominating the lovely plain of Messara. Only the foundations remain, yet with the memories of Knossós fresh in mind it is possible to conjure up a picture of what the palace must have looked like. To sit on the grandiose staircase in the moonlight, resurrecting past splendor, is one of those unforgettable experiences which only few sites can provide. Still closer to the sea lies the royal villa of Agia Triada, the elegant country house of a Minoan prince.

The remains of the 1600 B.C. villa near Arhanés, nine miles south of Knossós, are less interesting than the 14th-century frescos in the two village churches, or Mt. Iouktas, supposedly Zeus' tomb.

Geography determined the choice of Knossós and Phaestos at

the beginning and end of the only relatively easy north-south passage in the island's center. Crete is 160 miles from east to west, dissected by an unbroken range rising to almost 8,000 feet in the western White Mountains, the central Mount Ídi (Ida) and the eastern Dikti Mountains. Yet the island is never more than 38 miles wide, narrowing to eight miles on the isthmus of Ierapetra.

From Agía Varvára, on the highway connecting the two palaces, a branch right (west) opens up the spectacular southern slopes of Mount Ídi. The frescos of the Vrondísi monastery and of Agios Fanourios at Valsamonéro are attributed to El Greco but were most likely painted in an earlier century. High above is the Spíleon Kamáron, the cave in which the loveliest Minoan pottery, the *Kamáres,* were found.

Górtys, between the northern vineyards and the fertile plain of Messara, was the Roman capital of Crete. Ruins of an Egyptian sanctuary, a temple of Apollo and a Christian basilica are scattered among the olive groves. Embedded in the wall of the Roman Odeon is the famous 5th-century law code of Gortys, the fountainhead of Greek justice. The port of Phaestos, Mátala, was taken over by Górtys and lately by a nudist colony, which appropriated the caves carved as refuge against pirates into the cliff towering over the fine beach. To the north, at Kommos, American and Canadian archeologists are bringing to light the Minoan port, connected by a wide paved road with Phaestos. Flourishing from 2000 to 1300 B.C., it revived as a sanctuary with a unique proto-geometric temple, succeeded by an archaic and a Hellenistic shrine, to be finally abandoned in about A.D. 125.

The Minoan royal villa of Agía Triáda stands on a hill near the beach of Tymbáki. To the west, Agía Galíni (St. Serenity) lives up to its name as the South's safest harbor. The quickest drive back to the north coast is via Spilí to Réthymno; the finer scenery, however, is along the Platiés river, passing a unique medieval bridge and a minor Minoan palace at Monastiráki, to Platánes.

The Hidden Highland

It is 35 miles from Iráklio to Ágios Nikólaos, a deservedly popular summer resort between the sea and a theatrical lagoon. The road follows the coast east past the beaches of Háni Kókini, Góurnes, Góuves, Liménas Hersoníssou and Stalída to the golden sands of Maliá (22 miles), where foundations of another, less elaborate Minoan palace crown a headland; then passes through a 270-yard tunnel to Neápoli. At Hersónissos a 20-mile-long branch road climbs to the Lassithi plateau. A row of picturesque Venetian windmills—disused for centuries, but restored as a backdrop for the film of Kazantzakis' *Christ Recrucified*—guards the ridge of a dramatically barren mountain. Behind that some 15 square miles of an idyllic tabletop plateau open up at an altitude of 2,400 feet, with some ten thousand flowerlike wheels whose sails turn in the constant breeze to draw the water from the wells irrigating the potato fields. The road skirts the plain linking Tzermiádo with most of the other 17 villages, to Psihró (The Cold), named after the icy spring beneath the huge plane tree in the village square. You can drive almost to the entrance of the perpendicular cave (guide required) on Mount Díkti which disputes with one on Mount Ídi the honor of being the birthplace of Zeus. The numerous votive offerings (now at the Iráklio museum) that were found at the bottom of the frightening chasm bear witness to the importance of the sanctuary in antiquity. The eastern descent from the highland to Ágios Nikólaos is a few miles longer.

Opposite Elóunda, seven miles north of Ágios Nikólaos, is the island of Spinalónga, protected by an imposing Venetian fortress for 100 years after all Crete had fallen to the Turks. The grim ramparts enclosed a leper colony till 1958.

The same distance southeast is Goúrnia, the best-preserved ruins of a Minoan town as distinct from the palaces. The most striking feature is the narrowness of the streets and the smallness of the domestic quarters. Turning right (south) at Pahiá Amos you reach the south coast at the excellent beach of Ierapetra after only eleven miles. To the east, at Koutsounári, an experiment to increase the villagers' livelihood from tourism, has been made by doing up some genuine cottages. The north coast highway follows the magnificent gulf of Mirabéllo to Sitía, the easternmost port, with a good beach and pleasant seaside taverns.

Though Toplóu Monastery contains a magnificent icon painted by Kornaros in 1770, the fortified Cretan monasteries cannot rival the splendor of their mainland counterparts. The road continues to Paleókastro on the east coast. The branch north ends at the ruins of antique Itanos after passing the palm grove of Vaï on a beautiful sandy bay. The branch south leads to the remains of a 17th-century B.C. palace, near the beach of Kato Zákros. The palace conforms to the traditional plan, but the bathtubs were supplemented by a small swimming pool in what seems to have been the main Minoan naval base. The site had never been plundered, but huge lumps of volcanic debris had been flung across the 80 miles from Thira, which greatly strengthens the theory that the fall of the Minoan Empire was primarily due to the aftermath of the Thira eruption and not a Mycenaean invasion.

Arkadi and the White Mountains

The 90 miles west from Iráklio to Haniá fully display the varied beauty of the Cretan landscape. From the inland road you may branch left to Anogia and then a spectacular 14 miles under towering peaks to the Idéon Ándron, Zeus' alternative birthplace, continue westwards to the village of Melidóni, where a large cave has now been opened to the public.

Bypassing the beach of Agía Pelagía, the coastal highway rejoins the sea at Fodéle, where Domenikos Theotokopoulos, the famed El Greco, was born in 1541. After passing Pánormos, a branch leads 11 miles inland (southeast) to the monastery of Arkadi, an interesting example of Greek-Venetian rococo. Believed to have been founded by the Emperor Heraclius in the 7th century, the monastery played a prominent part in the successive risings of the 19th century. On November 7, 1866, the Turks were on the point of taking it by storm, when the Abbot Gabriel ordered the refectory to be blown up, killing the defenders together with 3,000 assailants. This heroic sacrifice is commemorated every year as the national Cretan holiday.

Réthymno, halfway to Haniá, has the liveliest waterfront below the arcades of 16th-century houses. St. Nicholas and the Rector's Palace have been restored within the ramparts of the huge Venetian fortress, on the acropolis of ancient Rithymna. The small archeological museum in the Venetian Loggia contains an interesting coin collection. The annual Wine Festival is held in the Municipal Park in the second half of July.

The foothills of the White Mountains straggle closer to the sea than those of Mount Ídi, and the road follows the coast till Georgioupoli. At Vrýsses (Springs) huge plane trees shade the roadfork to Sfakiá, where the tall blond descendants of the Doric invaders of 1000 B.C. have preserved their racial purity and characteristics in a way unique in much-conquered Greece. Sfakiá is often likened to the Mani in the Peloponnese, and there are indeed many points of resemblance in these two wild and inaccessible regions, where the way of life has hardly changed over the centuries, where vendetta exterminated whole families and put the women into perpetual mourning for some relative killed.

On the whole both districts were little bothered by the foreign overlords, but successive waves of refugees diluted the ancient Hellenic stock in the Mani, and the continuous savage feuds there were not relieved by the homeric carousing and feasting of Sfakiá. Enormous quantities of a fierce liquor have to be consumed, this *tsipouro* often even taking the place of morning coffee. To fall behind one's host is considered a sign of contemptible effeminacy, so the choice lies between scorn and drunken stupor.

The road ascends through increasingly barren and desolate country by a steep gorge, snowbound for many weeks each winter. Remote, inaccessible hamlets can be barely distinguished on the precipitous slopes. At Sfakiá, a fairly large village on the southern sea, the road turns east to follow the rugged coast which abounds in lonely coves and sandy beaches, to link up with the south axis near the fishing village of Plakiás.

Close to the shore stand the ruins of Frankgokástello, sole reminder of a vain Venetian attempt at ruling the ungovernable mountains. Scene of particularly heavy fighting, culminating in a wholesale massacre of the local population by the Turks in 1828, the castle has been haunted for over a century. At dawn during May knights in shining armor have been observed by a large number of people manning the crumbling walls and towers.

After a visit to this land where time has stood still, it needs a violent wrench to return to modernity at Soúda, the important naval base in the large northern bay. Atop a hill lie the ruins of ancient Áptera, Apollo's Doric and Demeter's Hellenistic temple, a Roman theater and vast underground cistern, still partly encircled by ramparts. Soúda is now the harbor of Haniá, as the Venetian port round which the town was built cannot accommodate modern steamers. The old port is now given to caiques and smaller craft, which makes an evening in the taverns encircling the harbor-basin, or in the café in the former mosque, all the more picturesque. The Cretan's capital's tall 18th-century houses lend it the befitting dignity, which extends to the well-planned modern suburbs. The Venetian Church of San Francisco has been turned into an archeological museum, the historical museum is dedicated to mementos of Venizelos, and the naval museum in the Old Port displays ships' models from the triremes of antiquity onwards. In the small zoo in the Public Gardens are some kri-kri, the wild goats of Crete; nearby are the foundations of a Minoan town.

From the vast government building a shady avenue leads to the Halépa suburb facing the open sea, a favorite stroll of young and old in the evening. The road continues up the rocky promontory of Akrotiri, separating Haniá from Soúda Bay. Among the pine trees lie the tombs of the illustrious Cretan statesmen Eleutherios Venizelos and his son Sophocles, likewise prime minister. Higher up you get some breathtaking views of Haniá before turning inland to the monastery of Agía Triáda, or crossing over to the airport.

The coastal road continues west via Agia Marina Maléme, which saw some of the heaviest fighting in 1941, to Kolymbári, where the Orthodox Academy's huge congress hall near the 15th-century Gonias monastery is used for international conferences. An ancient temple and theater stand in the 16th-century Venetian castle above the long but shadeless beach at Kíssamos in the western bay.

Several scenic roads lead from the north coast into the mountainous interior and to the splendid beach of Paleohóra on the south coast. Even the great White Mountains are easily accessible by a road that climbs via Fóurnes and Láki to Omalós, where a zigzag path descends steeply 2,500 ft. to the tremendous Samaría Gorge—closed November through March—that splits the cliffs for eight miles down to Agía Roúmeli on the Libyan Sea, where Greece's first sun-thermal station provides electricity. Boats convey the weary walker to Sfakía. Yet even more remarkable than the landscape is the vitality of the inheritors of the oldest European civilization.

PRACTICAL INFORMATION FOR CRETE

 WHEN TO COME. Crete is big enough to offer a variety of attractions all the year round. Winters are mild and hotels in the bigger towns are equipped with central heating, so that there is no obstacle to exploring the Minoan sites undisturbed by the crowds of the tourist season. Though snow lies on the high mountains till May, it practically never snows on the coast. Spring is the best time: it comes about the end of March. Wine Festival at Dafnés, near Iráklio, mid-July.

 HOW TO GET ABOUT. Iráklio international airport is connected to several European capitals. There are also six flights daily from Athens, one from Rhodes, Mykonos and Thira in summer. There are also three flights every day between Athens and Hania. The daily ferries from Piraeus to both Iraklio and Hania, about 11 hours, are complemented by a catamaran taking 200 passengers in 5 hours from Piraeus to Rethymno.

On the island itself, there are excellent roads along both the north and the south coasts. These are linked by a number of good north/south roads. Buses are cheap and frequent, but car hire is expensive.

 HOTELS AND RESTAURANTS. Crete has a large number of modern hotels and bungalows. Some hotels in the towns stay open during the winter, offering reductions of between 10 and 40%. Package tours dominate the scene at all times. There are also furnished flats and rooms in private houses.

Except in the luxury hotels, food varies from the uninteresting to the downright unappetizing. But seaside taverns provide fresh fish, grilled or fried. In season, *lagós* (hare) will often be on the menu. If you like goat's cheese, try *manóuri; myzíthra* is a creamy sheep's cheese. Both are eaten with honey by the locals. *Anthótyri* and *graviéra* should also be sampled. Of the local wines, *Mirabello* and *Minos,* red or white, are best. But beware topping up too liberally with *tsikoudiá*, a Cretan ouzo with a kick.

AGIA GALINI. *Astoria* (I), tel. 91 253. 22 rooms. The only (I) hotel, among some 15 others, with a restaurant; also largest and closest to beach.

AGIA MARINA. *Santa Marina* (M), tel. 48 460. 66 rooms. On beach.

AGIA PELAGIA. *Capsis Beach* (E), tel. 233 395/7. 554 rooms in central block and bungalows. Pool, tennis, minigolf and disco.

AGIA ROUMELI. *Agia Roumeli* (I), tel. 91 293. 9 rooms. No restaurant.

AGIOS NIKOLAOS. *Minos Beach* (L), tel. 22 345/9. 118 bungalows, not airconditioned. Minigolf. *Minos Palace* (L), tel. 23 800. 151 rooms, on headland facing town. Both on small beaches, pools. *Mirabello Village* (L), 131 rooms in central block and bungalows. Pool, tennis and minigolf.
Hermes (E), tel. 28 253/6. 204 rooms. Minigolf and disco. On the town seafront. *Mirabello* (E), tel. 28 400/5. 174 rooms.
Ariadni Beach (M), tel. 22 741/4. 76 bungalows. *Coral* (M), tel. 28 363/7. 170 rooms. On seafront, with roofgarden pool. *El Greco* (M), tel. 28 894. 38 rooms. *Rhea* (M), tel. 28 321/3. 113 rooms. Disco on 10th floor.
Akratos (I), tel. 22 721. 31 rooms. *Almyros Beach* (I), tel. 22 865. 38 rooms. *Apollon* (I), tel. 23 023. 60 rooms. *Creta* (I), 28 893/4. 27 rooms. *Du Lac* (I), tel. 22 711. 40 rooms. No restaurant.
Restaurants. *Ariadni*, *Cretan* and *Vassilis* at 18, 10 and 16 Iosif Koundourou, as well as *Avra* and *Rififi* in Akti Koundourou, are all Moderate.

AKROTIRI. *Tzanakaki Beach* (I), tel. 64 363. 35 rooms.

AMOUDARA. *Agapi Beach* (E), tel. 225 501. 203 rooms. Beach, pool, tennis. *Creta Beach* (E), tel. 286 301/5. 114 rooms. Pool. *Dolphin Bay* (E), tel. 821 276/7. 141 rooms. Not airconditioned; pool, tennis.

ELOUNDA. *Astir Palace Elounda Bay* (L), tel. 41 580/5. 297 rooms, 3 suites. On beach with pool, tennis, minigolf and nightclub. *Elounda Beach* (L), tel. 41 412. 301 rooms. Beach, pool, tennis, minigolf and nightclub. *Elounda Marmin* (E), tel. 41 535. 58 rooms. *Aristea* (I), tel. 41 300. 37 rooms. On beach, with tennis and minigolf.

GEORGIOUPOLI. *Gorgona* (I), tel. 22 378. 38 rooms. Disco.

GÓURNES. *America* (M), tel. 761 231. 44 rooms. 550 yds from beach.

GÓUVES. *Candia Beach* (E), tel. 41 241/6. 217 rooms. Public rooms only airconditioned. On beach, with pool, tennis, minigolf and disco. *Marina* (E), tel. 41 361/5. 250 rooms. On beach, with pool, tennis, minigolf and disco. *Aphrodite* (M), tel. 41 271. 234 rooms. *Christi Apartments* (M), tel. 41 278. 32 furnished flats. *Mon Repos* (I), tel. 41 280. 37 rooms.

HANIA. *Kydon* (E), tel. 26 190/4. 117 rooms, 8 suites. Disco. *Doma* (M), tel. 21 772. 29 rooms. *Porto Veneziano* (M), tel. 29 311. 63 rooms. In a converted Venetian mansion on the old port; airconditioned. *Samaria* (M), tel. 51 551. 58 rooms. Airconditioned; no restaurant. *Xenia* (M), tel. 24 561. 44 double rooms. In the Venetian fortress; closest to the town beach. *Canea* (I), tel. 24 673. 49 rooms. No restaurant. *Kriti* (I), tel. 21 881. 88 rooms. Pool. *Aptera Beach* (I), tel. 22 636. 46 bungalows. 2 miles west.

Restaurants. The setting of the openair taverns round the old port is more pleasing than the fare; likewise for the original tavern cum cafe, *Aposperida*, on several floors in a 17th-century soap factory. All Moderate.

HANI KOKINI. *Arina Sand* (E), tel. 761 349. 233 rooms in central block and bungalows. Tennis. *Knossos Beach* (E), tel. 288 450. 106 rooms in central block and bungalows. Partly airconditioned. *Themis Beach* (E), tel. 761 374. 124 rooms. All with pool, minigolf and disco. *Danae* (I), tel. 761 375. 18 rooms. Small pool.

IERAPETRA. *Ferma Beach* (E), tel. 28 418. 89 rooms and bungalows. Pool; tennis. *Petra Mare* (E), tel. 23 341/8. 150 rooms, 78 suites. Beach, pool, nightclub. *Atlantis* (I), tel. 28 555. 69 rooms. Airconditioned.

IRÁKLIO. *Astoria* (E), tel. 285 025. 141 rooms. *Atlantis* (E), tel. 288 241. 164 rooms. *Galaxy* (E), tel. 236 421. 148 rooms. All with pool and disco. *Esperia* (M), tel. 288 211. 54 rooms. *Mediterranean* (M), tel. 289 331. 55 rooms. The only airconditioned hotel with restaurant in this category. *Asterion* (I), tel. 224 981. 60 rooms. Roofgarden. *Athinaïkon* (I), tel. 234 834. 40 rooms. *Castello* (I), tel. 241 771. 64 rooms. Roofgarden. *Daedalos* (I), tel. 224 391. 60 rooms. Airconditioned; no restaurant. *Grabelles* (I), tel. 235 086. 37 rooms. Airconditioned. On the sea but no beach, and one mile out at Poros is *Galini* (I), tel. 288 223. 52 rooms. *Poseidon* (I), tel. 285 859. 26 rooms.

Restaurants. Platia Venizelou is a prettier setting than Daedalou in the same central pedestrian zone, but the food is equally poor in all the openair Inexpensive establishments. *Caprice* is closest to the lovely Morosini fountain, *Klimataria* in Daedalou has efficient service, but the less said about the food the better. Fresh fish at the *Maxim Fish Tavern*, Koroneou 5, and *Ta Psaria*, opposite the sea fortress. All are Moderate.

Kandra Kitchen of San Francisco organizes badly-needed 6-day cooking classes Apr.–Oct.

KALO HORIO. *Istron Bay* (L), tel. 22 850/1. 106 rooms. Pool, tennis. *Elpida* (M), tel. 22 854. 46 rooms.

KARTEROS. *Minoa Palace* (E), tel. 225 333/6. 124 rooms. *Karteros* (M), tel. 225 231. 54 rooms. *Motel Xenia* (M), tel. 281 841. 42 double rooms.

KATO GALATAS. *Panorama* (E), tel. 54 200/5. 150 rooms. Partly airconditioned; pool and disco.

KÍSSAMOS. *Kastron* (I), tel. 22 140. 11 rooms. *Kissamos* (I), tel. 22 086. 16 rooms. No restaurant.

KOLYMBARI. *Rose Marie* (I), tel. 21 220. 9 rooms.

LIMÉNAS HERSONÍSSOU. *Creta Maris* (L), tel. 22 115/30. 516 rooms in hotel and bungalows. Pool, tennis, nightclub. *Belvedere* (E), tel. 22 010/5. 296 rooms in central block and bungalows. Pool, tennis, disco. *Lyttos* (E), tel. 22 575/8. 326 rooms. Beach, pool, tennis, disco. *Glaros* (M), tel. 22 106. 141 rooms. *Heronissos* (M), tel. 22 501. 89 rooms. *Nora* (M), tel. 22 271/5. 181 rooms. Pool, disco. *Sergios* (M), tel. 22 583. 75 rooms. *Albatros* (I), tel. 22 144. 74 rooms. *Eva* (I), tel. 22 090. 33 rooms. Airconditioned; disco. *Ilios* (I), tel. 22 500. 47 rooms. *Iro* (I), tel. 22 136. 41 rooms. *Palmera* (I), tel. 22 481. 72 rooms. *Zorbas* (I), tel. 22 075. 22 rooms. The best-equipped of some 20 (I) hotels on or near the beach.

LINOPERAMATA. *Apollonia Beach* (E), tel. 223 766/9. 309 rooms in central block and bungalows. Disco. *Zeus Beach* (E), tel. 223 761/5. 395 rooms. Both on beach, with pool, tennis, minigolf.

MALEME. *Crete Chandris* (E), tel. 91 221/8. 414 rooms in central block and bungalows. Pool, tennis, disco.

MALIA. *Ikaros Village* (E), tel. 31 267/9. 179 rooms in a German-designed "typical" Greek village. *Kernos Beach* (E), tel. 31 421/5. 246 rooms in central block and bungalows. *Sirens Beach* (E), tel. 31 321/5. 228 rooms. Disco. All have beach, pool and tennis. *Kostas* (M), tel. 31 485/8. 30 rooms. *Malia Beach* (M), tel. 31 301/3. 186 rooms. *Sofokles Beach* (I), tel. 31 476. 44 rooms. The largest among some 20 Inexpensive hotels near the beach.

MATALA. *Matala Bay* (I), tel. 22 100. 55 rooms. Disco; 500 yds. from beach.

PAHIA AMMOS. *Golden Beach* (I), tel. 93 278. 12 rooms. Beach and pool.

PALEOHORA. *Elman* (M), tel. 41 412. 23 furnished apartments. Disco. *Livykon* (I), tel. 41 250. 15 rooms.

PANORMOS. *Lavris* (M), tel. 51 226. 28 rooms. Pool, tennis, minigolf. *Panormos Beach* (I), tel. 51 297. 31 rooms.

PLAKIAS. *Kalypso Cretan Village* (E), tel. 23 655. 102 bungalows on beach. *Alianthos* (I), tel. 31 227. 18 rooms. Airconditioned; beach, disco. *Lamon* (I), tel. 31 205. 23 rooms.

RAPANIANA. *Olympic* (I), tel. 22 483. 34 rooms. 300 yds from beach.

RETHYMNO. *Braskos* (M), tel. 23 721. 78 rooms. Disco. *Cretan Star* (M), tel. 22 056. 211 rooms. Airconditioned; tennis. *Ideon* (M), tel. 28 667. 71 rooms. *Xenia* (M), tel. 29 111. 25 rooms. The only directly on the excellent town beach. *Minos* (I), tel. 24 173. 46 rooms. The largest of some 20 adequate Inexpensive hotels; none with restaurants. *YWCA* (HEN), tel. 23 324, 26 rooms.

On beaches east of the town: *El Greco* (E), tel. 71 281. 307 rooms. *Rithymna* (E), tel. 29 491. 538 rooms. Both with central block and bungalows, pool, tennis, minigolf, disco.

Restaurants. Fresh seafood in the Inexpensive-to-Moderate fish taverns in the arcades along the waterfront; eat in the open at night.

RODIA. *Rogdia* (I), tel. 22 763. 22 rooms.

SITIA. *Sitian Beach* (E), tel. 28 821/4. 162 rooms. Only public rooms airconditioned; pool, tennis, disco. *Maresol* (M), tel. 28 933. 20 bungalows. Pool, tennis. *Itanos* (I), tel. 22 146. 72 rooms. Airconditioned; the only hotel with restaurant and largest among some 10 other Inexpensive establishments.

STALÍDA. *Anthoussa Beach* (E), tel. 31 380/2. 167 rooms. Pool, tennis. *Amazones Villas* (M), tel. 31 488. 51 furnished apartments. *Blue Sea* (M), tel. 31 371/4. 197 rooms in bungalows. Beach, pool, disco. *Heliotrope* (I), tel. 31 515. 70 rooms. *Stalis* (I), tel. 31 246. 44 rooms.

TYMBAKI. *Penelope* (I), tel. 51 621. 10 rooms. No restaurant.

TZERMIADO. *Kourites* (I), tel. 22 194. 7 rooms.

ZAKROS. *Zakros* (I), tel. 28 479. 16 rooms, no restaurant.

YOUTH HOSTELS. These are at: *Agios Nikolaos,* 60 beds; *Iraklio,* 120 beds; *Malia,* 35 beds; *Sitia,* 30 beds.

MOUNTAIN REFUGES. Two in the White Mountains, one on Mount Idi.

USEFUL ADDRESSES. GNTO, Akti Tombazi 6, Old Port, Hania, tel. 26 426; Xanthoudidou 1, Iraklio, tel. 222 487.

TOURIST
VOCABULARY

TOURIST VOCABULARY

Pronunciation. Our Greek orthography is as phonetical as is practicable. The tonic (heavy) accent is indicated everywhere. Certain letters are pronounced as under:

a—as in father
e—as in help
i—as in hit
l—as in sleep
u—as in soon

o—as in hot
gh (or g)—as in get
kh (or ch)—a guttural h
th—as in theory

GENERALITIES

Do you speak English . . . French . . . German?	Miláte angliká . . . galliká . . . germaniká?
Yes—no	Málista or Né—óchi
Impossible	Adínaton
Good morning—Good day	Kaliméra
Good evening—Good night	Kalispéra—kaliníkta
Goodbye—*Au revoir*	Kalí andámosi
Mister—Madam—Miss	Kírie—kiría—despinís
Please	Parakaló
Excuse me	Me sinchórite *or* signómi
How are you?	Ti kánete *or* pós íste
How do you do (Pleased to meet you)	Chéro poli
I don't understand	Dén katalavéno
To your health!	Yásas!
Thank you	Efcharistó

381

TRAVELING

I am traveling by car . . .
   train . . . plane . . . boat
	Taxidévo mé aftokínito . . . me
	   tréno . . . me aeropláno . . . me
	   vapóri

Taxi, to the station . . .
   harbor . . . airport
	Taxi, stó stathmó
	   limani . . . aerodromio . . .

Porter, take the baggage/luggage	Akthofóre, pare aftá tá prámata

Where is the filling-station?
   (gas) (petrol)
	Pou íne o stathmos vensínis?
	   (vensíni)

When does the train leave for . . . ?	Tí óra thá fíyi to tréno ya tin . . . ?
Which is the train for . . . ?	Pío íne to tréno ghiá . . . ?
Which is the road to . . . ?	Piós íne o drómos ghiá . . . ?
A first-class ticket	Éna isitírio prótis táxeos
No smoking (compartment)	Apagorévete to kapnízin
Where is the toilet?	Póu íne í toaléta?
Ladies—Men	Ghinekón—Andrón
Where?—When?	Póu?—Póte?
Sleeping-car—Dining-car	Wagonlí—wagonrestorán
Compartment	Diamérisma
Entrance—Exit	Íssodos—éxodos
Nothing to declare	Den ékho tipota na dilósso
I am coming for my holidays	Érchome ya tis diakopés mou
Nothing	Típota
Personal use	Prossopikí chrissis
Must I pay duty?	Prépi na plirósso telonío
How much?	Pósso?

ON THE ROAD

Straight ahead	Kat efthían
To the right—to the left	Dexiá—aristerá
Show me the way to . . . please	Díxte mou to drómo . . . parakaló
Where is . . . ?	Pou íne . . . ?
Crossroad	Stavrodrómi
Danger	Kíndinos
Drive slowly!	Sigá
Look out for the train (railroad crossing)	Prósseche to tréno

IN TOWN

Will you lead me? take me?	Thélete na me odigísset? Me pérnete mazí sas?

Street—Square	Drómos—plateia
Where is the bank?	Pou íne i trápeza?
Far	Makriá
Police station	Asstinomikó tmíma
Consulate (American, British)	Proxenion (Amerikanikon, Anglikon)
Theater—Cinema	Théatron—Kinimatografos
At what time does the film start?	Tíóra archízi to film?
Will you dance with me?	Thélette na horépsete mazi mou
Where is the travel office?	Pou íne to touristikó grafío?
Where is the tourist information office? . . . tourist police?	Pou íne o tourismós . . . i touristiki asstinomia?

SHOPPING

I would like to buy	Tha íthela na agorásso
Show me, please	Díxte mou, parakaló
How much is it?	Pósso káni? (*or* kostízi)
It is too expenseive	Ine polí akrivó
Have you any sandals?	Échete pédila?
Have you foreign newspapers?	Échete xénais efimerídés?
Show me that blouse, please	Díxte mou aftí tí blouza
Show me that bag	Díxte mou aftí tí valíza
Envelopes—Writing paper	Fakélous—grafikí íli
Roll of film	Film
Map of the city	Hárti tis póleos
Something handmade	Hiropíito
Wrap it up, please	Tilíxeto parakaló
Cigarettes, matches, please	Tsigára, spírta parakaló
Ham	Zambon
Sausage—salami	Loukánika—salami
Sugar—salt	Záchari—aláti
Grapes—cherries	Stafília—Kerássia
Apple—Pear—Orange	Mílo—achládi—portokáli
Bread—Butter	Psomí—voútiro
Peach—Figs	Rodákino—síka

AT THE HOTEL

A good hotel	Éna kaló xenodochio
Have you a room available?	Échete eléfthero domátio?
Where can I find a furnished room?	Pou boró na vró epiploméno domátio?
A room with one bed, with two beds	Éna monó domátio, éna dipló domátio

With bathroom	Me bánio
How much is it per day?	Pósso kostízi tin iméra?
A room overlooking the sea	Éna domátio prós ti thálassa
For one day, for two days	Ghiá miá méra, hia dió méres
For a week	Ghiá miá vdomáda
My name is	Onomázo me
Here are our papers (passport)	Edhó íne tá chartiá mas (diavatíria)
What is the number of my room?	Piós íne o arithmós tou domatíou mou?
The key, please	To klidí parakaló
Where is the chambermaid?	Pou íne i kamarghiéra?
Breakfast, lunch, supper	Proínó, messimerghianó, vradinó
The bill, please	To logariasmó, parakaló
I am leaving tomorrow	Févgo (*or* anachoró) ávrio

AT THE RESTAURANT

Waiter	Garsón
Where is the restaurant?	Dixé mou to estiatório?
I would like to have lunch, dinner	Tha íthela na fáo messimergianó, vradinó
The menu, please	Dós mou ton katálogo
Fixed price menu	Menú
Soup	Soúpa
Bread	Psomí
Hors d'oeuvre	Orektiká
Ham omelette	Omelétta zambón
Chicken	Kotópoulo
Roast pork	Psitó chirinó
Veal cutlet	Moskhári
Potatoes (fried)	Patátes (tiganités)
Tomato salad	Domatosaláta
Vegetables	Lachaniká
Watermelon—melon	Karpoúzi—pepóni
Cakes	Gliká *or* pástes
Fruit—Cheese—ice-cream . . .	Fróuta—tirí—pagotó
Fish—Eggs	Psári—Avgá
Serve me on the terrace	Servírisse me sti terátza
Where can I wash my hands?	Pou boró na plíno ta chéria mou
Red wine, white wine	Krasí áspro—krasí mavro
Unresinated wine	Krasí aretsínato
Beer—bottled water—tap water	Bíra—gazóza—neró
Turkish coffee	Kafé toúrkiko
Coffee with milk—milk	Kafé evropaikó—gála

(For the names of Greek specialties see our 'Food and Drink' chapter).

AT THE BANK—AT THE POST OFFICE

Where is the bank? . . . post office?	Pou íne i trápeza? . . . to tachidromío?
I would like to cash a check	Thélo ná isspráxo éna tséki
I would like to change some money	Thélo ná chalásso chrímata
Stamps	Grammatóssima
I want to send it by airmail	Thélo na to stílo aeroporikós
I would like to send a telegram	Thélo na tilephonísso
Postcard—letter	Deltárion—grámma
Letterbox	Grammatokivótio
I would like to telephone	Thélo na stílo éna tilegráphima

AT THE GARAGE

Garage—gas (petrol)	Garáz—vensíni
Filling station	Pratírion vensínis
Oil	Ládi
Change the oil	Alaksete to ládi
Look at the tires—a tire	Rixe mia matiá sta lástika—ena lástiko
Wash the car	Plíne to aftokínito
Grease the car	Grassarissé to aftokínito
Breakdown	Vlávi
To tow—to repair	Rimulkyísse me—epidiorthóno
Spark(ing) plugs	Búsi
The brakes	Fréno
Gearbox	Kivótio tachítiton
Carburetor	Karbiratér
Headlight (headlamp)	Prowoléfs
Starter	Ekinitis
Axle	Akson
Spring	Sústa
Spare part	Antalaktikó

MOUNTAIN CLIMBING—SAILING

Guide	Odigós
Horse—Mule	Álogo—moulári
Food	Fagitó
I want to eat, to drink, to sleep	Thélo na fáo, na pió, na kimithó
Hut or refuge	Katafíyio
Do you want to guide us?	Thés na mas odigíssis?
How much do you want per day?	Poso thélis tin iméra?

Sunrise—sunset	Anatolí—thíssis
Sun—moon	Ilios—fengári
Day—night	Iméra—nýchta
Morning—afternoon	Proi—apóyevma
Skipper—engineer	Kapetános—michanikos
Port—Port commandant	Limáni—Limenárchis
Port—starboard	Aristerá—dexiá
Aft—forward	Prýmni-próra
Boat—sail	Várka—paní
North wind	Meltémi
Course of the yacht	Poría
Speed	Tachítita
Creek—beach—rocks	Órmos—ammoudiá—vráchia
Engine breakdown	Zimía michanís
We are touching port	Fthánome stó limáni
We are sailing for . . .	Apopléome . . .
The weather is good—bad	Ó kerós íne kalós—kakós
The sea is calm—rough	I thálassa íne kalí—kakí

NUMBERS

1 éna	9 enéa	80 ogdónda
2 dío	10 déka	90 enenínda
3 tría	20 íkossi	100 ekató
4 téssera	30 triánda	200 diakóssia
5 pénde	40 saránda	300 triakóssia etc.
6 éxi	50 penínda	1000 chília
7 epta	60 exínda	2000 dió chiliádes
8 októ	70 evdomínda	3000 tría chiliádes etc.

INDEX

INDEX

The following abbreviations are used in this index: E-Entertainment; H-Hotels; R-Restaurants; YH-Youth Hostels

See also Practical Information at the end of each chapter for local information on camping, shopping, special events, sports, transportation.

Facts at Your Fingertips

Air travel
  from Britain 15
  from Europe 17
  from North America 14-15
  in Greece 31-2
Archeological sites & terms
  29-30
Auto travel
  car-sleeper expresses 16, 18
  from Britain 16
  from Europe 17-18
  in Greece 34-6
  rentals 35

Businessmen's hints 24
Bus travel
  from Britain 16
  in Greece 34

Camping 12
Climate 5
Clothes & packing 12-13
Costs 3-4
Cruises 33-4
Culture
  classical 90-101
  modern 41-51
Currency & exchange 3
Customs
  arriving 18
  returning home 36-8

Ferries 18, 35-6

Food & drink 102-8

Health certificates 14
History 52-71
Holidays 23
Holiday villages 21-2
Hotels 20-1
Hours of business 23-4

Language 19-20
Laundry 24

Mail & telephones 23
Medical services 25
Museums 29
Mythology 72-89

Newspapers 24

Off-season travel 5

Passports 13-14
Photography 24-5
Pollution 25-6
Public facilities 24

Rail travel
  from Britain 15-16
  from Europe 17
  in Greece 32
Restaurants 22

Seasonal events 6-7

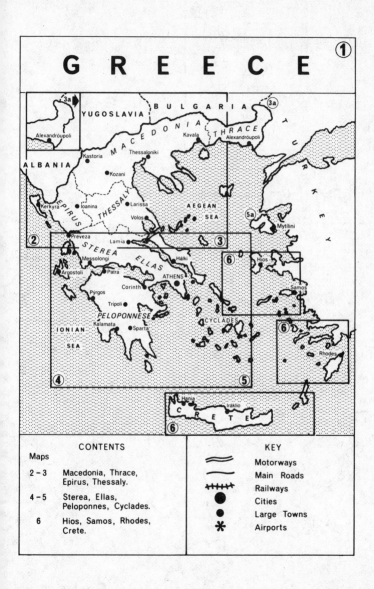

G R E E C E ①

③a

YUGOSLAVIA   B U L G A R I A   ③a

Alexandroupoli

MACEDONIA   THRACE

ALBANIA

Kastoria   Thessaloniki   Kavala   Alexandroupoli

Kozani

EPIRUS   THESSALY   Larissa   AEGEAN SEA   ⑤a

Kerkyra   Ioanina   Volos   Mytilini

②   Preveza   Lamia   ③

STEREA   ⑥   Hios

Messolongi   ELLAS   Hálki

Argostoli   Patra   ATHENS   Samos

Pyrgos   Corinth

Tripoli   ⑥

PELOPONNESE   CYCLADES   Rhodes

IONIAN   Kalamata   Sparta

SEA

④   ⑤

Hania   Irάklio

C R E T E

⑥

KEY

〰️ Motorways
— Main Roads
🚂 Railways
● Cities
• Large Towns
✳ Airports

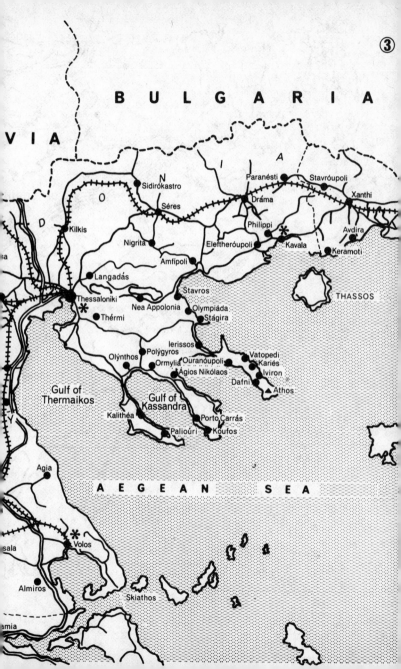

SKÝROS

EVIA

Kými

Halkída

Ágii Apóstoli

Thíva

Oropos

L   A   S

Dafní

Marathon

Megara

Kifissia

Kárystos

Salamis

ATHENS

Piraeus

Voula

Vouliagmeni

Souvala

Varkiza

Egina

Lavrio

Moni

Agía Marína

Poros

Sounio

OLIS

Kéa

Andros

mioni

Tinos

Ydra

Spetses

Sýros

Mykonos

KYNTHOS

Possidonia

Ermoupoli

DELOS

CYCLADES

mvassía

Serifos

Naxos

Paros

gía

NAXOS

MILÓS

THIRA (SANTORINI)

Thira

5a

Vassiliki

Mytilíni

LESVOS

Plomári

CRE TE

⑤

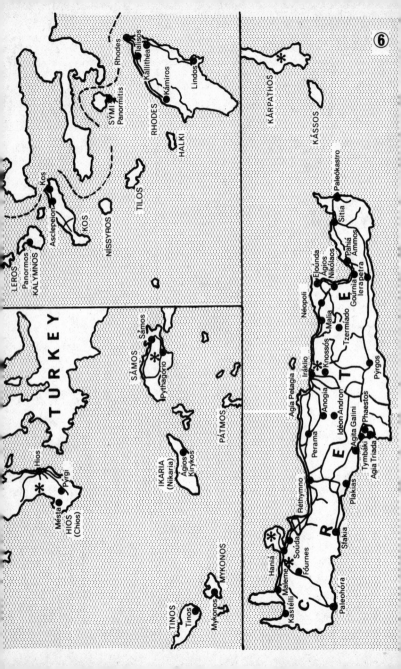

⑥

TURKEY

LEROS
Panormos
KALYMNOS
Kos
Asclepeion
KOS

NISSYROS

TILOS

SÝMI
Panormitis
Rhodes
Tallsos
Kállithea
Kámiros
RHODES
Lindos
HALKI

KÁRPATHOS

KÁSSOS

Hios
Pyrgi
Mesta
HIOS
(Chios)

IKARIA
(Nikaria)
Ágios
Kirykos

SÁMOS
Sámos
Pythagório

PATMOS

MYKONOS
Mykonos

TINOS
Tinos

Agia Pelagia
Réthymno
Souda
Haniá
Maleme
Kastélli
Foúrnes
Paleohóra
Sfakia
Plakias
Perama
Anogia
Idéon Andron
Agita Galini
Tymbáki
Agia Triada
Phaestos
Pérama
Neópoli
Irákilo
Knossós
Tzermiado
Malia
Eloúnda
Agios
Nikólaos
Gournia
Pyrgos
Ierápetra
Pahiá
Ammos
Sitia
Paleokastro

C R E T E

Paleokastro